T0342361

THE RISE OF CENTRAL BANKS

THE RISE OF
CENTRAL BANKS

State Power in Financial Capitalism

LEON WANSLEBEN

HARVARD UNIVERSITY PRESS

Cambridge, Massachusetts & London, England

2023

First printing

Library of Congress Cataloging-in-Publication Data

Names: Wansleben, Leon, author.
Title: The rise of central banks : state power in financial
    capitalism / Leon Wansleben.
Description: Cambridge, Massachusetts : Harvard University
    Press, 2023. | Includes bibliographical references and index.
Identifiers: LCCN 2022011350 | ISBN 9780674270510 (cloth)
Subjects: LCSH: Banks and banking, Central. | Monetary
    policy. | Capitalism—Government policy. | Financial crises.
Classification: LCC HG1811 .W365 2022 | DDC 332.1/1—dc23/
    eng/20220609
LC record available at https://lccn.loc.gov/2022011350

To Rahel

Contents

Preface

When I decided to work on central banks about ten years ago, a colleague from political science brushed me off with a single sentence: "We already know almost everything about them." How could I disagree? I knew that central banks were curiously neglected in sociological studies of the economy and financial markets. But I was also aware that in economics and political science works on the topic filled whole libraries. What could a sociologist add to this vast literature?

A distinct strength of my discipline, I thought, was to look at central banks as organizations, how people interact within them and with outside groups, and how those who work there think and come to decisions. More specifically, my initial focus was on how central banks have become "scientized," that is, how they have turned into organizations that excessively produce, use, and promote macroeconomic knowledge. With this idea in mind, I applied for a grant from the Swiss National Science Foundation (SNSF) in 2013. In the hearing, I received a challenging comment from a committee member. How would I be able to address the big questions about neoliberalism and capitalism with such a study? What could I say about the role of capitalist interests in influencing economic and financial policies? Again, I did not have a good answer. While I was lucky enough to receive the grant and was committed to the idea of following actors and focusing on organizational processes, the added value of this perspective for the case of central banking was not yet clear.

Strikingly, what I did *not* do when starting the project was to draw a connection between central banks and the Great Financial Crisis. I knew—and had seen firsthand as a participant observer—that traders in financial markets pay enormous attention to central banks, watch press conferences with their leaders, and make guesses about their future interest-rate decisions. In my first book about currency markets, I had discussed these "mirror games" between policymakers and financial actors. But how these interactions mattered more broadly, including for events associated with the crisis of 2008, remained unclear.

I spent a lot of time in the next years in central bank archives. Most of what I know about the subject is from reading notes, policy drafts, meeting protocols, and so on, from files buried in these places. I started out by looking at the research divisions, how they expanded from the 1970s onward, how they became breeding grounds for a new sort of policy expertise, and how actors in these divisions communicated with decision-makers. When I was based in Switzerland, I regularly visited the archives of the Swiss National Bank (SNB) in Zurich and the Bank for International Settlements in Basel. At the SNB, I benefited from lengthy conversations with the archive's head, Patrick Halbeisen, as well as with many other members of the organization. Contacts intensified and I was invited at one point to present preliminary findings at an SNB research seminar (together with Matthieu Leimgruber). In 2014, I became assistant professor in sociology at the London School of Economics and Political Science (LSE). I had selected the Bank of England as another case for my project, and this new job gave me the opportunity to regularly descend into the basements at Threadneedle Street to go through thousands of pages of typewritten documents. Curiously, I found that, in the Bank's case, officials wrote a lot of letters. For instance, in the 1970s, the Bank's economist Charles Goodhart had exchanged thoughts with an impressive array of disciplinary colleagues representing diverse schools (Frank Hahn, John Hicks, Karl Brunner, and David Laidler, to name just a few). More importantly, I could see through these letters how officials commented on others' policy proposals or research papers; how they engaged in collective deliberation on key issues; and how they communicated with actors from other institutions, particularly the Treasury (the UK's finance ministry). Tellingly, some of the most interesting letters were never sent.

Gradually, and primarily through the UK case, I came to realize that, while scientization has indeed changed the inner workings and faces of central banks, there is another area of transformation with far more important consequences. Since the 1970s, central banks have fundamentally changed their relationships with finance. By redefining their own roles within an emergent regime of financial capitalism, these organizations have made their own ascendency possible. Perhaps, I had initially overlooked this issue precisely because the connection is so obvious. Academic discourse, particularly the more critical one, suggests so. It was not by chance that the committee member at the SNSF had argued that central banks were beholden to financial interests, and that these interests were dominant in an era of financial globalization.

But through the archival files, I discovered that the relationship between central banking and finance is far more problematic and interesting than the standard view suggests. Documents covering seemingly boring issues such as policy implementation in money markets and central banks' participation in sovereign debt management revealed that, in the period from around the 1970s until the 1990s, central bankers had been extremely concerned with and been putting a lot of effort into redefining their roles within rapidly changing financial systems. The advent of new instruments, the rise of nonbank financial companies ("shadow banks"), and the enormous growth of balance sheets and trading volumes on financial markets had initially challenged officials' traditional notions of authority and their governing practices. Coming to terms with, and ultimately capitalizing on, the advent of market-based finance thus was an important if difficult step in central banks' rise.

I give just one example. In an internal Bank of England deliberation in the preparation for "Big Bang" (the UK's financial sector reforms in 1986), one official asked his colleagues, "Hitherto our traditional approach . . . has inclined to institutional specialization . . . Are we in fact ready, in principle, to see a conglomerate offering a complete range of all kinds of financial services?"[1] This question indicated that the Bank staff were deeply concerned about Big Bang because the reforms were expected to undo the very structures and cultures in London's financial sector that the Bank was so strongly attached to (the cartel-clubs of clearing banks, Discount Houses, etc.). For that reason, Bank officials initially did *not* welcome the arrival of American and other overseas investment banks in London that would follow Big Bang. In fact, for a significant period, Bank officials were at a loss because they did not know how to adapt their own monetary management techniques to these sectoral developments. In retrospect, we know that financial globalization has helped the Bank of England and other central banks to enhance their policy roles and political authority. But from the perspective of actors involved at critical historical junctures, this "win-win" scenario was not so clear.

I thus gradually came to see what my research would be about. I would still pay attention to how central banks have remade themselves with the help of macroeconomic expertise. And I would contextualize their changing roles within broader political developments and structural economic change. But the specific question of my research became how central banks have redrawn their connections with financial sectors for the purposes of policymaking. Central banks ultimately are "the banks' banks"—state bodies operating from the midst of financial systems. The question is how they have leveraged this particular role to secure and increase what Michael Mann calls "infrastructural power": the power to govern "through" markets as vehicles to influence the economy at large. As the other side of this same process, I also wanted to explain how reconfigurations of these concrete connections between central banking and markets have influenced the structures of, and dynamics within, finance. I had already recognized in my earlier research that central banks were extremely relevant for financial actors. But what had remained unclear was how specific modes of coordination shape structures, expectations, and risk-taking behaviors in markets. Moreover, I wanted to understand in more detail what happens in spheres like interbank money markets, where it is almost impossible to separate the "public" (central banking) from the "private" (commercial banking) sides. This second set of questions about repercussions within financial sectors finally helped me to better grasp the events around 2008—a financial crisis that I had experienced as an ethnographer of finance, but whose deeper origins and consequences had completely escaped my understanding.

Let me add that case comparisons were a crucial method for detecting and analyzing contingencies in, and problems of, central banks' relationships with finance. The SNB served as a contrast foil to the Bank of England, particularly for the 1970s and 1980s. For instance, in the SNB archive, I discovered a protocol documenting a meeting between central bank officials and private bankers from the early 1980s, in which both groups agreed that they wanted to *prevent* the emergence of money markets—the very markets that drove financial globalization at the time and whose developments motivated policy innovations in the United States and UK. This indicated to me that, at least up until the 1990s, the SNB relied on very different infrastructural foundations than its Anglo-Saxon peers. Exploring this thread further, I included the German case in my analysis as another context, where a powerful central bank had emerged from the Great Inflation on the grounds of operational linkages with a still relatively regulated, conservative banking sector.

When I presented preliminary thoughts on these institutional differences in April 2018, I was fortunate to have Philip Manow, an expert on German political economy, in the audience. Philip's comments provoked me to better incorporate the role of wage settlement into my analysis, a topic that had been studied by political scientists Robert Franzese, Torben Iversen, and others. But Philip also helped me to see that these scholars, while they had identified how differences in bargaining institutions affect monetary policy, had curiously neglected finance. Here was a contribution that I could make beyond my familiar scholarly context. My colleague in political science, who had advised me against studying central banks on the grounds of epistemic saturation, had been wrong.

In an interview in December 2017, Paul Tucker, the Bank's former Deputy Governor, gave me another piece of good advice. Without explicitly including the US case, he said, I would only be able to tell part of the story. In fact, as I recognized myself, officials from the Bank of England during the 1980s had explicitly talked about the "Americanization" of the City of London and had adapted their policies accordingly. I thus took Tucker's suggestion to heart and studied the dynamics in the United States that had brought into being the instruments, techniques, and organizational forms, which subsequently shaped UK and international markets. Additionally, I realized that I needed to look yet again at what is probably the most researched event in central banking history: the Volcker shock. Through a careful reading of historical accounts and archival documents, I saw that, in the early 1980s, Federal Reserve chairman Paul Volcker had innovated practices of interest-rate setting and information signaling with markets, which provided the blueprint for policy solutions in market-based systems, and which were later adopted (and refined) in the UK and elsewhere. A similar dynamic occurred after 2008. The Fed again became the locus for significant policy innovations that then spread internationally. Just as Tucker had suggested, analyzing these innovations, their preconditions and consequences, became a crucial element in my story.

The result of all of this is a comparative study of central banking since the 1970s, which primarily (though not exclusively) looks at four formative cases: the Bank of England, the Bundesbank, the Federal Reserve, and the Swiss National Bank. The questions being asked are how these central banks acquired more power as economic policymakers and, particularly, what role their varying relationships with finance played in this ascendency. I also explore how particular forms of central banking enabled and supported the development of market-based financial systems that we now find (in different variants) in most advanced economies.

As indicated, when conducting this research and writing this book, I searched for new insights, but I also constantly challenged my own thinking and preconceptions. In my little research diary, I repeatedly reformulated research questions, articulated provisional arguments, and adjusted my research strategies based on these reflections. Encounters like those with Philip Manow and Paul Tucker were formative because, beyond what these particular persons intended, they cast long shadows over my reflections and influenced the directions I chose. Intense and memorable encounters, especially with my many interview partners in places like investment banking boardrooms, homes for the elderly, private houses, airports, or my shoebox office at LSE, have provided invaluable insights and enabled me to go through a steep learning curve.

The project began in Switzerland, continued in London, and concluded in Cologne, Germany, at the Max Planck Institute for the Study of Societies. My acknowledgments begin with this Institute because it has by now become my true intellectual home. I greatly appreciate how the Institute's current directors, Jens Beckert and Lucio Baccaro, bring economic sociology and political economy together to facilitate research (like my own) at the interstices of these fields. I also benefited greatly from the high standard of earnest intellectual exchange with many colleagues here. Benjamin Braun is one of them, with whom I have been in conversation on central banking since 2013. I also benefited from the broad and deep knowledge of the Institute's former director and active emeritus, Fritz Scharpf. Georg Rillinger helpfully commented on drafts of the introduction and Chapter 4. Members of my own research group have played a special role in this project, including Arjen van der Heide (now at University of Leiden), Vanessa Endrejat, Edin Ibrocevic, Camilla Locatelli, and Toby Arbogast. I have repeatedly hijacked research group meetings to get feedback on draft chapters, and this has helped me a lot in the final stages of writing this book. Finally, my confidence in getting this project completed came from emotional and logistic support at the Institute. Research assistants Nils Neumann and Fabian Pawelczyk collected the last pieces of evidence that I needed during the write-up phase; Sharon Adams teamed up with James Patterson to copyedit all draft chapters; and all of my colleagues together created an environment at the Institute in which I enjoy working.

Before joining the Max Planck Institute, I spent some months at the Institute for Advanced Studies of the University of Konstanz, where I met Philip Manow as well as Boris Holzer and Christian Meyer. I am extremely grateful for those months at Lake Konstanz, which were a turning point for the project. Before that, at LSE, I benefited from conservations with colleagues in the Department of Sociology, particularly Fabien Accominotti (now at University of Wisconsin, Madison), Nigel Dodd, Rebecca Elliott, Monika Krause, Juan Pablo Pardo-Guerra (now University of California at San Diego), and Mike Savage. Precisely because these colleagues have diverse research interests, I was challenged time and again to translate my findings into broader sociological arguments. Just as beneficial for me was that Charles Goodhart still actively practiced academic research when I was at LSE. My conversations with him, as well as with other (former) central bankers and academics at and around the LSE, have made this project possible. I want to particularly mention Duncan Needham and Anthony Hotson, both economic historians at Cambridge. I learned the most from them about UK finance and central banking. Last but not least, LSE provided me with funding to conduct exploratory research into the Bank of England's regulatory role, a project that I conducted jointly with research assistant Andreas Grueter. Discussions with him gave me a backstage context to explore directions of research and greatly enriched this project.

As mentioned, this work began in Switzerland, at the University of Lucerne, where I became a postdoc in 2011. Cornelia Bohn enabled the early stages of this research; more generally, she has played an important role in supporting my intellectual and professional development. Funding from the SNSF helped me to get on my own feet with this project at a point at which I had not even yet settled on a convincing research question. Together with Matthieu Leimgruber from the University of Zurich, I explored the curious role of Karl Brunner as one of the most influential monetarists, and I learned much from him about Swiss economic and financial history. Martin Wyss was my first research assistant and did extensive research on the development of macroeconomics in Switzerland. In the Swiss context, I also did a lot of highly productive interviews with central bankers to whom I am grateful.

I benefited enormously from exchanges with various colleagues at conferences, research seminars, and other intellectual encounters, more than I can list here by name. I collaborated closely with Timo Walter for parts of this project and am in regular exchange with Matthias Thiemann on the topic. At various points throughout the process, Richard Bronk, Bruce Carruthers, Christian Joppke, Oliver Kessler, Karin Knorr Cetina, Andreas Langenohl, Donald MacKenzie, Alex Preda, and Tobias Werron gave extremely helpful feedback. Moritz Schularick kindly helped me with balance-sheet data. Together with Ian Malcolm at Harvard University Press, I developed this project into a book, and he confidently guided me through the publication process. I also want to mention Joe Zammit-Lucia, my friend and frequent conversation partner on central banking, whose thinking is as generous as it is sharp.

Last but not least, I want to acknowledge the work of those unknown reviewers who commented on the manuscript and on papers that provided an initial foundation for this book. Chapter 2 draws on ideas first presented in "How Expectations Became Governable: Institutional Change and the Performative Power of Central Banks," *Theory and Society* (2018) 47: 773–803. Chapter 3 is informed by "How Central Bankers Learned to Love Financialization: The Fed, the Bank, and the Enlisting of Unfettered Markets in the Conduct of Monetary Policy," coauthored with Timo Walter and published in *Socio-Economic Review* (2020) 18(3):625–53. Chapter 4 expands on discussions introduced in "Formal Institution Building in Financialized Capitalism: The Case of Repo Markets," *Theory and Society* (2020) 49:187–213. Lastly, Chapter 5 advances research put forward in "Divisions of Regulatory Labor, Institutional Closure, and Structural Secrecy in New Regulatory States: The Case of Neglected Liquidity Risks in Market-Based Banking," *Regulation and Governance* (2020). Getting insightful feedback on these submissions has been essential for advancing the project.

At about the time I began the research for this book, Rahel became part of my life. We have by now spent ten intense, extremely enriching, and at times challenging years together. In February 2018, our beloved son Janis was born prematurely and died. He will always be part of our family. Clelia, the most wonderful girl, joined us in April 2020. In about a month, we expect another child. This book is dedicated to Rahel because her enormous courage, personal strength, and love have made all this possible.

THE RISE OF CENTRAL BANKS

Introduction

AS INFLATION ROSE rapidly in the early 1970s, Western governments were at a loss. In July 1972, Helmut Schmidt, Germany's finance minister and later Chancellor, proclaimed that higher inflation was tolerable because people cared more about retaining their jobs.[1] But only two months later, Schmidt raised doubts about the underlying economics of his own statement by admitting that "[o]ur economic policy is much more limited than our old textbooks used to tell" (cited in Gray 2007: 318). Indeed, as the 1970s progressed, more and more leaders accepted that action was needed to tame the incessant rise in prices. The question was, how could this be done? In October 1974, US president Gerald Ford unveiled a comprehensive package of measures before Congress. But while promising vigorous action against "our public enemy number one," Ford exposed himself to ridicule when recommending that his fellow citizens grow vegetables, produce less waste, drive less, and embrace the role of "inflation fighter" by wearing buttons with the acronym "WIN" or "Whip Inflation Now."[2]

Central bankers offered an answer. In December 1974, the Bundesbank announced unilaterally that it would set a limit for the money supply so that "no new inflationary strains are likely to arise."[3] By 1978, the German inflation rate had dropped to 2 percent. In July 1979, Paul Volcker became chairman of the Federal Reserve (the Fed), America's central bank. In October, he initiated a policy turn to eliminate excessive inflation quickly and drastically; it did not return for the next forty years. As John Singleton notes, "The Great Inflation and Disinflation restored central banks to a vital place in the economic policy community. Almost everyone now accepted that monetary policy mattered, and that central bankers were the professionals in this field" (2011: 203).

But the story does not end there. Over the 1990s to the 2010s, central banks assumed broader responsibilities. In February 1999, after financial crises in Southeast Asia and Russia, Fed chairman Alan Greenspan appeared on the front cover of *Time* magazine, positioned between Treasury Secretary Robert Rubin and Rubin's deputy (and successor) Lawrence Summers. *Time* called the three the "committee to save the world." True, the interconnected crises of 1998–1999 were dramatic, but minor events compared to those ten years later, when the Fed offices in New York and Washington again turned into control rooms for rescue operations, this time to save the North Atlantic financial system from collapse (Tooze 2018). In overnight sessions, billion-dollar programs for illiquid (as well as insolvent) firms and defunct markets were designed, and transnational networks were established to distribute international dollar funding to the world's major financial institutions. But rather than withdrawing after the fire had been extinguished, the Fed went on to innovate "quantitative easing" (QE) as the most experimental, expansive monetary policy practice in history. The more elected leaders scaled back their fiscal programs, the more the Fed and other central banks stepped up their QE interventions to fight persistent stagnation and unemployment. At this point, several observers noted that, when it came to macroeconomic policy, central banks remained "the only game in town" (El-Erian 2016).

Where we stand at present is less clear. In October 2020, shortly before the Covid-19 pandemic's second major wave, Chris Giles of the *Financial Times* argued that Covid-related public health and supply-side problems had finally relegated monetary authorities to second place: fiscal policy and other forms of government steering were in higher demand.[4] And another pro-business paper, the *Economist,* wrote in its July 25, 2020, edition, "In the 1990s and 2000s a synthesis of Keynesianism and Friedmanism emerged. It eventually recommended a policy regime loosely known as 'flexible inflation targeting' . . . Fiscal policy, as a way to manage the business cycle, was sidelined . . . Now it seems that this dominant economic paradigm has reached its limit . . . Devising new ways of getting back to full employment is once again the top priority for economists."[5] Nevertheless, central bankers remained at the center of crisis management. Their responses to the pandemic's financial and economic fallouts have been more aggressive than ever. The Bank of England's asset purchases in 2020 outsized all its previous QE combined; the Fed, in a unique emergency action, purchased one trillion dollars of US government bonds in just a few days; and without aggressive bond buying by the European Central Bank (ECB), Italy and Greece would have seen a return of the debt troubles experienced in the early 2010s. With enormous levels of public and private debt, ever more fragile and bloated financial markets, and the return of inflation, it is hard to see when and how the age of central bank dominance will really end.

But rather than speculating about the future, this book follows a long tradition in the social sciences of engaging in a historical inquiry. I reconstruct the story of, and offer an explanation for, the rise of central banks over half a century, from around 1970 to 2020. The book thus looks closely at a distinct group of state organizations in an effort to understand how their roles and policies have changed. This particular explanandum is embedded in a broader question, which has bothered social scientists for many years: How do state institutions and economic policies co-evolve with transformations in capitalism? Building on Karl Polanyi, John Ruggie (1982) famously engaged with this problem and identified the period following the two world wars as "embedded liberalism." Other scholars characterized the very same period as "Fordism" (Boyer 1990). In any case, the decades in question saw the consolidation of organized industrial capitalism, regulated North-to-North trade, demand-driven growth, and remarkably low levels of intrastate inequalities. This regime came with a distinct set of policies and institutions: expanding welfare states, activist fiscal stabilization, strong labor unions, fixed (but adjustable) exchange rates, and (selective) capital controls. Central banks mattered as managers of the international currency order, but they were not the key movers and centers of power in this regime.

Enter the 1970s, and we can place central banks' ascendency squarely within broader processes, which led to the demise of embedded liberalism or Fordism and the emergence of a new order. Globalization in finance,

value chains, and in corporate organization increasingly restrained state
action in fiscal, regulatory, and other domains. But a select group of state
actors was to benefit from, and reinforce, globalization (Sassen 2006), and
central banks were among them. As the social and institutional infrastructures of industrial capitalism weakened, societal mechanisms to coordinate corporate interests with sociopolitical demands ran dry. Central
bankers capitalized on this crisis to *expand* their own coordination capacities, particularly with the rapidly growing financial sectors and markets.
And even if some key objectives of postwar Keynesianism, such as output
stabilization, were not discarded entirely, relative priorities shifted, and the
kinds of instruments being used to achieve these objectives changed fundamentally. Instead of redistributive tax policies and public spending, central banks increasingly used monetary policies for these purposes. "Neoliberalism" is an imperfect label for these profound transformations. But
if we want to understand the realignments between capitalist structures,
state institutions, and economic policies after 1970, we should pay particular attention to what happened at and with central banks.

Embedding the study of central banks within these broader transformations also allows us to see why their ascendency matters. For while monetary authorities gained power, capitalism became more unequal, unstable, and unsustainable.[6] In no economy was the Great Disinflation in
the 1980s painless, and in most countries, central bankers determined the
price that societies were to pay. The Bundesbank was famous for disregarding the labor-market consequences of its policies, and persistently
high unemployment became the key political-economy problem in West
Germany after the early 1970s (Manow 2020: 85). Volcker was equally rigorous in maintaining high interest rates during the early 1980s, while the
US economy was plunging into its worst recession since the 1930s; people
sent him keys from cars they had bought on consumer loans that they could
no longer afford.[7] In some countries, disinflation reinforced a rapid and
brutal decline of traditional industries that changed their economic structures for good. In the 1990s and 2000s, central bankers saw the fruits of
their labors in what they called the "Great Moderation," a period of low
volatility in economic output and inflation. However, during this very
period, new patterns of globalization, corporate reorganizations, and a
growing disparity between salaries in high-end service jobs (particularly
in finance) compared to the rest of the economy all contributed to a rapid

increase in inequalities. Private credit growth accelerated, a dynamic that would ultimately lead to the financial crisis of 2008. In the storm of this crisis, central bankers then exerted enormous influence to determine the survival (or insolvency) of firms and, in the European context, even states. This raised widespread anger about the palpable distributional effects of choices being made by unelected leaders, who seemed to favor the biggest, best connected economic actors over those, who struggle to get by. We then saw how financial markets quickly recovered after the crash while "real" economies barely showed any productivity gains; jobs with decent wages became increasingly scarce. As studies suggest, QE supported this pattern in the 2010s as most of its benefits accrued to equities and other asset markets.[8] People recognize that something has gone wrong. In a survey in December 2020, 70 percent of French respondents and 50 percent of US Americans, UK citizens, and Germans expressed the view that their economic systems need a major or complete overhaul.[9]

What's Missing in Neoliberalism Critiques

Because central banks assume such critical positions in broader transformations of capitalism, state institutions, and the practices of macroeconomic management, I am not the first to note their importance. Indeed, hardly any social scientist who tackles neoliberalism neglects their crucial role. But as I will show in this book, when positioning central banks in these larger processes, it is worth studying in more detail how they act as bureaucratic organizations, what is distinctive about their governing practices, and how these practices are intertwined with particular capitalist institutions and structures. With this focus, I particularly depart from two prominent research streams that study key forces in political economy while abstracting from the concrete practices and processes through which constellations of power emerge.

The first of these strands looks at the conflicting economic policy interests of different groups in capitalist democracies. From this vantage point, we observe an intensification of distributional struggles in the 1970s over relative shares of income between capitalists and workers (Goldthorpe 1978). Capitalists tend to get their way because they have greater instrumental and structural power—they can exercise "voice" and threaten to "exit" from national economies (Streeck 2014). For that reason, governments only temporarily resorted to inflationary policies before giving in to capitalists' demands. Central banks became the advocates and executers of "hard-money" policies. Their positions then remained unchallenged in the subsequent decades as globalization, deindustrialization, and a seemingly inevitable wave of deregulations entrenched the dominance of capital over labor.

To be sure, this story captures the rough contours of "regime change" since the 1970s. But it has several defects. First, by focusing on conflicting interests, we cannot explain how and when central banks emerged as dominant actors in economic policymaking. In Germany and Switzerland, this turn happened in the mid-1970s. In 1979, Paul Volcker dramatically increased the Fed's importance; but the American central bank only really consolidated its role within neoliberalism under Alan Greenspan in the late 1980s to early 1990s (Goodfriend 1993: 16). In the United Kingdom, the Bank of England had to wait until 1993 to assume de facto (though not yet de jure) authority over monetary policy. It is not clear how the predominance of hard-money interests could explain this pattern. Moreover, the term "hard money" covers considerable variation in terms of how monetary policies are implemented. In the German and Swiss contexts, central banks used money supply targets to convey their stabilizing intentions to corporatist institutions, while this particular version of "practical monetarism" was no part of central banks' rise in the United States or United Kingdom. Instead, what mattered in the latter countries was to enhance and maintain "the credibility and reputation of macroeconomic policy [in global financial markets, LW] so that [these] markets behave in a way which generally supports it," as noted by a prominent UK Treasury secretary from the Thatcher era (Middleton 1989: 51). Most importantly, while scholars in the interest-based literature describe the core conflict in terms of groups struggling over policies allowing or restraining inflation, they cannot capture the extent to which expansionary policies in past decades have failed to generate inflation or to improve the structural conditions for workers, while doing much to boost financial growth and increase wealth concentration at the top (Petrou 2021a). In order to understand these patterns, a more detailed study of central banking and its nexus with capitalist structures and institutions is needed.

Similar problems permeate the second prominent strand in political economy, which looks at the evolution of macroeconomic policy ideas. This literature classically argues that "[i]n the wake of the 1973 OPEC oil crisis . . . Keynesianism was thrown into question, economists and policy-makers searched for answers, and more conservative approaches carried the day, often referred to as neoliberalism or market fundamentalism" (Campbell 2020: 793). There is some discussion of the specific vehicles of ideational change. In some versions, scholars argue that politicians such as Margaret Thatcher built new political platforms on neoliberalism and changed the configuration of policies and institutions in the wake of their electoral victories (Hall 1993). In other versions, scholars prioritize the influence of economic experts in international organizations, epistemic communities, "thought collectives," and / or national technocratic bodies (e.g. Jones 2012; Marcussen 2009; Seabrooke and Tsingou 2009). Moreover, some authors recognize considerable ideational variation under the broad tent of neoliberalism, from monetarism in the 1970s and 1980s to New Keynesianism during the 1990s and 2000s (Clift 2020; Van Gunten 2015). But notwithstanding these internal differences, we can identify a number of general shortcomings in this second political-economy branch. First, any scholar familiar with policy procedures and organizational processes in bodies such as central banks recognizes the limited and qualified relevance of economic ideas. A striking example is Thatcher, who successfully campaigned for the rigorous implementation of monetarism in the late 1970s but quickly recognized the inoperability of this approach in practice. It is undeniable, however, that concepts, models, and styles of reasoning from macroeconomics matter in central banks and have helped these organizations to innovate policies and redefine their roles. However, ideational scholars do not have the proper tools with which to analyze how central bankers use these epistemic elements creatively to support particular governing techniques. We have to go beyond ideas to understand how this works.

In sum, the dominant ways of studying neoliberalism in political economy can help us to identify the material / political conditions of central banks' ascendency and to describe the broad intellectual climate during the late twentieth century in which this ascendency took place. But they neither adequately account for central bankers' agency in the process, nor do they spell out how central banking is intertwined with institutions and structures in the economy at the level of actual governing. For these reasons, the timing and mechanisms of central banks' ascendency, the specific conditions conducive to these processes, and the consequences of particular versions of monetary policy dominance remain unclear.

General Approach

In order to address these shortcomings, I adopt a distinct analytic perspective on central banks, which builds on recent work in sociology and political economy and is grounded in an understanding of what is particular about these organizations (Braun 2018a; Braun and Gabor 2020; Walter and Wansleben 2019). For central banks are situated at the intersections of state apparatuses and financial systems. They are bureaucratic bodies *and* banking organizations that operate in private markets (Braun, Krampf, and Murau 2021). Max Weber already recognized this peculiarity when he drew a distinction between authority based on coercion versus authority based on constellations of interest. Weber saw central banking as a prominent example of the latter: "[E]very central bank . . . exercises dominating influence via its monopolistic position in the capital market" (Weber 1976 [1921]: 542).[10]

Building on these ideas, we can study central banks' ascendency as the result of innovation processes within specific opportunity structures, which have enabled central banks to put to use their specific governance capacities. This implies, first, that central banks have learned to use their banking functions for economic policy purposes. The particular tools and methods of central banking vary widely between contexts and over time. But conventionally, monetary authorities lend reserves to banks, conduct repurchase operations, and buy or sell assets directly on the market. This is combined with certain regulations that define eligible collateral, the classes of purchased assets, and reserve requirements, among other things. Crucially, while financial transactions (combined with statutory regulations) provide the operational basis of monetary policy, it is not straightforward how central banks can use these operations effectively to influence macroeconomic variables such as the rate of inflation or economic output. The functional use of financial transactions for such purposes raises formidable implementation and transmission problems. Monetary authorities need to establish stable transactional routines with their counterparties and understand the policy implications of their own as well as private banks' operations. Moreover, central banks rely on private actors and markets to transmit local operations to the broader financial and economic systems in order to affect the economy at large. As I aim to show in this book, innovations at this seemingly mundane, operational level of policy have had decisive consequences for how monetary policies have been institutionalized and how central banks capture "infrastructural powers" (Mann 1984; Mann 1996: 59–60), that is, how they enlist private actors and markets in their own practices to increase their governing capacities.

But the effectiveness of central bank operations as acts of governing also depends on another factor, their ascribed meaning. The anticipations of economic actors, political decision-makers, as well as third-party observers with regard to these operations and their consequences can undermine or greatly enhance efficacy. If market actors do not believe that a hike in a central bank's refinancing rates will tame inflation, then this hike remains without its intended effects. The challenge for central banks is thus to gain purchase over the broader field of beliefs and anticipations and to align them with their own policymaking intentions. To this end, central banks need particular expectation-management tools, and the development of these tools has been another crucial area of innovation in its own right (Holmes 2013). It is important to note, however, that these innovations have not happened in a vacuum. How people think about money, how they coordinate expectations, which versions of political authority appeal to them, and, not least, how central banks can reach them with strategic communication all depend on the structural and institutional configurations in a polity and economy. In that sense, central banks' expectation-management tools are just as deeply embedded in capitalist structures and institutions as are their financial market operations. Indeed, we can speak of stable foundations for central bank governing only if operational technologies and expectation management make up a coherent whole. Once we observe such coherence, we can assume that central banks have successfully inscribed their policies and institutional roles into prevailing capitalist orders.

In short, then, this book pursues a new avenue of analysis at the intersections of political economy and sociology that foregrounds how bureaucrats innovate tools (Carpenter 2001); how these tools are woven into the fabrics of economic structures and generate infrastructural power for particular state organizations (Mann 1984); and how such intertwinements produce intended as well as unintended effects (Walter and Wansleben 2019).

A Comparative Study of Policy Innovations

As I aim to demonstrate, we can better describe and explain the rise of central banks since the 1970s from this angle. My demonstration relies on a detailed and comparative study of a few cases. The story that emerges from this analysis goes as follows.

Starting in 1970, the problem of high inflation provoked central bankers to engage in policy experimentation to figure out how they could gain output legitimacy for inflation control. But the initial conditions under which monetary authorities engaged in these experiments were quite different. This affected their room to maneuver, strategy choices, and the results of particular trials. Only in countries in which existing institutional configurations could be repurposed for the conduct of monetary policy and turned into its infrastructural foundations did monetary authorities achieve policy success and manage to enhance their authority. Especially the German Bundesbank and the Swiss National Bank benefited from such configurations. They used stable credit and liquidity management routines in their respective banking systems to make authoritative claims over the controllability of the money supply—that is, to practice an institutionally adapted version of practical monetarism. Stability in banking combined with another crucial feature, namely continuity in wage bargaining institutions. These institutions helped the respective central banks to coordinate the expectations of relevant economic groups around monetary targets, producing stability as a self-fulfilling prophecy.

In other countries, new problem pressures and disruptive structural processes in the 1970s undermined extant policy routines and complicated the search for new solutions. We see these difficulties most clearly in the United Kingdom, where several experiments in practical monetarism failed. Centralized macroeconomic management raised formidable problems of coordination, especially in light of reduced growth rates and intensifying industrial conflicts. But just as problematic for the Bank of England were rapid structural changes in British banking, which rendered unclear how monetary and financial management could work at all. We find a somewhat similar constellation in the United States, where central bankers enjoyed much stronger independence but failed to see how they could use the Fed's intervention tools to control inflation at acceptable costs. Based on these frustrating experiences, Fed chairman Arthur Burns noted upon retirement at the end of the 1970s that "central banks alone [are] able to cope only marginally with the inflation of our times" (1979: 21).

But Burns's successor, Paul Volcker, incidentally discovered in his search for effective solutions that, in the US context, it was futile to expect citizens to voluntarily reduce consumption or to rely on Congress or the president to solve problems of monetary instability. It was equally impossible to adopt the kind of monetary policy practiced in Germany and Switzerland. Trade unions would not coordinate with the Fed, as they did with the Bundesbank and Swiss National Bank; nor were monetary and financial developments sufficiently stable to conduct practical monetarism. Instead, the Fed's solution lay in capitalizing on the market-based nature of the US financial system. For that purpose, a turn away from monetarism and toward a particular use of the Fed's influence over short-term interest rates in money markets was needed. Indeed, as gradually became clearer over the 1980s, financial globalization and innovations *enhanced* the infrastructural power of this particular tool. This was because the price signals that the Fed sent through alterations of its rates rippled more quickly through markets when these were more price-sensitive and more tightly connected. Moreover, with the disempowerment of workers and dismantling of unions, the Fed could engage in a different version of expectation management that focused not on wage bargainers, but on capital markets. Based on the attainment of credibility for stable inflation in these markets, the US central bank managed to exercise conditional influence over longer-term interest rates that determined broader financial conditions in the economy. Moreover, with larger and more fragile markets, Fed's rate changes assumed direct signal value for financial actors. This then opened up possibilities for countercyclical stabilization policies during the 1990s and 2000s.

The Bank of England, which had been pessimistic about the effectiveness of its interventions and its own possibilities to act as an independent policy authority, soon recognized that these Fed innovations promised solutions for the particular problems that it had encountered during the monetarist experiments of the 1970s and early 1980s. The UK central bank saw the potential for emulating the Fed as it became apparent that a deregulated domestic financial sector and deeper financialization of the UK economy (primarily through mortgage debt) increased the effectiveness of policy-rate manipulations. The problem then was how to steer these rates purposefully and transmit price signals effectively to the broader system. A first prerequisite was to redesign those markets that were of immediate relevance for monetary policy implementation and transmission (particularly the government bond and short-term money markets). A second hurdle concerned how the Bank, rather than the government, could gain the authority to engage in expectational coordination with markets. The opportunity to gain influence over expectation management came in 1992, when the government and particularly the Treasury suffered a loss of legitimacy after the United Kingdom's involuntary exit from the European Exchange Rate Mechanism. Clever officials at the Bank used this occasion to introduce inflation targeting as a particular technique to relate decisions over interest rates to inflation forecasts authored by the Bank. The newly introduced *Inflation Reports* were a decisive new instrument because, beyond serving policy deliberations with the Treasury, they engaged financial markets in explicit ways; through the reports, it became easier for markets to detect how the Bank desired to steer interest rates and react to expectational changes in bond markets. As a result, the Chancellor was brought into a defensive position because he had to argue for his own interest-rate preferences against the Bank (with its sophisticated forecasts) *and* the markets. The incoming Labour Party Chancellor Gordon Brown acknowledged this de facto power shift when conferring operational independence on the Bank in 1998.

German and Swiss central bankers resisted the importation of American liability management techniques and instruments to their home markets long after these had arrived in London. This resistance was based on an understanding that market-based banking would undermine the conditions needed for successful conduct of practical monetarism, which also secured the historical settlements between monetary authorities and universal banks. But as the largest of these banks became more active in international and particularly US dollar markets, the infrastructural foundations of monetary targeting crumbled. The Bundesbank and Swiss National Bank therefore turned to the Anglo-Saxon solutions for policy implementation and transmission at the end of the 1990s. This not only changed the operational foundations of policy, but also redefined central bankers' relations with finance. Rather than sticking to the distinct tradition of money market politics, the newly founded European Central Bank and the Swiss authorities became supporters of a global market-building project from the late 1990s onward that solidified the infrastructural foundations of inflation-targeting techniques and simultaneously strengthened the conditions for market-based finance. During this period, the Fed chairman Alan Greenspan appeared on the front cover of *Time* magazine, and central bankers secured their status as the state actors who offered solutions to the intricate governability problems raised by globalizing finance.

Notwithstanding the fact that the Global Financial Crisis called into question basic assumptions built into this precrisis trajectory of central banking, we observe a striking continuity of post- with precrisis patterns. Central bankers used their freedom of maneuver at this historical moment to innovate new policy tools that were adapted to postcrisis financial and economic conditions and that would secure and consolidate their own authority. The Fed's innovation of quantitative easing is a case in point, which deepened this nexus of central banks with financial markets beyond "classical" banking. But at the same time, over the 2010s, the infrastructural limits of this macroeconomic policy approach became ever more apparent. Reinforcing financialization processes no longer generated the macroeconomic benefits that had undergirded the regime's legitimacy before 2008. The book thus ends with a predicament: Central banks' positions of power are entrenched, but their output legitimacy has weakened.

Innovations like those at the Bundesbank and Swiss National Bank in 1974–1976; at the Fed in 1979–1982, 1993, and 2008–2009; and at the Bank of England in 1992–1993 helped monetary authorities to introduce policies that worked effectively under specific finance-internal and broader political-economic conditions. Based on the successful introduction of governing practices that tapped context-specific infrastructural powers, central bankers then assumed greater influence and legitimacy in their respective polities. Particularly in the Anglo-Saxon settings, these innovations concentrated on market-based finance. By connecting their own techniques of banking and expectation management with these prevailing structural trends, central bankers in the United States and similar countries learned how to generate finance-based infrastructural power for monetary policy purposes. Under conditions of financial globalization, more and more central bankers then turned to these Anglo-Saxon solutions. It is important to note here that this focus on policy innovations, their contexts, and infrastructural foundations does not imply that other factors were irrelevant. To be sure, decreasing growth rates, capitalist counterrevolutions, new electoral coalitions, and unresolved intellectual problems in postwar Keynesianism all mattered for central banks to assume prominent positions in neoliberal regimes. My argument, rather, is that by looking at these factors from the perspective of central banks, and studying in detail how larger structural forces were translated at these organizations into specific policy solutions, we can better capture country-specific trajectories, relevant conditions for monetary policy dominance, and its varying effects.

Champions of Finance

Accordingly, one reason why it is worth reconstructing these processes with more precision and from the angle of practical policy innovations is that such analysis gives us a distinct perspective on the consequences of central banks' rise. As I have discussed above, looking back at half a century of rising inequalities, severe financial crises, and growing debt, we are not short of pessimistic retrospections on neoliberalism. But what is the precise role of central banking in all of this? Seen from the angle of existing political-economy accounts, monetary authorities are to be charged with two faults. Scholars focusing on economic policy interests particularly draw attention to central banks' deflationary bias in the period up until the 2000s. This bias arguably supported the unsustainable growth of finance because, as households suffered relative losses in wage income, they turned to unsustainable credit-financed consumption. There is evidence to support this argument, particularly for the US setting. The limitation here is that central banks' deflationary bias disappeared at some point, while financialization continued. A second argument is that central bankers have been vocal and influential advocates of financial deregulation. Without the shackles of New Deal laws or "financial repression" (Turner 2014), financial firms indulged in an aggressive search for yield, which has fed the boom-bust cycles seen since the 1970s. Again, there is much to recommend this view. But what remains unclear is why and when central bankers favored (what kinds of) deregulation and when they did not; for instance, compare the Fed position on repo markets (pro) to that of the Bank of

England (against) during the 1980s; or that of the Bank of England on the same markets during the early 1990s (pro) to that of the German and Swiss central bankers (against). More importantly, the deregulation perspective misses the fact that central bankers have not just liberalized finance; they have also helped to co-construct some essential parts of it.

This then leads me to look at the consequences of central banks' ascendency from a different angle, namely through the concrete linkages between central banking and financial systems at the level of governing techniques. First, from this angle, we can shed new light on central banks' contributions to the rise of active liability management and associated money-market instruments, which have provided essential infrastructures for financial expansion. Indeed, if we look back at the 1970s, most central bankers perceived the introduction of such practices and instruments as threats. Postwar banking regulations were undermined and extant monetary-management routines were disrupted by firms trading liquidity across borders and offshore. But as the authorities came to grips with these innovations through the adoption of new operational techniques, their politics of money markets changed. In the event, monetary authorities emerged as designers of more formal institutional foundations for these markets that helped consolidate and stabilize a globally integrated system. For instance, in many countries, officials helped to develop repo markets as the core segments for liquidity lending and borrowing in a market-based financial regime. Tragically, these particular venues for trading liquidity developed into the Achilles heels of financial systems. When problems occurred in American real estate, money markets such as asset-backed commercial paper and repo worked as super-spreaders, amplifying local "corrections" in asset valuations into downward movements within the entire North Atlantic financial network. Out of their distinct policy interests, authorities had thus co-constructed financial structures that proved to be extremely fragile as the financial cycle of the late 1990s and early 2000s came to a (temporary) halt. Anticipations of these systemic risks had existed in the central banking community, proving that efficient market beliefs had not always prevailed. But monetary authorities had decided to disengage from *prudential* regulation because strategic dissociation from this area helped to safeguard their monetary policy authority and the mutually beneficial settlements with market-based finance.

A complementary mechanism through which central banking supported financial expansion was the cognitive expectational structure that central banks had created in order to render their monetary policies effective. In particular, with the adoption of inflation targeting, becoming predictable for financial audiences emerged as a chief policy concern. Predictability was seen as important because when markets can anticipate upcoming official interest-rate decisions, there will be less disruption in the underlying governing relationships between short-term and long-term rates (the so-called yield curve). But rendering policies predictable means downplaying substantive uncertainties that exist in capitalist systems, as Jens Beckert and Richard Bronk (2018) have plausibly argued. Actors adapt to fictitious visions of the future and will be all the more disappointed when their illusions fail. Arguably, what we saw in 2008 was partly that: the implosion of a systemic stability illusion. Financial firms suddenly realized that it was not sufficient to calculate the expected marginal changes in policy rates to understand their true liquidity risks. More importantly, the reality of secular stagnation after 2008 has led central banks and financial firms to continuously err on inflation, interest rates, and growth. This has forced central banks to become increasingly expansionary in order to uphold asset values that have unwarranted expectations about future returns built into them.

More generally, and as became most apparent under QE, contemporary central bank instruments operate via financial markets. As Mario Draghi, the ECB president, put it in a press conference in 2013, at a time in which youth unemployment in Greece was at 50 percent, financial markets "are the only, the necessary channel, through which monetary policy is transmitted."[11] If at all, contemporary central banking thus influences the "real" economy through its effects on financial market values that, it is hoped, may improve financing conditions for companies and enhance household wealth. QE makes it particularly evident that such central banking creates considerable effects before ever achieving the intended objectives, for example, by reinforcing wealth concentration and financialized corporate strategies. It is by understanding these implementation and transmission effects of monetary policy that we can better capture how central bank dominance has contributed to unequal economies with bloated financial systems and low growth.

The Study

In this book, I look in detail at a selection of cases because I am interested in what I consider to be formative instances of central banking innovations. Thus the Bundesbank and the Swiss National Bank serve as exemplars of successful practical monetarism, and the Fed and the Bank of England represent important innovators of inflation targeting. Looking comparatively at a few cases and for longer time periods will also reveal the precise sequences through which central bankers reacted to circumstances; how contextual features became relevant (constraining or enabling) conditions for policy innovation; and what consequences particular monetary policy practices have had. Besides exploiting comparisons to identify these enabling conditions and varying effects, I also connect the cases in an integrated narrative. For the innovations at particular central banking organizations induced broader learning processes and policy adaptations in the sample of cases that I study. Moreover, we cannot understand the convergence of monetary policy techniques in the 1990s and 2000s without accounting for the formative role of American financial institutions and practices for other financial systems in the developed world. I draw on Philip McMichael's concept of *incorporated comparisons* to develop this particular comparative methodology.

The material I use has been collected in a seven-year research effort, involving numerous visits to central bank and national archives and over thirty oral history interviews with current and former officials, as well as other relevant actors. Archival work was important to go beyond polished presentations of finished policy designs to the shop-floor level, at which officials express uncertainty, negotiate conflicts, and make practical judgments. The interviews serve as complementary sources that provide invaluable insights into central banks' internal lives and enable me to reconstruct in more detail the organizational processes through which governing techniques have been constructed and employed. As a nonexpert, I also used interviews to learn about the intricacies of central banking and to test propositions that I developed during the research process. Personal fame was not my criterion of selection. I focused rather on the actors who were actually involved in developing central bank tools. I should say that the response rate for requested interviews was exceptionally high—out of all my interview requests, only one went unanswered. I do not attribute this to my own cleverness or to the particular relevance of my study, but to the fact that central bankers are generally proud of what they have achieved. A list of archives and interviewees, together with some biographical information, is provided in the appendix.

More broadly, I see the combined use of archival sources and oral history interviews as a viable strategy to study practices of central banking as a core unit of theorizing and analysis in my work. These include practices of money-market management, practices of modeling and forecasting, practices of interest-rate setting in senior decision-making bodies, practices of strategic public communication, and so on. While ethnographic work would be preferable for this analytic purpose, it is simply not feasible to get access to core domains in central banks (senior decision-making contexts, trading desks, etc.) for the purposes of participant observation. Moreover, ethnography has the additional problem that, even when researchers spend extended periods "in the field," they will observe only snapshots of longer transformative processes. This is a problem when the research question being asked is about interrelated changes in policies, institutions, and capitalist structures. I thus also see this study as a test case for a kind of qualitative sociology that foregrounds bureaucratic practices, their (re-)configuration, and their shifting locations in between broader fields of politics and markets as crucial elements for explaining macro-transformations, like the rise of central banks.

Chapter Outline

Chapter 1, "Neoliberalism and the Rise of Central Banks," develops the book's theoretical backbone. I argue that the development of new governing techniques at central banks was one key driver of neoliberal policy and institutional change. The book's approach thus diverges from, and addresses problems in, dominant ideational, interest-based, and institutional perspectives on neoliberalism and monetary policy dominance. The chapter develops a new vocabulary to analyze how governing techniques are constructed on the basis of central banks' operational entanglements with finance, and reflexive engagements with expectations in the economy. Lastly, I justify my comparative research design and case selection.

Chapter 2, "Monetarism and the Invention of Monetary Policy," gives an original account of the era of widespread monetarist experimentation from 1970 until the early 1980s. It is largely uncontested that modern monetary policy has its origins in this period of high inflation. However, popular ideational, interest-based, or institutional accounts cannot make sense of the patterns of successes and failures among central banks in this period. Only in Germany, Switzerland, and to some extent Japan did monetary targeting become an effective operational technique and communicative strategy for anchoring inflationary expectations. In most other countries practical monetarism failed. The main section of this chapter compares Switzerland and the United Kingdom to explain these divergent outcomes. Using original data, I show that monetary targeting in these two countries developed as policy experimentation under fundamental uncertainty. But only in Switzerland did such experimentation encounter felicity conditions that enabled the innovation of new governing tools. These conditions were (a) significant room for experimentation for the central bank; (b) a fiduciary role for the central bank vis-à-vis corporatist institutions; and (c) stable routines in banking that undergirded apparent causalities between central bank interventions, bank liabilities, and inflation. All these conditions were absent in the United Kingdom, where macroeconomic management remained centralized, the Bank of England remained disconnected from constituencies outside the "City of London," and the banking sector underwent a period of rapid innovation and transformation during the 1970s. The final section of this chapter then turns to cases following similar as well as different trajectories—I discuss Germany and Japan as similar to the Swiss case, Canada as encountering problems also confronted in the United Kingdom, and France as providing yet another story of failure. These comparisons help to strengthen the chapter's main claim.

Chapter 3, "Hegemonizing Financial Market Expectations," then turns to the development of inflation targeting in two significant incubator settings, the United States and the United Kingdom. I recount this development in three steps. First, I unpack Thatcherism to demonstrate an incoherence between her government's pro-financialization policies and her monetarist framework for macroeconomic management. I then turn to the United States to show that Paul Volcker as Fed chairman discovered a policy technique that was more appropriate for governing financial and monetary relations amid globalizing and integrating markets. This technique involved the Fed reacting to bond-market movements, which were interpreted as authoritative judgments on the appropriateness of interest-rate decisions. In a final step, I return to Britain to show that while the Americanization of bond markets and the establishment of futures markets created structural prerequisites for a Volcker-style policy, the Bank of England overcame the obstacle of centralized macroeconomic management after the UK's exit from the European Exchange Rate Mechanism in 1992. In the aftermath of this event, the central bank capitalized on the Treasury's loss of authority to assume independent forecasting competencies and moved on to publish its own inflation reports. With these reports as critical devices, the Bank could enroll financial markets into coordination games that led to the informal shift of policy authority from the Treasury to the central bank; operational independence followed logically in 1998. The final section of the chapter discusses the German and Swiss rejections of the Bank of England's and other inflation targeters' desire for predictability in interest-rate movements in order to highlight significant differences between monetary and inflation targeting. In this final section of the chapter, I also discuss New Zealand's and Sweden's early adoption of inflation targets to support the major findings of my analysis in another, formative setting.

Chapter 4, "Money Markets as Infrastructures of Global Finance and Central Banks," turns to a complementary aspect of the development and consolidation of inflation targeting that deserves special attention. For inflation targeters, money markets with ample liquidity, which are highly interconnected among each other as well as other parts of finance (for example, capital and stock markets), are an important prerequisite for the implementation and transmission of policies via interest-rate signals. Accordingly, as I discuss in this chapter, inflation targeters have been political advocates and practical architects of market-based financial systems. I demonstrate this significant role by discussing a shift in central bank attitudes and actions toward money markets during the neoliberal era. Up until the 1960s, and less consistently in the 1970s to 1980s, the authorities still aimed to put regulatory limits on the expansion of Eurodollar and banks' active liability management. But with the widespread adoption of inflation targeting in the 1990s to 2000s, these regulatory concerns disappeared, and central banks became active supporters of the expansion of key money markets, particularly "repo" (repurchase agreements). Monetary targeters such as the Bundesbank and Swiss National Bank initially remained critical of these developments and successfully inhibited money-market innovations in their domestic financial systems until the 1990s. But the growing practical and political difficulties in maintaining this position ultimately led to the abandonment of monetarism and motivated the adoption of inflation targeting across Continental Europe.

Chapter 5, "The Organization of Ignorance: How Central Bankers Abandoned Regulation," looks at the relations between monetary policies and the regulation of finance and banking in light of the 2007–2009 crisis—an event that dramatically falsified the precrisis view that, if "central banks succeed in stabilizing inflation in the short term[,] . . . the economy will broadly take care of itself" (Borio 2011: 2). While there has been a lot of discussion on regulatory failure and the lessons of the crisis, the chapter draws on original data from the Swiss and the British cases to make two contributions. First, I look beyond formal regulatory policies to show that, up until the 1970s, central bankers held informal authority over regulatory matters; central banks' subsequent withdrawal from that role left a vacuum. Second, the chapter demonstrates that this vacuum particularly affected the regulation of banks' liability management, rather than capital requirements. Because central banks are in daily operational contact with banks to provide liquidity and act as lenders of last resort, they naturally possess competences and powers to shape regulation in this domain. Disastrously, the differentiation of financial supervision from monetary policy led central banks to abandon these responsibilities. Policymakers also failed to integrate liquidity-related regulatory concerns into the Basel framework of international prudential rules for banks. For these reasons, liquidity issues and the regulation of money markets fell through the cracks. The fact that the crisis of 2007–2009 was a global bank run—that is, a breakdown of market-based liquidity—brings home why this neglect was consequential.

Chapter 6, "Plumbing Financialization in Vain: Central Banking after 2008," finally turns to the postcrisis era to argue that, because monetary policy as macroeconomic management has become predicated on financialization, central banks have busied themselves in vain "repairing" financialization to reestablish governability under the conditions of sluggish growth, debt overhangs, and financial fragility. This applies on two levels: (1) the level of finance-internal institutions and market structures, and (2) the level of the macroeconomy, where finance is supposed to function as the

conduit for growth. These orientations toward finance are particularly reflected in central banks' practice of QE. The chapter concludes with a
detailed analysis of these problematic policies by arguing that, as financialized capitalism has developed into an unsustainable regime, central
banks risk losing the output legitimacy upon which their ascendency has
been based.

Finally, the Conclusion revisits core findings from this book and relates
them to two broader agendas: (1) to advance the state-centric tradition of
studying economic policies that goes back to Theda Skocpol and Margaret
Weir, and (2) to compare the case of central banks in financialized capitalism with that of Fordism as a regime in which institutions, policies, and
capitalist structures first strengthened each other, before entering into a
vicious feedback loop of endogenous self-destruction.

CHAPTER ONE

Neoliberalism and the Rise of Central Banks

Why is it that the economy is governable by means of monetary policy?
—BRAUN 2018B: 196

THIS BOOK DISCUSSES how the powers of particular state bodies have increased vis-à-vis other elements of the state, how this is associated with policy change, and what role the evolving structures of capitalism play vis-à-vis these institutional and policy-related transformations. The starting point for this analysis is a well-established finding from political science, economic history, and sociology: We have seen significant, transformative changes across all these dimensions in advanced capitalist economies over the past fifty years (Streeck and Thelen 2005). Industrial capitalism has weakened (Boix 2015), together with its organizational infrastructures (Baccaro and Howell 2017). This process has durably reduced real growth rates (Rachel and Summers 2019). We have also seen massive changes in corporate strategies that have led to the reorganization of production, consumption, and financing activities along "value" (Baldwin 2013) and "wealth chains" (Seabrooke and Wigan 2014). Also, the period since the 1970s is one of massive expansion of financial activities and the "re-coding" of significant economic processes and welfare systems in accordance with financial logics (Krippner 2005; Offer 2017; van der Zwan 2014). Financial crises have become more frequent and severe as a result (Schularick and Taylor 2012). Lastly, and perhaps most importantly, inequalities of income and wealth have grown (Milanovic 2019; Piketty 2014; Saez and Zucman 2019), undermining postwar growth models (Baccaro and Pontusson 2016) and the class compromises that underpinned political stability in the West (Rosanvallon 2013).

Complementary to these diagnoses of capitalist transformation and its different crystallizations across countries and regions, we have seen significant changes in how states intervene in, regulate, and govern economies. Subsumed under the concept of neoliberalism, authors have observed processes of state retrenchment and the rise of markets (Fourcade-Gourinchas and Babb 2002). A more nuanced interpretation posits that governments continue to conduct active economic and social policies, as well as market regulation. However, while states have given up or scaled back political authority over some domains (e.g., redistributing wealth and limiting income inequalities) (Lynch 2020; Saez and Zucman 2019), they have increasingly acted to build, strengthen, and secure markets as privileged vehicles to address economic as well as a wider set of social, environmental, and other concerns (Langley 2015; Morgan and Campbell 2011). Moreover, the aims and activities of state bodies have increasingly been articulated according to specific mandates, with independent technocratic agencies serving as preferred institutional vehicles (Jordana and Levi-Faur 2004; Majone 1994). Associated with this are state-internal shifts in the centers of power, from lateral coordinating units and elected officials, toward those organizations that can most effectively cooperate with powerful social and economic actors, such as executive bodies with relationships to financial markets and multinational firms (Sassen 2006).

I thus premise my analysis on the well-established observation of transformative change in Western countries toward new capitalist structures, the adoption of neoliberal policies, and the rise of market-oriented executive bodies. Unquestionably, the growing importance of monetary policies since the 1970s and the expanded influence of central banks are a case in point. But if library-filling works on this broad topic already exist, why produce another one? The rationale for this book is that, despite the widely accepted diagnosis of concurrent changes in capitalist formations, policies, and institutions, scholars in political economy and sociology have paid relatively little attention to the problem of how precisely authorities have managed to establish new ways of governing capitalist economies, which have undergone significant structural change. How do public authorities go about engaging the ever-changing objects of their concerns so that public interventions actually produce reliable, politically desired effects? In other words, how can some state organizations—such as central banks—claim that they effectively produce the outcomes that give them legitimacy? This is not just a question about the motifs and forces that create and settle political fights over who can decide over what; it also raises the problem of how state organizations establish and stabilize (cognitive, material, social) relations with the markets, sectors, and actors whose aggregate choices bring about the macroeconomic outcomes that authorities claim to be responsible for.

The research that I cite here has neglected this problem because the prevalent analytic strategies being employed in political economy and most of sociology provide hardly any means of studying governing practices. The underlying mechanisms cited in most studies instead have to do with the ideational or interest-dependent forces determining choices over policies and institutions. For instance, many social science scholars suggest that law makers and authorities have adopted neoliberalism as a new ideology because they learned that previous policy paradigms were ineffective and because they believed in the promises of deregulatory and monetarist ideas. The usual alternative explanation is that the demands of changing electoral coalitions or the employment of strategic and structural power resources by corporations and wealthy groups have altered the calculi of decision-makers and the centers of power within the state. In more nuanced versions, institutional path-dependencies are introduced to explain the set of constraints and opportunities under which ideas or interests are able to induce change (e.g., Beramendi et al. 2015). But these different explanatory strategies do not get us to the core of the governing problem. For policy ideas or demands are not the same as policy practices and the organizational forms through which these are enacted. There is a wide gap between a proposal on paper or a claim being voiced by an elected official and the "instrumentalization" (Clift 2020; Lascoumes and Le Galès 2007; Rose and Miller 1992) and "infrastructuration" (Edwards 2019) of concrete macroeconomic interventions. Moreover, as we know, many policy ideas and demands actually fail. Proposed measures end up producing unexpected results, leaving authorities in a rather awkward position. In her famous book

Capitalizing on Crisis, Greta Krippner (2011) structures her whole argument around such unintended consequences. Measures whose purpose was to make capital available for the broader economy and to restrain inflation had actually unleashed financialization. Policymakers were taken by surprise, but they accepted the unintended outcome because it rendered invisible the problems that had motivated their reforms in the first place.

But beyond an implicit yet unrealistically linear theory of policy and institutional change, running from ideas and / or interests to implementation, or an improved conception based on the study of unintended consequences and expediency, there is yet another possible avenue through which we can analytically engage with the problem. To learn about this other option, we need to turn our attention to the actual conduct of economic policies and the actors responsible for it. These usually are the officials within executive organizations, who design particular interventions and implement them. In sociology and political science, we have a strong tradition of scholarship that looks at these state authorities, their interests and rationalities, and their patterns of action (Carpenter 2001; Carruthers 1994; Skocpol 1985). A plethora of theories can answer the question of how state officials use their room to maneuver and what interests they actually pursue. For instance, some scholars argue that bureaucrats try to advance their personal careers inside or outside the state apparatus (Adolph 2013; Van Gunten 2015). Others believe that officials' primary objective is to show their allegiance to leaders and parties; or that bureaucrats enact ideologies and cultural templates that are dominant in national institutional configurations (Fourcade 2009); or that state bureaucrats follow the *esprit de corps* of their elite group (Bourdieu 1996 [1989]).

My own perspective on public officials by and large follows Daniel Carpenter's (2001) concept of bureaucratic autonomy. I assume that, because bureaucrats have some room for discretion and control significant organizational resources, they will try to expand these resources and put them to use in order to advance their organizations' influence and legitimacy. This usually, though not exclusively, means searching for conditions under which their organizations can claim policy success, however defined. Accordingly, officials mobilize the instruments that they control (Weir and Skocpol 1985: 118) to actively engage with the governing problems that they confront, with the aim of finding viable solutions (Dewey 1915; Haydu 1998). Under conditions of uncertainty and / or when confronted with new dilemmas, this search leads to experimentation and innovation. Policy-makers retool their instruments and engage in policy trials to find new ways to render their interventions effective and legitimate. This requires incremental learning from (sometimes unintended) successes and failures (Carpenter 2001: 21–22, 30–31), and it leads to the development of new techniques that can contribute to effective policymaking. When state actors are capable of innovating such techniques and retain exclusive control over them, their organizations gain considerable intrastate influence and legitimacy.[1]

By foregrounding the role of bureaucratic actors and their governing techniques, one may think that I am focusing only on a subset of questions associated with neoliberal policy change: technical issues of bureaucratic capacity and implementation, rather than the big questions of paradigmatic change and its linkage to macrostructural transformation. After all, the very idea of bureaucracy is that its officials act under multiple, political and state-structural constraints, expressed in predefined mandates and duties and divisions of institutional labor, hierarchies, and formal accountabilities. But my aim is to challenge the principal-agent view of policymaking, which has often provided the lens through which the respective institutional features and actors are theorized. For not only do policies succeed or fail at the level of actual governing, requiring experimentation and pragmatic learning at that level. If policymakers can show through their experiments that they can realize objectives and solve problems for which their principals or other officials have no ready answer; and if they can communicate such efficacy internally as well as toward relevant publics, they can leverage their influence within the state (Carpenter 2001: 32–33). Often, this involves redefining mandates and tasks, as well as reframing the terms of success. Over time, policy experimentation can thus lead to fundamental reassessments of what is regarded as feasible and legitimate state authority under certain conditions of capitalism. The suggested, reversed causality thus runs from experiments in policy implementation, to the codification of new governing techniques, to the redefinition of policy jurisdictions, to the redistribution of intrastate influence among different bureaucratic actors.

Importantly, however, I do not conceive of this reverse causality as a kind of meritocratic contest among bureaucrats for the best available solutions. In order to make plausible why such an interpretation would be misguided, it is useful to draw on Michael Mann's concept of *infrastructural power* (Mann 1984; Mann 1996). Mann introduces this concept to distinguish states' monopolistic control over lethal force from their capacities to penetrate civil society and to engage social actors in the process of governing by shaping the circumstances of their actions and the resources that they draw on in daily routines. For instance, the infrastructure of streets, lanes, traffic lights, demarcations, and so on makes traffic governable by giving citizens the contexts and resources they need to drive from A to B. Because whole territories are penetrated by this infrastructure, governing large-scale traffic movements becomes feasible. Moreover, Mann argues that the resources undergirding infrastructural power may not actually be invented or generated by public bodies; they can come from civil society as well. States often tap infrastructural power sources opportunistically by inscribing their own projects of governing into emergent social structures, routines, and technologies.[2]

In contradistinction from the state retrenchment literature, Mann maintains that Western states and their infrastructural powers remain strong in the post-1970 world of "globalizations" (Mann 2011). But to my mind, a more adequate application of his concept to neoliberalism would suggest that changes in capitalist economies have reconfigured and redistributed the sources of infrastructural power that are available to different parts of the state and for different projects of governing. In some areas, bureaucracies with particular responsibilities and institutional positions may find that they can achieve policy success and leverage their own influence by using intervention tools that effectively engage new corporate forms, new techniques of calculation and marketization, and the transformed orders and institutions of markets (Fligstein 2001). In other domains, capitalist change has reduced previously available infrastructural powers. For instance, strong organized labor unions (Blyth and Matthijs 2017) and / or cohesive networks of corporate elites (Mizruchi 2013) were essential for Keynesian and / or corporatist governing in the Fordist era, but they are no longer available in the neoliberal age.

To be sure, the suggested conception offers only a selective perspective on the plethora of relevant factors influencing the reformulation of policies and institutions. It is undeniable that the redistribution of power resources in financial capitalism (Baccaro and Howell 2017), the formation of new electoral coalitions (Beramendi et al. 2015), and / or broader processes of "social learning" among elites (Fourcade-Gourinchas and Babb 2002) have also played a role. What I contend, however, is that under certain scope conditions, concrete changes in policies and institutions are driven primarily by innovations in governing practices and become consolidated through the capacity of particular bureaucratic organizations to enroll powerful market constituencies in the enactment of particular techniques. To take one illustrative case from another realm, think about twenty-first-century defense policy. Remote-control drones equipped with lethal weapons, combined with ever more precise geolocational information, have not just transformed the set of options available to the principals deciding on attacks and war efforts; they have actually transformed the entire process of defense policymaking. Executive agents controlling technologies have more say, and the very blurring of boundaries between war and peace means that formal declarations of war often become unnecessary to initiate significant lethal action.

The empirical case that I use in this book is less deadly, but nonetheless highly consequential. I analyze the rise of central banks and the growing importance of monetary policies. There is hardly any question that, in recent decades, these particular policymaking bodies have gained in prominence and that their policymaking has increasingly gained traction. Some scholars even go so far as to argue that monetary policy dominance is the defining feature of neoliberal macroeconomic policy regimes (Blyth and Matthijs 2017). The process leading to that outcome started in the 1970s under conditions of collapsing international currency orders and high inflation. Central banks' power grew more consistently from the 1990s onward, with the spread of inflation targeting (Wasserfallen 2019) and the adoption of operational independence as hegemonic institutional form (Bodea and Hicks 2015). This led Saskia Sassen to argue that over "the last decade [central banks] have become the institutional home within the national state for monetary policies that are necessary to further the development of a global capital market and, indeed, more generally, a global economic system" (2006: 233). The unsettled years that followed—between the financial crisis in 2007–2009 and the outbreak of Covid-19 in 2020—have only reinforced these trends. Indeed, for some years, it appeared that central bankers were "the only game in town" (El-Erian 2016).[3]

Why central banks and monetary policy? Answering this question will give me the opportunity to spell out in more detail my argument about officials' policy experimentation, the codification of governing techniques, and infrastructural power, and to distinguish the argument in more precise terms from propositions and arguments about neoliberalism and monetary policy in other research strands. The chapter will thus continue with a review of prominent views on how central banks have benefited from, and contributed to, neoliberal change. Based on a critique of these scholarships, I will contend that only by studying and problematizing central banks' highly specific tools of governing and their distinct infrastructural relationships with finance, can we understand how these organizations emerged as dominant governing bodies within contemporary capitalist orders. I will further argue that, rather than encouraging a neglect of broader structural developments, a detailed study of central banks' governing techniques actually offers a specific lens on political-economic change. These techniques are highly context-dependent—monetary authority tools rely on the structures of financial systems and on the broader institutional configurations that influence expectational dynamics in the economy. By identifying how central banks have successfully exploited the expansive development of financial infrastructures since the 1970s, and how they have inscribed their policies into hegemonic "politics of expectations" (Beckert 2016; Beckert 2020), we can analyze how growing central bank power is intertwined with broader transformations of capitalism. This will then give us tools for comparing country-specific trajectories and ultimately also for problematizing neoliberal governmentality, as deeply implicated in financialized capitalism. The chapter will close with a discussion of the problems of central bank dominance and introduce "incorporated comparison" (McMichael 1990) as a particular methodology that I will draw on in this book.

How Do We Explain Central Banks' Dominant Roles in Neoliberalism?

The book's core argument is that central banks' rise during neoliberalism is the product of monetary authorities' successful enlistment of finance as an infrastructural vehicle for effective governing, an outcome that required intensive policy experimentation by central bankers themselves. This perspective contrasts with dominant strands in political economy that have usually relied on interests, ideas, and institutions as conceptual building blocks to explain changes in monetary policies and their status in neoliberal regimes. It also differs from the conceptions of central bank technocracy found in most sociological works. I will now introduce and criticize these different approaches.

Distributional Conflicts and Politics of Money

A first body of works starts with the assumption that every political "choice about money reflects the outcome of a political contest" (Kirshner 2003: 646). This political contest is thought to consist of struggles among "macrogroups" (Ingham 2004: 55), which have competing interests in monetary affairs and different sources of social power to influence politics. The relevant social actors can be social classes (Goldthorpe 1978) or sectoral groups (Frieden 2002). Whoever prevails in these struggles will reap benefits in the form of policy decisions, regulations, and institutional arrangements that favor their monetary interests over those of others. Since the prevailing politics of money, prevailing interests, and sources of social power mutually reinforce each other (Pierson 2014), we can find more or less durable regimes of monetary policies in capitalist societies with particular distributional effects.

This is the skeleton of the argument. It is then specified for two, mutually related, aspects of the politics of money: for decisions that influence a currency's relative value versus other currencies; and for decisions affecting the (future) value of a currency in terms of goods. For instance, exchange-rate policies are seen to depend on the relative importance and power of export-oriented sectors versus those for nontradable goods, as well as the relative weight that these groups give to exchange rate versus price stability (Bernhard, Broz and Clark 2002; Frieden 2002). In more export-dependent growth models, dominant interests can thus be expected to favor policies that prevent an appreciation of domestic versus foreign currencies (for example, Germany), as compared to debt-driven regimes, where exchange-rate policies either matter little (for example, the United States) or create capital flight pressures, in which case powerful financial interests will demand policies that prevent the domestic currency's devaluation.

But because of the perceived ineffectiveness of exchange-rate stabilization, in recent years most attention has been devoted to the politics of (dis)

inflation. Indeed, Geoffrey Keith Ingham (2004: 78) claims that the conflict over "hard" (that is, stable) versus "soft" (that is, inflationary) money,
and its distributional implications for creditors and debtors, is the oldest and
most profound in capitalist states. Beyond that, a key reason for scholars'
attention to inflation lies in the assumed trade-offs that are inherent in
macroeconomic management. In other words, decisions about future rates
of inflation supposedly imply political choices over the relative weight
to be given to price stability versus other policy goals—in particular, employment and growth. There is a trade-off between different macroeconomic stabilization objectives that requires hard choices over what goals are
prioritized. This leads different groups, which are differently affected by
macroeconomic developments, to desire different (dis)inflationary policies
(Hibbs 1977; Scheve 2004). Workers and poorer segments of society are
seen to be the first victims of hard-money disinflationary policies and are
thus inclined to accept inflation if it helps secure employment and redistributive growth. By contrast, owners of capital funds are thought to favor
hard-money policies. Wealthy groups evidently also benefit from growth,
and they own real assets that protect them from inflation; but their financial wealth (for example, holdings in government debt) will depreciate as
prices increase. In doubt, they therefore favor measures that stabilize the
monetary value of their wealth.

On the basis of this distributional conflict and monetary policy framework, one can develop a succinct narrative about central banks' rise to
power and their growing importance in neoliberalism. The narrative pre-
sents recent developments as reflecting the superiority of capitalists' structural power over democratic demands, a superiority that they have been
able to mobilize in the neoliberal era through credible threats of "exit" and
the exercise of "voice" (Hirshman 1970; Lindblom 1977). As a consequence,
hard-money policies have come to prevail. This has not just reinforced the
dominance of capital but has gone hand in hand with a power shift inside
advanced capitalist states. Central banks, as the advocates and enforcers
of hard money, have gained influence and power vis-à-vis democratically
elected governments with more contradictory priorities. Because central
bank power and capitalist hegemony reinforce each other, hardly any government in the Western capitalist world dares to challenge the power of
central banks, the doctrine of low inflation, and mobile capital.

There is much to say for the politics of money approach as an explanatory template in political economy. It connects macrostructural changes in capitalism—growing capital mobility, income shifts from labor to capital, and so on—to conflicting preferences among social groups, to widely observed processes of policy change toward disinflation after 1970 (Streeck 2014). Moreover, recent work in economics vindicates the distributional emphasis in monetary policies and contradicts the neoclassical and New Keynesian assumption that low inflation is neutral for long-term growth (e.g., Auclert 2019).

But one key problem with the politics of money framework is that, in its coarse version, it cannot explain variations in the role and substance of monetary policies. For instance, if it were true that "high class conflict leads to elite unity and orthodox economic policy" (Maxfield 1991: 420), then the United Kingdom would be the prime example of the rise of hard-money policies, whereas countries such as Germany, with muted class conflict, would provide more fertile ground for soft-money approaches. But the opposite was the case in the 1970s, as I will discuss in more detail in the next chapter. In Germany, the central bank was much quicker to assume authority and pursue draconic disinflation than the Bank of England. In an interest-based framework, one may respond to this puzzle by introducing finer and more complex distinctions in relation to group interests. For instance, while Germany is a country with a significant group of middle- and even working-class savers, as well as internationally competitive producers (who are objectively interested in low domestic inflation), the share of mortgage holders (interested in higher inflation) was rising rapidly in Britain during the 1970s.[4] Moreover, in contrast to German banks, British banks were somewhat protected against inflation because their loans were granted with variable rates—accordingly, the key financial players were little hurt by high and volatile inflation and could sometimes even profit from it.

I here pursue another strategy to move beyond the simple framework of money politics and structural power. I start from the empirical observation that policies that are functionally beneficial for powerful groups have not always been adopted for that purpose. In fact, sometimes the respective groups have not even understood their objective interests sufficiently, or their influence on policies has remained limited.[5] Peter A.

Johnson therefore advises that we study the "relationship between institutions, interests and goals in each country as the principal actors understood them to be" (1998: 22)—that is, to focus on the public decision-makers and how they act in complex environments that send incommensurable and sometimes unclear signals. I follow his advice to obtain a realistic picture of the concrete dilemmas and conflicts associated with monetary policies and to understand why concrete courses of action were adopted in different countries.

Why should we care, however, about the actual motives and details of policy change if the hard-money literature correctly identifies a general trend? A more significant reason for moving beyond hard versus soft money is that it restricts our perspective to developments in inflation rates and the interests behind them, but black-boxes the precise policies, what consequences they had, and what roles different state actors played in their implementation (Braun 2018a). For instance, by simply juxtaposing hard versus soft money, we would have a hard time understanding why the disinflationary policies pursued by Margaret Thatcher in the United Kingdom actually went hand in hand with a rapid expansion of financial activity (Offer 2014), while leaving the Bank of England relatively powerless in the process. In the United States, disinflation happened through a rapid policy shift initiated by Paul Volcker in 1979. To understand the timing of this shift and how this happened, it is important to recognize the central role of bond markets and their "inflation scares" at the time (Goodfriend 1993). By contrast, the German Bundesbank cared little about monetarist ideology, nor did it worry about bond markets. It rather initiated disinflation in the mid-1970s by introducing a kind of corporatist monetary targeting that entailed strong elements of wage restraint and limits on fiscal spending (Rademacher 2020; Scharpf 1987). In all these cases, the politics of money perspective sees the same outcome (hard money and disinflation), while disregarding significant differences in the patterns and contents of policies, as well as the roles of central banks.

More important still, since the mid-1980s, nominal and real interest rates have come down significantly (Rachel and Summers 2019). Inflation in the prices of consumer goods has remained subdued, but financial activity, far from being discouraged by softer money, has actually exploded. Moreover, since 2010, central banks have engaged in very expansionary policies, but these interventions have primarily benefited those groups (the rich with a lot of financial wealth) who, according to discussed literature, usually demand and profit from hard money (Petrou 2021a). Only by overcoming the neglect of "the operational details of central banking" (Braun and Gabor 2020: 243) can we hope to explain these trajectories and decipher the recent patterns of easy money, low inflation, and rampant financial growth. My suggestion thus is that we should not just refine our understanding of monetary policies in different countries, but also engage with the question of how policies got operationalized and inscribed into their immediate financial and broader political-economic environments.

Ideational Accounts

Just as neoliberalism is often portrayed as a set of ideas about the efficiency of markets, the futility of regulation, and the virtues of "disciplined" state intervention (Campbell 2020; Mudge 2008), scholars standardly reconstruct the emergence of monetary policies and their growing prominence as the outcome of ideational change. For these scholars, the key moment was Milton Friedman's Presidential Address at the annual meeting of the American Economic Association in 1967, when he turned the Keynesian argument on its head. Rather than stating that market failures require proactive government intervention, Friedman (1968) saw the economy as consisting of efficient markets that were temporarily disrupted by governments' inflationary—and self-defeating—measures. The policy implication of this fundamental theoretical "gestalt-switch" was for governments to withdraw from fiscal activism and constitutionally install a money-supply rule. Harry G. Johnson (1990 [1971]) called this project a "monetarist counter-revolution" against Keynesianism; and many historians, political scientists, and sociologists have followed his lead. For instance, the prominent works of Mark Blyth (2002), Peter Hall (1986), Daniel Stedman Jones (2012), and Marion Fourcade-Gourinchas and Sarah Babb (2002) are all concerned with the influence of monetarist ideas on states' responses to the inflationary crises of the 1970s. More recently, the economist Paul Krugman has argued that macroeconomists' ideas have had a fatal impact on macroeconomic policy. He laments that mainstream economics followed Friedman's key tenets, assuming that economic actors have rational expectations and that markets achieve their equilibria in the long run (for the orthodoxy, see Goodfriend 2007; Woodford 2003b).[6] Based on these ideas, monetary policy was given priority over fiscal policy; and in the conduct of monetary policy, central bankers prioritized inflation control because they thought that little else than market-clearing prices were needed to keep or bring back economies to their optimum states (Borio 2011). This macroeconomic mindset arguably also led to the neglect of disequilibria and market imperfections within finance in the run-up to the Global Financial Crisis (Fligstein, Brundage, and Schultz 2017).

To be sure, there are important differences between the cited works. Peter Hall (1993) has suggested a particular model of ideational change. He argues that, during conjunctures of structural economic and political crises, we can sometimes observe "third order" changes that lead to shifts from one all-encompassing paradigm to another. The mechanisms driving such shifts are cognitive inconsistencies and contradictions in the old paradigm, as well as successful electoral mobilization with the help of radical new ideas. Hall interprets the UK's abandonment of Keynesian demand management in favor of Thatcher's monetarism during the late 1970s as a case in point. Other works diverge from Hall's model by emphasizing the role of "organic intellectuals" and / or experts inside bureaucracy and international organizations, who translate ideas to serve strategic interests and / or to offer concrete policy solutions (Ban 2016; Van Gunten 2015). Such translation presupposes a certain malleability and bricolage of ideas as they travel from academia to policymaking contexts (Clift 2018).

The subsequent analysis will show that Hall's paradigm-shift story is wrong, even for the UK context that he singles out as his own critical case. As others have already noted (Best 2019; Clift 2020; Prasad 2006), monetarism never became a true macroeconomic policy program in Britain, despite Thatcher's public endorsement of Friedman's ideas. This failure can be interpreted in accordance with the distinction between the sphere of politics, where actors make electoral promises and promote widely appealing policy ideas, and what Ben Clift (2020: 284) calls the "'thwarted operationalisation' of monetarist precepts." The Thatcher government failed to meet its own monetary targets and quickly gave up early trials to hit them, as the economic historian Duncan Needham (2014b) has shown. And Thatcher also failed to reach key constituencies with her monetarist promises: Neither labor unions nor bond traders gave much credibility to the government's targets. If we follow monetarist ideas, we thus have a hard time understanding how the UK's neoliberalism emerged and how the Bank of England found a place for itself in this regime.

It should then be apparent that the "post-paradigmatic" ideational per-spectives promoted by Cornel Ban, Ben Clift, Tod Van Gunten, and others are more helpful for my analysis. For instance, they draw attention to the translation work carried out by economists within central banks, who de-velop concrete policy proposals. They also urge us to try to understand how authoritative New Keynesian concepts and models came to inform the practice of inflation targeting. Again, however, I contend that we may learn more about monetary policy and its employment of economics by focusing directly on the cognitive, but also operational and political, problems of central bankers *as they try to make their governing work.* From this angle, we will see that organizations such as the Bundesbank enacted a kind of monetarism that had little to do with Friedman's proposals, but owed much to a strategy of engaging and disciplining corporatist institutions. We will also see that Volcker, certainly no advocate of New Keynesianism, inno-vated an informal version of inflation targeting out of his interaction with bond markets (Hetzel 2008). Ideas mattered in these developments, but in ways that cannot be captured fully within an ideational frame.

Institutionalist Perspectives

One strategy for moving beyond ideas and interests is to introduce insti-tutions as mediating elements and sources of stability in specific national configurations. To be sure, we should not simply presuppose that institu-tions are stabilizing and serve as sources of national differences, as neo-institutionalists in sociology warn us. But before engaging with the latter position, let me here discuss the more established, traditional conception of institutions that still enjoys strong intellectual and empirical support. From this vantage point, institutions are path-dependent artifacts. They stabilize the outcomes of past political struggles and decisions, and thereby shape how current and future conflicts are resolved (Pierson 2004). Actors may be oriented toward their self-interest, but the assumption is that these actors "interpret their self-interest [through institutions, LW] and thereby define their policy preferences" (Steinmo 1993: 7). Moreover, institutions help these actors to address inconsistencies between short- versus long-term interests and resolve collective action problems (Hall and Soskice 2001). Institutions also guide the selection of ideas that align with the frameworks through which actors interpret the world and adopt plausible courses of action. For instance, proposals for activist macroeconomic management may be more appealing in countries such as the United Kingdom with a strong and centralized executive, while the manifold institutional checks and balances found in a federalist country such as Germany give more intuitive plausibility to ordoliberal ideas (Allen 1989).

For my own analysis, this conception of institutions is useful, but not in the dominant way in which it has been employed in central banking and monetary policy research. Most often, scholars in this field assume that the institutions in the story are central banks themselves. The rationale behind this view is that, as institutions, central banks enshrine political commitments to monetary stability. Such commitments may, in turn, reflect dominant forces in a polity (Goodman 1992) or express expert opinions on optimal policy (King 2005). Formal independence for central banks in the pursuit of monetary policies then gives these choices a credible and durable form.[7] In consequence, independent central banks can resolve inconsistencies between politicians' short-term interests in high economic output and the long-term societal benefits of stable money. This is the classic central bank independence argument that much of the economics and political science literature has endorsed (Barro and Gordon 1983; Persson and Tabellini 1993; Rogoff 1985; Tucker 2018).

But central banks are not institutions—they are policymaking organizations that intervene in an evolving economy under conditions of uncertainty. No stable optimal formula is available for them, and whatever these policymakers decide to do will have distributional as well as structural consequences for the economies in which they govern. Moreover, as a large body of scholarship has shown, the conventional central bank independence argument fails to position monetary policies within larger polities with multiple stakeholders (Conti-Brown 2016; Wooley 1984). In this regard, what matters are (formally or informally) institutionalized terms of interaction not just with governments, but also with other groups—commercial banks, wage bargainers, powerful corporations, other central banks, and expert groups with epistemic authority over monetary policy questions. All these groups matter as they influence not only the preferences and orientations in a polity, but also conditions of policy implementation and central banks' legitimacy.

To my knowledge, only one body of literature has engaged with such a broader understanding of institutions and how they matter for monetary policy. Using game-theoretic underpinnings, varieties of capitalism (VoC) scholars have proposed that the precise procedures and outcomes of monetary policies depend on the complementarity between two institutions. The first is the conventional variable, the degree of central bank independence in a specific polity; and the second concerns the degree of coordination in wage bargaining. In line with mainstream economics, VoC scholars believe that independent central banks are more capable of reducing inflation than those under government control. But they add that this advantage depends on the degree of centralization of wage-bargaining procedures. Central banks that autonomously pursue monetary policy rely on coordinated bargaining in order to effectively communicate with economic actors and induce them to incorporate the expected effects of future policies into current wage settlements (Hall and Franzese 1998; Iversen 1998). This communicative coordination around low inflation helps in avoiding the unemployment costs that would otherwise result from unilateral disinflationary policies, which become necessary in purely market-based regimes.

VoC scholarship thus introduces a language that enables us to explore how broader institutional configurations provide conditions that are conducive to, or create obstacles for, central bank–specific policy interventions. It thereby provides analytic tools to explain why independent monetary policies are more successful in some settings than in others; that question is largely ignored in mainstream economics, but also is sidestepped in the literatures on monetary policies and ideational change. However, to arrive at these important insights, VoC scholars adopt an overly restrictive theoretical and empirical framework. A first issue is that, in VoC theory's game-theoretical thinking, economic agents must have rational expectations about central bankers' policy choices *and* outcomes. For instance, trade unions are assumed to rationally calculate how central banks will behave in response to wage settlements and correctly anticipate the implications for employment and growth. I do not follow the rational expectations view here as I assume that collective actors such as unions have socially conditioned and nonoptimizing strategies of expectation formation (Beckert 2016; Beckert and Bronk 2018). Second, for the VoC framework, it makes no difference whether central banks use monetarism, inflation targeting, or quantitative easing (QE) techniques to implement their policies: The simple choice in this framework is among hard, disinflationary, and soft inflationary options. But this view of policy implementation is problematic because it abstracts entirely from central banks' relations with the financial sector, which condition how central banks intervene in the economy and with what consequences (for example, via the effect of policies on credit and capital markets). These latter limitations of the VoC approach become particularly problematic if we aim to understand central bank policies in the context of *financialized* capitalism, in which the authorities' relations with finance emerge as primary, while those with wage-bargaining institutions lose importance. While offering a more productive way of using the institutionalist lens, the VoC framework thus proves theoretically and empirically too constraining.

Central Bank Technocracy

I conclude my review by discussing a number of sociological approaches to central banking. These overlap more strongly with my own approach here, as I will point out. But before turning to these research strands, it is first worth noting that sociological interest in central banks has waxed and waned. Our classics actually dedicated considerable attention to these organizations and gave them pride of place in their analyses of the intertwined institutionalizations of modern states and capitalism.[8] But at the very moment in history that central banks became more important and powerful (in other words, after 1970), sociologists curiously lost interest in them. New Economic Sociology turned away from the study of the macroeconomy and its institutional regulation and instead prioritized endogenous institutions within markets, social networks, as well as economic behavior. Social studies of finance also failed to take up the topic. Leading scholars in this field conceptualized finance as a distinct domain of markets, featuring distinct types of practices (such as arbitrage and speculation) and market-internal governance mechanisms (for example, trader cartels in stock exchanges) (Abolafia 1996; Knorr Cetina 2007). No concepts were developed to understand the creation of credit money, capitalist circuits, and the role of state power in finance. Political sociologists were equally neglectful, by and large considering central banks outside their remit.

But, fortunately, these gaps have been addressed through new research. A first, neo-institutionalist body of scholarship turned to central banking because of the rather curious and rapid convergence in legal frameworks, organizational forms, and monetary policy strategies across a diversity of countries during the 1990s. For instance, neo-institutionalists have shown how central bank independence (Bodea and Hicks 2015; Polillo and Guillén 2005) and inflation targeting (Wasserfallen 2019) spread quickly to diverse nations. This convergence raises the question of how central banking can become so similar on the surface when concrete monetary problems, struggles over prioritized solutions, cultural dispositions, and state structures mediating political processes are rather specific in each national context. To explain convergence, neo-institutionalists focus on states' attempts to gain legitimacy within an increasingly integrated world culture. As these scholars argue, such culture is constructed and promoted by experts from epistemic communities and intergovernmental organizations, as well as "rationalized others" from the private sector (Kapstein 1992; Marcussen 2009; Roberts 2011). Neo-institutionalists assume that governments accept the recommendations of these "rationalized others," not because their proposals make sense in terms of local monetary problems. Rather, having legitimacy in the eyes of these observers is important in its own right to maintain status and to display rational, "agentic" features (Meyer et al. 1997). Moreover, authorities may decide to adopt the proposed scripts because they help convince financial market participants, international organizations, or trade partners to give positive assessments that facilitate economic trade relations, public borrowing, and private investments (Gray 2013; Mosley 2003). In short, the central banks' high status, according to neo-institutionalism, is a combined effect of experts' production of neoliberal policy scripts and the growing force of this scientization in increasingly integrated political and capitalist systems (Fourcade 2006).

Complementary to this research strand, sociologists have recently developed two different perspectives on central bank technocracy. A first, Bourdieusian tradition highlights a key gap in neo-institutionalism as it reintroduces the notion of conflict into processes of neoliberal policy change and state reorganization. But in contrast to the politics of money literature, Bourdieusians do not focus on conflicts between interest groups but on struggles among state elites over who dominates macroeconomic policy (Maman and Rosenhek 2009; Mudge and Vauchez 2016; Van Gunten 2015). Accordingly, they interpret the rise of central banks as the outcome of a successful "field strategy." By accumulating scientific capital and other power resources, central bankers were able to carve out their own policy competencies at the expense of other state organizations, such as finance ministries. Supportive of this field-internal change were processes in adjacent fields, such as the shift of power from industry toward global finance in the economic realm, or the "changing of the guard" from Keynesians to neoclassical thinkers in macroeconomics. Combined, these processes have raised the relative value of technocratic central bank governance vis-à-vis other strategies of macroeconomic policy.[9]

But like neo-institutionalists, Bourdieusians say very little about the practices of governing, that is, the processes through which central bankers ensure that their actions actually achieve outcomes that support claims to political authority. Fortunately, a third sociological strand of research has emerged to tackle this problem. This is the performativity literature on central banking (Best 2019; Braun 2015; Holmes 2013; Nelson and Katzenstein 2014). According to this research, we should conceive of central bankers' extensive use of academic concepts, models, and econometric forecasting neither simply in terms of rational ways of conducting policy, nor as symbolic acts to gain legitimacy or strategic moves to dominate competitors in national economic policy fields. Rather, performativity scholars interpret the use of epistemic elements as governing devices (Hirschman and Berman 2014) that undergird central bankers' reflexive communication with their relevant publics. Such communication is successful when it engages economic actors' *fictional* expectations and beliefs, and thus produces monetary stability as a performative effect: Economic agents acting upon central bank communications will adapt their wage claims, product prices, interest rates, and so on so that the desired results—monetary stability—come about (Beckert 2016; Orléan 2008; Simmel 1989 [1900]).

My own approach is informed by these ideas, but it rests on a critical appraisal of the three sociological research strands introduced here. First, I do not adopt a neo-institutionalist perspective on policy change. The reason for this has to do primarily with my empirical focus. As neo-institutionalists have themselves acknowledged, their theory is less applicable to core capitalist countries that are less concerned with world cultural legitimacy and have relatively durable national configurations of institutions that do not lend themselves to the wholesale import of new scripts. Every time central bankers or other authorities from these countries engage with proposals from international expert groups and policy solutions from other countries, they carefully consider how to translate the respective scripts into national settings (Ban 2016; Bockman and Eyal 2002). Moreover, neo-institutionalists themselves acknowledge that the adoption of authoritative scripts does not yet resolve problems of governing—they therefore introduce the idea of *decoupling* of authorities' ritualistic adoption from their idiosyncratic practice on the ground. But the decoupling perspective is not very helpful for understanding central banking in the neoliberal era. In fact, until recently, central bankers' authority was buttressed by their apparent successes in delivering low and stable inflation, a constellation of successful "output legitimacy" (Scharpf 2004) that is hard to explain with neo-institutionalist tools.

My view of changes in policies and institutions is much closer to that of Bourdieusians in that I focus on central banks' growing influence and authority within larger, national macroeconomic policy contexts. But we need to be careful with conceptualizing such developments as a straightforward zero-sum game, in which one public body takes ever more competencies from the other. In fact, central bankers usually do not want to assume overt, visible responsibility for fiscal matters; their objective rather is to establish and protect a monetary policy jurisdiction that they can control (Abbott 1988).[10] More importantly, by focusing solely on actors' motivations and strategies, Bourdieusians leave out the programs, procedures, and technologies through which central bank governing is actually done (Lascoumes and Le Galès 2007).

As performativity scholars have rightly stressed, the invention and remaking of these programs, procedures, and technologies have been critical for the rise of central banks, often eluding authorities' strategic intentions (Joyce 2013: 22). But I do not follow the performativity approach because it endorses a too actor-centric and teleological narrative of policy success that resembles the one found in internal central banker discourses (Bernanke and Mishkin 1997; Goodfriend 2007; Mishkin 2007). In these latter discourses, the view prevails that central banks need only to introduce the most sophisticated techniques of scientized expectation management and are thereby empowered to align the public's expectations with their own macroeconomic stabilization goals. This way of thinking about the governability problem neglects how broader political-economic conditions define which techniques can become performative in which settings. Because the performativity scholarship relies mainly on frontstage presentations by central bankers, we also learn very little from this research about dimensions and effects of central banking that are excluded from the macroeconomic frameworks that undergird the dominant expert discourse.

In short, despite the growing interest in central banking among sociologists, they have failed so far to challenge established abstractions of how monetary policy works. For instance, none of the three strands offers insights into how central banks can govern macroeconomic phenomena with their fairly specific and limited tools of intervention, which ultimately consist of financial transactions with banks. This failure to account sociologically for the concrete relations and processes undergirding central bank governing has led scholars to ignore or misunderstand central banks' relationships with finance—an issue that deserves full attention in an age of financialization. In addressing these shortcomings, as well as those in the dominant political-economy strands, I will develop my own conceptual foundations in the following section.

Toward a New Sociology of Central Banking: Bureaucratic Actors, Policy Instruments, and Financial Systems as Governing Infrastructures

The key tenet of this book is that, in order to understand why central banks have risen to power within contemporary formations of capitalism, we need to understand how monetary authorities have learned to employ the particular tools of intervention available to them for achieving politically legitimate and desired results. This has involved tapping central banks' exclusive sources of infrastructural power, particularly those provided by financial systems. It has also meant that, based on central banks' claims over the governability of capitalist processes, the very objectives and criteria of policy success have shifted. Over time, central banks have assumed an ever more prominent position in broader macroeconomic policy frameworks.

Central Bankers as Bureaucratic Actors

This argument entails three components. First, I see monetary policies to be decisively shaped by central bankers themselves, rather than by their principals or external interest groups. Central bankers are state bureaucrats

(Braun, Krampf, and Murau 2021). Abstracting for a moment from significant institutional variations—for example, organizations' different degrees of control over their own operations—all central bankers enjoy some room for maneuver, and their organizations have distinct resources at their disposal. In the most abstract terms, central bankers use this room and their resources to secure and strengthen the status of their organizations as relatively autonomous entities within the state (Carpenter 2001). To achieve that, they aim to create and stabilize conditions under which they can causally relate their own practices to objectives that are positively sanctioned in the polity and society—in short, to construct a favorable framework of "output legitimacy" (Scharpf 2004).[11] For that purpose, central bankers use their room to experiment with and innovate policy tools. These tools not only structure their regular policy conduct, but also help central bankers to causally relate policy actions with outcomes—they embody what political scientists standardly call capacities to implement economic policies. The fact that these capacities are not just given, but themselves are results of policy experimentation and learning makes this a case of "policy feedback," as theorized by Paul Pierson (1993: 603–4). However, it is important to note that, just as capacities can be constructed, output legitimacy needs to be defined. Central bankers will thus try to attain or maintain some influence over the framing and definition of the tasks ascribed to them, the causal frames through which observers make sense of policies, and the criteria applied to judge on failure or success. This also involves work around the boundaries of their own policy jurisdictions—control over the separation or association of tasks and over institutions and decisions outside their jurisdiction that directly or indirectly shape the conditions of policy success.

Policy Instruments

A second element of my approach is to prioritize the processes through which central bankers try to answer the following question: How can we (re)design, activate, and employ instruments exclusively available to us that we can then use to claim reliable causal influence over outcomes that are positively sanctioned in the polity? In other words, before seeking responsibility for objectives, and before engaging in the definition of boundaries around their policy jurisdictions, central bankers need to have an idea of their own governing capacities. As I show in subsequent pages, answering this question is not straightforward. How can central bankers claim that their own actions contribute to stable inflation, economic output, and / or other desirable effects in the economy? A key challenge for monetary officials thus consists of developing their own organizational practices into functional tools of governing. As I will show, economic experts, money-market operators, and other officials in central banks from the 1970s onward engaged in creative problem-solving to address this task. To provide the foundation for this empirical analysis, I introduce two concepts here that will help us to compare different innovation processes and to explicate what is distinctive about central banks' governing (Braun and Gabor 2020).

First, *operational technologies.* When conducting policies, central banks in most situations act as banks' banks (Braun 2018a). The fact that they have their own balance sheets; that they can issue state-backed liabilities; and that they are positioned at the heart of financial systems gives central banks an "expansive toolbox of multiple instruments," as Alexander Barkawi and Simon Zadek write. The authors note that central banks "not only set short-term policy rates, but make use of a vast array of interventions. They decide to which extent to deploy their balance sheets for asset purchases. They define what public and private assets are eligible for such purchases and how to allocate their balance sheet across them. They determine to what extent to buy sovereign and corporate bonds, asset-backed securities, exchange traded funds and other assets. They set conditions under which commercial banks can seek refinancing with them and what collateral is eligible in such operations . . . In their role as financial supervisors, they also define capital and liquidity requirements and make use of a whole additional set of regulatory measures."[12] This indicates that most central banks can draw on a wide range of statutory powers and balance-sheet transactions to conduct policy. But the question here is not only which operations central banks control, but how they can "functionalize" (Kallinikos, Hasselbladh, and Marton 2013) or "technologize" (Rose and Miller 1992) these operations to claim governability over broader financial and macroeconomic processes. Most central banks, most of the time, have used their influence on banks' access to refinancing for that purpose. That is, central banks deliberately alter conditions under which financial actors get access to the state-backed, ultimate means of settlement (Jobst and Ugolini 2016; Mehrling 2011: 3). More precisely, this means that authorities alter their own refinancing terms and influence conditions in the private markets in which commercial banks trade ultimate means of settlement among themselves. The latter are interbank markets for very short-term (usually overnight) funding; as Claudio Borio notes, these are the "relatively unglamorous and often obscure [corners] of the financial markets where the ultimate source of the central banks' power to influence economic activity resides."[13]

Two crucial operational problems are associated with this type of governing. First, how can central banks claim sufficient influence over refinancing conditions among private actors as the foundation for operational control? This is what monetary technicians call the "implementation problem" (Bindseil 2014). Second, central banks need to make sure that their local operations sufficiently affect broader conditions in financial systems and the economy to influence macroeconomic variables—the transmission problem. As we will see, one implication of this is that monetary policy looks different depending on the particular shape of money markets, financial systems, and the institutional settlements that have historically emerged between private markets and states. It also means that, while transformations within financial systems (for example, the invention of new funding instruments) change the operational conditions of central banking (Minsky 1957), so will central banks try to intervene in these developments to align market structures with their own practices (Jobst and Ugolini 2016). Relevant choices concern who central banks transact with; what collateral they accept for secured lending; in which markets they intervene; and what regulatory obligations they attach to particular borrowing privileges. As we will see later in the book, monetary authorities even sometimes engage in the co-construction of new markets to secure their operational efficacy and proper "pass-through" of operations.

It is important to note here that, while refinancing transactions with banks and control over short-term money markets remain the core operational technology for central banks, since the 2008 crisis authorities have experimented with a new and distinct instrument, namely large-scale asset purchases, or QE. These asset purchases depart from traditional policy implementation and transmission because they aim primarily to influence financial conditions among *nonbanks* rather than authorities' traditional counterparties. Moreover, with these operations, central banks do not influence the refinancing conditions that affect the issuance of credit and money; rather, the objective is to nudge investors in their portfolio choices to buy similar, more risky assets. As we will see, QE was a response to new policy dilemmas after 2008 and has reinforced the rise of shadow banking and the disintegration of traditional center-periphery structures in financial systems.

But central banks also use a second set of instruments, associated with *expectation management.* The importance of these instruments reflects the fact that economic actors, political actors, and observers hold beliefs and expectations about monetary order, about economic futures, and about the processes of monetary governing itself.[14] Such sense-making has a *retrospective* dimension, when actors interpret current conditions as outcomes of past policy decisions; and it has a *prospective* dimension in that actors interpret future developments by reading authorities' intentions and actions and anticipate their effects. Moreover, such sense-making has a *reflexive* dimension in that actors are aware that others' expectations have consequences for actual outcomes (Stasavage 2003).

Expectations about the impact of economic and monetary policy on monetary processes can lead to crises, for instance when economic agents collectively lose trust in the future stability of monetary values, or when observers recognize contradictions in political aims or between policymakers' aims and actions. But the very growth of central banks' power indicates that these organizations have found ways of mobilizing the respective processes of belief- and expectation-formation to their advantage, as an important source of governing power in its own right.[15] This is why performativity has become a such a popular notion in the sociology of central banking, and why even hard-nosed economists refer to expectation management, credibility, and transparency as critical components of any successful monetary policy regime (Laidler 2007; Woodford 2003a). But what *are* the processes through which actors are made to accept and subscribe to authority-enhancing expectations and beliefs? To elucidate these processes, I use Jens Beckert's concept of expectational politics (Beckert 2016; Wansleben 2018). This notion draws attention to the struggles through which hegemonic beliefs and expectations emerge in a particular political-economic setting. The notion challenges us to reconstruct a field of economic and political actors, as well as experts and observers, who have different degrees of influence over the processes of expectation formation in a particular currency area. In some settings, the decisive actors might be the wage-bargaining institutions; in others, bond traders and financial analysts might have more purchase. Central banks will adopt different strategies of engaging expectations in response to these institutional variations of hegemonic discourse.

The concepts of operational technologies and expectation management refer to what central banks can do in concrete terms to intervene in the economy, and they indicate that any central bank action is implicated in and preconditioned by the structures of financial systems and the broader economy. Rather than thinking of policy in one-directional causal terms, I thus see policy instruments to be endogenous to the very structures and processes that central banks govern. This implies that intended and unintended effects of such governing reflect rather complex entanglements between transactional and communicative interventions, their enabling conditions, and the ecologies that they (co)produce. In short, instruments become effective through what Paul Edwards calls "infrastructuration"—the establishment of relatively durable linkages between policymakers and their environments and associated routines that reproduce them. As I will describe in this book, this happens by mutual adaptations between central banking, its practices and instruments, and their environments. Policy success consists in exploiting such stability and framing interventions in terms of legitimate and desirable outcomes, such as low and stable inflation.

Another important question is how operational technologies and expectational politics relate to one another. I here differentiate between two juxtaposed states: Stable techniques of governing presuppose that central banks' operational interventions in financial infrastructures, and their symbolic interventions in expectational politics, fit together—or, to use a notion introduced by David Laidler (2007), that they make up a "coherent" whole. Coherence does not mean that the imaginaries and cognitive frameworks used in expectation management are true representations of how central banks actually intervene in financial infrastructures; it also does not mean that central bankers truthfully implement what they claim or promise to do. Rather, the operational and symbolic dimensions of governing contribute in complementary ways the constitution of effective techniques. From an operational standpoint, what matters is that, under varying circumstances, central banks can decide on highly controllable financial interventions that they can causally associate with intended, politically desirable results. Accordingly, there is a tendency toward "technologization" and black-boxing in this domain (Bowker and Star 1999). If operational control works as expected, not just external observers, but even senior decision-makers within central banks lose interest in these matters. Expectation management follows a different logic. It works in the service of central banks if significant stakeholders collectively expect the outcomes promised and predicted by authorities, even if the operations used to achieve these outcomes have not yet been implemented or should only have material consequences a few years hence; this is why central bankers are so concerned about "credibility" and about their purchase over inflationary expectations, as dimensions of governing that explicitly concern future, imagined states. Coherence means that these different but complementary dimensions of operational control and authoritative sense-making reinforce each other, with the result that the respective central banks gain generalized legitimacy and that their governing techniques become structurally engrained in the economy that they purport to control. We can contrast these states with situations in which operational relationships are unstable, and in which expectations and beliefs are in conflict, preventing the emergence of a hegemonic discourse. In these crisis situations, we not only observe disagreements about the *aims* of economic and monetary policy, as emphasized in politics of money accounts. On a deeper level, crises are associated with an inability to establish the very conditions of governability.

Opportunity Structures after 1970

Building on these concepts and ideas, the empirical claim of this book is that central banks have been able to activate, articulate, and integrate their operational technologies and expectation management tools into coherent techniques that underpin their macroeconomic governing capacities. This brings me to the third element of my theoretical approach. The question I ask here is: What has initiated the central banks' *rise*, that is, an evident process of change in the status and power of these particular state organizations? Why did central bankers, after 1970, launch policy experiments that would ultimately help them to construct a new version of output legitimacy and to redefine macroeconomic management more broadly? I address this question by differentiating two crucial historical developments that created favorable opportunity structures for central banks: crises of Keynesian (or functionally equivalent corporatist) approaches and the strengthening of those economic domains that particularly provide infrastructural power to central banks.

With regards to the crisis of Keynesianism, I share a widely held perception that the 1970s mark a turning point. Currency crises, high inflation, and stagflation undermined its legitimacy and efficacy (Fourcade-Gourinchas and Babb 2002; Hall 1986; Scharpf 1987). While this varied between countries, constituencies and interest groups demanded that the state act to reduce and stabilize inflation. High and variable inflation rates not only hurt the economic interests of powerful groups and constituencies (Hibbs 1977); they also had a very damaging symbolic dimension. Governments apparently were not in control anymore, unleashing a crisis of confidence that was exacerbated when promised measures to restore monetary stability failed to achieve tangible effects. As many authors have noted, this was the hour of the central banks, having played a subordinate role in macroeconomic management before the 1970s. As guardians of the currency, they naturally felt entitled to fight inflation at this point in history (Singleton 2011). It is important to note, though, that the Great Inflation in the 1970s initially was no more than a window of opportunity. Whether or not central banks could capitalize on this crisis depended on their ability to develop and institutionalize techniques that could perform stabilizing functions that were functionally equivalent to those of Keynesianism in Fordist regimes. The opportunity thus came hand in hand with radical uncertainty as to how governability could be achieved. Policy experimentation was initiated by this constellation and led to different patterns of failure and success.

Less recognized is a second aspect of Keynesian crisis. After the end of a postwar boom enabled by high growth rates, peace-time dividends and positive demographic trends, Western governments ran into fiscal difficulties (O'Connor 1973). These undermined the legitimacy and efficacy of proactive fiscal policy beyond the inflationary period of the 1970s (Buggeln, Daunton, and Nützenadel 2017; Pierson 2001). In consequence, what had been the dominant instrument of macroeconomic stabilization became defunct. Again, central bankers were cautious when stepping into fiscal policymakers' shoes. Their first step involved figuring out how their own techniques could provide foundations for macroeconomic stabilization. In the event, however, as inflation risks receded, central banks increasingly committed themselves to being wholesale macroeconomic stabilizers and claimed an expanded policy jurisdiction. This change took place primarily during the 1990s and made possible the extreme expansion of central bank power observed in more recent decades.

In short, then, the crisis of postwar Keynesianism created favorable opportunity structures after 1970 for central banks to claim ever broader responsibilities over macroeconomic policy and to construct a comprehensive version of output legitimacy for themselves. But for central banks to *use* these opportunities, they additionally needed favorable conditions to develop their own practices into effective governing tools. This is where Michael Mann's (1984) concept of infrastructural power comes in. This concept helps us to understand that central bankers' instruments work only when they encounter favorable structures and institutions in the economy that undergird their efficacy. Central banks use very little coercion and therefore rely strongly on economic actors to engage in voluntary policy coordination—either because cooperative behavior is rational for them, or because actors hold beliefs that motivate such cooperation, or because certain circumstances simply make them act cooperatively as a matter of routine. The set of relevant actors whose cooperation is needed varies between political-economic contexts and also depends on the specific policy techniques employed by central banks.

In general terms, we can distinguish two constellations in which central banks gain the infrastructural powers needed to make their interventions effective. In a first constellation, the respective economy and polity already offer favorable conditions for monetary policy conduct, and the challenge for central banks is "only" to capitalize on the crisis of Keynesian governability by initiating new coordination processes with their own instruments. This is the least disruptive version of central banks' rise as they inscribe their own instruments into existing orders. But it is also an unlikely constellation, for several reasons. First, postwar orders implied a certain alignment between Keynesian policies and the institutional conditions that undergirded their efficacy (Blyth and Matthijs 2017). Central banks could only inscribe their own techniques into postwar orders, where these alignments were weak to begin with (on the German case, see Allen 1989). Second, as the historical literature on the 1970s shows, the very crisis of Keynesian governability in that period was the result of disintegration processes and disruptions that weakened or destroyed postwar institutional orders (Fourcade-Gourinchas and Babb 2002; Hall 1986). Accordingly, to reclaim governability, state actors needed to introduce techniques that were aligned with changing conditions. The far more prevalent, important constellation therefore was one in which central banks gained infrastructural powers through the very changes that were taking place in advanced capitalist economies after 1970. As I aim to show in this book, the development that turned out to be decisive in this respect was financialization. The concept has various facets (van der Zwan 2014), many of which I will not explicitly engage with in this book. But two aspects of finance's rise are critical for understanding the growing importance of central banks and their new infrastructural powers. First, households and firms became increasingly dependent on debt financing and / or incomes from financial returns (Jordà, Schularick, and Taylor 2014; Krippner 2005). This also means that overall economic activity became more sensitive to changes in borrowing conditions and / or to fluctuations in asset prices. This enlarged the potential infrastructural power of central bankers, whose instruments are designed primarily to affect financial activities (Petrou 2021a: xviii). A second relevant dimension of financialization concerns transformations within banking. Students of finance have described this change as the dissolution of nationally contained and cartelized sectors toward market-based practices, which particularly alter the ways in which financial firms manage their liabilities. The new way to do this is called active liability management and involves seeking funds for particular, tradable positions in money markets (Konings 2011: 123; Minsky 1975). What we thus see is a fundamental change in how financial firms manage their balance sheets and a corresponding growth in the markets in which they acquire and provide liquidity. Hence the rapid growth of markets for short-term borrowing and lending, such as asset-backed commercial paper and repo.[16] One important implication of this is that the funding liquidity available in these markets becomes closely intertwined with the liquidity and value of securities that firms hold on their balance sheets. This is because in firms' balance-sheet management, assets and liabilities are treated as marketable and market-priced items. Moreover, in *secured* borrowing and lending, banks use assets directly as collateral, which implies that the value and liquidity of these assets directly affect access to funding liquidity. The shift to market-based banking has had important structural consequences, further blurring the boundaries between what are banks and nonbanks—in the respective markets, traditional depository institutions can transact with money-market funds or broker dealers (Pozsar et al. 2010; Thiemann 2018).[17] As central bankers discovered in the late 1980s to early 1990s, these transformations at the core of financial systems actually increased their own infrastructural powers: "Concern has been expressed that . . . deregulation and innovation [in financial markets, LW] may have weakened the mechanisms through which changes in monetary policy . . . affect aggregate demand and inflation . . . contrary to [these] concerns, the impact of interest rates . . . is now *more* powerful than in the past."[18] In particular, central bankers discovered that the pass-through of their manipulations of banks' refinancing costs to broader markets—the processes of policy implementation and transmission—worked *better* in market-based than in the postwar regulated systems (Adrian and Liang 2016).

In short, then, the third component of my theoretical approach involves identifying particular opportunity structures—the crisis of Keynesian macroeconomic management and changes in the infrastructural foundations of economic policymaking—that created favorable conditions for central bankers to render their own instruments effective and to claim an independent and increasingly broad economic-policy jurisdiction. The following section gives a brief sketch of the historical narrative that I develop on this basis and includes a table to facilitate comparison of different central bank governing techniques and their supportive political-economic conditions.

Innovations in Central Banks' Governing Techniques since 1970

In the 1970s, this process of experimentation started with *monetarism*—authorities around the OECD world attempted to use quantitative targets for the money supply to repurpose central banks' operational technologies and / or as symbols to convey their intentions to reestablish price stability. But the conditions for successfully using practical monetarism were demanding. For instance, capital flight, destabilizing financial innovations, labor conflicts, and / or conflicts over macroeconomic policy priorities rendered these experiments unsuccessful in most countries. Accordingly, as I argue in Chapter 2, only in countries that maintained corporatist wage coordination, and in which banking systems were relatively unaffected by

TABLE 1.1 Central Banks' Macroeconomic Governing Techniques

Central bank techniques for macroeconomic governing	Operational technologies and their felicity conditions	Expectation management and its felicity conditions	Formative cases
Monetary targeting	Central banks help maintain and rely on conservative banking routines	Central banks act as independent fiduciaries to wage-bargaining institutions and fiscal policymakers	Germany; Switzerland; (Japan)
Inflation targeting	Central banks leverage price sensitivity of market-based financial system and significant effects of changing asset values	Central banks use transparent communication with forecasts to "anchor" market expectations	United States; New Zealand; United Kingdom; Canada
Quantitative easing	Central banks nudge nonbank investors in their portfolio choices and act as market makers of last resort	Central banks commit to supporting asset appreciations and to avoid any reversal in market trends	(Japan); United States; United Kingdom

early waves of financial globalization did monetary targeting succeed (see table 1.1). In short, then, and contrary to what many authors assume, practical monetarism was an antidote to the market-oriented and pro-finance techniques that became prevalent during the 1990s.

This also means that, in the broader context of central banks' rise, these early successes with monetary targeting in a few countries were consequential only in indirect ways. For instance, the Bundesbank's and the Swiss National Bank's rise to fame during the 1970s indicated that central banks can successfully establish their own jurisdictions based on monetary policy practice. But the particular route taken by the Germans and Swiss remained closed to most other central banks. This then brings me to the main story I aim to tell in this book, which is how *inflation targeting* emerged after failures of monetary targeting, and under quite different institutional and structural conditions.

By the 1980s, stagflation problems, initial neoliberal reforms, and shifts in the balance of power from labor to capital (Baccaro and Howell 2017) had dealt a death blow to Keynesian macroeconomic management. Particularly in Anglo-Saxon countries, central banks could capitalize on these developments through their own policy innovations, which relied on the emergent financialized capitalism as infrastructural foundation. This connection between central banks and finance had two dimensions. First, the growing authority of capital markets defined a viable expectational co-ordination game for central bankers that could work without corporatist institutions. Inflationary expectations incorporated in bond and futures rates became central bankers' primary concern. As Fed historian Robert Hetzel writes, "Under Volcker and Greenspan, the FOMC [the Federal Open Market Committee, the Fed's policymaking body, LW] measured its credibility by the behavior of the long-term bond rate" (2008: 253). The primary tool used for this purpose was the publication of inflation forecasts that revealed the central banks' awareness of inflationary risks and, more importantly, indicated that monetary authorities would adapt their short-term financing rates to avert these risks. Predictability in decision-making, and a corresponding use of macroeconomic models to achieve this (Braun 2015), became critical for this particular version of expectation management.

Second, central bankers learned to exploit the changing infrastructural conditions within financial systems, particularly the rise of active liability management. The role of these developments for monetary policy is usually neglected because most people are uninterested in policy implementation, and those who care about these "plumbing" issues (Fullwiler 2017) approach them with a set of problematic assumptions. But as my analysis will show, this neglects how financial globalization in general, and the emergence of wholesale money markets in particular (from Eurodollar to repo), led to significant changes in the infrastructural foundations of central banking (Jobst and Ugolini 2016). A key driver of policy change consisted of central bankers learning about the particular options of operational control that the new finance regime offered, and internalizing the constraints and opportunities that a market-based system imposed on them. Even more, upon realizing the increased leverage that they could gain in such a system, monetary authorities became its key institutional architects (Gabor 2016; Wansleben 2020).

After monetarism and inflation targeting, QE constitutes another, distinct central bank technique. I here describe it as an incremental innovation by inflation-targeting central banks after 2008, which strengthened and expanded their nexus to market-based finance. Upon exhausting their possibilities for supporting growth and employment via changes in the banks' refinancing conditions, monetary authorities thus turned directly to shadow banks and their investment decisions. Large-scale asset purchases were supposed to nudge these investors to buy riskier assets to refill their portfolios after sales of government securities to central banks. As more and more financing happened via capital markets, and more and more (also nonfinancial) firms engaged in portfolio management, the idea was that such nudging could induce expansionary effects on the broader financial systems, improve firms' financing conditions, and enlarge households' purchasing power with financial wealth. Complementarily, with words and actions, authorities strengthened confidence among financial market participants that central banks were acting to support further appreciations in asset values and forestall any adverse market movements. This enabled the fairly remarkable financial market boom after 2010. As I will discuss, as much as QE expands and radicalizes central banks' connections with market-based finance, it also signals a deep crisis of governability that now, in the 2020s, has come back to haunt central banks.

What Is the Problem with Central Banks' Rise?

But so what? Why does it matter that central banks have been able to claim jurisdictional authority over much of macroeconomic management? While central bank policies have complex first-, second-, and third-order consequences, my book concentrates in particular on the question of how the rise of central banking, which in my analysis has increasingly become predicated on financialization, has in turn fostered unsustainable financial growth, including the creation of oversized financial systems, bloated asset markets, and excessive debt.

As I see it, we can discern five mechanisms through which central banks' increasingly dominant policies since 1970 have contributed to such unsustainable financial growth (table 1.2). As I mentioned earlier, the political economy school associated with hard money has conceptualized one of

TABLE 1.2 Central Banking and Unsustainable Financial Growth

Central banking and excessive financial growth: mechanisms

Deflationary policy bias	Growth in household debt via distributional effects
Deregulations	Incessant search for profit; boom-bust cycles
Improving monetary policy "pass-through" via interconnected money markets	Supports procyclical liquidity cycles and creates trust in unlimited liquidity ("liquidity illusion")
Instituting market expectations of stable interest rates, growth, and inflation	Encourages aggressive term transformation and position taking ("stability illusion")
Central bank puts for asset markets / backstops for (shadow) banking	Creates an upward bias on asset markets, subsidizes those with financial wealth, and creates moral hazard problems in financial sectors

them. According to this literature, central banks generate debt growth through the distributional implications of their deflationary policies. This argument is relevant primarily to the 1980s and must be specified differently for two different kinds of economies (Baccaro and Pontusson 2016). First, in debt- and consumption-based growth regimes such as the United States and the United Kingdom, excessively restrictive monetary policies created income losses for middle-class and poorer households from labor, with the consequence that these households turned increasingly to debt (Blyth and Matthijs 2017). In a second group of export-led growth regimes such as Germany and Switzerland, restrictive monetary policies helped the respective tradable goods sectors to enhance their competitiveness and to "capture" a growing share of demand from the more consumption-oriented economies, including those relying on public and private debt to finance such demand. In consequence, an important avenue through which export-led countries were entangled in financialization was their dependence on (often debt-financed) external demand and their banks' growing engagement in US markets (Beck 2021).

A second prominent discussion focuses on central banks' advocacy for, and independent decisions over, financial deregulation. The idea here is that the transition from highly regulated or "repressed" financial systems of the postwar period, to the globalizing systems after 1980 intensified competition among financial players, led to more aggressive search for profits, and higher leverage. This in turn generated more volatile boom-bust cycles. As natural partners of financial firms, as organizations with control over some crucial regulatory levers, and / or as believers in efficient markets, central bankers bore some responsibility for this change. For instance, the Fed significantly contributed to undermining the Glass-Steagall Act, which had been introduced in the New Deal period to avoid excessive risk-taking on the part of banks and restrain access to funding for investment firms (Menand 2021). It is important to add, though, that central bankers have *not* consistently advocated deregulation and sometimes been major forces to restrain it (e.g., Paul Volcker at the Fed or the Bundesbank up until the 1990s). This raises the question when and why central bankers do or do not favor deregulation—a question that I aim to address by introducing central banks' quest for infrastructural power. Moreover, even market-based finance relies on institutions (Carruthers 2015) and central bankers arguably have played a decisive role in constructing them. Again, to understand how and why, it is important to analyze central bankers' own interests in financial systems as vehicles of policy implementation and transmission.

To complement the deflationary bias story (which has become less and less relevant) and the deregulation perspective, my book thus discusses three further effects of central banking on financial growth, which are direct consequences of central banks' deep operational and symbolic entanglements with finance. In addition to central banks' hard money and deregulation bias, I thus add a third mechanism that consists of a recursive causality between the global expansion of money markets, central bankers' discovery of the benign consequences of this expansion for monetary policy efficacy, and authorities' subsequent support for market-based banking (Braun 2018a). For instance, repo markets grew massively from the 1980s onward, partly because the Fed had helped market participants to secure the legal foundations for them. A true *global* expansion in repo then came in the 2000s (Gabor 2016), when monetary authorities from all major economies joined the project of constructing an architecture for global liquidity (Birk 2017). As part of this process, ideas for reining in or restricting money markets were dropped. The outcome was a multi-trillion-dollar (or euro) system of funding markets, in which some firms rolled over a quarter of their balance sheets on an overnight basis, using collateral with procyclically changing values. As we all know, these markets failed in 2008, ushering in a truly dangerous phase of financial crisis (Tooze 2018). Only massive public interventions in repo and other markets saved them, and central bank support has become a more general perquisite for money-market stability since 2008.

Fourth, as touched on above, inflation targeting relies on coordination between central banks and market actors around forecasts for inflation, growth, and the assumed equilibrium (so-called real natural) interest rates. To render such coordination effective, central bankers make their future actions as predictable as possible for financial audiences (an objective that preceded "forward guidance") so that long-term interest rates reflect anticipated future policy changes and move only in response to "real" economic shocks. In turn, central bankers take the incorporation of low and stable inflation expectations into long-term interest rates as the most important indicator for their policy success. But the consequence of this expectational coordination is that the system as a whole increasingly disregards the fundamental uncertainty that is inherent in capitalist developments, raising the possibility that expectations incorporated in economic decisions may be disappointed. One unforeseen event obviously was the financial crisis of 2007–2009, which led to a temporary and dramatic rise in money-market rates. Financial corporations had conducted aggressive term transformation (better called "maturity mismatching") because they had assumed that future refinancing costs were calculable, based on confident estimations of future policy rates; arbitrage on even very small interest-rate differentials had become profitable (Adrian and Shin 2008). But when the crisis hit, financial transactions of billions of dollars suddenly turned red. Overconfidence bred fragility, just as Hyman Minsky (1986) had foreseen. More importantly, though, both central bankers and market actors have been continuously disappointed since 2008 because growth, inflation, and risk-free interest rates have turned out to be *lower* than expected. Here, the endogeneity problem becomes truly systemic. The political production of (over)confidence among financial actors by central banks becomes self-defeating because it has produced oversized credit and debt that have become structural burdens for economies. Fueling more confidence, through expansionary measures, thus only drives the economy into deeper trouble, a fact that has come to haunt central bankers in the guise of secular stagnation.

As a fifth point, this then ushers in a phase of central banking in which these organizations essentially become regime preservers of an increasingly fragile, crisis-prone financialization process. This role became more relevant under Alan Greenspan in the 1990s (Axilrod 2009: 138), and since then, other central bankers have joined the Fed to uphold the values of financial assets and act as market-makers for particularly critical market domains with aggressive interventions when crises loom. A reasonable widespread concern is that such actions generate moral hazard, as financial firms respond to such policies in the knowledge that their downside risks are capped. But central bank "puts" increasingly go beyond this. Research indicates that, as economies financialize and households depend more and more on asset values for consumption, asset-price drops and frictions in credit issuance actually entail significant macroeconomic risks (Cieslak and Vissing-Jorgensen 2018). Going beyond the "Greenspan put," QE and associated policies thus imply that central banks address this growing weight of financial wealth and try to ensure whole economies against the downside risks of fragile financialization. However, as I discuss in the final part, such regime preservation policies perpetuate the unsustainable financial growth that renders crisis interventions necessary in the first place.

Incorporated Comparison

The book traces how we got to this point. For that purpose, it relies on a particular version of the comparative historical method that social scientists use to explain "substantive, high-stakes outcomes" (Pierson 2014: 129) that are products of complex causalities (Abbott 1992; George and Bennett 2004) playing out over longer time sequences. In my framework, the cases are central banks, in particular in advanced capitalist economies, and the process of interest consists of trajectories toward monetary policy dominance within this population of cases. Observing structural and institutional changes within countries through time (Rueschemeyer 2003), as well as differences between them, will help to reveal the diverse and changing conditions of possibility for this process. But in contrast to the classic analytical approach to comparison, I will not treat cases as independent units that serve to control variation and isolate causal factors. Instead, adopting Philip McMichael's (1990) method of *incorporated comparison,* I aim to show that developments at the various central banks hang systematically together. The ways in which these interconnections have primarily been theorized in international political economy are as structural interdependencies between units and the "system": The policies of significant players not only reflect, but also shape international monetary and economic relations, continually redefining the conditions of possibility under which all actors operate. My own emphasis will be more on how central bankers observe monetary policy developments in other countries in their search for domestic solutions. How policymakers respond to successful experiments in other countries then depends on how they can translate what they regard as a viable, legitimate policy solution. As we will see, in some cases, learning from others means finding equivalent but fundamentally different methods of intervention. In other cases, emulating others' techniques presupposes foundational changes to the respective financial systems and broader institutional configurations—in other words, a remaking of the infrastructural foundations of governing. For instance, the adoption of inflation targeting in many countries required significant money-market reforms. Indeed, the closer we move toward the twenty-first century, the more we observe the latter variant, namely the active production of similar institutional conditions that facilitated the adoption of almost identical techniques.

Since the 1970s, only two paths have opened up for central banks to gain macroeconomic governing power: monetarism or inflation targeting, later superseded by QE. I therefore focus on the central banks that have been most formative in the development of these techniques. Moreover, I exploit the fact that the felicity conditions for these two techniques differed radically, allowing us to reveal these conditions through a comparison of the respective paths of innovation and enactment. First, there are Switzerland and Germany. The rationale for grouping these two countries is that they followed very similar paths. The Swiss National Bank and the Bundesbank were the pioneers in institutionalizing practical monetarism. In these two countries, monetarism remained the primary macroeconomic governing technique until the late 1990s, when the Swiss National Bank finally adopted inflation targeting and the Bundesbank joined the Euro system. Many view this late adoption as a sign of backwardness: The German and Swiss central bankers supposedly had failed to recognize the advances in macroeconomics in the 1980s and 1990s and had adhered to monetarism even after it had fallen out of fashion. The story that I tell is a different one. Monetarism in these export-oriented economies depended on and was supportive of very distinct institutional configurations: strong corporatism, close banking-industry ties, and "conservative" banking methods. Accordingly, the gradual disintegration of monetarism must be seen not as catching up with the latest macroeconomic advancements but as a reflection of changing institutional and structural conditions, particularly in finance. The factors I put most emphasis on are pressures from domestically located international banks to bring "modern" money markets and "innovative" funding practices to home markets (reinforced by European integration). Accordingly, in order to remain ahead of the game, Swiss and German central bankers came to accept and endorse reforms that gradually shifted the institutional conditions toward financial integration and inflation targeting.

The second group of closely related cases are the United Kingdom and the United States. While there are important differences in the trajectories of these two countries, they share important similarities, have strong historical ties, and have competing financial centers (New York and London). In both countries, the 1970s brought monetary crises that were not resolved until the 1980s. To be sure, these crises were different in origin, as Britain faced balance of payments troubles unknown to the American hegemon, with its global reserve currency. But a key parallel arose from the fact that untamed industrial conflicts and coordination dilemmas associated with Keynesian macroeconomic management combined with a wave of financial innovations to render ineffective monetarist attempts to address stagflation problems. Ironically, these problems contributed to the rise of a radicalized monetarist discourse in the Anglo-Saxon sphere that was not observed in Germany or Switzerland. Such ideologies legitimized drastic measures against inflation. But durable solutions to the countries' governability problems were found only when the respective central banks turned to other options. In particular, Volcker led the way in identifying advantageous features of financialization that provided distinct opportunities to manage expectations and achieve operational control. Volcker was helped by the fact that American finance had already established key market-based institutions to undergird these practices: a variety of interconnected money markets and huge, liquid markets for default risk-free (that is, sovereign) debt. These conditions were not present in the United Kingdom, however, which leads me to pay special attention to this country and treat it as a special case. The Bank of England would eventually emerge as the key architect of inflation targeting. But on the way, it not only challenged and redefined established intrastate policy procedures, but also contributed to the redesign of money and sovereign debt markets. In short, because innovations in central banking involved radical transformations in the country's institutional fabric, Britain is a particularly useful case for studying the processes and conditions that led to a central bank–dominated neoliberal policy under conditions of financialized capitalism.

I will refer to other cases selectively when they assume particular relevance for the process of mutual learning among "my" central banks. But this should not be misunderstood as a shortcut to cover central banking across the entire universe of advanced capitalist states. What I present here remains an exercise in contextual explanation (Tilly and Goodin 2006) that aims to facilitate an incremental, case-by-case oriented process of gaining general insights.

Appendix: What Are Central Banks?

If this book's analytical strategy is to view broader transformations in capitalism's governing through the eyes of particular organizations, it may be helpful to give a preliminary idea of what these organizations are. However, it proves extremely difficult to pin down central banking—and many existing definitions would only lead us astray. Instead of starting with a definition, I therefore begin by looking at the historical trajectories through which these particular organizations have come about. I then discuss two distinctive features of central banks that will frame the subsequent analysis: First, central banks occupy singular, interstitial positions between states and financial systems and play a major role in regulating their interdependencies. Second, central banks are special because they conduct balance sheet operations with banks and thereby create modern economies' ultimate means of settlement—their own liabilities.

Some central banks have already been around for a few hundred years, while most were founded about 150 to 100 years ago. The purposes and motives for founding the respective organizations reflected the particular political and economic concerns that prevailed during these different times. For instance, as stressed by Broz (1998), up until the mid-nineteenth century, all central bank foundations happened in the context of wars. As these wars demanded ever larger expenditures, rulers responded not just by building more effective bureaucracies (Ertman 1997); they were also forced into new settlements with an emerging capitalist class (Tilly 1990). In Europe, this class had incrementally developed modern techniques of finance from the early medieval period onward (Braudel 1992 [1979]; de Roover 1946). Starting with the late seventeenth century, these techniques had come to be identified as critical for extending access to financial resources and for prevailing in fierce military competition. But in order to use credit issuance for such purposes, rulers had to enter into "institutional bargains" (Broz 1998: 233) with the classes controlling modern forms of credit. Central banks arose from these bargains; they were either newly established for war financing or transformed from existing commercial banks. Rulers would market sovereign debt through central banks and the financiers providing the funding were given control over the respective organizations. Crucially, through central banks, financiers acquired privileges and strategic competitive advantages in their commercial undertakings.[19] The most important of these was the monopoly of note issuance, that is, the exclusive right to fund claims on governments by issuing paper liabilities, denominated in fixed units of account.

Later in the nineteenth and early twentieth centuries, central banks were founded for purposes other than war finance, such as uniting fragmented currency areas or as "symbols" of national sovereignty (Fisher 1994). Despite considerable diversity, however, we find that the privilege of issuing legal tender or, put differently, the special status of central bank liabilities as ultimate or penultimate "settlement money" (second only to gold) gave the respective organizations an exposed political role.[20] As credit and monetary processes became more expansive and more tightly integrated in the nineteenth and early twentieth centuries, systemic crises in financial sectors recurred with devastating effects. As it turned out, financial corporations and their customers in these crises rushed to acquire settlement money: gold or, in countries with already well-established central banks, the latter's "IOUs." Many scholars therefore date the rise of central banking "proper" with the emergence of multilayered financial and monetary systems, in which central banks accept their role as countercyclical providers of widely accepted forms of liquidity to the banking sector (Calomiris and Laeven 2016; Goodhart 1988; Gorton and Huang 2002; Sayers 1976).

Precisely because central banks emerged from institutional settlements between state and finance to regulate their various interdependencies, what they actually do has remained ambiguous and uncertain for most of modern history (Riles 2018: 10). To be sure, from their early days, central bankers were advocates, promoters, and beneficiaries of fiscal discipline and prudent banking, if only because excessive deficit-spending by governments or excessive credit issuance in the banking sector would expose their own balance sheets to considerable financial risks. Moreover, in the course of the nineteenth century, through disputes in the United Kingdom, we can observe the emergence of an incipient notion of *monetary* stability, based on the idea that central banks should manage a country's reserves carefully (Wood 2005). But how exactly central banks should manage a currency in light of broader economic developments and in the public interest remained unclear and ill-defined. Central banks thus only became partially and ambiguously included in the practices of macroeconomic management that developed from the 1930s onward. Accordingly, well into the postwar period, we find that central banking was often described in terms of vague legal mandates (for example, to ensure the "stability of a currency") and/or by "laundry lists" that included multiple, underspecified tasks. Singleton (2011: 5–9) lists no fewer than ten, including issuance of legal tender; monetary policy; public debt management; custody of the cash reserves; banking regulation, including lending of last resort; exchange-rate management and custody of the national reserves; promotion of economic development; cooperative international monetary arrangements; and the ominous "other functions."[21]

While in this book we tackle a historical period (1970s and onward) in which central banks have assumed powerful roles in macroeconomic management—first through the exercise of monetary policy, and increasingly as the primary managers of the economy at large—we thus need to bear in mind these organizations' rather peculiar institutional trajectories. This is important not just for historical reasons. For *how* central banks govern, how they intervene in the economy is conditioned by the interstitial positions they have historically assumed in between financial sectors and the state. At bottom, governing, for central banks, means conducting financial transactions and relying on the privileged, state-backed status of their liabilities as ultimate settlement money for commercial banks (Jobst and Ugolini 2016: 148). Moreover, because of central banks' interstitial position, they continue to perform a diversity of roles and tasks, some of which are hardly ever mentioned in policy discussions. But as we will see, it is critical to recognize how central banks, even as they conduct macro-economic policy, remain deeply entangled in finance; for it is through these entanglements that they have been able to develop the powerful governing techniques that are at the heart of contemporary policy regimes.

CHAPTER TWO

Monetarism and the Invention of Monetary Policy

> [W]e need to flip the current economic orthodoxy on its head, seeing inflation targets not as the timeless and asocial anchors for economic actors' rational expectations, but rather as one among many possible constitutive rules for inflation games, which must ultimately be anchored through concrete social and political practices.
>
> —BEST 2019: 635

IN THE LATE 1960s and 1970s, a new theme emerged in the social sciences. Was capitalism still governable? Marxist social scientists took up this issue to argue that Western governments had exhausted their capacities to compensate for the inherent contradictions of democratic capitalism (Offe 1973: 24). Their liberal colleagues suggested that intensified politicization of distributional outcomes had come to affect states' legitimacy and policy effectiveness, symptomized by taxation crises, rising inflation, and new dilemmas in macroeconomic management (Bell 1967). It seemed that the Keynesian compromise between social democracy and private capital was broken.

These sweeping diagnoses of crisis were associated with broader ideological controversies within and beyond the social sciences. But they resonated with actual problems in the more circumscribed field of macroeconomic management. The postwar economic boom had come to an end (Maier 2004), and with it, the Fordist regime of self-reinforcing economic growth (Baccaro and Pontusson 2016). Diminished output, combined with an exhausted "peace dividend," created new problems for fiscal policy

(Pierson 2001). Revenues stagnated and appeared to hit a ceiling as governments encountered fiercer opposition from corporate and private taxpayers (cf. the "tax revolt" in California) (Buggeln, Daunton, and Nützenadel 2017). Expenditures, promised during boom years, began to weigh more heavily on public budgets and reduced politicians' fiscal room for maneuver. Budget conflicts among political parties intensified (Quinn 2017), and optimistic expectations about the stimulus effects of additional spending remained unfulfilled. Meanwhile, the regulatory and institutional frameworks of "embedded liberalism" (Ruggie 1982), essential for governing market and nonmarket relations, began to crumble. Such disintegration was rendered visible in financial markets, where rule circumvention proliferated (Reinicke 1995). Moreover, those with capital turned in growing numbers to the tax-dodging industry (Saez and Zucman 2019) to escape from national fiscal contracts. Fiercer industrial conflicts over the distribution of firms' revenues also had disintegrating effects (Goldthorpe 1978). Internationally, growing pressures within the Bretton Woods system of pegged exchange rates led to the exhaustion and ultimate failure of financial diplomacy. American president Richard Nixon opted for "soft money," while the "hard-money" bloc, led by Germany, remained opposed to significant exchange-rate adjustments. In this situation, widely employed or just implicitly shared notions of economic governing, suggesting to policymakers how to balance prosperity and full employment with domestic as well as external monetary stability, no longer provided effective solutions. As the economist Robert Lucas noted, "[I]n 1966, it seemed to many that we had one theory which could quantitatively link fiscal policy to economic performance with sufficient accuracy that it could be responsibly applied to policymaking. In 1977, we know we have none" (1981: 264).

Monetary issues were at the heart of these economic-policy predicaments. Not only did it prove impossible to coordinate the interests and policy solutions favored by deficit countries exposed to devaluation pressures with those of surplus countries within the framework of Bretton Woods. Even after the abandonment of internationally regulated exchange rates, policymakers remained highly skeptical about the options they had available to address monetary ills. Inflation rates had increased significantly over the late 1960s in almost all core capitalist economies, and they kept rising during the 1970s. Central bankers in small and open economies thought that this dynamic originated partly from international financial and monetary forces beyond their own control. And policymakers in larger economies, such as the United States, became increasingly convinced that domestic inflation was so deeply entrenched that "central banks alone [would] be able to cope only marginally with the inflation of our times" (Burns 1979: 21). To be sure, central banks—if they had the autonomy— could "simply refuse to provide enough money" to finance the economy, but in a democracy, as Paul Volcker noted in 1976, such a policy choice would pose a "risk [not just] to the political life of a particular government, but to our way of government itself" (cited in Lindsey, Orphanides, and Rasche 2013: 528).

As we know today, the 1970s did not bring macroeconomic governing to an end, nor did state power over the economy recede. What happened instead can be captured with the notion of "foundational realignments," introduced by Saskia Sassen (2006: 144). Core capitalist economies entered a post-Fordist period of divergent growth regimes (Baccaro and Pontusson 2016); arbitrage strategies to avoid taxes and financial market practices of rule circumvention became constitutive elements of the internationalized economic order; value chains were restructured globally (Baldwin 2013); and labor's bargaining power decreased (Baccaro and Howell 2017). States proved that they could maintain considerable governing capacities in the face of these transformations. But this required significant reorganizations and redistributions of power inside the state. Among the winners from these changes were central banks. While exchange-rate volatilities and inflationary waves during the 1970s had overwhelmed them, central bankers would ultimately benefit from the restructurings provoked by the Great Inflation. Monetary policy became more important, and the organizations with capabilities to use such policy would sooner or later gain power (Singleton 2011: 184).

How can we link our understanding of the 1970s as a period of crisis to the subsequent processes that have led to the adoption of neoliberalism and the rise of central banks? The interest-based, ideational, institutional, and organizational perspectives discussed in the previous chapter all offer their own answers to this question. For instance, interest-based "politics of money" scholars consider the intensified distributional conflicts during the 1970s as key. As they argue, the rise of central banks and the associated shifts from expansionary fiscal to restrictive monetary policies reflected the inherent bias in these distributional conflicts in favor of capital. Ideational scholars emphasize the importance of state elites and organic intellectuals and suggest that monetarist ideas promised these elites new solutions to the encountered dilemmas (Blyth 2002; Fourcade-Gourinchas and Babb 2002; Hall 1986). In this story, central bankers rose, if not as champions, then as exercisers of highly appealing neoliberal solutions. For institutionalists, by contrast, the question is which countries were able to overcome stagflation and regain monetary stability. What they find is that differences in the status of central banks, most notably their independence, plus a few other factors, were essential prerequisites (Hall and Franzese 1998). Lastly, sociologists such as Mitchell Abolafia (2012) see the 1970s as the birth hour of central bank technocracy. The influx of monetarism into central banks initiated the scientization of monetary policy.

In this chapter, I am going to offer a different account of what happened at this critical juncture. What I exploit, for that purpose, is an oft-overlooked fact: At the end of the 1970s and well into the 1980s, in most countries, monetary policy remained a problematic, if not feeble economic management technique, and only very few central bankers were able to capitalize on the crisis directly. Even where disinflation happened (for example, in Britain between 1980 and 1983), these developments did not necessarily lead actors to give credit to monetary authorities, or to assume that monetary policies were superior to other tools for achieving disinflation (Prasad 2006). In fact, in only a handful of cases did central banks not only contribute to disinflation, but also establish a distinct political authority based on their new policymaking. This happened consistently only in Germany, Switzerland, and to some extent Japan. In all other countries, we have to wait until the 1980s or even 1990s to observe the rise of central banks and the institutionalization of monetary policy dominance.

The existing approaches that I cite above have a hard time explaining this pattern. For instance, if we assume that distributional conflicts were key drivers of change during the 1970s, it becomes difficult to explain why countries with the fiercest industrial conflicts, such as Britain, were not among those where central banks became particularly important for resolving these conflicts in favor of capital. Also, countries with intense ideological mobilization around monetarism were *not* those where monetarism provided a basis for central bank power. Explanations based on institutional variables provide more leverage to explain why only a small number of central banks capitalized on this crisis—usually, these were countries where the central banks already enjoyed strong institutional status (Goodman 1992). But the respective analyses remain incomplete if we do not probe further into how different institutions interacted to provide supportive contexts for a new, previously unknown *practice* of monetary governing under flexible exchange rates (Johnson 1998). Lastly, sociologists Mitchell Abolafia and Douglas Holmes rightly point to the influx of monetarist ideas during the 1970s. However, these scholars cannot explain why this influx led to vastly different policy outcomes and central bank roles in different countries.

My proposal is thus that, instead of singling out interests, ideas, institutions, or technocracy, we should recognize that central banks could capitalize on the Great Inflation if they succeeded in constructing new governing techniques that were anchored in their concrete operations, and provided focal points to coordinate expectations and beliefs in the wider economy. The salience of the inflation problem, and growing political pressure to address it, opened a window of opportunity for these innovations. And for innovations to be successful, institutions mattered as they guided policymakers toward feasible solutions and defined the (in)felicitous conditions that determined the effectiveness and legitimacy of chosen techniques. But it is not the institutions in isolation that mattered, but how they supported or prevented central banks from enacting new operational and communicative interventions, with emergent ordering effects. Moreover, as we will see, in the attempted construction of new governing techniques, macroeconomic expertise played a decisive role. Without engaging in the experiment of guiding policy decisions by monetarist concepts—an unheard-of practice in the world of central banking—authorities would not have learned that announcing prospective targets for monetary growth could serve to coordinate expectations. However, the usefulness of targets was far from inevitable. Rather, the more difficult step consisted in enlisting the constituencies that mattered in a particular political-economic setting to buy into monetary targeting as a new macro-coordination game.

What Is Monetarism?

In short, the proposition here is that only central banks, which could translate monetarism into governing techniques that were felicitously adapted to local conditions, were capable of using the inflationary crisis of the 1970s as a window of opportunity. In other cases, the crisis initiated a more complicated search for policy solutions, and monetarism influenced this search only insofar as it remained an episode of failed experimentation. This claim makes it necessary to clarify what I mean by monetarism and to justify my focus on experiments with monetarist concepts and techniques. In orthodox academic monetarism, authors such as Milton Friedman and Karl Brunner state that there exists a causal path from money, measured as a quantity, to output and inflation. These authors assume that an expansion of money in relation to economic output induces more demand in the economy; the problem then is that excess demand, caused by excessive money creation, leads to a rise in the inflation rate (Friedman 1956; Friedman 1970; Friedman 1990 [1961]; Friedman and Schwartz 1963).[1] Monetarists further argue that, in one way or another, central banks have control over the relevant monetary aggregate. This can be via control over their own reserves (the so-called monetary base) (Brunner 1968) or via changes in interest rates that affect propensities to consume or save (Friedman 1970). In consequence, hard-nosed monetarists claim that excessive inflation indicates that central banks have failed to use their available options for exercising monetary control.

Since the 1980s, post-Keynesians, practitioners, and increasingly also mainstream economists have abandoned these ideas and have argued convincingly why orthodox academic monetarism does not work in practice (Bindseil 2014; Fullwiler 2013; Snowdon and Vane 2005). The common denominator of this literature is that money creation is by and large a process that happens in the banking sector in interaction with various customers (households, firms, public actors). Accordingly, predominant monetary forms evolve constantly, in response to innovations in finance, customers' changing preferences, and structural changes in the economy. This makes it impossible for policymakers to define money consistently and to rely on stable relationships between the measured monetary quantity, economic output, and inflation. Moreover, in contrast to monetarist notions of control, the new literature argues that central banks are severely constrained in their practical influence on monetary expansion. That is because private banks expand credit and their deposit liabilities first and then concern themselves with funding later. In consequence, central banks are in a bind to satisfy the reserves that banks demand at any given time, and they would produce a financial crisis if they failed to do so. Endogenous money, the money created within the banking system, thus drives exogeneous money issuance, not the other way around. By implication, the power of central banks in the conduct of monetary policy does *not* derive from their ability to control the money supply. It originates in their ability to influence the *price* of credit, namely interest rates (McLeay, Radia, and Ryland 2014). Not by holding back money, but by making it more or less expensive do central banks influence aggregate demand and the general price level.

These critical appraisals of monetarism in more recent economic literature and the historical experiences of monetarist failures have led many political economists to argue that, even in the high times of monetarist debates in the 1970s, monetarist concepts were irrelevant for central bankers' real-world actions. If at all, monetarist idioms such as "too much money chasing too few goods" or "closing the money tap" served as ideological veils for real choices over interest rates (Krippner 2011). I depart from this view here, not by returning to the theories of Friedman or Brunner, but by offering a sociological interpretation of monetarism as a historically situated phenomenon. Jacqueline Best gives a succinct summary of such an approach; she writes that "there is nothing inherently credible [or invalid, LW] about a quantitative rule or target as a way of managing inflation. For monetary rules to work they need to be both understood and made to be credible—which means that key actors need to learn that this is how a given inflation game works and put into place a whole range of supporting practices that reflect and reproduce this conviction" (2019: 624). With the distinction between the operational and expectational dimensions of central bank governing introduced in the previous chapter, I have suggested a concrete method of analyzing such "inflation games" and the conditions of their failure or success.

Accordingly, the key question is not whether monetarism can or cannot work in principle. The question rather is which central banks, in a period during which monetarist concepts and precepts provided the available repertoires to think about and articulate monetary policy, were able to translate these concepts and precepts into devices that empowered authorities to govern monetary processes and gain influence over processes of expectation formation in the broader economy. I will argue that this felicitous use of monetarism was possible only if the central banks operated in an environment characterized by relatively coherent, cartelized banking sectors, which managed reserves conservatively and controlled access to credit and savings products for households and firms. If that was the case, there was a possibility that monetary statistics provided the basis for defining loosely controlled, but plausible targets for monetary policy. Whether such targets gained credibility among core constituencies further depended on the structure of expectational politics in the respective political economy—the extent to which interest groups articulated incommensurable or compatible claims and expectations and what role the central banks assumed vis-à-vis these constituencies. In particular, it was essential for successful central banks that there were corporate actors willing to coordinate wage bargains with an eye on the central banks' announcements (Höpner 2019), and that monetary authorities acted as trusted fiduciaries that credibly signaled their policy intentions to them.

Practical Monetarism and Its (In)felicity Conditions

Monetary targeting thus worked if central banks could draw on conservative banking structures to claim "proprietary" control over money supply and if they could engage directly with corporatist wage bargaining in order to orchestrate expectations about future inflation rates; this presupposed some autonomy in decision-making or, more precisely, the capacity to act as independent fiduciary in the larger polity (Evans 1995). By contrast, in many countries, practical monetarism could not be made to work precisely because experiments with monetarist concepts did not encounter these felicitous conditions. For instance, where banks had already transitioned to active liability management, and where the boundaries between banking and the wider financial system had become porous, monetary targets did not provide plausible abstractions from underlying monetary and financial processes. Moreover, in most countries, strong corporatist institutions as carriers of expectational coordination were absent, or militant industrial conflicts undermined their willingness to coordinate around shared expectations of future inflation. Lastly, in many countries central banks could not claim proprietary use of monetary targets and/or were unable to convey their intentions to the relevant constituencies.

In short, then, this chapter shows why we see such strong divergences between central banks that could or could not capitalize on the inflationary crises of the 1970s. The following analysis shall establish this argument by drawing on the two extreme cases that I introduced in the previous chapter, Switzerland and the United Kingdom. After these in-depth case studies, I will turn to Germany to illustrate its broad similarities with the Swiss case before discussing some intermediate cases to strengthen my claims. This section will also spell out two important implications of my analysis. First, contrary to much of the debate on monetarism and neoliberalism (Mudge 2008), I show that monetarist central banking was actually incompatible with liberalized, financialized capitalism and relied on the continuity and stability of nonmarket arrangements in the domains of banking and wage bargaining. Moreover, the substantive meaning of central bank independence in the "successful" monetarist cases was not synonymous with technocracy but is better captured by what Peter Evans (1995) calls "embedded autonomy." Emphasizing these aspects of felicitous monetarism is not to deny the problematic political implications of the Bundesbank's or the Swiss National Bank's dominance in their respective polities, but to make explicit that their restrictive policies and sources of legitimacy were categorically different from those that became essential for the marriage of financialization and central bank power during the 1990s and 2000s.

The second, more important implication then relates to those countries in which monetary targeting did *not* work and the requisite supportive conditions for its enactment did not exist. Failure of monetary targeting in those latter contexts informed a search for alternative techniques that could rely on different infrastructural foundations. In contrast to most of the literature, I do not assume that central bankers in these latter countries subsequently turned to inflation targeting and interest-rate policies simply because these were the more rational, straightforward ways to conduct monetary policy. Rather, the turn to inflation targeting had its own supportive context, its own infrastructural foundations, and rested on an equally demanding "inflation game." Financializing economies and their emergent systems of market-based banking played a formative role in the development of this new technique. Through the transformation of finance since the 1970s, central banks learned to tap market-based infrastructures as transmission belts for their policy interventions and to capitalize on expectation coordination with capital markets as the hegemonic game; concepts such as the "natural rate of interest," far from providing some unconditional, noncontingent basis for central bank efficacy, established fragile symbolic foundations for this particular game. It is in relation to this latter version of monetary policy that we can speak of a complicity between financialized capitalism and central bank power.

By opening this chapter with the governability crisis as it was perceived by social scientists and policymakers around 1970, I want to point out right from the start that experiments with monetarism were launched in situations of crisis and on the pretext of fundamental uncertainty. At the beginning of the 1970s, monetary targeting was not a clearly defined technique and the conditions that might contribute to its success were unknown. Trials in different settings were therefore like attempts at solving a jigsaw whose pieces constantly changed shape and whose final picture remained unknown. In some contexts, the pieces felicitously fit together, but in most others they did not. It is in this spirit that I approach my empirical sources.

The Swiss National Bank: From Elite Mediation to Corporatist Monetarism

The Swiss context was in many ways conducive to the adoption of monetary targeting. Federalist struggles over nation-building had established a central bank with strong independence; a large constituency of savers made disinflation a widely shared political aim; cohesive producer groups in the export sectors provided the institutional conditions for coordinating inflation expectations; and a universalist banking sector maintained stable routines throughout the 1970s, facilitating operational coordination with the central bank. At the same time, the practice of targeting and the ways in which different institutions would fall into place to support the policy's efficacy were unknown to actors and observers when the decade began. Until the mid-1970s, central banking rather consisted of moderating different elite interests and contained no forward-looking decision-making; the kind of strategic communication needed to coordinate expectations was not available. Moreover, the idea that central bank authority could derive from persuasive public communications around monetarist policy targets was unfamiliar to any Swiss central banker before 1975. The following analysis will thus focus on the concrete and unpredictable process whereby monetary targeting developed into a governing technique that became thoroughly embedded in the Swiss political economy, turning the Swiss

National Bank into one of the first agentic, authoritative policymakers of the late 1970s.

Swiss Central Banking before 1970

The Swiss National Bank (SNB) is a peculiar organizational construct, whose legal status, external governance, and internal decision-making procedures reflect the protracted and twisted trajectories of Swiss state formation during the nineteenth and twentieth centuries (Tanner 2015). Up until the late nineteenth century, banks in the various Swiss cantons had maintained control over note issuance, which was centralized only with an amendment to the Swiss Constitution in 1891. The subsequent plan was to establish a state institution to be granted the monopoly of issuing Swiss francs (Sfr.). But conservative forces and powerful trade associations successfully lobbied against this proposal, and the electorate endorsed these antistatist arguments in a popular referendum in 1897. Accordingly, a compromise was found between federal and cantonal, public and private interests, which involved establishing the Swiss National Bank as a private stock company, whose ownership was distributed among three groups: the cantons (40 percent), private investors (40 percent), and the former note-issuing cantonal banks (20 percent) (Bordo and James 2007). Because of this complicated legal form, the SNB has enjoyed relative independence from the federal state and politics since its foundation in 1907. The government's influence is restricted to nominating the central bank's governors (called directors) and to proposing amendments to the constitutional and statutory rights and obligations regulating the SNB's public role. The latter power is highly circumscribed, however, because legal changes must pass many veto players in the Swiss polity (various consultative committees, two parliamentary chambers, strong provisions for popular referenda).

But yet another feature has defined the SNB's position in the Swiss polity and economy. Since its foundation, powerful interests in Swiss society have been represented in the central bank's organizational structure, particularly the SNB's governance and oversight body, the Bank Council. Before the introduction of monetary targeting led to a stronger concentration of decision-making powers with the organization's expert staff and executive body (the Direktorium), major central bank decisions were deliberated on and formed within this Council. The importance of these deliberations derived from the fact that elites legitimately representing broader political and economic interests participated in them. For instance, representatives of the various trade associations—the general industry association "Vorort" or those representing important sectors (machines; watch manufacturing; hotels)—always participated in Bank Council discussions. Representatives of different local and federal chambers of commerce were also present. The key actors, however, were CEOs or chairmen of Switzerland's major banks (Credit Suisse; Swiss Bank Corporation; Union Bank of Switzerland; the latter two later merging into UBS). These elites represented the interests of the powerful banking sector, but also spoke in the name of large industrial firms on whose boards of directors they were represented (Bühlmann, David, and Mach 2012; Ginalski, David, and Mach 2014). In effect, the various CEOs and nonexecutive directors assembled in this body represented around 20 percent (21.5 percent in 1943; 18 percent in 1960; 18.5 percent in 1980) of the overall market capitalization of Swiss stock companies. Liberals constituted the major group among the politicians and state representatives (Guex and Sancey 2010).

Accordingly, central banking before the 1970s largely meant mediation among economic and financial elites. The most powerful expression of this corporatist governing (Moran 1991) was the regular use of "gentlemen's agreements." The first such agreement had been reached between the SNB and the Swiss Bankers' Association (the body formally representing banking interests) in 1927 in response to growing domestic political pressure from farming groups and working-class politicians, who had blamed the banks for creating an artificial scarcity of capital because of their extensive investments abroad. In the following decades, the central bank governors and the Swiss Bankers' Association concluded numerous such voluntary agreements on a wide range of issues, including the import and export of gold and foreign currency, interest rates, and minimum deposits (Schweizerische Nationalbank 1982: 127–29). The importance of these agreements went hand in hand with the relative weakness of the SNB as an executive arm of the state. Its governors occupied moderately paid bureaucratic positions and had no special qualifications in monetary affairs (Guex and Sancey 2010). The other staff—200 (1950s) to 400 employees (late 1960s)—collected statistics, administered reserve holdings, implemented transactions with banks, and controlled the issuance of currency. Accordingly, as contemporaries describe it, working for the SNB was boring and people with ambitions quickly went elsewhere.[2]

The centerpiece of monetary stability that central bankers were supposed to protect and depoliticize was the Swiss franc's fixed external value (Bernholz 2007: 120; Straumann 2010). Up until the 1970s, the SNB *and* its major stakeholders never questioned the need to preserve stable exchange rates, first with gold, and following World War II, with the gold–US dollar standard that had emerged from the negotiations at Bretton Woods. The strength of the Swiss exchange-rate doctrine had already been evident during the Great Depression, which had forced Western countries to abandon gold. Among these countries, the Swiss had been the last to leave gold, supporting a strict adherence to monetary discipline with the idea that a currency is a transactional medium for the economy, but should not be manipulated for economic policy goals (Bordo and James 2007: 95). Importantly, despite the deflationary consequences of these Great Depression policies, there was no major break with this doctrine in the postwar era. Even though an expanded welfare state had emerged after 1945 (Tanner 2015), the Swiss federal state did not venture into activist macroeconomic management (Guex 2012). Accordingly, the SNB's almost exclusive concern remained the Swiss franc's external stability, now preserved through fixed exchange rates with the US dollar and gold.[3] Helpful for this doctrine was the fact that, just like Germany, Switzerland had evolved into what Martin Höpner (2019) calls an "undervaluation regime." Such regimes are characterized by the suppression of currency appreciation against those of trading partners, allowing industrial sectors to improve their competitive positions through stronger productivity growth and lower domestic inflation. Realizing these advantages, Swiss export firms developed a major stake in exchange-rate stability. For instance, when the Germans revalued the Mark in 1969, the federation of Swiss engine producers convinced the government that revaluating the Swiss franc would constitute a "catastrophe for Swiss industry."[4] The banks were equally committed to fixed exchange rates.[5]

From the 1960s onward, however, this regime came under growing strain. The diverging developments of "soft" (United States, United Kingdom, Italy) versus "hard" currency countries (Germany, the Netherlands, Switzerland) and the associated growth in current account imbalances articulated themselves in appreciation pressures and an involuntary

expansion of dollar reserves for the latter. These pressures increased with
trade liberalization and an associated weakening of capital account controls (Eichengreen 2008: 118ff.). Switzerland was strongly affected by these
pressures as a small economy with a large banking sector and safe-haven
currency. The big banks, private partnership banks, and increasingly numerous foreign bank affiliates were highly active in channeling capital into
the country (Giddey 2013). For instance, foreign liabilities of the big banks
increased with annual growth rates between 27 and 43 percent during the
late 1960s (Mazbouri, Guex, and Lopez 2012: 495). Most of these liabilities
were invested abroad, particularly in the Eurocurrency markets—Loepfe
(2011: 496) reckons that Swiss banks held between 30 and 40 percent of all
Eurodollar deposits for their offshore clients. But banks repatriated these
funds in the expectation of currency revaluations and in regular "window
dressing" operations (that is, to have larger reserve holdings on reporting
dates). The monetary expansion effects of these operations (every imported
US dollar from the Eurodollar markets needed to be matched by a Swiss
franc liability on the central bank balance sheet), combined with the stimulus provided by constant undervaluation, led to complementary domestic
monetary and economic-policy problems. There was soaring demand for
labor, credit, consumer goods, and housing, with inflationary pressure
gradually increasing over the course of the 1960s (Bernholz 1974: 116). A
few experts argued that the rise of inflation was inextricably linked to the
fixed parity.[6] But major decision-makers and stakeholders refused to consider exchange-rate revaluation as a serious policy option.[7]

If some growth of governing capacities can be observed within the SNB
over the course of the 1960s, this was as a result of concerted attempts to
preserve Bretton Woods and the Swiss undervaluation privilege within it
(Toniolo 2005: 429). But as elites gradually realized, international central
bank cooperation could only delay the ultimate breakdown of the international currency order. A large crack appeared in 1971, when Nixon decided to suspend gold convertibility and forced a much-disliked revaluation upon the Swiss.[8] Elites also came to realize that new commitments to
exchange-rate stability (for example, the Smithsonian Agreement) would
not stick.[9] But the most important reason why the Swiss turned away from
Bretton Woods came from the central bank balance-sheet effects of large
capital inflows. The central bankers became increasingly concerned that
their ballooning dollar reserves were providing a major impetus to domestic

inflation and bore considerable financial risks. With a further drastic in-
flow of dollars in 1972–1973 and the increasing likelihood of more dollar
devaluation to follow, the central bank balance-sheet risks began to look
daunting. This was less a budgetary problem than a political issue. The central bank's losses were covered by the federal government, a measure that
provoked political disputes over central bank independence.[10] For these
reasons, it was no accident that in January 1973, upon another massive
wave of capital inflows, the SNB, rather than the government, decided
to abandon fixed parity (Straumann 2010: 172). Besides fearing more inflationary pressures, the central bank also wanted to protect itself.

Switzerland's Haphazard Path to Monetary Targeting

The decision to float has been heralded in the literature as a major step by
the SNB toward regaining monetary-policy autonomy (Bernholz 2007). In
the early 1970s, however, neither the central bank's own governors nor Switzerland's elites perceived the decision in that light.[11] Instead, all major actors believed that Switzerland would eventually return to fixed exchange
rates. As argued above, maintenance of external Swiss franc stability had
helped to align powerful economic and political interests, and it had been
framed over decades as the legitimate way to ensure monetary stability; no
other coherent regime was in sight. The officials therefore accepted only reluctantly, and after several disappointing episodes, that a return to exchange-
rate stability was not a practical option. Swiss plans to join a European
regime of stabilized exchange rates ("the snake") were blocked by France
(Halbeisen 2005); and unilateral attempts to withstand appreciation pressures proved unsuccessful, by and large.[12] Moreover, reduced but continued
foreign exchange interventionism after the end of Bretton Woods threatened to enlarge the inflation problem—the rate had risen from 3.5 percent
in 1970, to 9 percent in 1973 and further to 10 percent in 1974. There was
also still the risk of losses on the central bank's reserve holdings.

Attention thus turned to domestic-policy options. But these options also
appeared highly constrained. Already since the late 1960s, the government,
together with the SNB, had attempted to strengthen legal capacities for
macro-stabilization policies, with the primary aim of reducing foreign capital inflows and domestic credit expansion.[13] These efforts intensified during
the early 1970s.[14] But the nature of distributed powers in a federal and

corporatist state and the resulting weaknesses of central policy planning capacities posed major obstacles (Halbeisen and Straumann 2012: 979).[15] For instance, the banks successfully lobbied against proposals that would have given the SNB statutory rights to adjust minimum reserves and impose credit quotas.[16] The SNB thus resorted to crisis management via the established corporatist route. But gentlemen's agreements proved equally ineffective. Bankers accepted highly limited restrictions only on their lending activities, and noncompliance became widespread.[17] The newly appointed SNB president, Fritz Leutwiler, therefore declared the end of Switzerland's version of "club government" (Moran 2003) in 1975.

The SNB's monetarism emerged from these failures and strategic dilemmas. Two parallel but separate developments preceded its introduction. First, for Swiss elites as well as for the SNB governors, monetarism had long offered an intuitively appealing "folk" vocabulary for articulating their strong anti-inflationist beliefs. For instance, parliamentarians from various parties stressed their concerns about inflation as national problem "No. 1" and drew widely on proto-monetarist interpretations of its causes.[18] The precise implications of these interpretations remained unclear, however. Reflecting such vagueness, Finance Minister Nello Celio could claim in 1972 that the government *was already* practicing a monetarism of sorts.[19] Many comments at the time imply that credit restrictions were seen as part of such broadly understood monetarism.[20] Similar attitudes were found inside the central bank. Its governors were committed inflation fighters and by and large thought about their contribution to disinflation in quantitative rather than interest-rate terms.[21] This also reflected the role of foreign capital inflows in increasing the central bank's own balance sheet in times of inflationary pressures. But even among these senior central bankers, there existed no clear idea of how to conduct forward-looking policy. To be sure, the central bankers knew that the less they purchased foreign reserves and increased the SNB's liabilities, the less the money supply would expand. In addition to concerns about the foreign exchange implications of such decisions, however, they had no yardstick for adjusting their current operations to achieve a controlled reduction of inflation; there was no forward-looking component in the management of the central bank's balance sheet.[22] Indeed, in the early 1970s, the governors still doubted that future-oriented policy could be implemented at all. They held an entrenched skepticism toward econometric calculations and forecasts and thought that central banking was too complex and uncertain to be guided by such expertise.[23]

It was thus essential for the SNB's adoption of monetary targeting in 1974 that, in parallel to the strengthening of popular monetarist sentiments, a more technical version emerged. At the time, a decisive shift in expert discourses and practices facilitated this development. In the postwar period, Swiss macroeconomics had remained by and large descriptive and historical.[24] But the situation changed during the early 1970s with the import of US scientific monetarism. Two Swiss-born, but US-based, economists were critical in facilitating this translation process (Bockman and Eyal 2002). One was Karl Brunner, a Swiss national who had taken up a professorship at the new University of Rochester Business School in 1971 (Fourcade and Khurana 2013); and the other was Juerg Niehans, also a Swiss citizen with a chair at Johns Hopkins.[25] Besides Milton Friedman, Brunner in a team with Allan Meltzer were the eminent figures in the advancement and promotion of monetarism.[26] In Switzerland, Brunner effectively served as the monopolistic translator of this US-bred economics (Brunner 1971). Despite Brunner's and Niehans's failures in convincing senior policymakers directly, these eminent economists exerted strong influence via another route.[27] Brunner, in particular, shaped macroeconomic research by educating and training several young economists. This "young guard" (Tilcsik 2010) then went on to establish a previously nonexistent space for domestic policy expertise around and within the central bank. For instance, a number of academic economists began confronting policymakers with previously unknown technical discussions of policy and concrete proposals gauged in scientific terms. Still more critical was Brunner's role in training economists who pursued careers inside the SNB. In 1972, Alex Galli embarked upon doctoral research to develop Switzerland's first systematic monetary statistics for the SNB's research division VOSTA.[28] Brunner played a supportive role in Galli's project to develop more comprehensive statistics that could support monetary policy. Kurt Schiltknecht became a second technically trained economist at VOSTA, who was encouraged by Brunner to develop money-supply forecasting and demand forecasting. Galli and Schiltknecht then went on to write the first proposal for monetary targeting for the Swiss economy. They suggested that the SNB could hit an M1 target by controlling the central bank's provision of reserves—what is called the "monetary base" (Brunner 1968). In order to achieve the respective target, the economists used GDP forecasts and rough estimates of monetary velocity as inputs to the classic quantity formula (GDP x inflation rate = M1 x velocity). From there, they deduced via a simple money multiplier formula how much supply of M0 would be appropriate in order to meet the forecasted value of monetary demand, with the aim of reducing the inflation rate moderately over the course of the following years.[29]

How Monetary Targeting Became a Successful Governing Technique

This proposal, with a corresponding M1 target, was adopted by the SNB governors in December 1974. In January 1975, the central bank issued a press release in which the target was publicly announced.[30] From the very beginning, however, the governors' commitment to the respective targets was based on different rationales than the ones entailed in the technical monetarist strategy proposal developed by Galli and Schiltknecht. In fact, senior central bankers remained highly skeptical toward forecasting, as well as precise money-supply control. Such control was incompatible, in their understanding, with the need to balance domestic with external stability concerns. Just like other central bankers, the SNB governors also thought that implementation via control of central bank liabilities would threaten established reserve management routines between the SNB and commercial banks.[31] But for the governors, supply targets had another useful purpose. They offered a way out of the political and strategic dilemmas that the SNB had confronted since 1973. The central bank could convey that it had developed a consistent strategy in line with its broader commitment to inflation reduction while avoiding and downplaying the conflicts and failings that were associated with credit control and foreign exchange operations. Acutely aware of the prevalence of popular monetarist ideas among Swiss elites, the governors thus counted primarily on the "psychological-political" effects that their commitment to money-supply control would have.[32]

Several supportive conditions led this strategy to generate beneficial effects. On the structural side, the SNB benefited from the fact that its reduced foreign exchange interventions and accelerated Swiss franc appreciation since 1973 led to an economic recession in 1974–1975 (Rich 1987: 5).

This recession stopped the domestic inflationary spiral that had been fueled in the last years of Bretton Woods. Meanwhile, much of the economic hardship produced by a 5 percent drop in real GDP could be externalized, to the Italian workers without social security protection who left Switzerland in large numbers (ca. 250,000) between 1974 and 1977 (Guex 2012: 162; Prader 1981: 422). Moreover, with foreign exchange interventions becoming less voluminous after 1973, and without the eminent threat of devaluation, the central bank was able to recover stable patterns of reserve management with the commercial banks. These usually held large amounts of reserves directly with the SNB, as buffers against customer withdrawals, as signals of prudent banking, and because there existed no domestic money market that would have allowed banks to economize domestically on excess reserves. Notwithstanding the frequent inaccuracy of econometric calculations and forecasts—for example, of money multipliers—the respective routines gave monetary targets a certain degree of plausibility because, from one year to the next, M0 as well as M1 growth rates did not vary strongly.

Under these felicitous conditions, SNB governors were able to promote money-supply targets as new focal points for coordinating the expectations of various stakeholders. Part of this coordination rested on a new, more proactive public communication. PR work was professionalized at the time. But the central bankers also mobilized their long-standing elite contacts to promote their new policies. Stable networks within and between financial, economic, and political spheres (Bühlmann, David, and Mach 2012; Kriesi 1980), as well as strong corporatist institutions (Katzenstein 1985; Oesch 2011), provided the basis for such coordination. For instance, the governors engaged representatives of peak associations in monetary targeting and thereby inscribed central bank policies within extant popular monetarist beliefs. On that basis, macro-coordination processes in the broader political economy were strengthened and enhanced. In particular, industrial workers and employers used targets to achieve wage settlements that maintained the competitiveness of export products; labor peace remained exceptionally strong throughout this period. This more specific translation of targets into collective wage bargaining was accompanied by an affirmative public discourse that associated the SNB's stabilization of the "money supply" with domestic monetary stability.[33] Still lacking its own macroeconomic policy apparatus, officials and politicians in Berne readily absorbed the monetarist message; fiscal policy became subordinated to the SNB's new monetarism (Baltensperger 1984; Guex 2012; Prader 1981: 566).[34]

The SNB thus emerged from the monetary crises of the late 1960s until the mid-1970s as an independent fiduciary (Bourdieu 2014: 37; Evans 1995) within the Swiss polity that set its own policy. It did so in ways that relied on existing sources of stability (within banking and industrial sectors) and that aligned with anti-inflationary dispositions and popular monetarist beliefs. As Leutwiler discovered over the course of these experiments, this version of central bank governing could even survive periods in which developments in monetary aggregates became more volatile. In the early 1980s, he noted that

> the volatility of monetary aggregates in Switzerland is *greater* than, for instance, in the United States. At the same time, the US monetary authorities face much harsher criticism than the Swiss. If you look for an explanation of that paradox, it is important to recognize that the *results* of monetary targeting are more favorable in Switzerland than the volatility in aggregates would suggest . . . We here have to acknowledge the importance of *psychology:* It is of secondary importance whether the monetary target is three, four or five percent. *What matters more is that the message sent together with the aggregates is properly understood:* This message consists of the declared will to be serious in fighting inflation; the primary issue thus is *credibility,* which—as shown in the US case—is easily destroyed but difficult to re-build.[35]

Indeed, the SNB's targeting record remained mixed. Several face-saving switches in the targeted aggregate had to be made throughout the 1980s and 1990s; and occasionally, the central bank shifted emphasis from inflation control to foreign exchange management to ward off pressure from export interests.[36] But, overall, monetary targeting helped to bolster the governing powers and political authority of the SNB.[37] In international circles, the SNB proudly promoted its monetarism as a solution to the policy problems that still haunted its central banker peers. And in a survey conducted in 1981, Swiss respondents expressed their high level of trust in the central bank.[38] Self-confidence was so high within the SNB that its officials believed that the central bank was the only authoritative policy institution in the country.[39]

The Bank of England: "Private Influence" as a Policy Lever and Fatal Strategic Choice

The situation at the close of the 1970s could not have been more different for the Bank of England. As one of its officials noted in 1977, the Bank "has in recent years been subject to abuse, misrepresentation, belittlement etc."[40] The Left saw the Bank as "a state within the state" whose purported intention was to advance narrow financial elite interests; and conservatives, monetarist academics, and prominent City analysts incessantly blamed the Bank for the inflationary excesses of 1973–1975 and the current account crisis of 1976.[41] When Margaret Thatcher came to power in 1979, the United Kingdom was as far away from authoritative central banking as it could be. The new Prime Minister centralized more decision-making at No. 10 Downing Street and treated Bank of England Governor Gordon Richardson as her subordinate; at one point, Thatcher called Richardson "that fool who runs the Bank of England" (cited in James 2020: 66). Thatcher's failed attempts at money-supply control and her choice for centralized decision-making over interest rates left the Bank of England's status as monetary policymaker uncertain for another decade, until 1992. Despite a drop in inflation rates during the early 1980s, the Bank of England still felt as late as 1987 that, compared with the German Bundesbank, it did "not yet have the same credibility."[42] The Great Inflation of the 1970s, and the Keynesian dilemmas, distributional conflicts, and ideological mobilizations associated with it, did not lead directly to an age of central bank dominance.

How did the British central bank end up in such a different position compared with that of its Swiss counterpart by the end of the Great Inflation? As the following narrative will show, a few conditions leading to this outcome are widely recognized in the literature—in particular the Bank of England's lack of independence and the conflicting imperatives of Keynesian macroeconomic management. But the fact that final authority rested with the executive did not prevent effective monetary policymaking per se, as the Bank of England would prove in the period from 1992 to 1997, when it still lacked formal independence, but successfully emancipated its policy approach and emerged as an authoritative central bank. The problems confronted during the 1970s thus were more specific and had to do with the solutions chosen during the crisis decade, in particular the experiments with monetarism in 1971–1973 and 1976–1979. These experiments failed because they reinforced a traditional division of labor between the central bank as advocate of austerity and the government as the arbiter of macroeconomic management, which was torn between conflicting demands from different constituencies. The central bank consciously reaffirmed this division in 1976 when it opted against "externalizing" its role and instead promoted monetary targets as a strategy to constrain *fiscal* policy. The central bank chose this role not just because this choice reaffirmed path-dependent institutions. Another reason was that central bankers had no idea of how to promote, let alone pursue, an independent monetary policy. The resurrection of global finance during the 1970s disrupted and changed domestic banking structures, credit practices, and money markets—a transformation that resulted partly from deregulatory policy choices that the Bank of England had itself made. In consequence, operative instabilities for monetary policy were heightened. With high volatility in monetary aggregates, monetary targeting did not offer a viable practical solution. These implementation problems, added to prevalent institutions, led to two unsuccessful episodes of monetary targeting in 1971–1973 and 1976–1979.

British Central Banking before the 1970s

How do we get there? To recognize the Bank of England's peculiar role within government and toward finance, it is necessary to go all the way back to its foundation in 1694, when the Bank was established as "a Whig finance company" (Walter Bagehot, cited in Wood 2005: 32), that is, as an organization whose social, political, and financial foundations lay in London's liberal financial oligarchy (Knafo 2013; Pincus and Robinson 2011). These origins meant that the Bank's shareholders pursued pecuniary interests via the central bank, which only reluctantly grew into a public institution (by accepting responsibility as a lender of last resort in the late nineteenth century) (Bagehot 1873; Sayers 1976). But the Bank's strong City affiliations also cast a long shadow over its position within the British polity, its modes of governance, and organizational structure. For instance, well into the twentieth century, the key locus of power at the Bank was the Court of Directors, which had been established to assemble the Bank's "Proprietors." These usually were merchant bankers, and so were the

Governors and Deputy Governors, who were recruited from the Court's ranks (Sayers 1976: 599; Wood 2005: 14).

A key change came with the failure of the gold standard in the 1930s. To be sure, famous Governor Montagu Norman had already begun to modernize the Bank of England in the 1910s and 1920s, strengthening its executive elements (Ahamed 2009). But Norman had remained a fierce defender of the gold standard and fundamentally opposed to activist economic policy (Ahamed 2009: 25–26; Collins and Baker 1999). An involuntary break with this doctrine came in 1931, when the Bank went off gold because of its (misplaced) belief that a resulting devaluation of the pound and exploding inflation would topple a Labour government and lead to the adoption of yet harsher internal devaluation (namely, reductions in real wages). But the opposite happened: Politicians and the public realized that, unconstrained by gold, there was more room for expansionary fiscal policies, supporting economic growth (Morrison 2016). The Second World War reinforced this trend (for example, Kingsley Wood's budget of 1941), ultimately resulting in the decision to nationalize the Bank.[43] This nationalization was part of a broader attempt to organize economic policy around domestic welfare goals and to use demand management orchestrated at the Treasury as the primary means to this end (Hall 1986; Weir and Skocpol 1985).

It is crucial to recognize, however, that, despite this departure from the Bank's financial oligarchy origins, its incorporation into the governmental apparatus remained partial. After 1945, the Old Lady of Threadneedle Street retained a "fair degree of independence over day-to-day affairs" (Collins and Baker 1999: 16), secured its own sources of income, and kept its historical role as "head-boy" of a still rather important and large financial center.[44] Competencies and authority for intervening in gilts (long-dated government bonds) and money markets remained within the Bank, and in particular with the Discount Office and the Chief Cashier, who constituted the operational heart of postwar British financial management. The Bank of England also maintained established practices of regulation that rested on transactional and social ties with direct (Discount Houses) and indirect counterparties (clearing banks) (see Chapters 4 and 5). The government had *no* control over these regulatory affairs, which rested on compromise formation among financial elites (Capie 2010: 590; Moran 1991: 63).[45] This explains why the postwar Bank, despite its nationalization, perceived itself as uniquely independent in banking matters compared with its peers: "In neither Germany nor the US—nor perhaps in any other country—is the independence and power of the central bank in regulating and supervising the banking systems equal to our own. Our role in managing the government's debt, both domestic and external, is also . . . unparalleled in other countries."[46]

On this basis, the Bank evolved in the postwar period from a City institution into a bureaucratic body that occupied a singular position between Whitehall and Downing Street to the West and the City of London to the East. Within the government apparatus, the Bank's exclusive City ties gave it distinct sources of influence over policies (Pepper and Oliver 2001: 32–33). To be sure, this influence had been considerably curtailed since 1931 and then again after 1945. The priorities of postwar British financial and economic policies were to reduce the large debt overhang (Allen 2014) and to manage domestic demand via a technocratic policy-planning process (Booth 2001; Peden 2000: 438). Charles Goodhart recounts that "the Chancellor was now treated as the absolute arbiter of the decision to set interest rates," informed by Treasury "forecasts and projections that formed the quantitative base for policy decisions, both on monetary and fiscal policies" (2004: 42).[47] But despite its diminished role, the Bank was able to maintain considerable influence because of its exclusive authority over City affairs and possession of "market expertise" (29). The Bank was particularly influential when voicing concerns over gilt-edged markets on which the government depended for its large refinancing needs (Allen 2019: 471; Capie 2010). The Bank also relayed to the government information about the foreign exchange situation, which was crucial for a country running a structural current account deficit. Lastly, because the government could not directly intervene in banking, it needed to cooperate with, and listen to, the Bank when implementing restrictions on private lending—a favored method of fighting inflation as long as interest-rate hikes were ruled out.[48] Cameron Cobbold, longtime Governor during the postwar period, articulated the Bank's resulting influence and independent position within the broader government machinery in the following words: "It would quite certainly make Bank relations with Government intolerable if discussion and argument were conducted by the Bank and Treasury in public instead of between us" (cited in Allen 2014: 208). In most circumstances, as a Deputy Governor remarked, public statements were to be entirely avoided and influence was to be exerted "behind closed doors, in private, not through newspaper headlines" (cited in Siklos 2002: 239). These words reflect that the Bank, in the postwar period, was *not* the "Treasury's East End Arm" (Grant 2002: 201), as so often claimed, but was the possessor of strong influence and had a distinct sense of purpose as an eminent, if informal, institution of the British state.

Starting in the late 1950s, however, this postwar order gradually disintegrated. In macroeconomic terms, Britain faced increasing pressure because of its entrenched structural account deficit under the Bretton Woods rules. The "excess demand" of the domestic economy (demand in excess of domestic output) (Jones 2012: 244) was caused partly by expansionary fiscal policy that in turn responded to Britain's lower productivity growth compared with trading partners. This put pressure on Britain's foreign reserves, which was reinforced by a process of disinvestments from foreign sterling reserves in the Commonwealth (Schenk 2010). Accordingly, under fixed exchange rates and increasingly porous capital controls, Britain was fully exposed to current account imbalance crises. Complementarily, expansionary fiscal policies and domestic credit expansion, together with supply shortages, created an endemic problem of inflation. This situation posed an acute dilemma for the government. There would have been the option to devalue sterling, in order to mitigate the current account deficit problem while avoiding internal deflation. But strong devaluation not only entailed the danger of harming financial sector interests, but also harbored the immediate threat of stronger inflationary pressures, via the foreign exchange-import channel.

The policy course that Britain instead settled on during the 1960s consisted of "stop-go" interventions, whose erratic nature reflected internal struggles within the "macroeconomic executive," between expansionary interests on one hand, and, on the other, the urgency with which rising inflation, chronic trade deficits, and pressures on foreign reserves needed to be addressed.[49] But even during crisis periods, governments generally remained resistant to raising the Bank rate. Chancellor Butler's reactivation of monetary policy in November 1951 remained an exception to that rule. In any case, there was no conception of how such hikes would affect economic output and inflation. The only political certainty was that higher rates meant higher borrowing costs for the government, businesses, and a growing class of mortgage holders (Allen 2015: 20). On the other hand, the Bank of England increasingly resented ceilings for private credit issuance—the preferred policy choice of governments. Moreover, implementation of such ceilings became ever more difficult with the internationalization of British finance and the exploitation of various loopholes in capital controls.

Britain's Two Failed Monetarist Experiments during the 1970s

Strong pressure to address these predicaments came in 1967, when the International Monetary Fund (IMF) provided support lending to Britain after another acute current account crisis and demanded measures to reduce excess domestic demand (for the model underpinning the prescriptions, see Polak 1997). UK officials resisted any external interference with British economic policy, though. They instead negotiated a tailored solution, namely to constrain what was called "domestic credit expansion" (Goodhart and Needham 2018). British engagements with monetarism originate from this situation. The central bankers were by now openly hostile to any quantitative credit ceilings for the banking sector, interventions that in their eyes had "been pressed to their limits" (John Fforde, cited in Needham 2014b: 30–31). The Bank thus seized the crisis moment and the growing popularity of monetarist ideas (also within the IMF) to develop an alternative plan.[50] For that purpose, it internally established a new research group (later called the Monetary Policy Group). Based on a critical evaluation of the extant American literature and first econometric calculations for the United Kingdom, this group concluded in 1970 that monetary policy changes could affect the money supply and that changes in money supply would trigger adjustments of prices and GDP (Goodhart and Needham 2018; Needham 2014b: 26).[51]

This cautiously framed finding supported the advocacy by senior Bank officials of an alternative strategy to credit ceilings, resulting in a common commitment to restrain the expansion of credit via targets for the broad monetary aggregate M3. Importantly, this agreement left open *how* such monetary restraint was to be achieved. The very choice of M3 as the relevant monetary aggregate meant that different policy tools could be used for that purpose. For M3 was a broad measure of banking-sector liabilities (customers' checking and saving accounts) whose volume was directly influenced by government borrowing, as the banks' major asset position.

Hence, fiscal policy and debt management, as much as monetary policy or banking regulation, provided potential tools for taming M3 growth (Goodhart 1986: 80). The British officials thus translated monetarism very differently from the Swiss, creating a monetary targeting framework that aligned with the high degree of centralization of its policymaking apparatus and the close interaction between public debt and monetary growth in the British banking system.[52]

But as a result of this specific translation, the role of monetary policy remained underspecified and uncertain. Needham speaks of a "misalignment of understanding between the Bank, the Treasury and the Heath government" (2014b: 169). In the Bank and some parts of the Treasury, there prevailed the hope that M3 targets would encourage restraint in credit-financed government expenditure (via reductions in the fiscal deficit and / or by selling more government bonds to the nonbank public), accompanied by hikes in the Bank rate. But restrictive monetary policy or reduced borrowing remained out of the question. The Prime Minister and the Chancellor instead decided in the early 1970s that Britain needed another "dash for growth." Cheap funding conditions remained essential for this policy, both for government and private business (ibid.: 70–71). Consequently, no attempt was made to enhance the status of monetary policy in order to hit the internally agreed target.

In the following years, the inflation rate went up to 25 percent, leading many academic and political observers to associate British economic policies with the problems of Keynesianism on the eve of the postwar boom—problems originating in political calculi guided by the exigencies of mass politics (Kydland and Prescott 1977) and / or erroneous conceptions of macroeconomic steering among Treasury mandarins (Hall 1986). While the "dash for growth" can indeed be interpreted in these terms, it is important to recognize that a complementary development in the financial sector, for which the Bank of England bore some responsibility, made an important contribution to the dramatic monetary expansion of the early 1970s. This was Competition and Credit Control (CCC), which was the Bank of England's response to growing pressures faced by British banking institutions vis-à-vis unregulated competitors, such as fringe and Eurodollar banks. The Bank in 1971 decided to help the regulated banks by leveling the playing field, allowing them to adopt active liability management and reduce their reserves. This decision unleashed a lending boom, which was by and large responsible for the massive overshooting of the first agreed M3 targets for 1972 (Offer 2017: 1058).

Moreover, it is important to recognize that Keynesian demand management came to play a diminished and severely constrained role in the second half of the 1970s, after the inflationary spike of the mid-1970s and another sterling crisis in 1975–1976. Britain again received IMF assistance, but this time, the government responded with significant policy changes (Jones 2012). The Callaghan government (1974–1979) adopted a harsh austerity course and committed to monetary targets for £M3. In contrast to 1971, these targets were made public; for instance, for 1978, Chancellor Dennis Healey announced a desired £M3 expansion of 12 percent. Ironically, it was this strategic choice that came to haunt and ultimately discredit the government, as well as the central bank, ending with the electoral victory of Margaret Thatcher in 1979.

One reason for the dramatic failure of this second monetarist experiment from 1976 to 1979 was that the government chose to commit itself publicly to monetary targets at the very moment at which these targets had assumed growing ideological significance, while their actual value for informing policymaking had deteriorated. The targets' symbolic weight resulted from how Conservative politicians, think tankers, some stock brokers, and a few radical monetarist economists came to frame the inflationary spike of 1974–1975 (Fourcade 2009: 45–46).[53] This group suggested that inflation rates had exploded during the mid-1970s because the government and the central bank had failed to curtail the money supply.[54] More gravely, observations of M3 statistics gained importance among these pundits and market participants in their assessments of the government's ongoing attempts to bring down inflation, a practice reinforced by the government's public commitment to £M3 targeting (Capie 2010: 676; Davies 2012; Oliver 2014: 214). Observers thus drew on the regularly published M3 statistics from the Bank of England to observe whether the government was on or off track with regard to its economic policies (Hotson 2017: 137–38).[55] The Bank's Chief Cashier at the time later recounted how these continuous credibility tests by the markets and critical observers destabilized financial and monetary processes:

> In the period before 1976, when money targets were not published, there was no publicly visible measure of the additional debt sales needed to satisfy

monetary objectives. From 1976 onwards, there was . . . For once the actual figure departed from the target path [for M3 growth, LW], the expectation formed that there would be a compensating change in the level of debt sales pressed on the market, with a resulting change in yields. Demand was either dampened, if the target was being overshot, or stimulated, if the target was being undershot, threatening an explosive departure from the target path and corresponding volatility in yields and interest rates.[56]

What Anthony Coleby here explains is that the government was increasingly judged based on whether or not it hit its own £M3 targets. The problem was, however, that the respective statistics were volatile, especially in the short term. Moreover, as economists at the Bank of England had already discovered before 1976, £M3 provided hardly any information on the development of prices or output in the economy. Already in a paper written for a conference in 1974, Goodhart had noted that "[i]t has not been possible to discern clearly in the UK the effect on the economy of altering the rate of expansion of the monetary aggregates."[57] At a later point, he would confirm this assessment, noting that "nowhere else . . . did the prior stability of the (short-run) demand for money function exhibit such a comprehensive collapse as in the case of £M3 in the United Kingdom in 1972 / 3" (1989: 314). In short, then, the government came to be assessed against a highly volatile and notoriously unreliable target on which it could only fail. While Thatcher benefited considerably from this visible failure during her 1979 election campaign, she would later encounter the very same problems.

Why, then, did Labour embark on this second, fatal experiment with monetarism in 1976, despite the fact that public targeting exposed the government to right-wing opponents and bond-market participants, who focused their attention on monetary statistics containing a lot of "noise"? The Bank's senior officials played an instrumental role in this decision. They were the key actors persuading Chancellor Dennis Healey that he should publish £M3 targets in 1976. As one Treasury official wrote in 1977, "[S]ince July 1976, the [Bank of England, LW] Governor has pushed the Chancellor further and further towards the acceptance of a target for M3 growth" (cited in Hotson 2010: 10). This advocacy, then, could not be founded on any consistent idea among the central bankers of how to practice economic policy with monetarism, given that the central bankers themselves had serious reservations about monetarist theory and had collected sufficient econometric evidence to question its applicability. Instead, the Bank of England Governors chose to advocate M3 targets because they hoped that announced targets would put "a tighter rope around the Chancellor's neck" (cited in Needham 2014b: 90–91).[58] In other words, monetarism was chosen as a means for the Bank to leverage its internal influence over monetary *and* fiscal policy. By motivating the Chancellor to adopt self-imposed restrictive monetary targets, the central bankers hoped that they could bring him to restrain spending and convince his Cabinet colleagues that fiscal austerity was inevitable. The Bank gave weight to its proposal with the argument that gilt markets had come to focus on published monetary figures as key information about government policy (Hotson 2010: 3, 9; Hotson 2017: 137–38). When advocating monetary targets, the Bank thus spoke again in its classic role as market expert, which authoritatively communicated to the Chancellor the prevalent "climate of opinion, expectations and attitudes" (cited in Oliver 2014: 218) in financial markets.

The Bank's choice to maximize its internal influence by pressing monetary targets upon the Chancellor with financial market arguments, however, made it more difficult to formulate a coherent economic policy. Monetarism was an inadequate language for that purpose, because of the unreliability of quantity statistics and monetarism's ideological baggage. There was the additional problem that monetarist proclamations provided no meaningful signal to nonmarket constituencies in the British economy, which played a decisive role in the process of monetary stabilization. For instance, trade unions in the public sector and beyond did not see monetary targets as focal points for adjusting their wage demands. The Labour government therefore reacted to inflationary wage demands with a very different response, namely the ill-fated attempt to strengthen income policies (Best 2019; Scharpf 1987). The idea was that moderate wage settlements would contribute to monetary stability, giving more breathing space to a government facing an upcoming election (Needham 2014a: 156). But these wage negotiations exhausted much of the government's remaining political capital. Disruptive strikes (the "Winter of Discontent") and apparent discrepancies between initial wage objectives and ultimate agreements fueled public distrust in the government's ability to hold the economy on course.

Given its continued reliance on internal influence, the Bank was implicated in this crisis of governability, which contributed substantially to Thatcher's election victory in 1979; as a result, the incoming government saw the Bank as part of the problem rather than the solution. But were any alternative strategic options available to the Bank to make its mark on economic policy, given its lack of formal independence? Internal documents reveal that another possible avenue was at least deliberated at the time. This would have entailed publicly communicating an independent stance on interest-rate decisions. As discussed among senior officials, this would have involved, for instance, seeking direct contact with Parliament and corporatist actors, such as the Trades Union Congress and the Confederation of British Industry; communicating the Bank's position via macroeconomic analyses; and intensifying press relations.[59] As one official mused, such a PR campaign would carry "the war [with Treasury, LW] into the open and this *could* be the right thing to do."[60] However, opposition to such "externalization" strategy prevailed because a large faction inside the Bank believed that "the Bank's reputation and influence [lay] in the highest possible professional competence and efficiency in all our operations," and that "speaking out publicly on policy could seriously harm private influence with governments."[61] In short, key decision-makers at the Bank during this period believed that it should preserve its informal authority within government and use the levers of bureaucratic politics; the dismal experiences with monetary targeting gave them little confidence that they even had an independent policy concept that they could publicly promote. In addition, it is important to note that the Bank of the 1970s was still in essence a City institution. Its policy strategies were grounded in its operational role in London money markets and its close relations with City firms.[62] It therefore appeared implausible to Bank officials that they could gain recognition and legitimacy with the wider public for assuming an independent policy stance. For example, among the thirty-two speeches given by the Governor and Deputy Governors during the 1970s, twenty-nine were to different groups of bankers, and only three were to nonfinancial audiences. In times of intense industrial conflict, this did not promise much leverage over significant constituencies involved in, and affected by, monetary policy.

Discussion

The analysis shows why the SNB could turn monetarism into a powerful governing technique during the 1970s, while the Bank of England could not. To summarize, the Swiss case reveals how the central bank was able to enlist different institutions into a self-confirmatory coordination around stability expectations articulated through monetary targets. The ideas for this strategy emerged from internal expert work by a young guard of economists in the SNB. Despite their reservations about scientific monetarism, the directors adopted this strategy in late 1974 because they held their own notions of "folk" monetarism, and because announcing a new targeting strategy diverted attention from the central bank's failures to address credit growth and foreign exchange volatilities after Switzerland's involuntary exit from fixed exchange rates. This choice for monetary targets proved successful because, after a recession had deflated the Swiss economy, targets provided plausible abstractions of the central bank's policy course of low inflation. In particular, banks kept large and regularly fluctuating volumes of reserves at the SNB, and they continued to monopolize customers' savings and credit provision. Under such conditions, targets for the monetary base and M1 maintained some credibility as symbols of monetary stability, even in the absence of tight central bank control (which, as today's critics of monetarism rightly note, is not feasible in practice). In the event, various stakeholders, including wage bargainers, adopted the monetarist language and accepted the SNB's underlying claim: Inflation will remain under the central bank's control. While the SNB's independence and the absence of electoral competition on monetary issues had given the central bank sufficient room to introduce monetary targeting, a weak federal bureaucracy in Berne soon acquiesced in the subordination of fiscal and other policies to SNB-defined goals.

By contrast, the Bank of England failed to capitalize on the inflationary crisis of the 1970s. The problem was not just that the Bank lacked the necessary independence to orient interest-rate decisions toward monetary targets and that the government was unwilling to accept any constraints. These were indeed problems, but they only clearly shaped policy developments around the "dash for growth" episode. Another, more significant problem was that the Bank's own CCC reform of 1971 unleashed a massive expansion of credit and brought active liability management to domestic British banking, with the consequence that monetary targets became unreliable. Without any clear idea of how to implement monetary policy under these unstable structural conditions, the Bank opted to raise its voice for prudent monetary and fiscal policy within the macroeconomic executive, using its role as a market expert to press austerity on the Callaghan government. But while the Bank's lobbying for publicized targets was relatively successful and enhanced its internal influence, this strategic choice exposed the government to credibility tests by markets and conservative pundits that it did not survive. Moreover, with its primary function of connecting fiscal decisions to bond-market expectations, UK monetarism never developed into a consistent framework for overall macroeconomic policy, a problem that became all too evident in the government's struggle over incomes policies in the "Winter of Discontent." As a result, the Bank found itself in a very uncomfortable position as the 1970s came to a close. The political Left continued to perceive it as a "state within the state" that promoted austerity and financial sector interests. More importantly, right-wing pundits, market experts, and the incoming Conservative government believed that Gordon Richardson and other senior bankers had contributed to excessive inflation by undermining a consistent implementation of monetarism as the cure for all ills.

More generally, what I emphasize with these two case studies is that the outcomes of crisis responses during the "long 1970s" (Maier 2004) in these two countries were the results of policy innovations and experiments under different structural and institutional conditions. In the Swiss setting, where such experimentation succeeded, the outcome had not been foreseen by actors at the start of the decade and consisted of a genuinely new practice of governing, which redefined the roles and relations of different stakeholders. Corporatist institutions and conservative banks emerged as the infrastructural foundations upon which the SNB's governing relied. By contrast, in the British case, there was a mismatch between the monetarist concepts used in policy experiments, and the conditions that determined the possibilities of successful monetary stabilization. Moreover, even though monetarist ideas infiltrated the Bank of England from the late 1960s onward, these ideas did not help actors to assume new agentic policy roles, but rather reaffirmed traditional identities and sources of influence. In short, because monetary targeting failed to generate new infrastructural power for the Bank of England, its officials, despite their considerable influence, saw no possibility to redefine the organization's status in the broader polity.

My focus on search processes and experimentation under varying conditions transcends the existing literature, which has usually assumed that structural variables, institutional conditions, or the traveling of ideas explain outcomes. All these factors matter, but in ways that become apparent only when following the paths of policy experiments and their (often unexpected) results. My analysis also suggests a distinct notion of practical monetarism. This was neither a set of economic theories or dogmas nor a political ideology to justify high interest rates. Rather, practical monetarism emerged out of locally specific processes of translation. In the Swiss case, this translation generated new central banker identities and previously nonexistent modes of expectational coordination—in the words of Jacqueline Best (2019), a new "inflation game." In the British case, the respective translation conflicted with ongoing structural changes in finance and reaffirmed traditional divisions of labor; this reinforced crisis constellations from which the actors knew no escape.

Even though my account emphasizes locally embedded experimentation under distinct conditions, there exist striking parallels with other cases (particularly the "successful" ones), which enable us to tease out some more general ideas from the findings presented above. For instance, just like the SNB, the German Bundesbank had been "obsessed with the idea of fixed exchange rates" (Karl Schiller, cited in Marsh 1992: 191) until the point when the international currency arrangements ultimately fell apart, and massive waves of capital inflows threatened domestic monetary stability (Emminger 1988; Gray 2007). Just as in Switzerland, monetarist ideas enjoyed a certain prima facie support because of an entrenched anti-inflationism and positive reception among a number of ordoliberal economists (Janssen 2006). But in the early 1970s, the Bundesbank was not keen on committing itself to a Friedman-style money-supply control. As Helmut Schlesinger and Friedrich Bockelmann stated at a gathering at the Bank for International Settlements in 1971, "Strict adherence to Friedman's monetary rule—if it were to be contemplated at all—would encounter serious practical difficulties."[63] Peter Johnson (1998) documents how the introduction of new expertise gradually led senior central bankers to change their attitudes and increasingly rely on monetarist concepts as the basis for policy deliberations. But the decision to announce a first money-supply target in December 1974 rested on a different rationale. The Bundesbank had failed to inculcate voluntary wage restraint during that year and decided to send an unequivocal warning to the trade unions: There would be no accommodation of high wages, and inflation would be conquered, if necessary, by letting unemployment increase (Goodman 1992: 101; James 2012: 180–82; Scharpf 1987: 101). Importantly, this move was no turn away from corporatism, but a modification of corporatist coordination processes, toward what Johnson calls "monetarist corporatism" (1998: 109) or what a Bundesbank official labeled "incomes policy in disguise" (cited in ibid.: 94). In fact, the Bundesbank itself explicitly demanded that all institutional actors join in the collective effort to stabilize inflation and realize the central bank's promise. As the authorities wrote at a critical juncture of monetary policy (in the year of German reunification), "The central bank, at all events, expects that all those responsible for *economic, budgetary and incomes policy* will work together with the Bundesbank in the interests of maintaining the domestic purchasing power of the Deutsche Mark."[64] According to Robert Franzese's description, this broader coordination under the Bundesbank's leadership worked in the following way: "The Bundesbank . . . directed its policy announcements specifically to wage-price bargainers and the government, thereby overtly threatening monetary contraction in response to upcoming settlements or budgets that it viewed as inflationary" (2000: 100–101).[65] One aspect of successful expectational coordination was that opposition to this central bank–dominated, strongly anti-inflationary macroeconomic policy coordination remained subdued. Trade unions incorporated the central bank's commitment to low inflation into their wage bargaining, thereby re-instituting the producer alliances that had emerged under the German undervaluation regime (Hancké 2013: 16; Höpner 2019; Issing 1997: 78; Johnson 1998: 99). And while activist economic policy was more strongly developed in Germany and more strongly politicized than in Switzerland, the government seldom opposed Bundesbank decisions openly, and if they did, regularly lost the fight (Goodman 1992: 87; Tognato 2012). Fiscal spending was restrained at critical moments in response to Bundesbank threats (Bibow 2003; Rademacher 2020).[66] Lastly, in similar ways to Switzerland, German financial structures were conducive to monetary targeting. The "Deutschmark (DM) money market [was] notably underdeveloped"[67] and "financial intermediaries

[were] essentially undifferentiated by type of portfolio, type of business, geographic locations, or type of clientele" (Johnson 1998: 9, 76). This gave monetary targets some degree of plausibility, even though the Bundesbank regularly failed to meet the targets and accommodated banks' reserve demands just like any other central bank.

At first sight, it seems more difficult to identify parallels between the German and Swiss cases, on one hand, and the Japanese, on the other. For the Bank of Japan was not legally independent and the financial system of the time entailed "bank- and market-based" (Allen, Chui, and Maddaloni 2004: 492) elements. Upon closer inspection, however, similarities with the Swiss and German cases are striking. First, during the 1970s, the Japanese central bank was able to link its reserve management to the volume of credit issuance because "[t]he loan rates of deposit banks [were] less flexible than inter-bank rates . . . Consequently, as the interest rates in inter-bank markets [rose upon BoJ intervention, LW], banks cut loans to customers, and instead [started] to lend or repay debts in the inter-bank markets. The Bank of Japan [absorbed] the resultant excess funds in the markets through sales of bills. The reverse [happened] when inter-bank rates declined. The Bank of Japan exercised 'window guidance' to encourage this portfolio adjustment of banks" (Suzuki 1985: 6). As a result, just as in Germany and Switzerland, monetary targets (here defined as M2 plus certificates of deposit) provided plausible abstractions from underlying financial operations. Moreover, the central bank did not directly announce targets because such targeting would have needed coordination with the government. But it used a different strategy to communicate its policy intentions, via "forecasts" of money growth. Widespread popular belief in the monetarist premises of the central bank's forecasting (namely, that stable inflation is anchored in stable money growth), combined with coordinated wage bargaining (Hall and Franzese 1998: 530), provided the conditions under which such signaling produced self-confirmatory expectational dynamics.

What about the cases of failure? Here, diversity is evidently greater. But by far the most frequently cited factor undermining experiments with monetary targets were liberalizations of financial sectors that rendered operational procedures ineffective and made forecasted quantity targets implausible (Argy, Brennan, and Stevens 1990). Concerning the Canadian case, David Laidler reasons that "wholesale deregulation of the financial sector had rendered the behavior of any money or credit aggregate totally uninformative"

(2007: 18). Another cause of failure can be observed in the French context (with parallels to Italy). The Banque de France was able to control the volume of credit issuance effectively because the (nationalized) banking sector directly funded such issuance via discounting at the central bank (Monnet 2015: 151). Additionally, because of the Banque's ability to differentiate the terms of discounting for different kinds of loans, it could exercise control over the *allocation* of funds. In 1973, the Banque decided that one way to formulate its credit policy was to set targets for the expansion of banking-sector liabilities (M2); from 1977 onward, these targets were made public. But despite strong central bank control over credit, monetary targeting did not strengthen the conduct of monetary policy and did not help to restabilize the franc's internal value. Given the high effectiveness of credit controls, central banking continued to be strongly associated with industrial and social policymaking. Under these conditions, the central bank could not employ its monetary targets to convey its monetary policy intentions because specific allocational choices overruled global target figures. Complementarily, communication with wage-bargaining institutions remained weak as labor unions understood money supply in terms of credit provision and allocation, not as entailing information relevant to their wage settlements (Monnet 2015: 168). Moreover, for French unionists, the state itself was the primary target for their wage demands; accordingly, the question of whether these demands were satisfied and justified was to be answered by the elected government, not the Banque. Under these conditions, the kind of expectational coordination observed in the Swiss and German contexts was inhibited, despite considerable public control over monetary processes.

The United States is the elephant in the room, and I will discuss the Fed's failed 1970s policies and the role of Volcker's famous turn to "nonborrowed reserves targeting" in the following chapter. But my cursory discussion of other cases suggests that success was generally encountered where conservative banking structures conferred some plausibility on monetary aggregates as targets for policy implementation, while corporatist institutions supported expectational coordination guided by central banks, which enjoyed embedded autonomy. In cases of failed experimentation, operational conditions for using monetary targets as guideposts for policy implementation were lacking, because of financial innovation; and / or expectational coordination between wage bargainers and central bankers found no supportive institutional conditions.

This brings me to the final point I want to make in this chapter, which concerns the implications of the 1970s monetarist experiments for subsequent developments, foreshadowing issues covered in subsequent pages. We need to discuss this question separately for countries with successful monetary targeting versus those in which monetarism failed. In the countries with successful monetarist policies, their legacies are highly ambiguous. On one hand, as noted by many scholars, the Bundesbank, the SNB, and the Bank of Japan assumed a dominant position over macroeconomic policy in their respective countries, which during the 1980s and 1990s led to an overemphasis on price stability at real social and economic costs, for domestic citizens, but also internationally, because of the adverse consequences of the countries' large export overhangs (Baccaro and Pontusson 2016). Central bank dominance also led to restrictive *fiscal* policies—the respective central banks exerted significant influence over government decisions and could threaten to raise governments' borrowing costs. This restrictive bias proved fatal in the 1990s, when all three economies—Germany, Switzerland, and Japan—went through periods of low growth and rising unemployment.[68] But we can also observe some positive consequences from monetary targeting. First, other than in Britain or the United States, the process of disinflation in the respective countries did not destroy corporatism and unionism; these institutions rather assumed a strategic role in central bank–led policy coordination (Franzese 2000). Second, because central banks depended on conservative banking structures for successful targeting, they resisted and delayed some financial innovations that would eventually turn into sources of instability.

There was thus more to monetarist central banking than meets the eye. But as I indicated at the beginning of this chapter, the central banks that could not exploit corresponding institutional conditions would be the ones to drive further developments. In the United Kingdom, the nexus between corporatist institutions and economic policymakers had been weak to start with (Hall 1986) but broke down after the "Winter of Discontent." As documented, the Bank, still a City institution, could not independently introduce corporatist elements. The UK chose another trajectory, which was initiated by CCC (1971) and further deepened by Thatcher's continued deregulation of banking and the broader financial markets. What was needed within this context of liberalized finance was a "monetary policy without money" (Laidler 2003), that is, a technique of policy formulation and implementation that dissociated coordination around price stability

expectations from regulating reserves and / or stable patterns of credit issuance. As I will discuss in Chapter 3, Paul Volcker incidentally discovered a solution that met these requirements and ushered in the development
of inflation targeting. The Bank of England was one of the first to embrace
this innovation, capitalizing on the emergent regime of financialized capitalism with an adapted version of monetary policy.

CHAPTER THREE

Hegemonizing Financial Market Expectations

[K]eeping inflation expectations contained is the most critical thing that we do.

—FREDERIC MISHKIN, FEDERAL OPEN MARKET COMMITTEE MEETING, DECEMBER 11, 2007

Over my time at the Fed, I came to worry that inflation expectations are bearing an awful lot of weight in monetary policy these days, considering the range and depth of unanswered questions about them.

—DANIEL TARULLO, CITED IN CHRIS GILES, "CENTRAL BANKERS FACE A CRISIS OF CONFIDENCE AS MODELS FAIL," *FINANCIAL TIMES,* OCTOBER 11, 2017

IRONICALLY, AS I showed in Chapter 2, it was the *absence* of financialized capitalism in its contemporary form that made some central banks' early experiments in monetary policy successful. The few monetary authorities who gained from the period of Great Inflation directly were those that managed to introduce practical monetarism during this period, using monetary targets as devices of asymmetric communication with corporatist institutions, and as plausible abstractions of their operational relationships with conservative banking sectors. On the other hand, where financialization had already progressed sufficiently in the 1970s, and / or where other obstacles prevented expectational coordination between central bankers and price-setting constituencies, practical monetarism failed.

I continue the empirical narrative in this chapter, deepening my analytic perspective and expanding the historical and comparative scope. For
even though the 1970s helped only very few central banks to rise to power,
the story does not end there. Starting in the mid-1980s, monetary authorities in most OECD countries gained in legitimacy and influence. One overt
sign of this development was states' widespread adoption of central bank
independence as a formal framework, which consolidated the separation
of monetary policy from other economic policies and passed exclusive control over this domain to monetary authorities (Polillo and Guillén 2005).
If the 1970s thus mark the uncertain beginnings of central bank power,
then we can consider the 1990s and 2000s as the central bankers' golden
age. Monetarism had by then been tried and abandoned in the majority of
core capitalist states. Beginning with New Zealand in 1990, then Canada
and the United Kingdom, central banks in a growing number of countries instead turned to inflation targeting as a new and promising way to
conduct policy. Indeed, its implementation proved so successful that the
respective central bankers and many experts soon claimed that inflation
targeting was far superior to monetarism, providing a more effective, reliable, and accountable way to deliver low and stable inflation. For instance,
in 2007, Marvin Goodfriend wrote confidently that "there is little alternative to inflation targeting: gold and monetary targets have lost favor as
nominal anchors for monetary policy [and] a fixed exchange rate is no
longer a viable nominal anchor in an era of increasingly mobile international capital" (2007: 56–57). By 2017, more than forty central banks had
adopted inflation targeting in one form or another (Jahan 2017; Wasserfallen 2019).

In this and Chapter 4, I will reconstruct the genealogy of inflation targeting. To embed this analysis in the literature, let me briefly introduce
the predominant ways in which political economists and sociologists have
discussed the topic, and how my own approach diverges from and con-
tributes to this literature. It is first important to note that many political
economists misrecognize the distinctiveness of inflation targeting. For instance, a significant proportion of studies equate both monetarism and inflation targeting with "hard-money" policies that cater to the interests of
capital (e.g., Streeck 2014). The ideas-oriented scholarship also sometimes
treats monetarism and inflation targeting as indistinguishable elements in
a broader neoliberal ideology (Blyth 2002: 273; Hay 2001; Jones 2012: 271).

While these views admittedly capture broad contours of neoliberal policy change—particularly the interrelation between monetary policy and weakening power of labor—a failure to distinguish inflation targeting from monetarism leads analysts to overlook differences in both the conditions for central bank power and its effects. For instance, as I have shown in the previous chapter, monetarist central bankers were dependent not just on corporatist institutions, but also on conservative banking and regulated money markets in order to maintain the credibility of monetary targets. By contrast, inflation targeters usually count on flexible labor markets and promote highly interconnected, fully marketized financial systems as infrastructural foundations for the rapid transmission of price signals.

If inflation targeting is distinctive from practical monetarism, how are we to reconstruct the history of this technique? There exist two approaches in political science and sociology that provide answers to this question. A first treats inflation targeting as a global norm that prescribes to governments and central bankers how to organize and conduct economic policies. While this literature refers to the role of experts, central bankers, and international organizations as developers and promoters, the scholars' primary question is how inflation targeting could diffuse among heterogeneous states. The explanation given to this question is similar to the one provided in studies of central bank independence (Bodea and Hicks 2015; Polillo and Guillén 2005). The key idea here is that, while some early adopters may have chosen inflation targeting for intrinsic policy reasons, later adoption resulted from states' and central bankers' motivation to signal credibility and legitimacy to international capital markets, official lenders (such as the International Monetary Fund), domestic constituencies, and transnational expert communities (Carruthers, Babb, and Halliday 2001; Hayo and Hefeker 2010; Wasserfallen 2019). Michael King (2005) tests these arguments for the British case. He argues that the key driver of the United Kingdom's adoption of central bank independence and inflation targeting was an emergent consensus among experts on the superiority of these norms. This consensus led the Labour Party to believe that granting operational independence to the Bank of England and consolidating its inflation-targeting approach was the best way for the party to signal its economic policy competence to electoral constituencies.

This chapter tells a different, complementary story. My focus is on the invention of inflation targeting and its early deployment among core capitalist states. I show that what drove the invention and first adoptions of inflation targeting was less a consensus among experts and a desire for legitimacy than the political and operational problems of conducting economic policies within financializing economies. I particularly stress the role of Paul Volcker, who developed a prototype of inflation targeting at a time when there was no expert consensus on monetary policy norms. The key discovery Volcker made was that he could influence the inflationary expectations incorporated in US bond markets directly by altering the Fed's operational target, the so-called Federal funds rate (Goodfriend 2007; Hetzel 2008). Similarly, and in contrast to King (2005), I argue that the primary driver of institutional and policy change in Britain was not epistemic community consensus. Rather, leveraging structural changes in the financial sector and frustration among state officials with monetarism and foreign exchange policies, the Bank of England innovated a formal inflation-targeting framework to strengthen its position of power within the polity. The crucial change did not come in 1997, with Labour's electoral victory, but in 1992–1993, after Britain's involuntary exit from the European Exchange Rate Mechanism (ERM). In this period, the Bank assumed de facto control over the key communicative relationship defining inflation targeting, namely the interaction between central bank signaling via forecasts and markets' formation of inflation expectations. This meant that the Bank had already become the de facto authoritative monetary policymaker in Britain *before* receiving formal independence in 1998.

More in line with my understanding of inflation targeting is the literature on communicative central banking and expectation management (Beckert 2016; Best 2019; Braun 2015; Holmes 2013; Nelson and Katzenstein 2014). This literature has interpreted this policy from two complementary angles. First, Douglas Holmes and others have emphasized that, with inflation targeting, central bankers started to engage more explicitly and reflexively with expectations as their primary objects of governing. This arguably led to a shift from transactions to communication as the primary tool for orienting price-formation behavior. Such emphasis on communication is combined with a second insight, namely that New Keynesian economics provides the props and devices for the new expectational governance (Braun 2015). In particular, tools such as Dynamic Stochastic

General Equilibrium (DSGE) models render unobservable variables such as the natural rate of interest (r-star) and an economy's output gap calculable. If central banks can authoritatively forecast these variables, market actors will readily make sense of and anticipate central bank decisions as appropriate actions within a shared cognitive framework. The success of inflation targeting is thus predicated not just on adopting widely accepted norms but on central banks' ability to gain "epistemic authority" (Maman and Rosenhek 2009) in the concrete conduct of policymaking.

The genealogy developed in this chapter expands on these ideas, but it also shifts the emphasis in significant respects. I first see the new core feature of inflation targeting less in the discovery of expectations; Bundesbank monetarists knew just as well as the champions of inflation targeting that economic agents' understanding and anticipation of monetary policies matter for the success of their interventions (Laubach and Posen 1997; Mee 2019: 242). But inflation targeting differs from monetarism because it is a practice of expectation management geared toward *financial* markets. Its key criterion of success is to get long-term interest rates to react predictably to manipulations of central banks' operational targets (short-term money-market rates), thereby confirming that inflationary expectations remain anchored at the levels defined as targets (for example, 2 percent per annum). As Ben Bernanke explains, "[T]he general public does not pay much attention to central bank statements, so robust policies should be designed to be effective even if they are followed closely only by financial market participants" (Bernanke 2020: 957).[1] This is what inflation targeting delivered, facilitating "a cooperative game [with] financial markets" (Ben Bernanke, cited in Mallaby 2017: 612). Ironically, the framework of this coordination process also opened a space for central banks to proactively support growth and unemployment, notably in situations in which authorities and markets agreed that such actions were consistent with assumptions of "output gaps" (capacity utilization below equilibrium levels) and therefore posed no risk to future inflation (Clift 2020: 298). Under inflation targeting, monetary policy dominance thus emerged not just as the institutional answer to excessive inflation, but to the broader problems of macroeconomic management in a globalizing economic system. The chapter reconstructs this process by emphasizing the structural and institutional conditions under which policymakers refocused their efforts on gaining

credibility vis-à-vis finance. I discuss these enabling conditions in my genealogy by embedding the emergence of inflation targeting in a broader
narrative of financialization and institutional change among the countries
that invented and adopted this technique.

This chapter thus begins to address more directly the book's broader
question of why central banks have most consistently expanded their governing powers in times of rampant financialization. The answer offered here
is that rendering policy predictable in the eyes of highly liquid and integrated money and capital markets became a powerful governing technique
during the 1980s to 2000s, not just to tame inflation, but also to support
growth. I will commence this account by returning to where I left off in
Chapter 2—to the United Kingdom in the year 1979. What I want to show
is how the incoming Thatcher government turned its attention away from
workers toward financial market constituencies and attempted to empower
policies through expectational coordination via credible targets. Thatcher's problem, however, was that monetarism proved inappropriate for that
project. I then turn to the development of inflation targeting, whose beginnings lay in Volcker's vigorous responses to "inflation scares" in US bond
markets during the 1980s. From there, it traveled to Britain and other economies and became codified as a technique that consists, at its heart, in an
anticipatory responsiveness to perceived inflation risks and the conduct of
proactive growth stabilization confined by a policy space determined together with financial markets. The key new element compared to Volcker's
informal, incipient version of inflation targeting was inflation forecasting,
which allowed central banks to associate their changes in operational targets with forward-looking signals to markets. The Bank of England made
a significant step toward developing this practice when it acquired the authority to publish its so-called *Inflation Reports* in 1992–1993. Based on the
ability to influence expectations with these reports, the Bank gained epistemic authority vis-à-vis the Treasury and created conditions under which
institutional reforms toward central bank independence were just a logical
next step. Then came the golden age of central banking, characterized by
high degrees of predictability in central bank policies for markets and
growing macroeconomic policy activism by central banks. One problematic unintended consequence was that such tight central bank–market coordination contributed to the growth of systemic risks. As some monetarists had warned in the 1990s, and as the financial crisis of 2007–2009 would

demonstrate, by creating the fiction of long-term stability in interest rates, growth, and inflation in markets, central banks contributed to excessive risk-taking among financial firms.

Contradictions between Thatcher's Monetarism and Politics of Financialization

As discussed in Chapter 2, highly centralized macroeconomic management with no defined role for monetary policy, combined with labor unrest, ideological contestations, and disruptive changes in finance, had made British monetary targeting a thoroughly disappointing experience during the 1970s. The Bank of England had played a significant role in the two failed experiments with monetarism because, during the first episode (1971–1973), it had first tried to liberate the regulated banking sector from competitive disadvantages, while in the second stage (1976–1979), it had reconfirmed its role as an internal voice of austerity. Thatcher was elected in 1979 based on the political promise to fix the inflationary problem, and she brought political force to this project by committing to disinflation, whatever the costs. While this ideological monetarism has received much attention (Hall 1986; Hay 2001), what is often neglected is that the early Thatcher years mark the ultimate failure of UK monetarism (Best 2019; Clift 2020; Prasad 2006: 102ff.). The Thatcher period also failed to resolve the underlying structural and institutional problems of UK monetary policy.

A first of these unresolved issues was that, in a highly centralized policymaking apparatus, the role of monetary policy remained uncertain and underspecified. This problem was reinforced under Thatcher since she further concentrated policymaking power at No. 10. Initially, she used such centralization to employ monetary and fiscal measures for the purpose of disinflation. But soon, high interest rates became unbearable because they pushed up the exchange rate and imposed punitive borrowing costs on business, leading the government to withdraw from interest-rate hikes. As early as 1980, Thatcher's Chancellor, Geoffrey Howe, therefore switched to restrictive *fiscal* measures (Prasad 2006: 118). Interest rates were lowered and the challenge of disinflation was addressed through procyclical spending and taxation policies. The key moment in this strategic turn was the infamous budget plan of 1981. In the midst of a recession, and arousing protests from numerous economists (Needham 2014a), the government revised some of its earlier tax cuts, in effect imposing austerity on the economy. Rachel Lomax, a Treasury official at the time, describes the rationale of this switch in the following words: "When we had a very high painful exchange rate [in the early 1980s], the thought was that we must take the strain off of interest rates by tightening fiscal policy, and that that will enable us to deliver the sterling monetary target with less damage in the traded goods sector."[2] There thus was no independent role for monetary policy, and it remained the weaker tool of macroeconomic stabilization. This situation reinforced the Bank of England's role as adviser and lobbyist vis-à-vis the government without independent authority. Thatcher was unwilling to change this awkward situation for the Bank and rejected proposals for central bank independence aired by experts and politicians (most prominently her own Chancellor, Nigel Lawson). She rather wanted to maintain a tight grip on interest-rate decisions, and she used this power to cater to the growing constituency of homeowner-mortgage holders (Hotson 2017: 146; King 2005: 103). Her successor, Prime Minister John Major, maintained this political stance.

A second predicament for monetary policy and the Bank of England, already too well understood by Bank of England economists, was that M3 statistics were highly volatile and held no predictable relationships with inflation. As I discussed in Chapter 2, Charles Goodhart had made this discovery as early as 1974. In 1979, however, the new government ignored these insights, sticking to an M3 targeting framework to deliver on its electoral monetarist promises. But already in the very first months of Thatcher's government, the inadequacy of such targeting became obvious. A real dilemma arose for monetarists when the economy went into a deep recession while credit continued to grow rapidly. In the face of a widening gap between reduced inflation and continued money growth, even the staunchest believers in monetarism had to admit that M3 targets provided misleading signals for economic policymaking (Hotson 2017: 144; Needham 2014b: 144–55).

A related dilemma arose from Thatcherite measures in the domain of banking and credit. From their first days in office, the Conservative government did everything it could to support the expansion of credit. This applied particularly to mortgages and consumer finance. In the 1970s, the

British version of consumer loans (hire-purchase) had remained restricted, and mortgages had been provided almost exclusively by building societies, which had only gradually expanded their assets and whose liabilities were not counted in M3 (Hotson 2017: 151). But the Thatcher government did away with these restrictions. The abolition of exchange controls in 1979 and of special supplementary deposits (the so-called Corset) in 1980 removed the remaining lending constraints on banks, in response to which the latter entered the mortgage market on a massive scale (Offer 2017; Payne 2010: 156–58). In consequence, from 1980 to 1982 the banks increased their market share in mortgages from 8.1 to 35.9 percent (Drake 1989: 46).[3] An acceleration of M3 growth was the inevitable result (figure 3.1).

Confronted with early signs of failure, some Thatcherites hoped to save monetarism by reframing its purpose. They suggested that the value of defining and publishing monetary targets was not exhausted by the government's early attempts to rein in M3 growth. Communicating restrictive money-supply targets was primarily supposed to shape *expectations* so that economic actors would anticipate a prospective reduction in inflation over a period of multiple years. In order to maximize these assumed

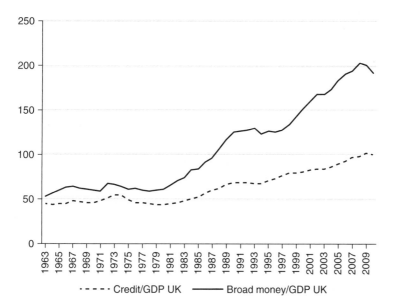

FIGURE 3.1. Growth of credit to private nonbank sector (black) and M3 growth (gray) as a percentage of GDP. *Data source:* Bank of England

expectational effects, the Treasury (and in particular Nigel Lawson), together with some key advisers (Tim Congdon, Terry Burns, and Alan Budd), developed a proposal dubbed the "medium-term financial strategy" (MTFS).[4] According to this plan, which Ben Clift understands as "the flagship policy embarked upon by monetarists" (2020: 291), the government would set out monetary targets, together with objectives for public borrowing, until the next parliamentary elections in 1983. The targets would tell a simple and unequivocal story. Consecutive reductions in the government's M3 targets would indicate that the political leadership had tied itself voluntarily and publicly to consistent inflation reduction over the entire electoral term, willingly sacrificing jobs and growth.

Sustaining these efforts, in light of considerable misgivings among some Treasury officials and the Bank of England (Best 2019) were beliefs that such comprehensive, publicly communicated targeting would exert an independent, positive effect. As Treasury official Peter Lilley explained, the "potential benefit [of MTFS lies in] moulding expectations and thereby reducing unnecessary unemployment," an effect that "depends on how rapidly wage bargainers learn to abandon habits acquired in a period when monetary policy invariably accommodated the going rate of pay increases."[5] Similarly, key economic advisers argued that "a medium term financial plan . . . would lend credibility to the government's counter-inflation policy, it would have favorable effects on inflation expectations, and it would reassure the private sector that the government did not intend to relax fiscal policy just because the [public-sector borrowing requirement] fell."[6] Signaling intent or a "communicative" approach to economic policy thus was supposed to make a distinct contribution to disinflation. As part of this new focus on, and attempted manipulation of, expectations, economists in the Treasury were advised in 1979 to adjust their forecasts accordingly, building into their models the assumption that wage bargainers adjust their inflationary expectations and wage claims according to the disinflationary promises entailed in the communicated MTFS targets (Needham 2014b: 148). The broader strategy was formally adopted in March 1980, when Chancellor Geoffrey Howe successfully advocated the virtues of monetarist PR to Thatcher and her cabinet.[7]

As quickly became apparent, however, wage bargainers would *not* adjust their wage claims in response to monetary targets—other than in Germany, Switzerland, or Japan, British trade unions attributed zero credibility to such targets.[8] Accordingly, hoped-for changes in expectations did not occur and expectational effects did nothing to remove inflationary pressures from the labor market. Disregarding the monetarists' communicative strategy, British steelworkers went on strike to demand a 20 percent pay rise during 1980 (Best 2019). Instead of a painless transition to lower inflation, the UK thus experienced a massive spike in unemployment, which climbed from 6 to 8 percent in 1980, and further to 12 percent by 1983. The government's attempt to enlist workers' expectations in the disinflationary process had clearly failed.

But rather than abandoning monetarism because of its operational and expectation-related failures, Thatcher, top Treasury officials, and their advisers tried to save the project with a last attempt at reframing. The cause of the lack of expectational changes, they argued, lay in the irrational behavior of workers, who were seen as unable to make reasonable wage claims in relation to the government's strategy. As the journalist Peter Jay had already argued in 1976, workers "need somehow to be 'dis-alienated' enough to become infected with the entrepreneurial realities which confront their present employers, so that they will accept a non-inflationary market-determined environment as setting the level of rewards that can be afforded" (cited in Payne 2010: 96). Based on this interpretation, Thatcherites adopted a "benign" view of the high levels of unemployment as a welcome push to weaken labor's political power and turned toward financial market professionals and private investor-consumers as the constituencies whose interests and views were better aligned with their own policy visions (Payne 2010). Accordingly, the government hoped that, if not via the labor market, its policies could become performatively successful with the help of these market- and consumer-investor constituencies.[9]

The problem was, however, that money-supply targets proved entirely unsuitable as devices for articulating policies and coordinating expectations in the context of an emergent debt- and consumption-oriented growth model. First, a growing number of bond and money-market analysts soon came to realize that monetary statistics were highly volatile, that the dividing lines between financial and monetary liabilities were blurry, and that the government did not respond consistently to changes in its own statistics (Cobham 2002: 48). Monetary targets thus could not serve to influence and anchor expectations among these professional actors.[10] Second, promising monetary constraint was inconsistent with promoting private credit growth and innovations to facilitate such expansion (Clift 2020: 292). For instance, building on the deregulations during its first years in office, the Thatcher government further pushed households into mortgage loans and credit through the privatization of council housing. This process was accompanied with more liberalizations. These particularly affected building societies, which up until the 1980s had been restrained in their mortgage issuance, due to restrictive regulations, the societies' particular company structures (small, cartelized, and regionally dispersed firms), and their particular funding models (based on savings). Over the 1980s, however, the building societies became indistinguishable from banks, with small firms merging into larger entities, competing nationwide for lending and deposits, and increasingly funding their activities on the wholesale markets.[11] Together with the clearing banks, the building societies led the way to a dramatic expansion of credit and money over the 1980s, and it became clear to most observers that, as long as the government supported and incentivized this process, it could not credibly claim to control the money supply (Pepper and Oliver 2001).

In short, then, the government ran into constant contradictions between its proclaimed monetarism and its pursuit of financialization. It became increasingly obvious that citizens could not be asked to debt-finance their houses *and* trust in government policies that were aimed at restricting credit and money growth. Monetarism had to be given up, not just in terms of practical conduct, but as a symbolic repertoire with which to articulate overall policy.[12] *Prima facie,* actual reductions in inflation between 1980 and 1984, from 18 to 5 percent, made this abandonment feasible. The "scourge" of inflation had temporarily disappeared, which made it slightly less embarrassing for a self-proclaimed monetarist government to turn its back on money-supply control. However, a deeper question remained: How would a government make sense of the new pattern of consumption-led, debt-financed growth (Baccaro and Pontusson 2016), and how would it conceive of macroeconomic stabilization in a context in which all significant restrictions on private money creation had been removed (Pixley 2018)?

This question was widely debated among British monetary experts before and after the so-called Lawson boom, a period of strong financial and economic expansion from 1985 to 1988, which was followed by another spike in inflation. A minority of experts came to believe that the boom exemplified a cycle, whereby oversupply of credit temporarily pushed up asset prices, which would eventually result in excessive consumption (Pepper and Oliver 2001: 48). The implication of this interpretation was that Britain should stick to monetarism and rein in financialization because accelerated credit-money growth would eventually affect the broader economy by way of overconsumption and monetary instability.[13] Chancellor Nigel Lawson and the majority of economic experts thought otherwise. They argued that, because private debt growth reflected a corresponding growth of private wealth that indicated shifting preferences and strategies for saving (for example, for old age), there was no problem from a monetary and macroeconomic stability point of view (Payne 2010: 154). Later, Lawson admitted that the years 1985–1988 had marked a cycle of overexpansion, resulting in subsequent spikes in inflation. However, he and most other economists considered contingent factors and temporary irrationalities—Lawson's own ostentatious optimism (Lawson 1992: 632) and consumers' "over-confidence and excess personal gearing" (ibid.: 166)—as the root causes of this boom. There was much less to fear from the *secular* growth of credit and asset prices, which would continue throughout the 1990s and 2000s (Shabani et al. 2014). The overall view settled in government and among experts that these developments implied structural adjustments to households' portfolios, with no material significance for macroeconomic policy (e.g., Minford 1991). Monetary and macroeconomic stability could be achieved in the face of rampant financialization.

What was thus required was a postmonetarist reformulation of macroeconomic policy that excluded credit from the list of relevant concerns while making plausible how a financializing economy would be rendered governable—or, as David Laidler (2003) has put it, to articulate a "monetary policy without money." But this reformulation would not happen at Whitehall or other centers of governmental policy planning. The genealogy of the new practice rather begins at the Federal Reserve under Paul Volcker, who incidentally discovered that he could exploit reactive and reflexive relationships between long-term bond and federal funds rate changes to stabilize inflation expectations. Learning from this experience, other central banks (the Reserve Bank of New Zealand; Bank of Canada; Bank of England) then codified inflation targeting during the 1990s. These innovations allowed the respective central banks to become the primary authorities in macroeconomic stabilization. Their ability to maintain expectations of low and stable inflation among financial market actors became the perceived key to rendering financialized economies governable. This is the story I shall turn to next.

Volcker's Proto-Inflation Targeting

The prehistory of the Volcker shock began in 1973. The Fed under Chairman Arthur Burns (1971–1978) faced an accelerating rate of inflation. As an independent institution long concerned with price stability, the US central bank attempted to address this problem through hikes in the federal funds rate, which is the rate for Fed reserves on the overnight interbank market. But the problem was that these hikes were outpaced by the inflation trend itself so that *real* interest rates—nominal rates minus inflation—dipped into negative territory in the mid-1970s and remained close to zero until 1979. There are different accounts of why the Fed lagged behind. Some authors argue that, still in the spirit of broadly, even if informally, coordinated macroeconomic policy (Mehrling 2011: 53), the Fed oriented its actions toward calculations of real growth and full employment that proved overly optimistic (Goodfriend 2007; Orphanides and Williams 2011). This combined with a belief within the administration (supported by Burns) that price controls and / or wage restraints were sufficient, even in combination with expansionary fiscal measures, to contain inflation (cf. the infamous "Whip Inflation Now" campaign under President Jimmy Carter) (Axilrod 2009: 44; Minsky 1988: 59). But as in the United Kingdom (Scharpf 1987), there was no institutional infrastructure in the United States to organize voluntary monetary restraint. This was also reflected in the fact that the Fed proved incapable of signaling its disinflationary intentions to relevant stakeholders, such as the trade unions (Johnson 1998: 127). Lastly, it is important to recognize that, from the Fed's perspective, there were financial stability reasons to avoid aggressive rate hikes. While parts of the banking sector clearly favored rigorous action against inflation, other parts (such as the savings and loan associations) were threatened by the potentially destabilizing effects of aggressive rate increases (Wexler 1981: 195). Incommensurable demands and prerequisites of a fractured financial system thus were a decisive factor in causing the Fed to pursue a cautionary, "interest-rate smoothing" course (Axilrod 2009: 95; Johnson 1998: 122; Karamouzis and Lombra 1989: 45).[14]

In 1979, these contradictory policy imperatives and associated conflicts intensified. Inflation accelerated further, while the Fed staff detected signs of a looming recession. The Federal Open Market Committee (FOMC)—the body that decides policy—was divided between those favoring some stimulative response to the economic downturn and those who wanted to implement rigorous disinflation. As president of the Federal Reserve Bank of New York (FRBNY), Volcker was a vocal participant in these discussions and clearly on the side of the hawks. His major concern was that the Fed would lose control over inflationary expectations as it continued to accommodate ever higher nominal rates, as confirmation of rising inflation rather than action against it. As he argued, "The greatest risk to the economy, as well as [to actual] inflation, is people having the feeling that prices are getting out of control."[15]

Volcker's hawkish position was known in financial as well as political circles. So when the short Fed chairmanship of G. William Miller (1978–1979) ended with his promotion to state secretary, Jimmy Carter knew that, by picking Volcker, he would get a chairman advocating a strongly anti-inflationary course.[16] In his acclaimed reconstruction of this nomination, William Greider (1987: 47) suggests that the administration still went for Volcker precisely because its aim was to placate financial markets.

But nobody at this point, not even Volcker himself, expected to be engaging in a veritable rupture in monetary policy. The "Volcker shock" was not part of a policy plan with which he came into office. The new chairman rather first attempted to address what he saw as entrenched inflationary psychology by tilting the balance of considerations within the FOMC toward a more restrictive course. But a revision of this strategy came a month into his tenure, in September 1979. Commodity prices (gold, silver, copper) spiked, together with falls in the US dollar value. The Fed at that point had no new macroeconomic data, and the latest wage settlements indicated no dramatic change on the inflation front. But the unraveling of inflationary *expectations* incorporated in asset prices triggered a fundamental rethink. At the fateful meeting on October 6, Chairman Volcker framed the Fed's challenge accordingly, arguing that "[o]n the inflation front, we're probably losing ground. In an expectational sense, I think we certainly are, and that is being reflected in extremely volatile financial markets" (cited in Lindsey, Orphanides, and Rasche 2013: 503).

The procedural change that was subsequently introduced meant that the FOMC would from then on articulate its policy instructions in new ways.

Setting targets for M1 growth, the committee defined appropriate levels of reserves. The Fed's system manager was supposed to subtract the reserves lent out by the Fed (via discount-window lending) to arrive at *nonborrowed* reserves as the immediate operational target (Bindseil 2004b: 29). These reserves are directly influenced by the Fed via its daily open market operations. Given that Volcker had himself expressed misgivings about monetary targeting, monetary historians and experts have heatedly debated the reasons behind this strategic choice. Notwithstanding considerable controversy, it is possible to discern a consistent motivation: As stated, Volcker's primary and most immediate concern was the possibility that expectations of high inflation would be incorporated into asset prices and long-term interest rates—as Robert Hetzel puts it, Volcker "looked at [the world] through the eyes of the financial markets."[17] Accordingly, the turn to nonborrowed reserves targets was a way to visibly assume responsibility for (dis)inflation, via the endorsement of monetarism, which was a first step toward gaining leverage over these expectations (Goodfriend 2007: 51). A related step then consisted in varying the federal funds rate more aggressively to signal a credible disinflationary course; nonborrowed reserves targets were supposed to provide the mechanism for the more flexible interest-rate policy that was needed in this signaling process (Axilrod 2009: 112; Krippner 2011: 117).

Assessed on these arguments, the Volcker shock failed. Again, as in the United Kingdom, inflation receded, not because the Fed managed to stabilize inflationary expectations, but because a dramatic loss in output and employment removed inflationary pressures from the economy: Real growth fell 6.2 percent in the fourth quarter of 1981 and by a further 4.9 percent in the first quarter of 1982. Inflation dropped concurrently, from 12 to 4.5 percent. As a graph produced by Fed economists in 1983 showed, this was not the relatively painless disinflation that many monetarists had promised (figure 3.2). The Volcker disinflation rather supported the Keynesian, Phillips-curve view of an inflation / employment trade-off that had become discredited among the vocal monetarist and neoclassical economists of the time.

But Volcker had probably anticipated that his monetarism would not be benign, but painful, with real macroeconomic costs. What seemed more puzzling and devastating to him was that, during this very process of painful disinflation, bond rates remained *on the rise*. In August 1981, the economists from the Fed noted, with some puzzlement, "The forces influ-

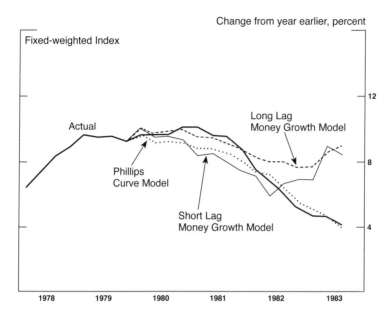

FIGURE 3.2. Comparisons of actual price developments against monetarist and Phillips-curve models, produced by Fed staff for the FOMC meeting on November 15, 1983. *Data source:* Board of Governors of the Federal Reserve, Washington, DC

encing interest rate levels seem to have been largely expectational in nature. Rates have remained high in the face of decelerating inflation and a slackening in economic activity."[18] Through to October, bond prices rose to a level 3 percent higher than in January. As Marvin Goodfriend observes, "One might reasonably have expected the aggressive disinflationary policy action taken in late 1979 to reduce long-term interest rate volatility by quickly stabilizing long-term inflation expectations at a low rate. Yet the reverse was true initially. Long rates turned out to be surprisingly volatile due to a combination of aggressive funds rate movements and inflation scares. Amazingly, it took until 1988 for the unusual long-run volatility to disappear" (1993: 16).

It was precisely this experience of volatile bond rates, combined with an increasingly defunct technique of nonborrowed reserves targeting, which led Volcker to develop a nascent version of inflation targeting. A first crucial step on this path was the realization that the apparent stability of US monetary growth (Friedman and Schwartz 1963) had broken down at the very moment that the Fed had begun to rely more strongly on predictions of money demand (Morgan 2006: 24–25). A report at the time stated that models "provide little reliable information regarding monetary control" (cited in Karamouzis and Lombra 1989: 37). Greta Krippner (2011: 119) plausibly attributes this structural break to financial innovations, particularly the introduction of NOW accounts—savings accounts with payment functions—that increased volatility between bank liabilities included and excluded from the monetary aggregate M1 (Adrian and Liang 2016). In effect, without reliable monetary forecasts, it was not possible to define meaningful nonborrowed reserves, or for that matter, any reserves targets. These internal problems were combined with the difficulty Wall Street analysts—the expanding group of "Fed watchers"—confronted in making sense of monetary statistics and predicting Fed action based on them (Axilrod 2009: 102).

But, more importantly, Volcker increasingly wanted to override the calculated nonborrowed reserves target in order to respond *directly* to "inflation scares" (Goodfriend 1993). This meant hiking the federal funds rate independently of the quantity target and even beyond what was deemed necessary to contain *actual* inflation. For instance, as Hetzel recounts, "in late spring 1983 . . . bond rates began to rise with an unchanged funds rate. Despite falling inflation, the FOMC increased the funds rate. With that increase, Volcker started the creation of a new nominal anchor. It was not the money target urged by monetarists, but rather the expectation of low, stable inflation" (2008: 163).

We can thus see that Volcker cared most about financial market expectations, and that he tried to convince the markets of future low inflation by vigorously altering the federal funds rate.[19] Monetarism was only a temporary and fugitive component in reorienting monetary policy to this objective. Eventually, aggressive rate responses *directly* contributed to stabilizing inflationary expectations. But it was also evident that Volcker's critical experiment (Walter and Wansleben 2019) had come at a substantial price: In the 1980s, the Fed repeatedly engaged in restrictive policies when the macroeconomic situation would have warranted a more expansionary course; and money-market volatility became exceptionally high. Alan Greenspan later consolidated Volcker's informal inflation targeting; the primary concern of the Greenspan Fed remained bond-market expectations (figure 3.3).[20] But Greenspan would incidentally discover how the Fed could

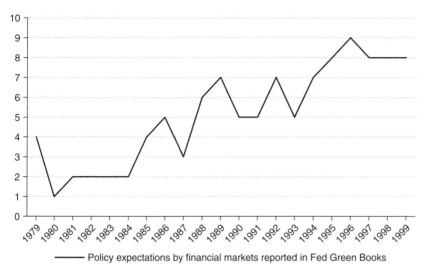

FIGURE 3.3. Number of Fed Green Books each year mentioning financial markets'
policy expectations. *Data source:* Board of Governors of the Federal Reserve, Washington, DC

conduct such policy with fewer and less extreme rate manipulations and
could even increase its policy space for counter-cyclical interventions.
Through releases of its internal deliberations, the Fed learned to signal its
determination to contain inflation risks, allowing long-term interest rates
to adapt in advance of, and sometimes without, any policy move (Krippner
2011: 127). This discovery led to a new preoccupation at the Fed and for
Greenspan: The key to felicitous coordination with markets, and hence for
successful monetary policy, was to become predictable (see below). The Fed
under Greenspan was still unwilling to announce a specific inflation target.
But by aligning the pattern of Fed responses to changes in its economic
outlook with the pattern of market reactions, the Fed came to practice inflation targeting in all but its name.

As I will show in the next section, it is this specific process of expectational coordination that makes up the operational core of formal inflation
targeting, and which gives a key role to macroeconomic forecasting in its
conduct (Braun 2015). But the full articulation of this technique did not
happen in the United States. Rather it was in the United Kingdom, in
response to reforms in New Zealand, that inflation targeting became fully
formalized.

The British Path to Inflation Targeting

Margaret Thatcher and the monetarists had contributed primarily to disinflation with their disruptive fiscal and economic policies, reinforcing a process of weakening labor power and deindustrialization. Retrospectively, the Bank of England recognized the importance of these structural or "supply-side" changes as facilitating the later success of inflation targeting. For instance, the former Deputy Governor, Paul Tucker, noted that "the more flexible an economy's product and labour markets, the less central banks have to do to steer aggregate demand in the face of nasty shocks to the economy" (2018: 440). As noted in Chapter 2, the opposite was actually true for monetary targeters, who relied on corporatist institutions to coordinate wage bargaining around their targets (Hall and Franzese 1998). But for central banks operating in contexts in which the enlistment of trade unions into coordinative games had failed during the 1970s, the alternative approach consisted of relying on "flexibilization," so that industrial conflicts could no longer interfere with a different coordination game that was centered on finance.

However, Thatcher herself did not have a recipe for such an approach. British monetarism had not just failed practically but was also incoherent as an ideology for a government supporting rampant consumer-credit growth. At the same time, across the Atlantic, Paul Volcker had learned the lesson that central banks *could* play a powerful role in macroeconomic governance in financialized settings. Coming out of his own disruptive disinflation and the structural weakening of labor that was part of it, he had shown how to rigorously orient decisions on the Fed's operational targets toward financial markets and thereby inscribe expectations of stable and low inflation into them.

Given the similar problematics and conditions for policymakers on both sides of the Atlantic, British officials understood that Volcker's experiments promised more suitable solutions for them than those of the German and Swiss monetarists. A key parallel between the American and British contexts consisted in financialization dynamics, which rendered monetary targeting impossible but *enhanced* the efficacy of interest-rate manipulations, creating the preconditions for highly effective monetary policies. Bank of England economists expressed this linkage between financialization and their policy effectiveness in 1990: "Concern has been expressed that . . . deregulation and innovation [in financial markets, LW] may have weakened the mechanisms through which changes in monetary policy . . . affect aggregate demand and inflation . . . Contrary to [these] concerns, the impact of interest rates on expenditure in the United Kingdom is now *more* powerful than in the past."[21] In the United Kingdom, a crucial source for this particular version of infrastructural power lay in the fact that, as more households incurred larger debts with variable interest rates (primarily mortgages), these households became more reactive in their consumption behavior to changes in financing costs. In turn, this had a significant influence on aggregate demand.

The problem was, however, *how* British central bankers could harness this potential infrastructural power of interest-rate policies. A key obstacle arose from what the technical literature calls "policy transmission" (Bindseil 2004a). Usually, central banks concentrate their interventions on short-term lending and exercise direct influence only over very short-term market rates. Volcker had found this limitation very painful. Despite his aggressive hikes in the federal funds rate, he had encountered difficulties in addressing erratic fluctuations in the interest rates on long-term Treasuries. Eventually, however, Volcker had solved the problem by using short-term rate decisions to signal to the bond markets what the Fed intended to achieve; this established an expectational coordination mechanism between the central bank and these highly liquid, informationally "sensitive" markets.

But up until the 1980s, establishing such expectational coordination was not possible for British policymakers because of the Bank of England's different role in the markets for government debt. Coming out of the Second World War, the Bank had assumed a major responsibility for helping the government to maintain "market conditions that will maximize, both now and in the future, the desire of investors at home and abroad to hold British government debt."[22] The problem addressed through this support was that, while public financing needs were huge, initially there was insufficient private demand. Moreover, the traditional market intermediaries—so-called jobbers—were too weakly capitalized to maintain liquidity in government debt trading. As a result, over the postwar period, the Bank operated as a very active market-maker (that is, it bought and sold gilts in the secondary market) and supported the jobbers in situations in which they proved unable to absorb supply or confronted solvency risks due to sudden changes in gilt prices and yields.[23] Reflecting these demand deficiencies and weak liquidity, the Bank had become convinced over the postwar period that the gilt markets were not self-stabilizing, but rather consisted of highly fragile transactional spheres. For instance, falls in gilt prices and concurrent higher yields could, in the Bank's view, initiate self-reinforcing crises: A "fall in the price of government securities may result in a decline rather than an increase in the quantity demanded in the immediate future."[24] Transmission of monetary policies from short- to long-term rates, via expectational coordination, was not possible under these circumstances.

It was in the 1970s that the parameters began to shift (Davies 2012). The Bank of England started to withdraw from its market-maker role. The motivation behind this was to tackle a dilemma. The Bank rejected lending limits for private banks as the method to tame inflation, and the government proved resistant to Bank demands for more restrictive fiscal and monetary policies. The Bank therefore hoped that more responsive interest rates on government debt could help to finally force the government to do something on inflation.[25] As discussed in Chapter 2, the initial framework within which gilt markets assumed this new role was M3 targeting. In this framework, gilt investors assessed government policy based on the purported success or failure of maintaining control over this particular monetary aggregate. The growing salience and significance of gilt-market reactions to monetary statistics then helped to create a new genre of financial analysis and journalism concerned with market assessments of government policies.

But as discussed, this new communicative relationship between market participants and policymaking exacerbated rather than resolved British problems of monetary stabilization, plaguing central bank and government officials throughout the 1970s and most of the 1980s. First, monetary statistics proved highly deficient as a language for coordinating expectations and actions. The statistics of monetary aggregates were erratic and entailed a lot of noise, sending inconsistent and misleading signals to markets about the government's policy stance. Moreover, there was problematic feedback between these signals and market reactions. When investors were concerned about higher future inflation, they stopped buying gilts, thereby further boosting an expansion in M3. The mechanism behind this was that, when markets reduced their uptake of government debt, Treasury had to resort to bank borrowing as a default financing option, a decision that in turn accelerated money growth (due to the expansive effects on banks' balance sheets).[26] Lastly, the procedures for responding to market expectations remained "ad hoc" and "disorganized."[27] No clear routine was available to adjust policy to changes in yields.

Financial sector reforms in the 1980s, together with the disenchantment with monetarism, gradually resolved these difficulties by shifting the focus from the relations between gilt yields and monetary aggregates to relations between yields and the Bank of England's short-term policy rates.[28] A first crucial institutional reform to enable this shift consisted in the establishment of derivatives trading at the London International Financial Futures Exchange (LIFFE). LIFFE enabled transactions in Eurodollar and gilt futures, which rendered observable "what the market thinks the policy rate will be in three months' or six months' time."[29] Equally critical were changes to the cash gilt market (direct trading in gilts) introduced with the "Big Bang" financial sector reforms. From 1986 onward, the Bank of England auctioned new gilt issues to the private market and ultimately abandoned its role as "jobber of last resort."[30] Interest-rate determination for gilts was entirely passed over to the primary dealers, who from now on comprised an enlarged group of domestic and international firms at the London Stock Exchange (called "gilt-edged market-makers," or GEMMs). These "Big Bang" reforms increasingly rendered plausible the notion that the yield curve reflected expectations of highly active, profit-seeking investors, who responded granularly to changes in expected monetary and macroeconomic information and thus gave such expectations an authoritative price. Moreover, arbitrage operations between the cash and futures markets undergirded the notion of efficient markets, which eliminated significant divergences between the expected future short rates in futures and cash markets.[31]

With a fully developed liquid bond market as a critical infrastructural foundation for policy transmission, and the Bank's own realization that appropriately set interest rates had significant macroeconomic effects, a last major obstacle remained. While the Conservative government under Thatcher, at least since the adoption of its Medium-Term Financial Plan, had set itself the goal of achieving "credibility and [stabilizing, LW] expectations in financial markets" (Middleton 1989: 49), continuing coordination problems and conflicting interests at the helm of government made this next to impossible in practice; Numbers 10 and 11 Downing Street (the

Prime Minister and the Chancellor) proved unable to coordinate with the markets through consistent, transparent decision-making. This problem remained unresolved because neither Thatcher nor her successor, John Major, were willing to contemplate central bank independence—that is, to hand control over interest-rate decisions to the Bank (King 2005). Despite the fact that the consensus among monetary experts had increasingly become supportive of central bank independence, both Thatcher and Major believed that monetary policy was political and that elected officials should maintain control. The Treasury responded tactically to the resulting problems, by using an *external* anchor. Chancellor Nigel Lawson decided informally to stabilize the pound's exchange rate with the German mark from 1987 to 1988; and the subsequent Chancellor, John Major, convinced Thatcher to join the ERM in 1990. The problem with this choice was that a peg exposed Britain to erratic developments of foreign exchange markets, which in turn reacted to uncoordinated policy actions by the different countries participating in the peg. These problems made the external anchor solution politically untenable, which the United Kingdom realized with its involuntary exit from the ERM in 1992 (Stephens 1996).

Inflation targeting emerged from this ERM failure, which opened an opportunity for the Bank to challenge the balance of power within the macroeconomic executive. Through incremental, but radical innovations, central bankers managed to introduce a new decision-making procedure that would eventually shift authority from the Treasury and Prime Minister to themselves. The point of departure of these incremental, radical innovations was the Treasury's loss of technocratic authority after the ERM failure (the second after 1976). In that moment of crisis, the Bank of England found new ways to enlarge its influence. Not only did the Bank have a Governor at that time who proved extremely capable of pushing for stronger monetary policy control, but, through a fortunate coincidence, Eddie George received decisive support in this project from a new figure in the Bank. Mervyn King had just been nominated as nonexecutive Director to the Bank's Court in 1991, the first economist in this body since John Maynard Keynes. The London School of Economics professor was an expert in public finance and had advised the government on tax reform. But because King had been unwilling to give up his research activities for a senior post in the Treasury, the government had offered him as a second option the Court position, which King could combine with academic work.

From there, King began to engage with monetary policy issues and was subsequently asked to join the Bank as its chief economist for a two-year stint. In this role, King supported Eddie George in high-profile discussions with the Treasury and the government in 1992–1993 on a new monetary policy framework for the United Kingdom. The two central bankers' initial, still rather cautious proposal was centrally coordinated inflation targeting, inspired by recent experiences in New Zealand. The Treasury would set an inflation target and would engage in regular formal consultations with the Bank on how to achieve it. The procedure for these interest-rate discussions would start at the central bank, which would produce analyses and forecasts of inflation and monetary developments that would then be sent to senior Treasury officials to discuss a joint policy proposal for the Chancellor (King 1994). In line with postwar tradition, and reflecting the Prime Minister's continuing rejection of central bank independence, the Chancellor would then have the ultimate say.

The precise implementation of this strategy in the following year then turned these initial ideas into radical reforms in policy procedures that would effectively redistribute power from the Treasury to the Bank. For the idea that the central bank should submit analyses to the Treasury for internal deliberations was not entirely new. This had long been done informally, with the crucial caveat that the Treasury usually edited the respective briefings in order to maintain control over the information sent to senior decision-makers. Also, the notion that the Chancellor should publicly announce a target range for inflation was not all that revolutionary at a time when such announcements had become policymakers' sport. The key change thus was less anticipated and consisted in the Treasury eventually giving up its practice of editing the Bank's analyses—forecasts of expected inflation and assessments of available policy options. In retrospect, Mervyn King argues that the Treasury took this step because it saw no way of editing the relevant graphs and charts. In any case, in autumn 1992 the Chancellor accepted that the Bank would henceforth submit only *final* versions of its macroeconomic and monetary assessments to the Treasury—just before they went to print and press. Out of these developments, the Bank of England's monthly *Inflation Reports* were born, which constituted the key expectation-management device of the new inflation-targeting regime. The first of these reports was published in February 1993.

The pieces of the jigsaw now began to fall into place: Price-sensitive financial markets had assumed an internal structure and political weight to become the authoritative judges on economic policy. And with the new *Inflation Reports,* the Bank finally had a tool to engage these expectations. The reports communicated the Bank's own view of future inflation and thereby made clear what decisions would be needed to achieve the targets adopted by the Treasury; the reports thus constituted the key device to convey the Bank's "commitment to low inflation" (Cobham 2002: 94–95). Coordination with markets from now on rested on their acceptance of the Bank's macroeconomic narrative as presented in these reports, which then led the markets to regard the respective inflation forecasts and the implied need for interest-rate adjustments as credible. This process could be considered successful as long as long-term interest rates reflected the expectation that inflation would remain within the decided target range. This criterion of success was explicit in the reports themselves, which always entailed an analysis of forward rates in financial markets in order to gauge whether "private sector expectations of future inflation are consistent with the stated aim of [the government's] strategy."[32]

To be sure, the *Inflation Reports* initially also had another purpose, namely to inform negotiations between the Chancellor and Governor George (in the "Ken [Clarke] and Eddie [George] show"). After all, the Chancellor still held formal authority over the policy rates and could thus decide in principle to ignore the implications of the Bank's published analyses. However, it soon became apparent that, with *Inflation Reports* published in its own name, the Bank of England had considerably increased its own policy leverage vis-à-vis the Treasury (Acosta et al. 2020: 13). For instance, if the Chancellor wanted a more expansionary course than Bank officials, this brought him into visible conflict with the increasingly sophisticated economic assessments produced by the central bank (McCallum 1997: 8). As the then chief economist, Mervyn King stated in somewhat menacing terms, "If the Chancellor rejects the Bank's advice, that will be clear" (1994: 126). Such visible disagreement had potentially damaging implications for the Chancellor because he risked disappointing market expectations. This new power dynamic manifested itself, for instance, in a meeting between Chancellor Kenneth Clarke and Eddie George in January 1997, when "[t]he Governor noted that, since there was a general expectation that rates needed to go up, and this in itself had an influence on people's expectations, they have in some measure achieved the effect of raising rates. It was for this reason that [the Governor] attached importance to continuing to press the case for a raise" (cited in James 2020: 374).

In a sense, then, the decision taken in 1993 to introduce *Inflation Reports* foreshadowed the subsequent reform of 1998. For when Labour came into office in 1997, it was evident that the government had little purchase over bond markets in comparison with a central bank that had already accumulated "credibility" in these markets since 1993 (Tucker 2018: 412). Accordingly, it was perfectly consistent for Gordon Brown to introduce operational independence as the missing piece to complete Britain's inflation-targeting regime.

Fewer Surprises

What unites Volcker's more informal tactics and the fully articulated and codified version of inflation targeting developed in Britain during the 1990s is a concern for credibility with financial markets, which emerged over the 1980s as the publics that mattered most for monetary policymakers. As Treasury official Middleton had noted, "[T]he main effort must be directed towards maintaining the credibility and reputation of macroeconomic policy so that financial markets behave in a way which generally supports it" (1989: 51). What changed from Volcker to Greenspan and King was a turn from reactive to future-oriented communication to gain such credibility. For Volcker had still been forced to materially alter the federal funds rate to ward off inflation scares, establishing a reputation in markets as an inflation hawk. By contrast, the Bank of England discovered the usefulness of communicating promises about its policy to influence expectations about future inflation and interest rates. These promises were entailed in the Bank's macroeconomic forecasts that implied the interest-rate changes necessary to attain the inflation target. Greenspan made the same discovery just a couple of years later, through a leaked protocol of the FOMC's internal deliberations in 1994. This leaked document led bond-market rates to move in the direction that supported the FOMC's considered policy course even before any decision had been taken.

This turn to prospective signaling naturally coincided with a desire for a new kind of second-order predictability in which policymakers and their

primary publics understood how central banks would respond to the forecasts that provided the focal points of coordination. This turn to predictability became explicit in how UK central bankers reasoned about the purpose of their *Inflation Reports*. These reports were seen to lead market
actors to become "clearer about the information set on which any individual
monetary policy decision is made, thereby making it easier for them
to identify the authorities' pattern of behaviour in response to news."[33]
As a result, "there should be fewer occasions on which the authorities'
behaviour—as opposed to the underlying economic developments—causes
uncertainty in the markets."[34] Mervyn King, while recognizing remaining
uncertainties, emphasized the same advantages of transparent communication as it helped "private sector agents predict how the monetary authorities will react to developments in the economy. The Inflation Report has
already improved public understanding of the Bank's thinking on inflation, and publication of the minutes of the monthly monetary meetings
should, in time, increase the accuracy of market expectations of the authorities' 'reaction function.' Indeed, the commentaries of City and Press
scribblers have already shown an increased awareness of official thinking . . .
As a result, over time the minutes should contain fewer surprises, thus contributing to the stability of macroeconomic policy" (1994: 125). Following
this same rationale, Fed Chairman Alan Greenspan became convinced that
"the market shouldn't be surprised. And if you minimize surprises . . . you
would minimize unpleasant side effects . . . [Greenspan] also wanted to
teach the market how the Fed was thinking and so that when the Fed indeed made a market move that it would be largely anticipated and then
the shock value would not be there . . . [T]he view really caught on that
the Fed should be as transparent as possible."[35]

Maximizing predictability was a coherent step toward fully articulate
inflation targeting as a governing technique. The new framework of macroeconomic forecasting, together with central banks' and governments'
commitment to steady future inflation, meant that the path of policy rates
going forward, and by implication the long-term bond rates, should be ex-
pectable for policymakers and market participants alike—at least until
economic shocks altered the picture. This approach found its way into central banker textbooks, where the virtue of predictability was endorsed:
"By controlling the overnight rate to a fair degree, and by making changes
to the overnight rate target predictable within a well-known macroeco-

nomic strategy of the central bank, medium and longer term rates, i.e. those judged to be most relevant for monetary policy transmission, will react in a predictable way to changes in short term rates" (Bindseil 2004b: 11). Inflation-targeting advocates and practitioners obviously understood that predictability had its limits, given the possibility of unexpected shocks and the need to adjust policies spontaneously in response to them. However, even if *practical* problems existed, maximum predictability was deemed a desirable feature of policymaking in principle. If market participants could anticipate future central bank actions and macroeconomic outcomes through conditional forecasts, and if they knew that others also formed their expectations based on these forecasts, expected inflation became "anchored," as policymakers like to say (see also Stasavage 2003). Ironically, this *increased* the space for discretionary policymaking. For instance, in a downturn, monetary authorities could react countercyclically, lowering their interest rates. Bond-market rates would follow these moves and shift the yield curve so that, while medium-term real rates were lowered more quickly to reflect the economic slump, long-term rates remained anchored at levels consistent with optimal output and central banks' inflation targets. In the words of the architect of inflation targeting, Mervyn King, "[a] central bank can take counter-cyclical actions to reduce fluctuations in output . . . provided that such actions do not alter inflationary expectations" (1997: 95).

But before this approach to central banking became universally accepted and unchallenged, a minority of monetary authorities raised some pertinent questions about its problematic implications. This happened at a conference at the Bank for International Settlements (BIS) on central banks' policy implementation in 1997. The Bundesbank officials speaking at this conference readily admitted that, even as a practicing monetarist, the German central bank played a decisive role in stabilizing short-term money-market rates. But what the German officials objected to was any involvement with capital markets: "[L]eadership in the capital market that dominates the real interest rate . . . cannot and is not to be achieved by means of the monetary policy instruments."[36] The German central bankers also conceived of communication and transparency differently from their Anglo-Saxon colleagues. The Bundesbank would stick to its unquestionable commitment to low inflation. But "transparency and accountability should not result in day-to-day monetary policy becoming completely calculable"; statements concerning economic and monetary conditions were made "under conditions of uncertainty" and did not forestall decisions "which come as a surprise to the markets."[37] Officials from the other monetarist institution, the Swiss National Bank, concurred with these views and even gave them a more radical twist. They felt "there is a need to leave the markets with some uncertainty about our short-term tactics" and that uncertainty was useful to avoid "opportunities for riskless (or near-riskless) speculative activities by market participants."[38]

These divergent attitudes toward the desirability of predictability resulted from the different roles that financial market expectations assumed in different central banking practices. For inflation targeters, predictable movements in mid- and long-term interest rates in reaction to predictable moves in their own operational targets (money-market rates) had become a key indicator of success. More predictable market reactions meant that more credibility was given to the central bank. For monetarists, by contrast, credibility lay with the wage-setting behavior of corporatist institutions and the willingness of fiscal authorities to practice restraint (see Chapter 2). Changes in bond yields were not a direct verdict on the Bundesbank's or the Swiss National Bank's policies. Moreover, because corporate borrowers could insulate themselves from interest-rate swings via long-term bank borrowing in these bank-based systems, there was no need to render yield changes predictable.

But soon after the reported BIS conference, inflation targeting developed into the globally dominant regime of macroeconomic policy (see Chapter 4), sweeping away monetarism even in Germany (via the European Central Bank, or ECB) and Switzerland.[39] This also meant that the controversy was decided in favor of predictability. This found expression in increasingly standardized ways of communicating with markets and of shared norms of "transparency." In a widely cited report on how central banks should "talk," central bank experts proclaimed as an unquestioned truism that "[t]he financial markets constitute the channel through which monetary policy actions are transmitted to the economy, and ultimately to achieve its goals. Since this channel is dominated by expectations, 'convincing the market' is part and parcel of monetary policy-making" (Blinder 2001: 25). This required that market "observers can understand each monetary policy decision as part of a logical chain of decisions leading to some objective(s)" (ibid.: 2), and that the central bank provide maximum transparency about these steps.

Only the financial crisis of 2007–2009 raised new questions about predictability as a virtuous feature of monetary policy. Ironically, the person to raise these questions was Mervyn King. As King suggested in public statements and writings after the end of his Bank tenure (King 2016), the crisis had shown that central banks faced radical uncertainties. Given such uncertainties, policymakers should renounce the "pretense of knowledge" and should reject "forward guidance" or comparable techniques (Braun 2018b). More technical studies supported the notion that a false pretense of predictability had led market actors to engage in long-term lending based on expected stable refinancing costs in wholesale markets (Adrian and Shin 2008). The possibility that short-term market rates could shoot up massively had not been discounted in the broader climate of expectations fostered by central banks.

Discussion

As was implicit in the monetarists' critiques of predictability, in the 1970s to 1990s, they still engaged in distinctive ways of governing expectations. For German and Swiss monetary targeters, it was critical that actors involved in price setting in the broader economy, especially wage bargainers, accepted and believed in the central banks' commitments to stable and low inflation. Accordingly, Otmar Issing explained the Bundesbank's success in establishing monetary stability in terms of a particular "interaction of monetary and wage policy. Even though wage trends all too often did not meet the high standards called for by those responsible for anti-inflation policy, ultimately management and labor repeatedly accepted the constraints imposed by monetary policy" (1997: 78). The monetary beliefs upon which such expectational coordination relied were rather vague, partly fueled by the "folk theories" of monetarism, partly based on communications between monetary authorities, economic actors and government officials tied together through corporatist institutions. Financial actors, particularly the universal banks, were important participants in these conversations, but they did not attempt to emancipate finance from the broader economic context. Nor did price movements on financial markets express authoritative verdicts on economic policy. In fact, monetarist central banks gave no privileged epistemic status to bond markets and bond yields. Inflation stabilization was possible while considerable uncertainty remained about financial market developments because what ultimately mattered was that corporatist institutions maintained wage growth below productivity gains, that fiscal authorities restrained public spending, and that banks effectively financed corporate investments (Höpner 2019).

As demonstrated in this chapter, entering the 1980s, the Anglo-Saxon central bankers found themselves in a different game. For them, the weight of industrial sectors and the bargaining power of labor had been reduced sufficiently so that they had to worry less and less about inflationary impulses from labor markets (Brenner 2006; Hung and Thompson 2016). The neoliberal governments in these two countries also accepted or even endorsed unemployment as a necessary cure to shift economic and political power relations (Minsky 1988: 61; Payne 2010). But despite these crucial policy changes, the sources for a new kind of macroeconomic stabilization policy remained ill-defined, at least until the latter half of the 1980s. Neither Ronald Reagan nor Thatcher had answers to the question of how to "stabilize dynamic credit-money economies with bloated financial systems" (Saad Filho 2007: 105). To the contrary, the respective governments even created fundamental contradictions between their own promises to control the money supply and their policies favoring financialization. For instance, Thatcher undermined her own monetarism by pushing credit-financed consumption and household investments, for example, by removing regulatory barriers to consumer and mortgage loans (Clift 2020). In the United States, mortgage-financed homeownership was subsidized through tax reforms and regulatory changes that supported securitization (Prasad 2012; Quinn 2019). There was a fundamental incoherence between promoting these versions of financialized growth while endorsing monetarism as the means to stabilize the economy and guarantee stable and low inflation. In addition to various practical and structural problems, this incoherence extended to the ideological realm because one and the same government could not credibly endorse credit expansion and be trusted to maintain money growth under control (Offer 2017). Accordingly, the Thatcher government withdrew from its monetarist mid-term financial strategy in 1985, just as Volcker had abandoned monetary targeting only two years after its adoption.

What eventually emerged as a viable strategy to claim governability was to use the central banks' influence over short-term interest rates to coordinate with financial markets around expectations of low and stable inflation. That was the "nominal anchor" (Hetzel 2008: 5) that could orient policy interventions within a context of financialization. Central bankers themselves arrived at this solution independently from the plans and ideas produced by neoliberal governments. This innovation developed in two stages. It began with Volcker's nascent inflation targeting, which consisted in aggressive hikes of federal funds rates in response to inflation scares. Then came the Bank of England's and others' translation of this strategy, which revolved around forward-looking communication. The crucial innovation in the United Kingdom was the *Inflation Reports*. In a context in which the capital markets (especially futures and sovereign bond trading) had become more liquid, price-sensitive, integrated, and independent from the Bank's own interventions, the central bank could use these reports to signal intended policy moves to investors and elicit quick and anticipated responses. This coordination game would ungird the Bank of England's epistemic authority vis-à-vis the Treasury and turn it into the de facto authority on monetary policy from 1993 onward. The act of granting operational independence to the Bank in 1998 was a public consecration of this power shift.

I have focused narrowly here on the US–UK trajectory. But it is obvious that, particularly in the second phase of policy innovations, governments and central banks of other countries also played a formative role. For instance, the country usually mentioned as the first and most radical adopter of inflation targeting is New Zealand (Holmes 2013: 69; McCallum 1997: 2). Here, just as in the United Kingdom, a turn away from full employment and expansionary fiscal policies toward liberalization, rampant credit expansion, and political toleration of unemployment paved the way for a new role for and practice of monetary policy. This shift had a different origin than in the United Kingdom. The trigger was a broader reform of the public sector, toward performance agreements with independent agencies. Inflation targeting emerged as a monetary policy that was consistent with this large-scale public-sector restructuring (Sherwin 2000: 17). Accordingly, key elements of New Zealand's regime consisted in enshrining price stability in law as the only Reserve Bank of New Zealand (RBNZ) objective; adopting so-called Policy Targets Agreements between the Finance

Minister and the RBNZ Governor; and granting operational independence for the Governor, combined with a threat of severe sanctions if the RBNZ failed to meet the targets. All these elements speak to a more politically driven and "master-planned" version of inflation targeting. Still, the symbolic and structural centrality of finance turned out to be decisive for the subsequent fate of New Zealand's inflation targeting. The RBNZ initially attempted to satisfy the new political imperatives by means of an indicator of monetary conditions that entailed a medium-term interest-rate and exchange-rate component. This made sense, given that exchange-rate movements were the primary drivers of inflation in this small and open economy. However, in addition to forecasting difficulties, using this indicator brought with it one key problem: "It seemed virtually impossible to give the market messages related to both interest rates and exchange rates . . . The MCI [the monetary conditions indicator, LW] did not solve the Bank's communication problems. When the Bank took a very different view from the market . . . , there was confusion of shifts in the MCI line and movements along it" (Mayes and Razzak 2001: 99–105). The RBNZ thus painfully learned that successful inflation targeting required, first and foremost, choosing a form of communication that was consistent with expectation formation in financial markets. Accordingly, it changed its policy practice in 1999 by making it more similar to the British version.

On the face of it, Sweden does not fit into this picture. This was the poster child of social democracy with its own tradition of corporatism; comparative political economists would not group this country with "liberal" economies such as the United States, the United Kingdom, and New Zealand. Nonetheless, the Riksbank, the Swedish central bank, was among the pioneers of inflation targeting, adopting a prospective objective for a range of inflation in 1993 and guiding interest-rate decisions toward this target from 1994 onward. An explanation for this adoption, I think, should focus on the problematic role of monetary policies in Sweden's political economy before the 1990s, the country's highly expansionary financial sector, and the disruptive phase of a banking and currency crisis from 1990 until 1993. For instance, in contrast to the central banks in Germany and Switzerland, the Riksbank did *not* enlist corporatist institutions in coordination games around monetary stability objectives. Instead, the Swedish central bank accommodated expansionary fiscal policies and wage increases above productivity growth with inflation; the currency, under these circumstances, was under constant devaluation pressure, leading to several adjustments during the Bretton Woods period and after. Moreover, while Sweden had a bank-based and highly regulated financial sector until the 1980s, household indebtedness rose considerably already in the postwar years. Growing competition from nonbank finance companies, plus the growth of money markets in the early 1980s, then led to significant deregulations during 1983–1985. We subsequently see an asset-price boom, particularly in real estate, followed by a banking crisis, and involuntary exit from the ERM in 1992 (Englund 1999). The Riksbank decided to adopt inflation targets in the midst of this crisis, when the budget deficit spiked at 12 percent of GDP, the currency continued to depreciate after the float, and inflation remained high (at around 5 percent). That was a window of opportunity for the central bank to abandon its accommodative "social democratic" role and commit to monetary stability; and it did so toward what had become an increasingly deregulated, market-based financial system. Accordingly, the Riksbank used very similar ingredients to the Bank of England. Regular inflation reports were combined with interest-rate decisions, whose purpose was to signal the commitment to price stability toward interconnected and open financial markets. This also led to an emphasis on "transparency and clarity" as "natural components in the smooth functioning of a market-oriented monetary policy," as Riksbank economists noted at the BIS conference on policy implementation in 1997.[40]

This implies that New Zealand and Sweden underwent similar structural and institutional changes than Britain, enabling the innovative adoption of inflation targeting. But this raises the more foundational question of how and why inflation targeting could spread far beyond this select group of pioneers, coming to be adopted in such diverse settings as Armenia, Brazil, Moldova, Uganda, and Switzerland (Jahan 2017). It is hard to see what unites these democratic and nondemocratic countries with fundamentally different economic regimes.

The diversity of inflation targeters thus provides *prima facie* support for theories that treat adoption of inflation targeting as the outcome of diffusion processes toward complying with a codified policy norm (Wasserfallen 2019). Without challenging the results of such analyses, I here want to point to a complementary aspect, which has to do with the nature of the conditions needed for successful inflation targeting. As argued, monetarism thrived within nationally embedded institutional configurations consisting of corporatist coordination and conservative banking. As many political economists have emphasized, it is difficult or even impossible to import such institutions or build them from scratch (for a discussion of this in the context of the European Monetary Union, see Hancké 2013). By contrast, inflation targeting thrives under institutional conditions that are compatible with, or themselves products of, financial globalization. For instance, coordinating expectations of low and stable inflation with financial markets requires highly liquid and forward-looking trading in sovereign bond markets that inform central banks about the expected rate of inflation. Organizing bond markets according to these prerequisites has emerged as one broad institutional trend across numerous and highly diverse OECD countries in the past thirty decades. Relatedly, what is critical for inflation targeting expectation management to succeed is that central banks develop and effectively communicate authoritative interest-rate and inflation forecasts. The resources for establishing such authority are themselves "global": They consist of academic degrees from prestigious (US) universities; sophisticated models such as DSGE; and forms of public communication that follow widely used scripts. With these elements in place, and in the absence of countervailing forces (such as strong labor unions, governments pursuing full employment policies, and so on), inflation targeting becomes possible across a wide diversity of contexts. Chapter 4 will single out one such process of institutional convergence undergirding inflation targeting, namely the remaking of money markets.

CHAPTER FOUR

Money Markets as Infrastructures of Global Finance and Central Banks

> Central banks depend on shadow bank activities for the implementation and transmission of monetary policy.
>
> —BRAUN AND GABOR 2020: 249

IN THIS CHAPTER, I argue that there is a recursive causality between the global integration of money markets and the spread of inflation targeting. Money-market integration created the operational infrastructures that allowed central banks to engage in signaling games with financial markets. The respective transformations began as rule-evading and offshoring processes that threatened postwar regulatory orders and policy routines, raising fears that states would lose their governing powers vis-à-vis globalizing finance. But monetary authorities soon discovered that they could capitalize on increasingly integrated and price-sensitive market environments to control short-term interest rates as their operational targets—financialization could thus be turned into an infrastructural source of governing power.[1] This led central bankers to come out as active supporters of financial globalization. Monetary authorities eventually assumed the role of architect of money-market institutions, facilitating the expansion of liquidity via these markets in a period of rapid financial growth. The money-market architecture that collapsed in 2008 thus was the product of a settlement between

private-sector and state interests that reflected the particular governing
motives of central banks.

Hyman Minsky (1957) was an early analyst of these recursive causalities between money markets and policy changes in the United States. Following his lead, Clemens Jobst and Stefano Ugolini have studied these interactions historically and comparatively, coming to the conclusion that
"money markets and monetary policymaking evolve over time: the way the
former work not only shapes, but is also shaped by the way the latter works"
(2016: 147). In his own writings, Minsky focused on how financial innovations altered the ecology of central banking. He observed that "the efficacy of any particular technique of monetary policy depends upon the financial institutions and usages that exist. If financial institutions do not
change significantly, then, once the efficacy of the various central bank operations is established, financial institutions can be ignored in discussions
of monetary policy. However, if a period of rapid changes in the structure
or in the mode of functioning of financial markets occurs, then the efficacy
of central bank actions has to be re-examined" (1957: 171). But the reverse
is also true, as Jobst and Ugolini note: "Once a central bank has chosen to
enter a given money market, the latter will no longer look the same. Because
of the monetary authority's involvement, in fact, crucial changes are bound
to take place in the microstructure of the market and, consequently, in
the behavior of prices" (2016: 149).

I want to draw on these ideas here to trace the interrelations between
money-market developments and central banking since the 1970s. The
starting point for this analysis is the observation that, in the countries included in my comparative analysis, the central bank–money market nexus
had historically taken very different forms, reflecting nation-specific settlements between state demands on finance and financial elites' interests
in maintaining profitable and protected markets, interspersed by rare democratic interventions in the politics of finance (usually after crises). In the
United States, the system that had emerged from these negotiations and
democratic processes was one of interconnected money and capital markets that served purposes of short-term financing and investment. The Federal Reserve attempted to steer this system by influencing the behaviors of
key intermediaries, which included regular banks as well as brokers who
"shifted" liquidity from one market to the next (Mehrling 2011). In the
United Kingdom, in the postwar period, we find a system of demarcated

market segments dominated by organized cartels, whose internal order was carefully safeguarded by the Bank. The core segment was that in prime and Treasury bills, which was run by specialist firms and regulated by informal rules (Sissoko 2016). Lastly, in Germany and Switzerland, central banks interacted with universal banks that controlled almost all aspects of finance (credit issuance, savings, and so on) and maintained money markets only for short-term settlement purposes.

As a large literature has documented, financial globalization challenged these national settlements (Burn 2006; Eichengreen 2008; Helleiner 1994; Strange 1998). Starting in the 1960s, new competitive pressures led banks to search for ways to circumvent domestic rules and move a growing share of their activities offshore. The Eurodollar markets developed as the key markets for lending and borrowing short-term funds without the need to comply with reserve requirements or other regulatory constraints. American finance was the first to be uprooted by these developments because its banks were particularly exposed to nonbank competition and proved highly innovative in circumventing New Deal regulations. Next came the United Kingdom, where Eurodollar markets were based and new techniques were imported from the United States. The large Swiss and German universal banks also entered the Eurodollar market at an early stage but initially attempted to maintain a lid on innovations in domestic markets, where they enjoyed a protected incumbent status. However, the more continental European banks entered into competition with their Anglo-Saxon peers, the less it was desired and feasible to maintain conservative banking practices at home (Beck 2021).

How did central bankers react to these developments? Banks' interests matter to monetary authorities. To the extent that domestic banks were exposed to competitive pressures and lobbied for deregulation, central bank officials were usually willing to give ground (Green 2015). Maintaining a hands-off approach vis-à-vis Eurodollars also brought some strategic advantages. These offshore markets performed important petrodollar-recycling functions, and their unclear legal status meant that central banks could maintain ambiguity about their responsibilities as regards last-resort lending. But there is no question that rule-circumventing innovations and offshoring raised challenges for public monetary and financial management. For the US case, Tobias Adrian and Nellie Liang note that "[m]oney creation in the shadow banking system is at the root of the breakdown of monetary relationships in the US. Until the early 1980s, the relationship between money growth and nominal output growth was very stable, a fact usually labeled as stable velocity of money . . . Credit began to grow rapidly and decouple from broad money since the early 1970s, via a combination of increased financial risk and leverage outside of non-monetary liabilities at banks" (2016: 12). The same observation holds true for the other countries. The more banks adopted active liability management, and the more porous the boundaries became between domestic and international markets, the less could authorities practice policies that were intended to control the volumes of money and credit in domestic economies.

However, as American and British central bankers discovered in the 1980s, financial globalization could be transformed from an existential threat to state power into a powerful resource in the conduct of monetary policy. The solution was to adopt the technique of maintaining tight control over the interest rates in domestic interbank markets. It was widely accepted that central banks could control these rates, which resulted from the fact that the scarce goods in these interbank markets are central bank balances that banks need to settle mutual debts (Fullwiler 2013; Mehrling 2011). But the new discovery was that policy worked best if central banks focused *only* on the price at which this marginal demand was met and relied on arbitrage relationships between the interbank and wider money markets to transmit price signals to a broader, economically significant range of actors and instruments. As a Bank for International Settlements (BIS) report at the time noted, "Central banks can normally rely on their influence on interbank rates being closely reflected in short-term interest rates on domestic markets with nonbank participation, in short-term interest rates in the offshore markets for the domestic currency, and in the rates applied by the banks for short-term lending to their customers" (Kneeshaw and Van den Bergh 1989: 21). In the event, the rise of active liability management and offshore markets *increased* the efficacy of monetary policy as a macroeconomic governing tool because an integrated system helps spreading price signals quickly to a wide range of financially involved actors; "[t]he shadow banking system, which is less constrained than banks by prudential regulation, leads to a *greater* [policy] transmission" (Adrian and Liang 2016: 12; see also Braun and Gabor 2020: 245).

The chapter will thus show that, induced by financial globalization, a powerful nexus was forged between market-based banking and inflation targeting between the 1980s and the 2000s. A new political-economic settlement had come about after "embedded liberalism," which integrated the global search for profit in finance with the particular governing motives of central banks. Central bankers in Germany and Switzerland accepted this settlement only belatedly and reluctantly. For the Bundesbank and the Swiss National Bank (SNB), in their practical monetarism, had capitalized on the relative isolation of their domestic banking sectors from financial globalization. But these particular settlements broke down over the course of the 1990s as the large banks in Germany and Switzerland adopted Anglo-Saxon active liability-management techniques. The Americanization of money markets thus finally brought the experiment of monetary targeting to an end.

A final element of the recursive causality argument is that, upon realizing the benefits brought by liquid money markets integrated through arbitrage operations and shadow banks, central bankers actively engaged in the consolidation of market-based banking into a proper global system. They did so through formal institution building in the realms of law, private governance mechanisms, and central banking itself. The problems addressed concerned how to lower transaction costs in increasingly large, transnational markets and how to reduce counterparty credit risks. The role of central bankers in this process reflected their belief in the monetary policy advantages of consolidating market-based banking; the Fed was the first in this process, followed by the Bank of England, and finally the Swiss and other continental European central bankers joined in. These efforts were highly successful in that the most thoroughly institutionalized markets, those for repurchase agreements ("repo"), expanded most rapidly in the 2000s.[2] However, these markets were also the ones that collapsed when the financial boom of the 2000s came to an end (Gorton and Metrick 2012). Implicit in my argument is thus the critique that, by co-constructing the fragile infrastructures of financial systems, central bankers bear some of the responsibility for what happened in 2007–2009.

The chapter proceeds as follows. I will first return to the United States to describe how deep-seated structural factors and the dialectic between New Deal regulations and their circumvention fostered innovations in

American money markets. I then turn to the United Kingdom to trace the dismantling of its "classical system" (Sissoko 2016), first *against* the Bank of England's interests and subsequently as part of the central bank's very own project to set up "modern" money markets as operational infrastructures for its interventions. I then reconstruct the opposition from the Bundesbank and Swiss National Bank against American money-market instruments and practices that faltered during the 1990s. The discussion section uses the empirical findings developed in this chapter to critique the prevalent framing of central banks' operational interventions in money markets as purely technical, rather than historically situated practices that are shaped by and co-construct the institutional architectures and dynamics of finance. In the final section, I also draw a link between central bankers' co-construction of markets and the breakdown of these markets in 2008.

The American Origins of the Contemporary Money-Market Regime

In the late nineteenth century, the absence of national branch banking, combined with political resistance to centralization (Wexler 1981), had created an American monetary system provisionally integrated through larger financial center banks and clearing houses, which managed the reserves of small regional or local banks. But as a mechanism to mitigate "money panics" (Gorton and Huang 2002), or even just to address the regular fluctuations of credit and money in an agriculturally dominated economy (Mehrling 2011: 32), these reserve management arrangements of the National Banking Era were inadequate. The Federal Reserve system was thus founded to enhance the "elasticity" of banking reserves within a fragmented financial structure (Burgess 1927; Willis 1914). Organizing such a system required establishing a network of regionally dispersed Fed branches. But the Fed also relied on markets to connect as many market participants as possible to its operations, leading to the development of a federal funds market in the years following the Fed's foundation in 1913 (Burgess 1927; Maerowitz 1981; Meltzer 2003: 164–65).

The nexus between the Fed and the money markets was reconfigured in the following decades by two crucial events. First, the succession of two world wars led to an unprecedented expansion of public debt and turned government securities into the primary assets for storing, transacting, and regulating liquidity. Fed open-market operations in Treasury securities substituted the "traditional" method of regulating the money markets via discounting commercial paper. Moreover, dealers emerged as the prominent actors in the US system from these early days, standing ready to buy and sell Treasuries from the banks (contributing to a "liquidity discount" for public debt). For that reason, it was critical for the Fed to reach these dealers, even though the latter were not direct Fed members. As a result, the Fed was concerned with money-market conditions beyond its immediate reach, and it ensured a smooth transmission from one market to another through what Perry Mehrling calls "shiftability," in other words, the exchange of liquid securities for funding liquidity.

The second development was the Great Crash of 1929 and the Great Depression that followed. In the 1920s, Fed action had primarily been passive. Policies had not been tightened because of coordination problems between regional branches, the Board in Washington, and the New York Fed as the system's informal leader (Meltzer 2003). Furthermore, regional Fed branches had failed to rein in a dynamic of competitive deregulation between states. US banking therefore proved vulnerable to mass failures in the early 1930s. For that reason, Franklin Delano Roosevelt and his political allies in Congress tried to embed the fragmentary market system in a proper regulatory framework with the Banking Act of 1933, the Securities Act of 1933, and the Securities Exchange Act of 1934. Banks received special protection through deposit insurance and were subjected to close supervision by the Fed, the Comptroller of the Currency, and the Federal Deposit Insurance Corporation. These arrangements were supposed to reflect the public-good character of money creation (Menand 2021). In parallel, securities markets and investment banks were legally separated from banking (in the so-called Glass Steagall Act) and regulated according to strict disclosure requirements and rules of conduct. The New Deal thus tried to realize the traditional English idea of banking regulation through functional separation, dissociating "the suppliers of money—the banks—from the users of money—commerce and industry," an approach that was (at least rhetorically) still endorsed by President Richard Nixon some forty years after the New Deal (D'Arista 1994: 70).

It is against this background that we observe an unprecedented proliferation of new money-market instruments and liability-management techniques in the 1960s and 1970s. The dynamics underlying this proliferation have been aptly characterized as a "regulatory dialectic" (Kane 1981; Reinicke 1995). The trigger of this dialectic was that various New Deal regulations—reserve requirements, interest-rate ceilings, the Glass-Steagall Act—had turned into competitive disadvantages for the regulated banks vis-à-vis nonbank finance companies or state-chartered institutions (Reinicke 1995: 30) and had caused reduced profitability in the conventional loan-making and deposit-taking business (Calomiris 1998). For instance, interest-rate ceilings on current and savings accounts made it attractive for savers to put their money into the newly established money-market mutual funds, which drained liquidity from commercial banks (figure 4.1).[3] With restrictions on banks' credit issuance and deposit rates, nonfinancial firms also increasingly turned away from classic bank intermediation, putting their surplus savings directly into money markets and organizing their short-term borrowing via commercial paper issuance. While smaller banks simply exited the Fed system to avoid restrictions (particularly reserve requirements) (Goodfriend and Hargraves 1983: 9), money center banks started to engage in ever more creative rule circumvention. This had a long tradition in the United States: Banks and nonbank competitors had already practiced regulatory arbitrage in the 1920s to exploit the fragmentary regulatory landscape of America's competitive federal system. But banks now intensified these efforts with "innovations [which helped] by 'opening up escape hatches through which alert market participants [could] flee some of the effects of financial stringency on their operations for a while'" (Wooley 1984: 74). For instance, commercial banks attempted to reacquire some of the liquidity drained by money-market funds by borrowing from these funds, issuing liabilities that appeared attractive to these increasingly prominent market participants. Banks also found ways to acquire funding through commercial paper, which offered attractive rates to investors and thus developed into an increasingly important segment of the larger money market. Depository institutions were not allowed to issue commercial paper directly, but from 1969 they started to use subsidiaries (later special-purpose vehicles, see Thiemann 2018: 30) within a holding company structure for such activities (Lindow 1972: 44). Before that, banks had already developed a funding instrument distinctly designed to circumvent regulation, namely the negotiable certificate of deposit, known as a CD (Cleveland and Huertas 1985). This instrument helped banks to pay rates above those allowed for

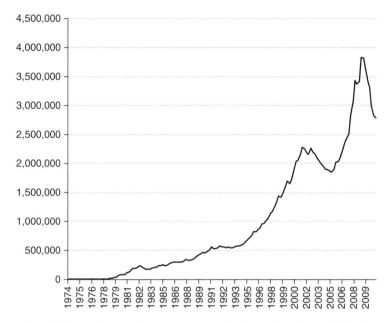

FIGURE 4.1. Volume of US-registered money-market funds (millions of dollars).
Data source: Federal Reserve Economic Data

savings accounts. When the Fed tried to rein in this business with restrictions on maximum CD rates, banks found yet another escape route, namely to the offshore Eurodollar markets, where they re-encountered American nonfinancial corporations, which had entered Eurodollars to invest surplus cash holdings with maximum return. Several laws issued in the mid-1960s, which were intended to contain capital flight, ironically reinforced this offshoring trend. Beck describes that, as banks expanded their arbitrage business between domestic money markets and Eurodollars, a "closely knit network" (2021: 11) emerged that provided the foundations of a financial globalization centered around US dollar markets.[4]

The Fed first tried to rein in these various rule evasions and offshoring activities, for example, by urging (unsuccessfully) the introduction of stronger restrictions on one-bank holding companies (D'Arista 1994: 69); by extending the liabilities against which it would charge reserve requirements; or by requiring *all* depository institutions to comply with uniform reserve requirements (Wexler 1981: 199). However, these attempts to reregulate banks' and nonbanks' reserve management, and to strengthen central bank capacities for credit regulation, remained ambiguous. The Fed confronted the endemic problem of enforcing national rules in a fragmentary regulatory and competitive system, and it had to safeguard the interests of its own counterparties, the deposit banks, if only to avoid a situation in which the shadow-banking sector took over, destroying the very basis of the Federal Reserve system. Additionally, the Fed faced the difficulty that some parts of shadow banking—particularly broker-dealers, who acted as primary dealers in the government bond market—had by the 1970s become ever more critical elements in the circulation of funding liquidity provided through Fed operations. Any drastic regulatory measure therefore risked destroying quintessential market infrastructures.[5] A sign of these internal contradictions at the Fed was the resignation of Paul Volcker (Mallaby 2017: 313–15), who had confronted growing opposition within the Fed against his own, rather strict regulatory approach (Menand 2021: 66).[6]

A key contributory factor in shifting the balance of forces inside the Fed toward deregulation was that, by the late 1980s, the monetary policy case (as opposed to the financial stability argument) in favor of reregulating banking and constraining active liability management had been weakened. Through Volcker's experiments, described in Chapter 3, the Fed had halted the inflationary spiral of the 1970s. As a result of this new situation, the Fed soon adopted an accommodative attitude toward money-market innovations.[7] The key to this shift was that commercial paper, repo, CD, and Eurodollar market participants all appeared to anchor their price determination in expectations of the Fed's federal funds rate target, giving the Fed greater leverage over refinancing conditions in a market-based system. Connecting central bank operations to banks' active liability management thus emerged as a way of *enhancing* the central bank's infrastructural powers (Adrian and Shin 2008; Braun and Gabor 2020; Nyborg and Östberg 2014). In Martijn Konings's words, "What had previously been a major problem for the Federal Reserve's ability to regulate the financial system—that is, banks' close institutional connections to financial markets—now emerged as a point of great policy leverage: The high degree of market depth and connectivity meant that changes in the Federal Funds rate were almost instantly transmitted to other markets" (2011: 149).

One domain in which this shift had palpable consequences was that of reserve requirements. These had been relatively high in the United States, requiring Fed member banks to keep 12 percent of their deposit liabilities in non-interest-bearing central bank reserves. Pressure to reform these arrangements had initially come from member banks, which had perceived these requirements as a competitive disadvantage vis-à-vis nonmembers and had engaged in various strategies to circumvent them. The Fed's ambivalence toward these developments was reflected in a trend of lowering requirements (not least to retain members) while demanding from banks that they stop "manipulating certain transactions 'to reduce reserve requirements artificially,'" as Volcker had complained (cited in Menand 2021: 66). But starting in the 1990s, the rationale shifted as the Fed increasingly believed that its attempts at stabilizing the volume of reserves in the system complicated its own procedures unnecessarily, and that monetary policy would be better served if the quantity of reserves was a passive reflection of banks' choices (and autonomous factors, such as tax payments) at a given policy rate. Reserve requirements were lowered in 1990 and virtually disappeared by the late 1990s without raising any central bank concerns (Fullwiler 2013: 181). Meanwhile, the Fed started publicly announcing its policy rate (Meulendyk 1998: 141–42) and encouraged banks to use discount window borrowing in situations in which open-market or repo operations failed to fully accommodate their reserve demands. The disappearance of reserve requirements is remarkable because, even though the political practice had not always lived up to the promise, the Fed had long claimed that reserve requirements and their regulation were essential components of its approach to taming excessive credit creation in the US financial system (Bindseil 2004b).

Another domain in which we can observe the concrete implications of the Fed's policy shift are the repo markets. Repo had originally emerged as a small segment of the larger money markets, in which government bond dealers acquired funding liquidity from banks by temporarily lending bonds to these cash providers (Garbade 2006; Sissoko 2010; Toma 1988)—a niche activity supported by the Fed (Menand 2021: 69). But the market dramatically changed in the 1970s, when commercial banks started issuing their own repos to reacquire some of the liquidity lost to money-market funds. This expansion brought new risks into a previously contained transactional realm, as the default of a securities dealer, Lombard Wall Inc., demonstrated in 1982. A bankruptcy court ruling had prevented Lombard Wall's repo creditors from using "their" collateral to secure exposure, thereby undermining the very purpose of collateralized transactions (Riles 2011: 55).[8] Therefore, securities dealer associations lobbied Congress to amend the Chapter 11 bankruptcy code in order to forestall similar rulings in the future (Walters 1982). The Fed gave decisive support for such legal amendments. Chairman Paul Volcker wrote a letter to the House Judicial Committee arguing that "because of the magnitude of the market . . . and *the importance of repos as an instrument of monetary policy,* it is desirable to restore an environment that will assure smooth functioning." He warned that "a repo market that has been narrowed by the withdrawal of participants that are unprepared to accept the risks inherent in the Lombard Wall decision could *limit the ability of the Federal Reserve to act promptly and in the large volumes necessary to achieve monetary policy objectives.*"[9] Congress followed this reasoning and created a legal "carve-out" for repo creditors that would give these actors "super-priority" status in subsequent US bankruptcy procedures (Roe 2011). Initially, this carve-out applied only to borrowing and lending that was collateralized with *government* securities, a specification that reflected the initial status of repos as the financing tool for a select group of government bond traders that were instrumental in facilitating the Fed's liquidity management with Treasury bonds. But crucially, the Fed continued to support repos in subsequent years as this market began to connect a far wider set of shadow and deposit banks. Rather than relying on, and supporting, functional separation, with its repo policies, the Fed came to endorse a fully marketized and increasingly concentrated financial system.

The Americanization of UK Money Markets

Before returning to the strategic role of repos, let me discuss the peculiar case of the United Kingdom. As is widely recognized (e.g., Green 2015), this country has played an instrumental role in bringing the new, American ways of "actively managing liabilities" to Europe. That the United Kingdom would play this bridging role is somehow intuitive. The country had developed the closest and deepest relationships with the United States in the financial realm. London and New York were the dominant financial centers of the late twentieth century, competing for primacy in different markets. Moreover, due to the liberal British approach to the arrival of the Eurodollar markets, American financial firms and offshore dollar activities had settled in London during the postwar period. At the same time, it is important to recognize that the United Kingdom had very distinct money-market traditions, going back to imperial times. These nineteenth-century conventions and techniques put the London money markets at odds with the American approach (Hotson 2017; Sissoko 2016). I will start by reconstructing these British peculiarities and the Bank of England's attachment to them in order to render visible how the Americanization of British money markets in the latter half of the twentieth century un-leashed a process of structural financial as well as policy change. The Bank of England would emerge as a central actor in this transformation. But this happened only after it had overcome various objections and opposi-tions from actors inside and around the central bank who were attached to the traditional ways of managing liquidity in the City of London. The discovery of effective capacities for interest-rate interventions, after the Eu-ropean Exchange Rate Mechanism (ERM) failure (see Chapter 3), was a decisive step in advancing a new settlement between inflation targeting and market-based finance.

The core London money markets from the late nineteenth century until the 1970s had different structures than those in the United States, and they also looked strikingly different from the globally integrated, market-based system that we have today. Three core features were responsible for this dis-tinctiveness. First, the entire financial sector worked upon a City-specific differentiation by function (Offer 2014). In contrast to the United States, functional separation had a proper foundation because firms in every seg-ment had different legal-organizational forms and were organized in cartels that brought together actors from distinct social status groups (Preda 2009). In the core money market, the most important participants were small part-nership firms, the so-called discount houses, which acted collectively as the London Discount Market Association (LDMA) (Fletcher 1976). In the late nineteenth century, these firms had emerged as the exclusive intermediaries of the bill market, practicing a peculiar type of wholesale liquidity transfor-mation. They offered withdrawable, secured deposits ("call money") to the clearing banks as their primary source of funding, and they backed these cash promises with the institutional privilege of selling bills from their in-ventories to the Bank of England at the latter's discount rate (Hotson 2017: 15). Moreover, the discount houses were granted the exclusive privilege of end-of-day borrowing from the Bank. In return for this privilege, the Bank kept the discount houses on a much tighter regulatory leash than other firms and used them to relay messages to the broader markets about the Bank's desired direction of interest rates.[10]

The second distinctive element derived from the prime bank bill as a particular money-market instrument. While a bill was negotiable just like CDs or commercial paper, issuance and trading worked differently. Every issuer or *drawer* of this instrument needed a bank as *acceptor,* which would promise full repayment of debts on the drawer's behalf. *Prime* bank bills were those accepted by the dominant merchant banks, also called "acceptance houses." These bills additionally contained the names of third parties, the *endorsers,* who had acquired and resold the bills, leaving their own names on them and thus providing an additional repayment guarantee. This practice of endorsement meant that, while illiquidity could be shifted among market participants through bill transactions, credit risk and due diligence responsibility of counterparties could not. This reduced incentive problems that we find in other types of money markets, most prominently in the repo arrangements discussed in more detail below (Roe 2011; Sissoko 2010; Sissoko 2016; Sissoko 2019). The Bank of England made a decisive contribution to these arrangements by discounting only prime bank bills that bore the signature of at least two "good names" (Fletcher 1976: 22). Anthony Coleby, the Bank's Chief Cashier during the 1970s, captured the informal nature of regulations in a retrospective account: "We did not publish a list of banks whose acceptances were eligible for rediscount here. It was well understood which bills were taken and which were not. The rules required that the acceptor be a British bank, but that term was interpreted loosely to include a number of banks in the old Commonwealth. Beyond that, the principal qualification was the ability to demonstrate that one's bills commanded the finest rate in transactions within the market."[11]

The third element underpinning London's money market was that prime bank bills should consist of self-liquidating paper. In its pure, not-quite-realized form, this meant that every bill should finance a commercial transaction, whose completion within a period of up to six months should extinguish the original debt (Goodhart 2011b).[12] Even in its less principled implementation, this rule meant that the bill market would never serve to fund long-term capital investments; the money market and asset markets were kept separate. Carolyn Sissoko (2016) argues that this separation helped reduce credit bubbles and that the Bank's policing over fluctuations in bill volumes can be considered an early version of macro-prudential policy.

The late nineteenth and early twentieth centuries are uncontroversially identified as the heyday of the classical system (Sayers 1976). It is less clear, however, how and when the system eroded. A radical change evidently resulted from the state's persistent funding needs after 1914. Treasury bills replaced commercial bills as the predominant money-market instruments; and for the Bank of England, particularly after the Second World War, priorities shifted from restricting speculative finance and protecting the gold reserve, to ensuring that the government's residual funding needs were met (Turner 2014). Quite literally, the Bank thus reoriented its interventions and reserve regulations toward the daily balancing of the government's and the market's accounts; as an unpublished Bank paper explained, "The management of the London money market is linked to the management of the central government accounts, because . . . the net daily flow of government payments to and receipts from the banks is generally the main cause of ease or stringency in that market."[13] But despite these transformations, key elements of bill financing persisted until the 1970s, anchored in entrenched class structures and daily routines and as a result of protective measures by its guardians. These were, in the first place, the Discount Office and Chief Cashier at the Bank of England, who upheld informal conventions and rules, enforced them through social influence over counterparties, and reproduced daily monetary management routines that integrated public financing, monetary policy, and prudential oversight (see Chapter 5).[14]

However, in spite of these forces in support of a "well-tried system," over a transitional period of about twenty-five years, lasting from 1970 until the mid-1990s, the bill market and associated central banking techniques disappeared, giving way to American instruments and techniques.[15] This process was much helped by the existence of Eurodollar markets and London's entrepôt status toward them. Initially, the Bank of England's idea had been that the offshore sphere, considered desirable as a source of revenue for the declining merchant banking business, could exist in neat separation from the regulated money market and thus leave extant regulations and routines unaffected (Burn 1999). But the Eurodollar expansion of the 1960s quickly undid this approach. Two mechanisms undermined the initial demarcations. First, American Eurodollar participants brought with them US techniques and instruments of active liability management that were gradually adopted by their British peers (Green 2015); certificates of deposit, commercial paper, and repos were all introduced to British finance via American firms.[16] Second, the offshore and unregulated sector had grown to an extent that threatened the incumbent firms in the City of London. For instance, the clearing banks had lost a considerable share of deposit liabilities during the 1960s (Ross 2004). As already mentioned in Chapter 2, the Bank of England therefore decided at the beginning of the 1970s to level the playing field between new entrants and incumbents. The CCC reform (discussed in Chapter 2) considerably lowered and (almost) unified reserve requirements on all firms conducting sterling business (the "reserve asset ratio") and thus gave clearing banks an entry ticket into active liability management.[17] As a result, together with M3 (the targeted monetary aggregate of the 1970s and early 1980s), wholesale liabilities in the domestic banking sector expanded dramatically within a few years. Nondeposit liabilities of British banks had been around 40 percent of all liabilities in the late 1960s; but their volume exploded to around 70 percent of all liabilities within a few years. One component of this expansion was the sterling CD, which had been virtually nonexistent in 1969 but grew to a volume of 4.5 billion by 1972.[18]

It is important to note, however, that these liberalization measures were initially adopted in order to improve the competitive position of British firms and the City of London as a financial center vis-à-vis its New York rival. Rather than providing new infrastructural foundations for monetary policy, it initially appeared that sectoral policies in favor of financialization and monetary stability objectives were in conflict. As discussed in the previous chapter, this was most evident during the early Thatcher period, when her government simultaneously accelerated financial liberalization while demanding that the central bank control the money supply. With regard to money markets, the most relevant Thatcherite reforms involved abandoning all remaining reserve requirements, ending restrictions on wholesale borrowing ("the corset") for the clearing banks, and allowing the building societies, which had been exclusively funded by retail savings, to enter the wholesale markets (Drake 1989). A few internal and external Thatcher advisers—for example, American economists Karl Brunner and

Allan Meltzer and gilt broker Gordon Pepper—argued that these money-market liberalizations posed no obstacle to monetary control; the central bank would simply need to terminate its practice of "lending of first resort" and restrict the quantitative provision of reserves to predefined targets (an approach called "monetary base targeting"). In reality, however, as Charles Goodhart bluntly stated at a Fed conference in 1982, when banks demand reserves to fund immediate settlement needs, "there is no question but that the reserves have to be provided . . . This, in fact, is *exactly* the same position which every . . . Central Bank is in."[19] Most officials in the UK Treasury accepted this position or at least sufficiently feared the destabilizing effects of monetary base control to support the Bank's rejection of it. Just as impracticable, however, was a compromise reform according to which the central bank should let the price of reserves be determined by market forces alone.[20] As the chief money-market manager remarked, "[O]perations [continue] to require official decisions on the rates at which bills are to be bought"; and "[e]very change in official dealing rates appears, to the market, to be a signal."[21] In light of these impracticable proposals and ill-fated reforms, the money-market managers at the Bank of England were left with the dilemma of how to reconcile the government's imperative of money-supply control with the explosion of funding liquidity in increasingly liberalized markets. When push came to shove, the officials had little choice but to monetize broader market liquidity with central bank reserves. As one member of the Bank's Money Market Division internally remarked in the early 1980s with some frustration: "What is clear at present is that the banks have us dancing to their tune. Despite assurances which they may have given about restraint on personal lending, they have no incentive to do so . . . Thus, on each occasion that a bank treasurer foresees a money shortage for his bank, his remotest thought is to seek ways of reducing lending; rather, he starts bidding for liquidity, while keeping an expectant eye on the news tape for our next package of assistance."[22]

Equally problematic for the Bank was that the abandonment of the reserve asset ratio in 1980 posed an existential threat to the discount houses, which were supposed to continue serving as buffers between the central bank and other banks. With increasing economization of reserves and plenty of other short-term borrowing and lending options available, there was less and less reason for clearing banks to keep "call money" with the Houses. The only remaining motivation for maintaining these traditional wholesale accounts was that they counted toward the fulfillment of reserve obligations. With this incentive gone, the fear was that the discount houses would face a depletion of their funding. For a time, the Bank's money-market operators managed to provisionally forestall this scenario by negotiating an agreement with the clearing banks to keep some "call money" voluntarily with the discount houses, henceforth called "club money" (to emphasize its voluntary nature).

But despite these improvised solutions, the central bankers gradually came to realize that the underlying social and institutional foundations of their classical system had been irreparably shaken, rendering liquidity management via the bill market system increasingly ineffective and problematic (Michie 2004). As Paul Tucker, a money-market reformer of the 1990s and 2000s, articulates, "The denizens of the city are no longer well-defined, no longer homogenous. We can't run this as an Elinor Ostrom club, [which has internally] cultivated a common good."[23] For instance, with ample other options available for managing their liquidity, banks increasingly questioned the discount houses' reason for existing. The latter were now portrayed as central bank–dependent firms that lived in a "corner of the City of London [that] has retained a reputation of short working days, long lunches and imperviousness to change."[24] Another problem was that, confronted with an increasingly internationalized marketplace, the Bank had difficulty defining "good names" on commercial bills, to differentiate quality, and to establish what paper was self-liquidating and what paper could be deemed "speculative."[25] A complementary argument against continuing policy implementation via bills transactions was that there were insufficient volumes of Treasury or commercial bills. While the government had moved to more long-term financing, Basel capital rules made endorsements of private bill instruments unattractive, due to the capital requirements incurred through these acts. Moreover, most of the remaining bills were held by just one particular bank, NatWest. "And so if I did my open market operation at 12 o'clock, at five, and [NatWest] decided not to borrow from me because they got all the eligible collateral,"[26] the market was left short of liquidity as a result. This meant that, even though money-market managers had found ways to provisionally stabilize their routines after the liberalizations and disruptive reforms of the early 1980s, they increasingly recognized the need for a radical overhaul.[27]

By that moment, the Bank of England had already gone through the Big Bang reforms in the 1980s, remaking the gilt markets and redefining its own role within them (see Chapter 3). These reforms marked a departure from the "traditional approach [of] institutional specialization" and toward recognizing the dominant role of international "financial conglomerates" operating across different "functions," as observed in internal Bank discussions.[28] Moreover, with its policy innovations after the United Kingdom's exit from the ERM, the central bankers had found ways to capitalize on these altered market structures, which rendered interest rates more sensitive to policy moves. What was now needed was a more effective pass-through of Bank interventions to these liberalized capital markets. Following this rationale, the Bank started to engage in money-market reforms during the early 1990s, based on the rationale of strengthening the involvement of international firms and dismantling the barriers that had defined the previous, cartelized system. The markets singled out for this purpose were those for repurchase agreements. Repo was emerging at the time as the "modern way of trading secured money," as Ian Plenderleith, the key official involved in the project, recounts.[29] Repo promised to provide a market infrastructure, in which funding liquidity could be distributed among a large number of market participants without massively expanding counterparty risk, due to the provision of collateral.[30] For the central bank, repo markets had the additional advantage that interest-rate changes quickly translated into rate changes in asset markets, because of the coupling of these markets through collateral. Central bank officials thus went around the City of London persuading firms to set up and join this market. Plenderleith remembers conducting "dozens of interviews with people in the market explaining them, you know, 'should we be thinking about having a government bond repo market like they do in the United States?'"[31]

So the Bank went on to encourage banks to start borrowing and lending via repo. Then it helped to set up a repo gilt market in 1996 (that is, a market in repos with gilts as collateral) (figure 4.2). Next, in 1997, it moved to implement its own market management via gilt repos, and as part of this final step, it started dealing directly with repo-market participants, not just with discount houses or domestic banks. In the event, the Bank, just like the Fed, experienced that linking its operations to the core liquidity management practices of banks and shadow banks made policy transmission

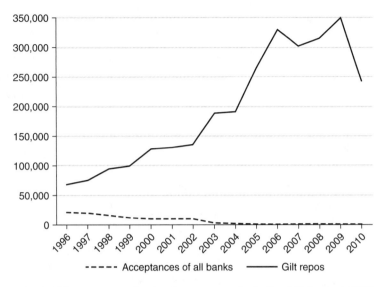

FIGURE 4.2. Gilt repos versus bankers' acceptances (including bill finance) (GBP million). *Data source:* Bank of England

faster and more effective. Combined with inflation forecasting, policy implementation via repo transactions became a consistent part of inflation targeting as a powerful way to govern the economy.

How Money-Market Innovations Unmade Monetarism

What thus becomes apparent from the UK case is that policy techniques evolved with market innovations, pushing central bankers toward inflation targeting as a viable strategy to improve the efficacy of their policy tools in increasingly integrated, deregulated markets. In response to their understanding of how to practice price signaling in such a context, central bankers then came to support the construction of money markets that appeared useful for such practice. In the case of the Bank of England, this is particularly evident in the context of development of the British repo gilt market. The Fed had played a similarly instructive role toward American repos since the early 1980s, a market that came to connect different components of a previously fragmented system. But while the Fed and the Bank of England had decided, by the early 1990s, that they wanted to foster market-based finance to help the sector *and* themselves, the situation looked different for central bankers in Germany and Switzerland. As I will discuss in this section, the comparable durability of practical monetarism in these countries resulted from different settlements between central banks and universal banking sectors that shielded public and private actors from the kinds of innovations that we observe in Anglo-Saxon finance. Over the course of the 1990s, however, these settlements came under threat through political and market-internal forces. This finally brought an end to practical monetarism and initiated the adoption of inflation targeting.

In the Swiss case, the distinct settlements between the SNB and private banks in the monetarist period rested on two pillars. First, public and private actors inhibited the development of a domestic money market. Corporations and public entities satisfied their funding needs with long-term instruments, relying strongly on bank loans. The banks themselves used retail deposits (savings and checking accounts) for their own funding needs.[32] This also meant that the practice of active liability management was virtually absent in domestic banking; most banks kept large volumes of surplus liquidity with the central bank and used interbank markets only for short-term settlement needs. These domestic structures were complemented, rather than undermined, by Swiss banks' engagements in Eurodollar markets, where they initially acted as creditors to invest surplus liquidity in higher yielding instruments (Loepfe 2011). When in the 1980s discussions came up about the possible establishment of a domestic money market, the joint interests of public and private actors were directed against this project.[33] Banks spoke out against establishing such a market because they aimed to maintain their oligopolistic control over domestic savings and corporate financing.[34] Likewise, within the central bank, doubts predominated because introducing alternative instruments for managing liquidity risked rendering the fluctuations in central bank reserves less predictable. For the same reason, the SNB had banned Swiss franc CDs.

A second pillar comprised reserve requirements. For the SNB, the function of these requirements lay in cushioning banks' volatile liquidity needs. Because a central bank must provide reserves when banks need them urgently to meet their payment obligations, larger reserves, which can be drawn down temporarily for settlement purposes (for example, because requirements are averaged), reduce such inelastic demand (Fullwiler 2017).

Accordingly, large reserves helped the SNB to conduct its monetarist central banking; demand-driven injections of additional reserves were needed less frequently. The downside was, of course, that large non-interest-bearing reserves constituted a cost for banks. But banks were willing to accept this aspect of the settlement because having large reserves was seen as prudent liquidity management and posed no material risk to banks' business models as long as competitive pressures from nonbanks were subdued.

The German settlement was very similar to the Swiss. The German economy and state equally relied on long-term financing. Short-term paper, such as commercial or Treasury bills, hardly existed at all; secondary trading in such paper was virtually unknown.[35] Through its regional banks, the Bundesbank had established "bilateral refinancing relationships" with hundreds of smaller and larger banks, which were complemented by an interbank market "before the Bundesbank's doors" (Häusler 1994: 256). In the 1950s and early 1960s, the Bundesbank had used its bilateral channels to exercise an informal version of industrial policy, refinancing bank credits that served "exports, small and medium-sized firms, and trade between the Federal Republic of Germany and the German Democratic Republic" on favorable terms.[36] From the late 1960s onward, the Bundesbank then increasingly moved to implement policy via repurchase agreements that were collateralized by long-term securities. However, other than in the United States, these operations did not rely on, or were supposed to foster, the development of a broader private repo market. Repo was an instrument to collateralize only short-term central bank lending, and German banks did not find much use in expanding these transactions between themselves. A principal reason for this was that counterparty risks were managed through relational ties rather than collateral. Just as in Switzerland, the banks had their own reasons for upholding these routines and suppressing financial innovation, primarily because they profited from the role as sole providers of savings products and corporate financing (Zysman 1983). Upon visiting Germany, a Bank of England official commented somewhat disdainfully that "[t]he banks find the present cosy relationship amongst themselves and with the authorities very congenial. In turn, the Bundesbank sees no reason to stir up a situation which is relatively easy to control."[37]

But these German and Swiss settlements came under pressure over the course of the 1990s, as opposition to extant restrictions mounted. Ironically, one key protagonist of change was the German government, which

TABLE 4.1 Reserve Deposits Held at Central Banks as a Share of Total Bank Liabilities*

Year	United States	Germany	Switzerland	United Kingdom
1980	1.6	7.2	4	0.3**
1985	0.8	5.6	3.1	0.1
1988	1	5.5	1.7	0.1
1991	0.6	5.5	0.7	0.1

*Annual average of end-month observations, in percentages.
**United Kingdom 1980: Figure is for year-end 1981 instead of year-end 1980.
Data source: Kasman (1993: 49).

wanted to expand Germany's financial sector and engage in global competition for the respective firms, market segments, and jobs (Zimmermann 2012). The Bundesbank tried to use its authority to slow this process. As Bundesbank official Gerd Häusler explained, "[T]he central bank, mindful of its responsibility for monetary policy, must give priority to monetary stability and to protecting the minimum reserve instrument over promoting national financial market interests, even if Germany is something of an outsider in this respect" (1994: 258). The central bankers' intention was thus to resist reforms by juxtaposing competitive interests with its stability mandate.[38] In concrete terms, this meant to oppose demands for the introduction of new money-market instruments and vehicles, such as CDs, commercial paper, or money-market funds.[39] It also meant protecting as far and as long as possible the Bundesbank's fairly comprehensive and onerous minimum reserve requirements that raised the costs of money-market intermediation and active liability management.

But this Bundesbank opposition, and equivalent positions adopted by the Swiss National Bank, became increasingly untenable as the 1990s progressed. The reason was that, in addition to political interests in strengthening financial markets, banks themselves abandoned the monetarist settlement that they had previously endorsed (Deeg 1999; Mazbouri, Guex, and Lopez 2012). Partly as a result of disintermediation in corporate financing, partly as a result of incumbents' adoption of transnational business strategies (UBS, Credit Suisse, Deutsche Bank, and Dresdner Bank), the banks became averse to reserve obligations. Rapid growth in Euro markets also meant that the previous separations between domestic and international money and credit markets became difficult to maintain. Beck writes that, as large banks aggressively attempted to enter US dollar (offshore and onshore) markets, "[T]he logics of US money market funding crept across those institutions . . . In the process of building links with US money markets, European banks first changed the way they raised their liabilities and, subsequently, how they constructed and managed their asset side" (2021: 13–14). As an economist had already noted in the 1980s, these developments gradually undermined the practice of German monetarism: "the money and credit creating potential of the Euro-market seems . . . to distort increasingly the information content of conventional monetary expansion statistics, which are based on domestic figures only. Therefore, there is a danger that the indicator function of the [domestic] monetary target (central bank money stock) and of other domestic monetary and credit aggregates deteriorates" (Gebauer 1983: 23–24). Additional pressure to dismantle domestic financial regulations came from European attempts to enforce monetary and market integration.

Swiss and German central bankers thus reluctantly gave in to these pressures. In both countries, reserve requirements were lowered and new instruments allowed for trading in domestic markets.[40] But with lower and consequently more volatile reserve holdings and growing use of new instruments, the relationships between different monetary quantities, between quantities and interest rates, and between quantities and inflation rates, became less and less predictable (Filc 1994; Rich 2007). Moreover, as large banks' operations integrated domestic with foreign markets, international money-market shocks and crises translated rapidly into volatile reserve behavior at home. In order to manage these crises, the monetary authorities not only temporarily suspended monetary targets, but also visibly intervened in order to stabilize short-term interest rates.

These experiences gave impetus to the transition from practical monetarism to inflation targeting in continental Europe during the late 1990s, at a point at which this strategy had already gained recognition among international experts as a more effective way of practicing monetary policy (Bernanke and Mishkin 1997). In Switzerland, throughout the 1990s, with monetarism losing its operative functionality due to financial market developments, its symbolic power became exhausted. Orthodox monetarists recognized that the SNB had considerably diverged from its own control promises (Albertini 1994), while trade unions grew increasingly frustrated about the SNB's rejection of the kind of modern economic stabilization policies that became possible with an activist steering of interest rates. These developments gave the impetus for a radical overhaul, leading the Swiss to adopt inflation targeting in 1999. The key components of the new strategy came to resemble those identified for the Anglo-Saxon countries (a primary mandate for monetary stability combined with output stabilization; implementation via price signals toward internationally connected money markets; transmission via financial market mechanisms), while corporatist institutions were embedded in the new inflation-targeting regime. In the case of the Bundesbank, the parallel transition to inflation targeting was tied up with European monetary integration. As many authors have argued, this process was dominated by the Bundesbank, which served as a role model for other central banks as well as the future European Central Bank (ECB). A key organizational vehicle, in this process, was the Committee of Central Bank Governors at the BIS in Basel, where European central bankers developed plans for the new central bank. Kathleen McNamara quotes a central banker on this committee, who stated in 1993 that "[t]he atmosphere in the Committee of Central Bank Governors is very professional; people do not come to meetings with distinctive national positions, but instead we all share a very common agreement on the correctness of a monetary policy model very close to that of Germany" (1998, 167). McNamara's account, and the general idea of the ECB following the Bundesbank template, overlooks, however, that by the late 1990s, the monetarist underpinning of German *Stabilitätskultur* had lost its practical and symbolic efficacy. Indeed, in the very committee preparing the ECB, discussions during the latter half of the 1990s turned to an assessment of monetarism's growing dysfunctions and the question of what could replace it. The growing integration of financial markets, particularly international money markets, was a key reason of why practical monetarism had stopped working and why it was advisable to turn to inflation targeting.[41]

A Global Market-Building Project

Financial globalization had undermined the postwar settlements between commercial and central banks in the United States and the United Kingdom already during the 1970s. By the 1990s, the central bankers in these countries had identified a new settlement based on synergies between inflation targeting and market-based finance. Because of the success of monetary targeting and the advantages of protected domestic markets for universal banks, we find that different settlements persisted in Germany and Switzerland until the 1990s; inhibition of money market-innovations, protection of reserve requirements, and shields that separated domestic from international markets were essential ingredients of the particular central bank–universal banking settlements that we find in these parts of continental Europe. However, banks began questioning and undermining these settlements in the 1990s, forcing monetary authorities to adopt monetary policy innovations from the United States and the United Kingdom as more viable strategies in the deregulated contexts in which they found themselves.

With this last opposition gone, from the late 1990s onward, central bankers in the G10 joined a common project of consolidating a liquidity system based on integrated markets (Gabor 2016). Central bankers' efforts particularly concentrated on developing and strengthening repo markets, which were singled out as effective conduits for monetary policies and as resilient, stabilizing elements in such a market-based system. Unsurprisingly, given the origins of this market segment, the push for repo initially came from the United States. After its 1982 advocacy of legal carve-outs, the Fed had emerged as a consistent supporter and builder of ever larger repo markets. In 1991, Congress had authorized the Fed upon its request to engage directly in repo operations with nonbanks (Ricks 2016: 197); in 1999, the Fed had started transacting in repos secured by mortgage-backed securities; and in 2005, Congress had responded to Fed demands to drop initial limitations on the kinds of repo contract to which legal carve-outs applied, encouraging a further expansion in repos undergirded by the fabrication of reputed safe assets within the financial sector (Gabor 2016: 982).

European central bankers joined the repo market-building project in the 1990s to early 2000s. As we have already seen in the British context, developing repo was regarded as a way to strengthen and formalize the linkage between central bank operations and market trading in liquidity. Repo also resolved operational problems for central bankers in small countries such as Switzerland because the SNB could now develop meaningful open-market trading by lending short-term funds secured by collateral that was not just issued domestically, but also in large currency blocks (US dollars; euros).[42] Accordingly, with all leading central banks converging to inflation targeting, there was strong support for developing repo into the core money-market segment that transmitted interest rates in the overnight interbank markets into financially more significant financing costs for the rest of the system. Reflecting this shift, a G20 report on repo argued that the instrument provided "an effective mechanism for signaling the stance of monetary policy"; "in a market with ample liquidity, price determination will be more efficient . . . for monetary policy."[43] These increasingly consensual views expressed the core motivation for central bankers to build institutional scaffolds for these markets and support their growth.

A complementary motivation for promoting repo resulted from the financial crisis experiences of the time (East Asian crisis; Russia's default; collapse of the investment firm Long-Term Capital Management [LTCM]; dotcom bubble; 9 / 11), which raised the question of how interconnected financial systems could be made resilient. The key solution offered in this period, and particularly promoted by the Fed, was that financial systems needed "sound and efficient repo markets" (Birk 2017: 45) in order to ensure efficient distribution and free access to funding liquidity, even under adverse circumstances. The goal was thus to encourage the development of a "stable system of liquidity" (ibid.: 7), whose constituent elements were market-making broker-dealers, freely circulating "safe" assets, central bank emergency backstops, and new tools of liquidity risk assessment. As a G20 central banker report during the late 1990s argued, repo brought "low credit risk while serving as a flexible instrument for liquidity management."[44] The perceived reason for reduced credit risk lay in firms' control over collateral, which, however, required frameworks in which such control was granted through private governance mechanisms and public law. Accordingly, as a working group led by the New York Fed concluded after the LTCM collapse, financial firms should reduce counterparty risk by ensuring that "close-out arrangements using commercially reasonable valuations can be carried out in a practical and time critical fashion during periods of market distress, with a high degree of legal certainty."[45] Such legal certainty was introduced in the European context through the Settlement Finality Directive (1998) and the Financial Collateral Arrangements Directive (2002), which demanded that member countries ensure "that certain provisions of insolvency law do not apply to [repo contract, LW] arrangements, in particular, those that would inhibit the effective realisation of financial collateral or cast doubt on the validity of current techniques such as bilateral close-out netting, the provision of additional collateral in the form of top-up collateral and substitution of collateral."[46] As I will discuss in Chapter 5, central bankers' promotion of such publicly consecrated private governance solutions against financial instabilities allowed these authorities to avoid any engagement with explicit *public* regulation, a step that they avoided because it would have endangered the newly found settlement between monetary policy prerequisites and the dominant financial interests in a market-based system.

While it is difficult to establish causality here, the evidence suggests that central banks' interventions in support of repo markets contributed to the dramatic expansion of trading in these instruments from the late 1990s onward (figure 4.3). In the United States, the volume of outstanding repo contracts grew from $833 billion in 1990 to $4.5 *trillion* ($4,498 billion) in 2007 (Roe 2011). In the European context, the rise was even more dramatic. These markets had been virtually nonexistent in most European countries for the best part of the 1990s. In the United Kingdom and France, before central bankers' engagement in market building, trading had been small

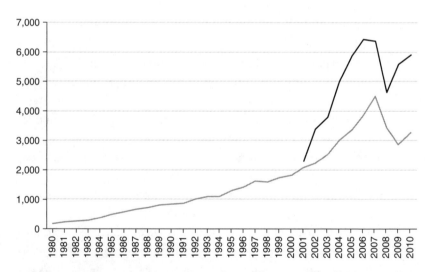

FIGURE 4.3. Volumes of outstanding repo transactions in the United States (in billion dollars: gray) and Europe (in billion euros: black). *Data sources:* Board of Governors of the Federal Reserve, Washington, DC (for US), and International Securities Market Association (ISMA) repo surveys (for Europe)

and informal, consisting of "word-of-mouth [communications, LW] . . . followed by telex confirmation" in small circles of mutually known traders.[47] But formal institution-building changed that, contributing to the expansion of repo markets from an estimated gross volume of outstanding contracts of 2.1 trillion euros in 2001, to 6.8 trillion euros in 2007.[48]

Discussion

Since the disappearance of the last monetary targeters in the late 1990s, "there [has been] little debate, at least among central bankers, [about] what a central bank decision on monetary policy means: it means to set the level of short-term money market interest rate that the central bank aims at in its day-to-day operations during the period until the next meeting of the central bank's decision-making body" (Bindseil 2004b: 7). We find evidence for this consensus in the task descriptions for operations officers at all leading central banks (Jobst and Ugolini 2016: 145). For instance, as Paul Tucker of the Bank of England stated in 2004, the mission of the Bank's officers was "to stabilize short-term rates at the policy rate."[49] Until the arrival of quantitative easing, system managers at the Fed (Mehrling 2011: 7) or ECB (Braun 2018a) would have given the same answer.

The dominant framework within which these choices are discussed is that of technical optimization—independently of context, it is just the most efficient way to practice monetary policy via price signals vis-à-vis a market-based financial system. My own account emphasizes the recursive causalities between financial market developments and central banking innovations, which gave rise to these particular views on policy efficacy and produced a particular settlement between financial and policy interests before the crisis of 2008. Going back to the 1970s, we actually find diverse settlements—different versions of central banking that went hand in hand with different financial market structures. For instance, in the United Kingdom, there was no all-encompassing, integrated market system. Instead, business practices, institutional statuses, and prudential regulations were carefully differentiated according to segmented and cartelized groups of firms. As part of these arrangements, only certain institutions, the discount houses, had access to the Bank of England's lending of last resort.

Money-market transactions remained restricted to prime bank bills—instruments with multiple creditors—which separated short-term funding for financial firms from capital investments. The British system up until the 1970s also featured a central bank that simultaneously steered market rates, regulated credit, and cultivated sound banking practices. For the operations officers running this system, it would have been absurd to suggest that their actions served solely to align market with policy rates. Whether as a matter of explicit regulatory interventions or latent effects of institutional arrangements, British banking was remarkably stable under the classical system, from the late nineteenth century until the 1970s (Hotson 2017; Turner 2014).

Another contrast can be drawn between contemporary orders and the universal banking structures that we find in countries in which central banks successfully practiced monetary targeting. In these settings, deposit liabilities were inert and there was little competition for retail savings. Accordingly, banks did *not* actively manage liabilities by bidding for funds on broader money markets. In fact, such markets existed only in very small, highly contained form. The main focus for the incumbents was to maintain margins between lending and refinancing conditions and sufficiently suppress competition in order to ensure customer loyalty. This implied specific interactions between banks and central banks. Money markets remained restricted and most banks maintained relatively large buffers of reserves directly with central banks. Even in these settings, just as in inflation targeting, central banks influenced the price of reserves. But the central banks' interest-rate leadership had a fundamentally different meaning compared to the contemporary "short interest rate doctrine" (Bindseil 2004b). The idea was not to give price signals to broader money and capital markets in order to align the policy rate with some macroeconomically calculated natural rate. Instead, by manipulating the fluctuations of banks' reserves, and by exerting direct influence over counterparties, central banks exploited relatively stable structural relationships between bank liabilities, funding costs, and credit issuance, thereby stabilizing (rather than narrowly controlling) the secular trend growth of monetary aggregates. Financial stability was a benign side effect of these monetary policies.

The British classical system and European continental monetarism thus offer some insight into alternative state–market settlements that defy the idea of neutral monetary policy implementation, which is optimal, irrespective of context. They also show how monetary policy was integrated with (implicit) financial regulation (see Chapter 5). More importantly, however, this chapter has shown that the kind of monetary policy that became dominant in the 1990s and 2000s is a product of recursive causalities, which were trigged by the reemergence of "prolific" finance. The development of Eurodollar markets and the introduction of new money-market instruments, which undermined postwar regulations, gave rise to a period of crisis and experimentation. In this period, the central bankers most affected by financial globalization discovered that, rather than disempowering their organizations, private-sector developments actually *enhanced* their governing powers. The primary reason was that market integration and arbitrage activities made market interest rates more sensitive to changes in central bank refinancing rates. The more economic actors were affected by, and thus responsive to, the movements in policy rates, the more leverage central bankers found they had. In contrast to what they had thought in the turbulent 1970s, central bankers thus emerged as the winners of financial globalization. The American experience, itself a result of the fragmented nature of its particularly large financial sector, was the example that others would follow.

This then gave rise to a phase of consolidation, in which inflation targeters from around the globe acted as architects of what they considered to be efficient and resilient infrastructures of market-based finance. Repo was chosen as the core segment for pricing and distributing liquidity in these broader infrastructures because it offered new operational possibilities and promised effective "pass-through" of interest-rate decisions. The Fed was the first central bank to actively support repo, due to its traditional reliance on securities dealers in transmitting price signals and shifting liquidity beyond the federal funds market. The existence of Eurodollar markets in London made the Bank of England a likely next promoter, but this required that the UK central bank shun a century-old system of compartmentalized and highly regulated finance. The continental Europeans, particularly the Germans and Swiss, were the last to join the repo project, for reasons associated with the success of monetary targeting and the traditions of universal banking. But by the late 1990s, we can identify a unified group of monetary authorities that collectively promoted legal changes and adjusted their own operational frameworks to facilitate repo's growth.

The consequences of this growth and of the political-economic settlement that underlies it were painfully felt in 2007–2009. Because the access to and costs of borrowing via repo depend on the value of collateral, devaluations of and uncertainties about whole asset classes (mortgage-backed securities) led to sudden spikes in haircuts and refusals to lend (Gorton and Metrick 2012). A whole (shadow) banking model, comprising the fabrication of seemingly "safe" assets through securitization and their cheap funding via repo markets, broke down; and a regime based on the belief that markets allow efficient sale and purchase of assets and provide unlimited funds for their financing suddenly collapsed (Sissoko 2019). During the crisis, repo functioned as an amplifier of self-reinforcing downward spirals rather than the system's resilient core (Brunnermeier and Pedersen 2009).

On the back of the story presented in this chapter, one realizes that central bankers were deeply implicated in this crisis. But as I discuss next, the institutional separation of monetary policy from prudential regulation created a protective shield for monetary authorities so that they could avoid assuming responsibility for the side effects and adverse consequences of the settlement that they had coproduced.

CHAPTER FIVE

The Organization of Ignorance

How Central Bankers Abandoned Regulation

> It was the cognitive denial of the links between monetary policy, LOLR
> policy and banking system stability that helped lead the world to the
> crisis from which it is still recovering.
>
> —TUCKER 2014: 36

IN MANY WAYS, the years preceding the World Financial Crisis were a
golden age for central bankers. Through the development and spread of
inflation targeting, they had effectively claimed control over inflation and
simultaneously found ways to become more active in macroeconomic stabilization (Goodhart 2011b: 145), enhancing their purchase over economic
policy. The success of inflation targeting, in the eyes of policymakers, was
reflected in long-term interest rates, which confirmed the authorities' capacities in anchoring inflationary expectations in target ranges. Money
markets such as repo were thoroughly institutionalized and enabled highly
reliable and effective policy implementation under conditions of deepening financial globalization. By comparison, other economic policy areas
appeared—or were regarded—in a less favorable light. In particular, fiscal
policy appeared to be a tedious politicized process (Wildavsky and Caiden
1992) without much macroeconomic leverage and facing serious constraints
from globalization (Cusack 1999; Swank 2016).

It was in this broader context that inflation targeting suddenly appeared
to be more than just a particular strategy for reining in the monetary

problems that had plagued Western societies during the 1970s and 1980s. Maybe, as Bernanke and others (Stock and Watson 2003) mused, price- and output-stabilizing central banking, together with some positive private-sector developments, had given rise to an era of "Great Moderation."[1] For as long as prices remained predictably stable, and fiscal policy stayed out of the way (Leeper 2010), the key cause of macroeconomic frictions had allegedly been removed, and markets could work their magic to equilibrate demand and supply, only occasionally requiring a nudge from monetary policy (Goodfriend 2007). As Claudio Borio noted, these discussions gave rise to the proposition, if not belief, that should "central banks succeed in stabilizing inflation in the short term (say, over a 2-year horizon), and absent major exogenous 'shocks' such as from fiscal policy, the economy will broadly take care of itself" (2011: 2).

The events of 2007–2009 and the subsequent Great Recession offered a dramatic falsification of these views. Successfully "anchoring" inflationary expectations, ironing out small output fluctuations, and occasionally propping up markets with the various tools of central banking was *not* a recipe for sustainable prosperity, as this crisis laid bare. In fact, the events in 2007–2009 revealed the severe imbalances and systemic risks that had built up from the 1980s to the 2000s. They included rising socioeconomic inequalities and (associated with this) secular stagnation. For all the acclaimed stabilization achieved by central bankers, the growth rates in the decades of monetary policy dominance actually turned out to be lower than those observed before 1980, and in the most advanced economy, the United States, the bottom 50 percent of the income distribution experienced virtually no economic improvements during the period. Meanwhile, the share of income going to the top 1 percent grew sizably, from just over 10 percent of overall income to almost 20 percent (Saez and Zucman 2019). Wealth inequalities grew in tandem: The top 10 percent increased its share from around 65 percent to over 70 percent of net wealth from 1970 to 2007. Admittedly, the United States is an extreme case, but the other countries discussed in this book have followed the same trend. Based on these (only retrospectively acknowledged) facts, International Monetary Fund (IMF) experts noted that "the period [termed the "Great Moderation," LW] was only great for a small portion of the population" (cited in Clift 2018: 114). Besides violating norms of equity central to the functioning of democracies (Rosanvallon 2013), growing inequalities in wealth and income also brought macroeconomic problems (discussed as secular stagnation—see Chapter 6) and raised the likelihood of financial crises, via growing demand for financial investments (among the rich) and debt (among the middle classes and the poor).[2] The crisis of 2007–2009 was thus not an accident of history, but a symptom of deeper dislocations in Western capitalism. And the policy institutions that had embraced and exerted considerable influence over these developments were central banks.

More immediately, however, central bankers failed to address the growing financial instabilities that built up in the period before 2007 (Allen 2013; Schularick and Taylor 2012). Systemic financial risks increased as credit growth accelerated from the 1980s onward, a growth that was decoupled from productive investment activity and deepened dependencies on ever-appreciating asset values. Transformations *within* finance played an instrumental role in enabling such credit expansion and simultaneously increased the vulnerability of market participants to any reversal in the interdependent, upward movement of credit volumes and asset prices. Authors have discussed these sector-related changes primarily with a focus on securitization and the development of subprime mortgages, but a crucial other part of the story concerns the ways in which financial firms came to fund their expanding balance sheets. In particular, the invention of active liability management in the 1960s (Konings 2011) and the rapid expansion of shadow banking from the 1980s (Thiemann 2018) made banks and other financial market participants ever more reliant on the availability of funding on wholesale money markets, as discussed in Chapter 4 (Hardie et al. 2013; Hardie and Maxfield 2013). In the years before the crisis (2000–2007), the proportion of total assets that investment banks financed with overnight repos doubled (Roe 2011: 552). At the same time, the share of deposit liabilities as a percentage of overall banking-sector liabilities fell, from about 80 percent in the immediate period after the Second World War to little more than 50 percent by the early 2000s (Jordà et al. 2017: 10). Holdings of crisis-tested liquid assets, such as government bonds, were reduced. In the United States, the growth of shadow banking was a driving force behind these transformations, while European "traditional" banks adopted active liability management, securitization, and US-style investment banking from the 1990s onward (Beck 2021). These changes made the tight transatlantic financial network ripe for the kind of (shadow) banking run that happened in 2007–2009 (Tooze 2018). The dislocations and hardships that resulted from these events have been widely discussed. Not only were billions of taxpayer money invested to contain domino effects within finance, but whole economies were taken hostage. The crash's immediate consequences were credit crunches, destruction of wealth, and pressures to deleverage (Schularick and Taylor 2012; Taylor 2015). More than ten years later, when the Covid-19 crisis hit, Western populations were still living with the consequences of this fallout. The forces of secular stagnation had become more deeply entrenched through the crisis, apparent in low productivity growth, growing inequality, and deflationary forces (see Chapter 6); and the government failures associated with the crisis have changed politics in fundamental ways.

What went wrong? There exist two lines of critique of central banking in light of 2007–2009. A first discussion takes up monetary policies and their implications for financialization. For instance, some scholars suggest that, with inflation targeting, monetary policies were constructed so as to "black-box" and depoliticize credit (Krippner 2011). Central bankers' targets, the respective indices for consumer prices, dissociated central banks' decision-making from significant developments in the monetary and financial spheres. This was politically convenient for central bankers because broader structural and political forces (weakness of labor's bargaining power; cheap imports from China) inhibited consumer price inflation while reinforcing financial expansion. But it also meant that policies became unresponsive to the build-up of systemic risks—a condition that was most apparent in the run-up to the 2008 crash, when evidence of a sudden downturn in housing markets failed to induce any significant policy change (Abolafia 2020; Fligstein, Brundage, and Schultz 2017). A related, more radical critique of inflation targeting holds that, through this approach, central banks actively *supported* financial expansion via macroeconomic and financial mechanisms. For instance, deflationary policies contributed to income losses for lower and middle-income workers, who in turn used credit to compensate for these losses—over time accumulating unsustainable debt. Moreover, central bank interventions in response to drops in asset values encouraged investors to assume larger and more risky positions. In the previous chapters, I have also pointed to some subtler mechanisms. Because central bankers increasingly saw stability expectations in financial markets as a reflection of their own credibility, they encouraged the formation of such expectations and thereby created a veritable *stability illusion.* This illusion had concrete consequences because it fostered a context in which financial firms could engage in ever more aggressive term transformation and adopted strategies to exploit even the smallest interest-rate differentials on markets (Adrian and Liang 2016; Adrian and Shin 2008; Borio and Zhu 2012; Walter and Wansleben 2019). Moreover, central bankers fostered the growth of market segments that helped policy-rate signals to travel more quickly through the financial system. These were the very segments, however, that became super-spreaders for financial risks during the crisis of 2008.

In this chapter, I concentrate on another discussion, which concerns central bankers' role in *regulation*—purposeful actions to maintain financial stability.[3] To be sure, in most jurisdictions, at the moment of crisis, central bankers were not the primary authorities responsible for this task. This had often been delegated to agencies with explicit mandates to issue statutory rules and conduct supervision (Goodhart and Schoenmaker 1992). In consequence, most criticism of precrisis regulation has been leveled against regulatory agencies. For instance, scholars argue that supervisory officials "excessively focused on seeking to improve the behavior and risk management practices of individual banks" (Brunnermeier et al. 2009: 6). In other words, financial regulation remained "micro-prudential," providing no answer to what are now understood as "cross-sectional" or "cyclical" systemic risks (Thiemann, Melches, and Ibrocevic 2021). Moreover, scholars have criticized the fact that the agencies' work focused only on registered domestic banks and thus was ineffective in addressing the growth of shadow banking and offshore markets (Thiemann 2014; Thiemann 2018; Thiemann and Lepoutre 2017). Deterioration in credit issuance standards was neglected, partly because supervisors readily believed financial sector statements that only "a few bad apples" were responsible for wrongdoing (Kwak 2014). Lastly, a point of criticism directed toward regulatory agencies is that the metrics used in supervisory examinations were constructed by the banks themselves, calibrated to frequent and minor losses rather than the kinds of scenarios that became a reality in 2007–2009. Agencies were unable, or unwilling, to challenge such benign risk assessments.

But making agencies solely responsible for regulatory failure is to neglect the crucial regulatory role of central banks. In some jurisdictions, these responsibilities are explicit and fairly comprehensive, as *was* the case in the United Kingdom (until 1997) and is still true for the United States.

In most other jurisdictions, agencies had been newly founded in the 1980s and 1990s or upgraded to conduct regulation and supervision in the context of the so-called Basel agreements—international minimum requirements on capital holdings negotiated in the Basel Committee on Banking Supervision (BCBS) (Goodhart and Schoenmaker 1992).

As I aim to show in this chapter, in neither of these settings should we exculpate central banks. There are two arguments for this. The first is informed by a historical institutionalist lens (Thelen 1999). Before the 1970s, central banks usually practiced prudential oversight as part and parcel of their other policy conduct, be it debt management or monetary policy. Even where separate supervisory agencies existed (often established during the 1930s), central bankers usually had more purchase over banks' practices than the formally assigned supervisors. When financial regulation moved to the center of attention during the 1980s and was increasingly articulated as a distinct task (Masciandaro and Quintyn 2013), monetary authorities failed to use their weight to make sure that the previously informal aspects of regulation were comprehensively translated into the new, increasingly formalized frameworks. Even when central bankers saw that these frameworks failed to address key aspects of banking that had been at the heart of their own regulatory activities, they failed to address this gap. Instead, they adopted what Diane Vaughan (1996) has called "structural secrecy."

The second argument for attributing responsibility to central bankers for regulatory failures is that these gaps in formalized regulatory regimes emerged precisely in those areas in which central banks possess exclusive expertise and competences (Goodhart 1988; Goodhart 2011b). These are the domains of banking liquidity and money markets—how commercial banks manage their liabilities and how markets for short-term funding work (see Chapter 4). In a detailed historical analysis, Charles Goodhart (2011a) shows how supervisory authorities proved unable to include these aspects in the Basel frameworks—even though risks associated with banks' liquidity and money markets had initially been on the agenda (see also Braun, Krampf, and Murau 2021). But, as Goodhart shows, besides resistance from some powerful committee members, the inclusion of liquidity regulation in the Basel frameworks failed because, after an agreement on capital adequacy rules had been reached, policymakers became complacent; relatively detailed plans on international liquidity rules were not seriously considered.[4] I see this failure, and / or the absence of any significant domestic rules (Bonner and Hilbers 2015), as at least partly a responsibility of central bankers because, as ultimate liquidity managers of financial systems, these authorities have the expertise, means of influence, and sometimes even the statutory powers to introduce or support prudential liquidity regulation. That is because central bankers inevitably have influence over who obtains access to reserve facilities, how scarce liquidity is, and which assets are singled out as acceptable collateral for central bank lending. Moreover, by engaging in liquidity management operations on a daily basis, central bankers acquire firsthand knowledge of banks' liquidity positions and market conditions. Finally, during financial crises, these authorities assume the role of regulators as an unavoidable dimension of their lending of last resort. Emergency lending always entails decisions on the firms that do or do not deserve rescue funding and the assets that should or should not be protected from market failure. The problem is that central bankers failed to act on their expertise and influence, or lenders of last resort competences, to enforce or support prudential rules. Instead, during the 1990s and 2000s, they converged toward what has been called the "Greenspan doctrine" (Golub, Kaya, and Reay 2015). It consisted of refraining from regulation but engaging in comprehensive and "liberal" lending, as well as market support in response to crises (Ricks 2016). In other words, central banks practiced an asymmetric financial policy, insuring financial firms against downturns, rather than stopping them on the upturn.

Why? Such complex historical processes never have single causes. Among the ensemble of crucial drivers, it was certainly crucial that decisions in the BCBS can be reached only unanimously; states voluntarily commit to Basel standards. In consequence, while some members (such as Germany) were in favor of reining in offshore markets and regulating liquidity, a minority of those states in which financial firms profited from offshoring and liability management (that is, the United States and the United Kingdom) could easily block any agreement (Oatley and Nabors 1998). States in which policymakers favored liquidity regulation then refrained from acting unilaterally in order to avoid competitive disadvantages. Moreover, some policymakers truly believed in efficient markets, the efficacy of private governance mechanisms (Riles 2011), and/or the welfare benefits derived from prolific finance (Kwak 2014).

Complementarily, in this chapter, I focus on another driving force. Starting in the 1970s, central bankers recognized that dissociating regulation from central banking and articulating monetary policy as a stand-alone policy jurisdiction brought several advantages for themselves. First, with apparent successes in reducing and stabilizing inflation, central bankers recognized that they could enhance their legitimacy by claiming exclusive "ownership" over price stability while shedding responsibility for regulation, which is "all too likely to tarnish the reputation of the supervisor" (Goodhart 2000: 20) and creates potential conflicts with banks. Hence, dissociating monetary from financial policy, even at the price of neglecting some issues at the heart of central banking, brought political advantages. But strategic dissociation also brought organizational benefits. By neglecting regulatory aspects, central bankers could streamline money-market operations for the purpose of implementing operational targets for short-term interest rates that corresponded to the macroeconomic views of senior decision-makers. This reduced organizational complexity considerably and made it possible to couple particular central bank operations with particular causal accounts of what monetary policy was about. In the same vein, successful strategic dissociation was a crucial barrier preventing central bankers from embracing their generic stability mandates during the 2000s, when the growing frequency of crises (Russian default; Long-Term Capital Management [LTCM]; dotcom) and new knowledge about systemic risks provided *prima facie* reasons for embracing these mandates (Thiemann, Melches, and Ibrocevic 2021). For instance, systemic financial stability policy was discussed in novel formats, such as the Financial Stability Forum or the Committee on the Global Financial System, and addressed with the issuance of new risk reports (Davies and Green 2010). However, because central bankers did not want to endanger their successful monetary policy role and practices, they failed to act upon the apparent problems and insights.

Drawing on my earlier comparison between monetarist versus inflation-targeting policies, I return to the cases of Switzerland and the United Kingdom in the subsequent two sections. The differences in institutional contexts and the distinct trajectories of policy experimentation are reflected in how these organizations dealt with regulatory issues, particularly in the domain of money markets. But we will also see that, identifying different opportunities for such maneuvers, monetary policy authorities in both countries practiced strategic dissociation because, at different points in their institutional histories, they were able to define a new le-

gitimate and powerful role in terms of inflation control. While monetarism had still entailed stronger *latent* elements of prudential financial
policy, these then disappeared entirely with the turn to inflation targeting. In consequence, during the 2000s, the Swiss and British central
banks followed very similar strategies to contribute to discussions on
systemic risks and macroprudential regulation without taking any substantive action. In the last section, I will extend my comparison, showing
that the fundamental insights gained from my comparison also hold for
other cases with different institutional setups, such as Germany and the
United States.

Switzerland: From Gentlemanly Regulation to Benign Neglect

For much of the twentieth century, there was no effective differentiation
between banking regulation and monetary policy, and formal institutional
mandates had little influence on how regulation was actually done. I discussed gentlemen's agreements negotiated between the Swiss National Bank
(SNB) and the Swiss bankers' lobby in Chapter 2 (figure 5.1). Dense elite
networks across banking, industry, and politics sustained this practice of
informal regulation in areas ranging from banking activities at home and
abroad, to measures for protecting the gold standard / dollar parity. The
Swiss National Bank together with the banking-sector representative, the

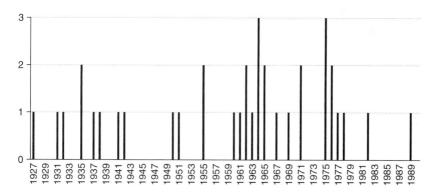

FIGURE 5.1. Annual count of gentlemen's agreements between the Swiss National
Bank and the Swiss Bankers' Association (the agreement in 1989 is the last one
recorded). *Data source:* Swiss National Bank

Swiss Bankers' Association, were the organizational carriers of such "gentlemanly regulation" because they provided the fora for elites to gather, cultivate an *esprit de corps,* and negotiate compromises.[5]

The banking law of 1934 had established a dedicated regulator, the Federal Banking Commission. But in many respects, this agency remained the weakest actor in the broader field of monetary and financial governance. This weakness was the agency's fate since its very foundation. The Swiss liberal and financial elite had established the agency for two complementary strategic reasons. On one hand, the government had bailed out a large Swiss banking institution (Schweizerische Volksbank), and a promise of stricter regulation was needed to calm public outrage on the part of farmers and the political Left about the use of public funds for rich bankers. The lawmakers chose to delegate the newly formalized regulation to a separate agency because the central bank had refused to take responsibility, arguing that it wanted to protect its confidential relationships with banks (Giddey 2012: 150). On the other hand, the act of establishing formal banking regulation allowed financial elites to codify Swiss banking secrecy as part of a larger legislative package. Such codification had become important for Swiss banks as a protective shield against tax investigators from neighboring countries (particularly France). These different motives brought forth a tokenistic regulator with weak supervisory competences and scarce resources.

This weakness persisted for much of the twentieth century. The Banking Commission's permanent personnel remained minimal. In 1942, almost ten years after its foundation, it counted only five employees, while the SNB had 392 (Giddey 2010: 150). This stark inequality remained in place for the entire period. Well into the 1970s, the regulator had no more than ten employees (including five secretaries) and a budget below one million Swiss francs (CHF). Its board members—"commissioners"—were part-time officials without relevant remuneration. Oftentimes, these commissioners were retired politicians, lawyers, or academics. In terms of supervision, the agency had hardly any competencies for sanctioning and rule enforcement (Mazbouri and Schaufelbuehl 2015). Its information was derived entirely from the annual reports of private auditing firms, which were often under the banks' control (ibid.: 60). The SNB refused to share banking data with the Federal Banking Commission (Giddey 2012: 152–53).

With weak formal institutions, banking regulation remained anchored in central bankers' and private bankers' informal exchange, consultations, and agreements.[6] This worked as long as reciprocal relations and common orientations to a shared national interest predominated among the Swiss elite. For instance, reciprocity implied that the SNB could elicit support for voluntary measures that helped the central bank to keep the fixed parity, protect its gold reserves, and stabilize domestic credit. In turn, the bankers demanded help in pursuing their domestic and international business interests. Engaging in reciprocity was a matter of defending a commonly understood national interest. Accordingly, the bankers presented themselves as "guardians of our national wealth," and the SNB proclaimed that it was a "question of *honor,* and at the same time solidarity, for each bank to do what is in the *general interest.*"[7] Bankers also accepted SNB demands because "the better we can prove our willingness to contribute effectively to voluntary measures, the more difficult it will be to justify state interventions. For the banks, there thus exists a realistic chance to prevent state policies with a clever strategy."[8]

Hence, even though the SNB had refused to accept formal responsibility for regulation in the 1930s, it actually retained influence over regulatory issues long after the establishment of a dedicated agency.[9] Regulatory and monetary issues were addressed in conjunction. But the situation became more uncomfortable from the late 1960s onward. In Chapter 2, I described how Switzerland ran into problems with an untenable currency peg and rising inflation. These monetary problems appeared, at the time, to be inextricably linked to weaknesses in regulation. For the enormous growth in capital inflows and instability in currency movements resulted partly from banks' aggressive business practices. These had expanded foreign exchange trading, a speculative activity, which not only made foreign exchange interventions more difficult, but also led to massive losses.[10] UBS lost CHF 124 million in 1973; Geneva-based Finabank had to shut down after a loss of $60 million; and in August 1974, a "rogue trader" from Lloyds in Lugano incurred a loss of £32 million (Schenk 2014).[11] Thus, foreign exchange speculation seemed to exacerbate monetary instabilities *and* produce crises within the banking sector. Additionally, the strong increase in capital inflows signaled an exponential growth of private offshore wealth on Swiss bank accounts. Not only did Swiss incumbents (big and private partnership banks, mainly based in Geneva) continually expand their management of foreign wealth. In the course of the 1960s, foreign banks also increasingly settled in Switzerland to participate in this lucrative business. Almost a hundred new banks or subsidiaries were established between 1950 and 1969. With the growth of offshore wealth management came more publicity about Swiss banking secrecy and its enabling role for tax evasion / avoidance and white-collar crime (Hug 2002); and such bad publicity combined with exchange-rate troubles and rising domestic inflation, which were partly attributed to the large waves of inflowing capital.[12]

By the 1970s, the capacity of elites to address these issues with gentlemen's agreements were exhausted. Bankers increasingly opposed agreements with the central bank that would have restricted their business, or they simply failed to abide by negotiated rules. Just as in other jurisdictions, ways were found to circumvent or ignore voluntary restrictions. SNB officials acknowledged this change, suggesting that voluntary agreements no longer provided an adequate foundation to address the country's monetary, macroeconomic, and financial instability problems. Switching to a more adversarial tone, the SNB president even argued that the Swiss banking sector had simply grown "too large."[13] This new situation also raised questions about the status of the Federal Banking Commission. One obvious problem was that the agency had let the banking sector expand massively, allowing a growing number of dubious firms to settle in the reputable Swiss market (Giddey 2016). Another fundamental problem concerned supervision. As bank failures, cases of fraud, and revelations of money laundering became more frequently reported in the 1960s and 1970s, the structural marginality and weakness of the regulatory agency turned into a liability (Loepfe 2011: 401). Central bankers were concerned about these failures because they were thought to affect Swiss institutions' broader reputation and create problems in domains that the SNB most cared about, namely foreign exchange developments, international capital flows, and inflation.[14] So the question was raised whether the central bank should rethink its decision from the early 1930s and eventually assume more regulatory responsibility.[15] This option was debated internally, while a working group of sectoral representatives and policymakers negotiated proposals on how to strengthen oversight.

In the event, the introduction of practical monetarism in Switzerland unmade these plans. Monetary targeting reframed the policy problem for the central bank and offered a less adversarial solution than statutory and regulatory approaches, such as formal credit restrictions and limits on capital flows. Realizing the PR success of its monetary targeting, the SNB not only abandoned its project of enforcing stricter regulations, but actively dissociated itself from regulation and supervision. This attitude was reflected in SNB President Leutwiler's statement in 1983 that "the SNB should focus on its actual task and draw a *clear line* between itself and the Banking Commission."[16] One year later, the SNB Directors noted that "the SNB can pursue its tasks best if it concentrates on one major task, monetary policy, and only supports regulation in decisive areas such as payment infrastructures. *This attitude should also increase our room for maneuver towards the federal government and the banks.*"[17]

Drawing a clear line became the SNB's new dogma. Leutwiler's successor, Markus Lusser, gave an ideological justification for this position. During a speech in 1994, he argued that the SNB would not be able to pursue such a successful monetary policy if it had to consider possible effects of rate hikes on banking stability—a farfetched argument in a country with constantly low interest rates and low inflation. Lusser also suggested that there was a clear distinction between liquidity and solvency and that, if the central bank was the responsible regulator, it would be induced to more willingly provide lending of last resort to insolvent banks—another questionable argument because nothing is as contested in a crisis as the separation between insolvency and illiquidity. Glossing over the true causes behind the existence of a separate regulatory agency, Lusser then concluded that establishing the Federal Banking Commission as a dedicated oversight body had been a "wise decision" and that the SNB's only, but decisive, contribution to financial stability should consist in ensuring low inflation—for "in the long run," as Lusser stated, "low inflation is the most important factor of success for a healthy financial sector."[18] Putting this ideology into practice, the SNB president refused to engage in cooperation with the regulators, even for the purposes of information exchange.[19]

But if monetarism allowed the SNB to strategically withdraw from regulation, there continued to exist at least one area in which disengagement was not easily accomplished. As discussed in the previous chapter, a practical monetarist such as the Swiss National Bank had a material interest in ensuring that banks managed their reserves and liabilities so that the SNB's own liabilities (the so-called monetary base) and broader aggregates (for example, M1) fluctuated in predictable ways. In turn, it was essential for the central bank that the banks kept considerable buffers of reserves with the SNB, because the larger the buffers, the less would fluctuating demand for cash and other liquidity drains affect the monetary base.[20] Relatedly, the SNB relied on banks avoiding business practices that would lead to erratic shifts in liquidity needs as these would translate into unstable interbank market rates.

In Switzerland, there was a relatively onerous rule, introduced in 1972, that supported the SNB's monetarism. It obliged banks to hold around 10 percent of safe "primary liquid assets" (including central bank reserves) and 45 percent of more widely conceived liquid assets against their external liabilities. This rule was welcomed by the central bankers as a supportive condition for their targeting. The problem was, however, that the regulatory agency was responsible for supervising this rule and willing to accommodate private-sector demands for lowering the requirements.[21] Especially the big banks intensified their lobbying in the 1980s as they gradually transitioned from a "stock" to a "flow" approach to managing their own liabilities—that is, moving to active liability management.[22] The SNB argued against such deregulation because its experts believed that "without adequate reserve holdings, the SNB's concept of monetary base targeting is doomed to fail."[23] The central bankers also reasoned that a drain of liquidity could happen even when firms' solvency situation appeared sound; hence the need for some safety cushion in the form of liquid reserves. But sticking to its policy of dissociation, the SNB was unwilling to invest political capital in the regulatory debate. The central bankers therefore accepted a compromise that weakened the liquidity rules in 1988.

Such a compromise was helped by the fact that, in 1988, Swiss banks still kept *more* central bank reserves than required by law. The SNB thus initially thought that persistent routines in banking would support its monetarism. But over time, banks began economizing on these reserves. The most important force behind this change was that the large Swiss banks increasingly developed into globally operating wholesale and investment firms (Bühlmann, David, and Mach 2012). For instance, two emerging behemoths of Swiss banking (Credit Suisse and UBS) expanded through acquisitions of US-based investment banking units and specialized firms.[24] This led to the adoption of US practices, including active liability management. In consequence, wholesale exposures on *both* sides of the balance sheet increased (see figure 5.2). Due to their reputation as conservative and

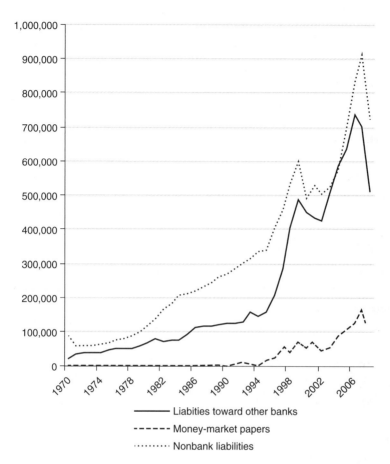

FIGURE 5.2. Balance sheets of large Swiss banks (in CHF); change in selected types of liabilities. *Data source:* Swiss National Bank

solid institutions, the large Swiss banks even enjoyed a comparative advantage in this new practice to other companies as they could borrow at the lowest possible rates. This induced balance-sheet expansion via wholesale funding; for instance, UBS became one of the largest issuers of asset-backed commercial paper in the United States.

The implications of these transformations materialized quickly. Financial frictions and crises began to translate into volatile demand for Swiss franc funding. In consequence, such demand and the respective money-market rates became more erratic. The SNB therefore increasingly had to intervene in order to stabilize money interest rates, irrespective of whether such actions could be justified as money-supply control. This eventually brought down the SNB's cherished monetarism and led to the adoption of inflation targeting. As discussed in the previous chapter, the new monetary policy strategy appeared to better align implementation with the banks' active liability management practices and promised high efficacy vis-à-vis increasingly integrated markets.

Meanwhile, regulation expanded into a policy jurisdiction of its own (Masciandaro and Quintyn 2013). In the Swiss case, this process was not driven by domestic "demand" for such regulation. In fact, after the SNB had withdrawn from gentlemanly regulation in the late 1970s, there was no powerful actor to effectively reform domestic oversight and prudential rules. For instance, the significant domain of offshore wealth management was left almost entirely unregulated.[25] The impetus for professionalization and formalization rather came from the negotiations and agreements at the BCBS. It was in the process of implementing the 1988 capital adequacy requirements ("Basel I") that the Federal Banking Commission expanded its accounting and legal knowledge to specify and supervise these rules; economic and financial knowledge at the agency remained marginal.[26]

This had consequences for how the regulator approached liquidity. There still existed the revised rule from 1988, which required banks to maintain 33 percent of accessible funding and liquefiable assets in relation to their Swiss franc liabilities. However, because the larger banks moved to active liability management in foreign currencies and adopted repo borrowing that did not count as a liability (it appeared as "securities lending" in the balance sheets), these banks did not face any material restrictions on their activities. The regulators recognized this deficiency but were unwilling to implement any significant reform. In line with the evolving discussion at the BCBS, the idea instead was to leave liquidity risk management up to banks and to support this process by codifying best practices developed by the leading firms.[27] In the event, the whole legal project of revising liquidity rules received so little attention that even a modest reform envisioned by regulators did not come to fruition before 2007–2009. This meant that the prudential liquidity regulation in place at the onset of the crisis was wholly inadequate to address the true sources of risk. In their report after a country visit to Switzerland in 2007, IMF experts recognized this deficiency, noting politely that "there exists some potential for improvement in monitoring the liquidity risks of large Swiss banks."[28]

One important reason for this regulatory failure was the SNB's persistent unwillingness to expose itself to prudential regulatory questions. To be sure, financial stability had come to receive more attention by central banks in the 2000s. The crises around the turn of the millennium had revealed the fragility of a growing and increasingly integrated financial system. At the SNB, a new Director, Nikolas Blattner, proactively took charge of the central bank's generic system-stability mandate in light of these developments. This brought forth a codification of the SNB's lender of last resort commitment toward systemically relevant banks and regular reporting on financial stability risks. But Blattner tried to go further and recognized deficiencies in the regulation of banks' liability management and money-market exposures. Rejecting the position held at the Federal Banking Commission, he argued that authorities should introduce rules for banks' liquidity management that went beyond private-sector solutions. Banks could not be trusted to manage these risks. Blattner's problem, however, was that his colleagues at the helm of the SNB did not support his expansive notion of the central bank's new regulatory responsibilities. They aimed to limit the SNB's financial stability role to information provision only, and concentrate policy work on inflation targeting. In particular, SNB Director and subsequent President Philipp Hildebrand argued internally for a purist monetary policy. Citing Greenspan, Hildebrand suggested that market efficiency would make crises rare; and when they occurred, the SNB would have sufficient capacities to provide liquidity and help ailing banks.

In the end, the large Swiss banks were among those with the most dramatic funding problems during the crisis of 2007–2009. Once perceived as the most prudent and conservative institutions in international banking, UBS and Credit Suisse ticked all the boxes as firms with deep and problematic exposures to systemic liquidity risks. Both held large volumes of securitized assets of questionable value and were engaged in massive dealer operations, all funded by short-term liabilities. They also ran money-market funds and special purpose vehicles that either held or were funded by massive volumes of asset-backed commercial paper. In media reporting during the crisis, the true size of these vulnerabilities did not become apparent; the only rescue measure that received broad publicity in Switzerland was the SNB's commitment to buy up CHF 60 billion in unmarketable assets from UBS, complemented by government's capital support. But in the background, the *American* central bank, the Fed, provided billions and billions of liquidity directly and indirectly to Credit Suisse and UBS. These Fed measures give some indication of how dramatically the two large banks' USD liquidity situations deteriorated in 2008–2009. On my count, Credit Suisse received USD 226.672 billion and UBS received 283.842 billion from the Fed's various programs designed for the US markets during 2007–2010. Additionally, the SNB borrowed USD 458.521 billion via currency swaps from the Fed: It is hard to imagine that this US dollar funding went anywhere else than to the big banks with large USD exposures. All in all, this implies that the US market exposures from just a couple of large banks amounted to a sum just under twice Switzerland's annual GDP.

The Bank of England: From Informal Leadership to Structural Secrecy

Before the Second World War, the Bank of England's own involvement in financial activities was mainly responsible for its prudential regulation of financial markets and firms. As the bankers' bank, the "Old Lady of Threadneedle Street" had a natural desire to maintain orderly market conditions, deal with sound counterparties, and trade in high-quality collateral.[29] In the early twentieth century, the Bank then considered the consequences of several smaller bank failures and started to conduct informal surveillance of the sector. Balance-sheet reporting to the monetary authorities began.[30] For the important firms in the City, such surveillance went so far to involve assessments of the suitability of top personnel (including personality traits) and occasional Bank interventions to influence its selection. The Discount Office at the Bank of England and the Chief Cashier were the responsible regulatory actors. Tight elite networks, transactional relations between the Bank of England and its counterparties, and the Bank's historical role as "jobber of last resort" provided the social and operational foundations for this informal regulatory regime (Capie 2010: 590; Moran 1991: 63).[31] Remarkably, while British policymakers had taken a painful lesson from the liberal Gold Standard era and moved to a government-controlled monetary policy, no equivalent steps were taken in the post-1930s or post-1945 periods to reorganize *regulation*.[32] Accordingly, it was in the "exercise of banking supervision and internal City diplomacy . . . [that] the Bank [could] be said to have retained independence as the determiner and not just the executant of policy."[33] Importantly, independence rested on the *avoidance* of formal frameworks and rules. Only the broader context of informality shifted with the Second World War, as the Bank increasingly demanded that banks comply with onerous requirements serving the government's financing needs—some authors even talk of a regime of "financial repression" (Allen 2014; Masciandaro and Quintyn 2013).

The highly compartmentalized and cartelized sectoral structures that I have already described defined what types of regulations applied to whom and what reciprocities justified these rules. One group that participated in these reciprocal relations were the London discount houses, which enjoyed the privilege of being the Bank's exclusive discount borrowers but, in exchange, were kept on a tight regulatory leash.[34] The Bank's influence over discount houses went so far to force weak firms into mergers with stronger ones (Capie 2010: 589). The Discount Office also held differentiated relationships with accepting houses (merchant banks) and clearing banks. The latter group enjoyed the privilege of managing the national payment system and was promised lender-of-last-resort support. In return, the Discount Office required that "clearers" hold about 30 percent of their assets as reserves.[35] Additionally, these banks held sizable cash balances directly with the Bank of England (Needham and Hotson 2018).

In the postwar period, we thus encounter a regulatory approach that was not differentiated from other policy areas, wholly embedded in the practice of central banking, and purely informal. But these social and operational foundations of regulation—familiarity and exclusive relations with different banking clubs—turned into a liability for the Bank of England as the financial sector expanded and internationalized in the 1960s and 1970s. With the growing presence of international banks and nonbank finance companies ("fringe banks"), the central bank came to regulate an ever-smaller part of overall financial activities (Goodhart and Schoenmaker 1992: 380). This caused two interrelated problems. On one hand, outsider companies could evade restrictive regulations and thus enlarge their market share vis-à-vis the clearing banks (Ross 2004: 316).[36] As a consequence, the incumbents lobbied for a change in regulatory requirements, which led to the abandonment of credit ceilings and a sizable reduction in reserve requirements in 1971. Second, because the unregulated fringe banks had mainly used their market opportunities for mortgage financing, they were the first to run into liquidity and solvency problems when, in the early 1970s, a housing bubble burst.[37] The "Secondary Banking Crisis" ensued, which was resolved only at high cost through concerted bailouts and take-over actions by the Bank of England, together with clearing banks (the "Lifeboat operation") (Reid 1982). It thus became increasingly evident that the informal transactional approach to regulation maintained by the Discount Office was insufficient in regulating competition between, and maintaining stability among, a wider set of firms.[38] Political pressure grew for regulation to be developed into a politically accountable public policy (Moran 1991).

In this context, the Bank of England aimed to maintain its authority and powers in the City and protect the relationships that underpinned its influence. After all, if there was one area in which the Bank had exclusive authority, it was in its dealings with City firms. As one senior official noted, "The Bank has, over years of close contact with fully recognized banks, fostered and, where appropriate, guided the ethic of [a] self-regulatory process. It would be a great shame if this process were halted or impaired by the advent of legislation."[39] The governors therefore responded to the growing political pressure and decided to separate out some of the Discount Office's competencies and fields of operation and to establish a specialized unit for Banking and Money Market Supervision (BAMMS) with a broader reach (Capie 2010: 610). Such organizational differentiation within the central bank had two purposes. First, as Forrest Capie notes, the establishment of "a new department . . . would demonstrate that the Bank was taking the current problems seriously" (ibid.)—there was a signaling value attached to organizational reform. Second, internal differentiation would give organizational space for supervision to develop into a larger central bank activity. In line with the latter intention, supervisory staff grew rapidly within the Bank. The BAMMS initially had seven senior members and thirty support staff, but grew to seventy-seven in 1979 and 200 in 1989 (ibid.: 611).

Crucially, while the Bank of England successfully defended its authority over regulation in 1974 and thereby also shielded the informal nature of UK supervisory practice, hardly any reflection went into the continuing interrelations between monetary policy and financial regulation and supervision.[40] Instead, the idea was that regulation and supervision would now be treated as functions of central bank policy that should remain "clearly separate from considerations of monetary policy."[41] Accordingly, as one key official claimed, regulation should be "exercised with judicial principles and not operating convenience in mind."[42] These notions reflected attempts to carve out a new jurisdiction. The problem was that the central bankers failed to address areas in which interdependencies and overlaps between regulation, supervision, and monetary policy were evident and unavoidable. One such area was the regulation and oversight of banking-sector liabilities and reserves.

These aspects had been integrated with the Discount Office's techniques, but they now became uneasily situated between money-market management and the newly institutionalized supervisory work. In the mid-1970s, the supervisors claimed formal responsibility for prudential liquidity provisions.[43] But at that point, due to its central role in restricting credit, the Money Market Division maintained all de facto powers; its managers controlled reserves in the banking system and had much closer contact with the relevant firms than supervisors. This discrepancy between de jure and de facto powers became a source of conflict in the 1980s. Money-market managers initially wanted to establish new liquidity rules after the Thatcher government had decided to abandon the 12½ percent reserve asset ratio.[44] But supervisors objected because the Money Market Division's proposal intruded onto their turf.[45] In the course of the subsequent years, the abandoned project was reactivated by a new head of the supervisory division, Peter Cooke, who believed that his Division's reliance on purely qualitative assessments of banks' balance sheets had become inadequate. In line with his work at the BCBS, Cooke's idea was to move to requirements for "Primary Sterling Liquidity" to be held as an insurance against money-market crises, calculated as a ratio of banks' maturity mismatches and wholesale borrowing.[46] But by the point that he was promoting these reform ideas internally and with the banking community, money-market managers had disengaged from liquidity regulation and failed to give Cooke the necessary support. The operational staff at the Bank had discovered ways of operating daily liquidity management without such regulations and therefore felt no need to reengage in this matter—not least because any regulation was opposed by the banks.[47] The absence of positive coordination (Scharpf 1976) between the respective units inside the Bank of England thus contributed to the failure of initiatives to reregulate liquidity in a situation in which the British banking sector underwent significant transformations toward a US-like market-based system.

Subsequent institutional closures of financial regulation and monetary policy then created "structural secrecy" (Vaughan 1996) around this unaddressed regulatory gap. A first process that contributed to this outcome was that, as financial regulation became formally codified, its jurisdiction was defined more narrowly and sealed off from the conduct of monetary policy. A first move toward closure was taken with the 1986 Financial Services Act, which rationalized regulation with a focus on deposit-holder and shareholder interests. According to Andrew Large, one of the architects of British regulation, the 1986 Act essentially followed the rationale of consumer protection.[48] Wholesale money markets—"which exclusively serve professionals"—were deliberately excluded from the "full rigour" of this Act.[49] This closure in national regulations reflected and complemented what was happening at Basel, where work by the Cooke and Sandberg groups was buried as policymakers narrowed their focus on capital adequacy requirements and defined rules to organize the supervision of transnational conglomerates. In consequence, while regulation and supervision remained under the Bank of England's responsibility during the 1980s, the one domain in which these practices could have substantially benefited from their organizational integration with central banking—that is, the realm of liquidity and of wholesale markets—was not addressed. The "synergy" between monetary and financial policy so often praised by Bank officials at the time was not much apparent in practice.[50]

In any case, Tony Blair's New Labour decided to create a fully self-contained jurisdiction for financial regulation in 1998, when it established the Securities and Investment Board and subsequently the Financial Services Authority (FSA). The supervisors, who had previously been recruited from the central bank's general staff, collectively moved to a separate organizational entity located in London's financial district, at Canary Wharf (Goodhart 2002: 2). Not just physically, but also institutionally, this move indicated a growing distance between central banking and financial regulation. As a separate organization, the FSA had its own mandate and operated within a distinct framework of accountability. Its practices largely consisted of scheduled supervisory visits at domestic banks, monitoring of internal management systems, and close coordination with the audit process; foreign firms with exposures to London's money markets remained outside its remit. If the assessment of risk management systems and accounting reports suggested that banks were solvent, according to Basel's capital adequacy rules, the supervisors' job was done properly (Goodhart 2011b: 144). In accordance with this practice, the FSA staff profiles changed. Lawyers and accountants increasingly dominated the organization and personnel with a central banking background disappeared. These developments turned initial problems with regulating liquidity into an entrenched institutional and organizational neglect. For instance, in 2003, "deficiencies in the existing liquidity regime" were noted. But the FSA "decided not to follow up" on this gap "because of the greater priority given to capital reform at that time."[51] This status quo prevailed until 2007.[52]

But closure was also pursued from the monetary policy side. Over a decade or so, the Bank developed from the "head-boy of the City" into a purist inflation targeter under the leadership of Mervyn King. His predecessor, Eddie George, had still stressed the interdependence of monetary and financial policy. As he had argued in 1993, "Financial stability, like price stability, is a public good. Central banks must pursue both objectives, because they are mutually dependent."[53] These arguments were not necessarily matched by actual synergies in practice, as I have noted above. But the institutionalization of inflation targeting finally led Bank of England officials to give up George's ambitions. A crucial force undergirding this transformation was the import and growing internal dominance of modern macroeconomics (Acosta et al. 2020). As described in Chapter 3, carving out the Bank's position as independent monetary policymaker in the 1990s involved gaining authority over economic and monetary forecasts and dominating the Treasury in macroeconomic policy discussions. The people around Mervyn King, who successfully pursued such scientization, changed the central bank's internal culture "beyond recognition," as one former official remarked.[54] One aspect of this change was a new institutional thinking about policy. The respective models and theories imported into the Bank depicted monetary policy as focused solely on macroeconomic variables (forecasts of NAIRU, real natural interest rates, and so on). Recognition of the central bank's infrastructural dependence on finance, as stressed by practical central bankers such as George, no longer found a place in this new language. To be sure, the Bank in principle held a second mandate besides monetary policy for financial stability (which was rearticulated after the FSA's foundation). However, as financial stability was addressed in a separate division, and most resources and the Governor's own attention went into monetary policy, the activities around this second mandate were marginalized. According to Chris Giles of the *Financial Times,* King told "colleagues to 'operationalise' [financial stability], by which he meant simply writing and publishing two financial stability reports every year. Sir Mervyn demonstrated the low status he attached to such reports by not presenting them himself, unlike the inflation report, which he [had] nurtured and presented as chief economist (1991–1998), deputy governor (1998–2003) and governor (2003 onwards)."[55]

The Bank's lack of a "culture of regulation" also had another, more subtle dimension.[56] Most of the expertise on regulatory processes had traditionally come not from economists but from the operators in the market divisions within the Bank. These divisions evidently did not disappear with the turn to inflation targeting because they were needed to implement interest-rate targets. However, the market expertise nurtured within this division was not sought for either regulatory purposes or monetary policy formulation. In the words of Bill Allen, "[T]here was a kind of major reorganization in which the Bank was really divided into two parts, a kind of thinking part and a doing part. And what once had been the Chief Cashier was part of doing, not part of thinking."[57] In other words, the practical expertise of operational staff, which had once defined the heart of British central banking, was only rendered relevant in the organization with one particular interest: to make sure that the decided policy rates were maintained in the markets.

As a result of these developments, the Bank of England not just proved incapable of addressing crucial sources of systemic risk in the run-up to 2007 (Northern Rock's failure). It also proved ill-prepared for the actual occurrence of a financial crisis and wholesale bank run, despite the fact that one of its senior officials had warned of the possibility of such events.[58] For instance, throughout 2007 and until early 2008, one can observe a curious disconnect between the discussions on inflation risks in the Monetary Policy Committee and financial market developments.[59] More importantly, King proved unable to respond appropriately to Northern Rock's liquidity problems and neglected the Bank's critical importance as a lender of last resort until the Lehman crash. A subsequent report documented coordination problems between the Bank, the Treasury, and the FSA in critical rescue operations.[60] And the Bank's own crisis response was slow because information flows remained deficient between the divisions responsible for policy formulation, financial stability surveillance, and money-market operations.

Discussion

In 2007, the monetary economist and central banker Marvin Goodfriend published an article entitled "How the World Achieved Consensus on Monetary Policy." This was a declaration of triumph. With inflation targeting, central bank practitioners and academic macroeconomists had finally found common ground. What worked in practice could be theorized in academic terms. Neo-Keynesian models showed *why* it was optimal for central bankers to practice inflation targeting: to align nominal with real interest rates with a prospective view toward a target for inflation, leaving some room for activist responses against exogeneous shocks (see also Woodford 2003b; Woodford 2009). But in the very same year of Goodfriend's publication, BNP Paribas reported large losses on its American subprime mortgage funds, and the British mortgage lender Northern Rock ran into fatal liquidity shortages. A deleveraging of the shadow banking system set in (Allen 2013). As we know today, the crisis that followed not only led to market failures and the collapse of banking behemoths; it also fundamentally challenged broader economic stability and deepened secular stagnation in core capitalist economies. These developments, together with more critical assessments of the "Great Moderation" as a period of rising inequalities and gradually accumulating systemic imbalances, provide a stark contrast to Goodfriend's optimistic, teleological narrative.

This raises the question of what went wrong with an allegedly successful model of central banking. In other parts of this book, I have approached this question by reconstructing the intrinsic connections between inflation targeting and the role of financial markets in determining macroeconomic expectations and in engineering accelerated credit growth. In this chapter, I have focused on the problem of regulatory neglect. To be sure, in many jurisdictions, central bankers did not have chief responsibility for banking supervision or the authority to issue ordinances for banks. But for two important reasons, this does not exculpate them. First, I have showed that, despite some variation in formal frameworks, central bankers had traditionally incorporated key aspects of regulation and supervision into their social and operational practices. After the 1970s, a growing number of monetary authorities became convinced that they could bolster their organizations' institutional power and legitimacy by disentangling monetary policy from regulatory issues and framing their actions exclusively in terms of inflation. While the new jurisdiction of financial regulation failed to incorporate key aspects of the central banks' previous practices, central bankers failed to address the emerging gap. This led to a structural secrecy around those issues that fell uncomfortably in between monetary and financial policy. Second, central banks could not entirely abandon financial stability responsibilities (if only because they remained the lenders of last resort) and often held generic mandates for this task. Due to the growing fragilities in financial systems in the course of the 1990s and 2000s, discussions intensified among central bankers about how to fulfill these mandates. But the strategic advantages of disengagement prevented them from taking proactive measures.

This chapter has reconstructed strategic disengagement in two relatively distinct settings. In Switzerland, we can see evidence for such behavior already during the 1930s, when the SNB refused to take over formal regulatory responsibility in its attempt to protect confidential relationships with banks. In fact, however, the central bank was the key banking regulator in Switzerland and relied, for that purpose, primarily on informal negotiations and agreements between elites. The establishment of a tokenistic supervisor supported this practice because the agency was too weak to challenge established practices, but it provided a protective shield against external political demands. After a brief period of crisis and rethinking, the SNB returned to strategic dissociation in the 1980s, which by that point was *not* complemented anymore with informal regulatory routines. Senior officials reasoned that the SNB should self-identify as a purist monetarist; as one official stated, such disengagement would "increase the room for maneuver towards the federal government and the banks." Even in domains in which dissociation was impossible—that is, in the regulation of reserves and liquidity—the SNB limited its exposure as much as it could. With the adoption of inflation targeting, reserve regulations became superfluous for monetary policy implementation, which supported this dissociation. As a few central bankers realized, there now emerged a strong *prudential* rationale for engaging in financial stability issues, particularly with regard to active liability management, due to the integration of markets and the growing frequency of crises. But adherence to dissociation was politically more convenient, and the SNB remained complacent about these issues until the 2008 crisis hit.

Strategic dissociation had much less of a tradition in the United Kingdom, because the Bank of England had historically self-identified as the leader in London's City and had based its political authority in the postwar period on its independent, if informal, role in regulatory affairs. In this context, a first step toward formal separation was taken in the 1970s, when the Bank established an internal supervisory division. With this step, the Bank wanted to signal its determination to address the failures of informal regulation, ward off political pressure, but also create organizational conditions for expanding its supervisory role. The attractiveness of formal separation soon became apparent to monetary policymakers as they came to appreciate the option of distancing themselves from contentious regulatory issues. Peter Cooke directly experienced the consequences of this dissociation. He aimed to introduce comprehensive liquidity regulation during the 1980s, but failed to gain support from Bank officials in operational divisions. Under Mervyn King, the Bank then ultimately abandoned its identity as regulator, despite intensifying discussions in international contexts about growing systemic risks and the adoption of financial stability reviews. In addition to King's single-purpose understanding of central banking, a complementary problem was that practical views on money-market developments were not fed back into policy discussions; "thinking" and "doing" had been organizationally separated at the Bank.

To what extent was strategic dissociation a more widely adopted strategy among central bankers before 2007–2008? The German case is striking for its similarities to and differences from Switzerland. Despite the establishment of a first formal supervisory framework and a dedicated agency in 1931, the Bundesbank's predecessor, the Reichsbank, maintained significant influence, for example, in its conduct of supervisory visits and in gathering balance-sheet information. After a period of centralization under the Nazis and a subsequent decentralization under the Allied Powers, the Bundesbank regained this influential, but informal regulatory role in 1961. Besides conducting supervisory visits, the Bundesbank also exerted strong influence over the principles and ordinances issued by the regulatory agency via interbu-reaucratic coordination. Lastly, by setting onerous reserve requirements, the central bank controlled a key regulatory lever, which restricted the banks' active liability management and prevented the introduction of new money-market instruments, such as repo or commercial paper. How-ever, as Hubert Zimmermann notes, the Bundesbank was "careful not to be drawn into the business of setting regulatory guidelines since such an inherently political task would potentially compromise its independence" (2012: 488). The public persona of the central bank, and its accountability as a policymaker, was thus framed exclusively in terms of its monetary targeting. Also, as parts of the political establishment and banking elites endorsed financial globalization, the Bundesbank became increasingly unwilling to risk its considerable political capital on its informal prudential role.

It is interesting to observe how the central bank's institutional strategy then changed in response to its loss of monetary policy authority with the establishment of the European Central Bank. Looking for new areas in which to claim a significant policymaking role, Bundesbank officials sud-denly started arguing in favor of a single regulator and for the central bank to be given that role. The central bank's inalienable responsibility for the payment system and lending of last resort were cited as arguments.[61] Stra-tegic disengagement from explicit regulatory responsibility thus became unattractive as soon as the central bank's institutional power and identity could no longer be articulated in monetary policy terms. For political rea-sons, though, the center-left government of the time opted to delegate responsibility to a new agency, the Bundesanstalt für Finanzdienstleistung-saufsicht (BaFin). Here, we encounter the very problems that have been widely associated with regulatory agencies: institutional weakness vis-à-vis bank lobbyists; a micro-prudential bias in its conception of regulation; and a lack of expertise on money-market and shadow-banking issues.

What about the American case? Lev Menand (2021) has argued that what he calls *the American monetary settlement* gave relatively free access to private firms engaging in banking (partly due to America's federal struc-ture and the nineteenth-century conflicts over finance), but enforced the franchise nature of money creation via strong and discretionary public reg-ulation. This settlement was centralized and upgraded with the establishment of the Federal Reserve in 1913 and New Deal regulations of the 1930s. As Menand writes,

> The legislators who established the Office of the Comptroller of the Currency, the Fed, and the Federal Deposit Insurance Corporation believed that the power to expand the money supply was too great to leave in the hands of elected bodies, that doing so would lead to corruption, stagnation, and a debased currency. But they were also afraid to allow the power to concentrate in the hands of a few unelected executives. So, they steered a middle course by diffusing the power and constraining it as much as possible. They set up a system of chartered banks whereby anyone willing and able to comply with certain terms and conditions could create money. The system has four pillars: (1) delegation—privately owned banks, not the government, create the bulk of the money supply; (2) open access—anyone can get a charter to expand the money supply if they are willing to comply with certain terms and conditions; (3) separation—banks cannot engage in commerce and vice versa; and (4) supervision—special government officials, empowered to stamp out "unsound" banking, ensure that banks fulfill their public purpose. (Ibid.: 7–8)

In its initial design, there thus existed a close nexus between monetary policy and banking regulation through the very nature of private money creation and its backstopping by deposit insurance and the Fed.

But the efficacy of these regulations and rules rested on maintaining the separation of different financial activities, which were regulated by the different agencies that focused on deposit banking, securities trading, and so on. Over the course of the postwar period, these separations collapsed, and so did a regulation based on functional separation (Funk and Hirschman 2014). I described circumventions of reserve regulations and interest-rate caps in the previous chapter, a process that undermined the distinction between regulated banking and the wider money markets. Derivatives constituted another important area of change. Commercial banks ventured into this market in order to acquire market shares in securities trading (Carruthers 2013). The Fed went from ambiguous responses to these developments during the 1960s until the 1980s (the last ambiguous regulation was the 1980 Monetary Control Act), toward full support for financial innovation and deregulation in subsequent years. For instance, "Alan Greenspan . . .

pressed Congress to repeal statutory barriers separating banks and securities dealers" (Menand 2021: 71); the Fed also allowed its members to establish "Section 20 subsidiaries" that gave them access to investment banking. While Commodity Futures Trading Commission President Brooksley Born wanted to bring over-the-counter derivatives trading onto regulated exchanges, the central bank was instrumental in stopping this project, mobilizing the dubious argument that better risk distribution would "lower systemic risk" (Özgöde 2021). By allowing Citibank to merge with Travelers Group, the Fed also facilitated the creation of a first financial mega-conglomerate, which would provide the role model for other firms (D'Arista 1994).

Importantly, while the Fed supported firms in transgressing boundaries, the regulatory landscape was *not* reformed. In the 1999 Gramm–Leach–Bliley Act that finally abandoned Glass-Steagall, the plethora of agencies with increasingly outdated and conflicting task descriptions was maintained. The Fed was charged with supervising banks' overarching holding structures but relied on the Securities and Exchange Commission (SEC) and other agencies to look at specific units within the new financial behemoths (Haubrich and Thomson 2008); discretionary supervision became an "anachronism" (Menand 2021: 71). Timothy Geithner would later note that this was a key source of precrisis regulatory failure because agencies such as the SEC were ill-equipped to understand the banking activities that firms such as Bear Stearns were engaged in; the SEC's traditional mandate had consisted of going "after market manipulation, fraud, and insider trading; they didn't focus much on financial stability" (Geithner 2014: 148).

The Fed itself gathered firsthand experience of the growing instabilities in finance that resulted from the very expansion of shadow banking and the creation of financial conglomerates that would ultimately lead to the 2008 crash. Repeatedly, in the 1980s and 1990s, the central bank intervened to backstop money markets and provide lending of last resort (after the 1987 stock-market crash; LTCM; the dotcom bubble; 9/11). Given this experience of growing instability, why did the public institution in the midst of an expanding, increasingly fragile system fail to act and instead even promoted the very innovations that undermined the efficacy of historical regulatory settlements? A plausible answer to that question is that, as lender-of-last-resort operations appeared sufficient to stabilize the functioning of markets and banking in a financializing growth regime, and as such interventions failed to conflict with the major source of central bank legitimacy, namely stable inflation, Alan Greenspan and other central bankers adopted strategic dissociation. Using its authority and powerful tools for regulatory and supervisory interventions would only create problems for an organization that enjoyed growing public legitimacy and prestige. As Greenspan's biographer, Sebastian Mallaby, writes, on several occasions, the Fed chairman "refused to allow the Fed to take on the mission of regulating . . . , preferring to prioritize its monetary independence" (2017: 660).

To be sure, it would be wrong to claim that central bankers were solely or even chiefly responsible for the failures in financial regulation prior to 2007. Too often, lawmakers were captured by bank lobbyists (Johnson and Kwak 2010) or saw financialization as the right path to economic growth and privatized welfare (Offer 2017). Supervisory agencies operated under limited mandates and were politically weak vis-à-vis the private sector. When negotiations on international agreements failed, the most powerful argument against unilateral action was to avoid competitive disadvantages at home. But central bankers *had* a role to play in all of this, especially in domains such as money markets and liquidity management, where they had more influence and expertise than any other public actor. What we see consistently across cases is that these authorities failed to use that influence and expertise because they saw more strategic advantage in delimiting themselves to price stability mandates and disengage from prudential regulation.

CHAPTER SIX

Plumbing Financialization in Vain

Central Banking after 2008

> If shadow money is a mark of the growing infrastructural power of private finance, then the crisis of shadow money in both Europe and the US provides several insights into the limits and potentialities of that infrastructural power.
>
> —BRAUN AND GABOR 2020: 248

> How could all these good intentions backed by so many trillions have had such a perverse result on the inequality that frustrates growth, increases the odds of renewed financial crisis, impoverishes so many Americans, and makes the nation ever more ungovernable?
>
> —PETROU 2021B: 2

CENTRAL BANKS HAVE assumed even more prominent roles since 2008. They have installed enormous and more or less permanent backstops for financial systems and transformed lending of last resort into comprehensive "first response" functions (Bernanke et al. 2020) against financial crises; and they have significantly increased the role of monetary policy as a macroeconomic stabilization tool. In fact, during the high times of quantitative easing (QE) discussed in this chapter, it appeared as if monetary authorities would be the only public bodies with the capacities and legitimacy to respond to crisis events and more persistent economic problems, starting with structurally weak, undercapitalized financial sectors, and including credit crunches, mass home foreclosures, insolvencies, skyrocketing unemployment, stagnant productivity rates, and sovereign debt troubles. In

2010, a political stalemate in Washington and Brussels produced the perverse situation that fiscal policy was rolled back, while central banks remained the "the only game in town" (El-Erian 2016). The predominant central bank response to this constellation consisted of lowering refinancing rates to virtually zero, adopting large-scale asset-purchase programs, and announcing prolonged periods of easy money.[1] In consequence, central bank balance sheets grew to sizes beyond what had previously been imaginable (figure 6.1). Initially, policymakers and observers thought that such forms and scales of intervention would remain confined to exceptional moments of crisis; hence their description as "unconventional" policies. But this expectation turned out to be premature. Authorities that had initially resisted QE soon gave up their opposition; and those that attempted to unwind QE and reduce balance sheets (as the Fed did in 2013) reversed course. Indeed, the Covid-19 crisis reinvigorated QE and led to previously unseen balance-sheet expansions within just a couple of weeks. Ben Bernanke, one of the chief architects of post-2008 policies, has therefore

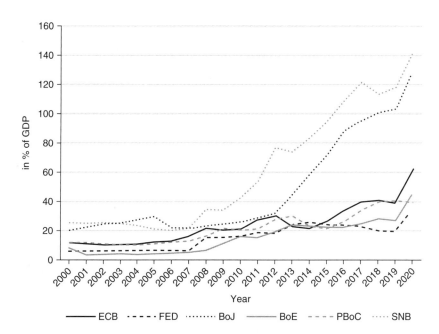

FIGURE 6.1. Central bank assets to GDP (percentages). *Data sources:* Annual reports from the respective central banks

changed terminology and speaks confidently about the "new tools of monetary policy" (Bernanke 2020).

This situation raises new challenges for analysts and critics of central banking. On the face of it, the new regime seems to mark a radical departure from pre-2008 policies and dogmas. Authorities have abandoned the predominant focus on inflation that was characteristic of the "Great Moderation." Responsibilities have been broadened, not just in the area of financial stability, where central banks now conduct (or at least contribute to) macroprudential regulation. Authorities have also departed radically from what political economists call "hard-money policies." The key central banks have all adopted very expansionary policies to support employment and growth. But more than that: Powerful central bankers have come out to explicitly embrace the objectives of maximum employment and support for the poor. Jerome Powell went so far in 2020 to argue that the Fed's expansive measures primarily served the most disadvantaged, Black and Hispanic communities in the United States;[2] and Vítor Constâncio of the European Central Bank (ECB) suggested that "the decline in unemployment that followed the introduction of the [ECB's quantitative easing, LW] had a disproportionately positive impact on low-income households."[3] Contrast this with the positions held by earlier central bankers, such as Alan Greenspan, Eddie George, or Karl Otto Pöhl, who would have seen such positions as a dangerous return of Keynesian thinking. During the Covid-19 crisis, authorities have gone even further to embrace encompassing financial and macroeconomic responsibilities. Early in the pandemic, they promised support for markets, businesses large and small, workers, the poor, and sometimes even governments, which relied on cheap funding for massive spending boosts. In conjunction with these significant policy changes, we observe remarkable developments in the realm of expertise. Central bank economists now hold conferences on climate change, financial fragility, inequality, fiscal policy, gender and diversity, and many more topics—gone are the days of single-minded New Keynesian modeling and inflation forecasting. What more could progressives desire? Democrats on the Left called for more dovish monetary policies and a commitment to maximum employment in their "Fed Up" campaign in 2015.[4] On most counts, these campaigners got what they wanted through revisions of Fed objectives and accelerated balance-sheet expansions implemented under Jerome Powell. In the Euro area, "Blockupy" marched against Troika-imposed austerity on southern Europe at the opening of the

ECB's new headquarters in Frankfurt in 2015.[5] By the time of this opening, however, ECB President Mario Draghi had already begun to relieve pressures from bond markets on the periphery with the adoption of aggressive QE. While he had initially advocated austerity and labor-market liberalization to go with these measures, Draghi and his successor gradually changed their positions on these matters and called for more active fiscal policies and wage increases (Braun et al. 2021).[6]

The problem is, however, that despite these apparent learning processes among central bankers, their abandonment of hard money and other dogmas, none of the deeper dysfunctions arising from central bank dominance in a financialized capitalism have disappeared. Between 2010 and 2020 structural imbalances and distributional injustices grew. The economic recoveries in this period (until the Covid-19 crisis) were one of the longest, but also weakest in history, entrenching the phenomenon that economists call "secular stagnation" (Rachel and Summers 2019).[7] Particularly in the Anglo-Saxon economies, employment levels rose, but "[m]any families [were] doing a bit better only because many more families now have more than one wage-earner and / or are working more hours" (Petrou 2021a: 70). This reflects the fact that, despite expansionary policies, income and particularly wealth inequalities grew. This is particularly true for the United States, where in 2020, the top 1 percent of wealthiest households owned more than 30 percent of household wealth, up from 26 percent in 2010.[8] In the United Kingdom, income and wealth inequalities also grew.[9] In Germany, the fact that unequal wealth distribution remained at a high level was all the more striking because overall household wealth in the period after 2010 (due to the dramatic appreciation of real estate) grew by 20 percent.[10] Additionally, while central banks expended enormous financial resources in 2008 to save financial institutions and markets, overall risks have increased. Most of this happened in shadow banking. Overall, with $200.2 trillion in assets on balance sheets in 2019, shadow banks have grown just as large as the entire traditional banking sector, up from a 42 percent share in 2008.[11] This has contributed to a growth of systemic risks, as the Financial Stability Board noted in its reports.[12]

This new constellation after 2008 has thus required scholars to revise their traditional perspectives on central banking. Most importantly, as a growing literature argues, expansionary policies since 2008, rather than supporting more equitable incomes, have reinforced inequalities (Coppola 2019; Fontan, Claveau, and Dietsch 2016; Petrou 2021a) (although it is worth acknowledging that some central bankers and economists reject these findings) (Haldane 2018).[13] A convincing argument from this new literature is that QE primarily benefits the very rich, who are disproportionate owners of financial assets. This group has profited directly and substantially from central banks' large-scale asset purchases and from interventions to stabilize stock and credit markets in situations of distress.[14] Karen Petrou spells out the perplexing implications of this situation: "Equality will advance with a smaller Fed portfolio and higher interest rates. These are counterintuitive to traditional thinking, which assumes that the bigger the Fed and the lower the interest rates, the better it is for bottom-up growth" (2021a: 15). Scholars have also increasingly drawn attention to central banks' roles in entrenching the path to ever larger and more fragile financial systems (Schularick and Taylor 2012). In particular, by saving firms against downside risks with huge market-making and lending operations, including firms such as hedge and money-market funds, and by failing to regulate significant parts of finance, monetary authorities have arguably contributed to the massive expansion of shadow banking in the years after 2008 (Petrou 2021a; Vissing-Jorgensen 2020).

These new themes in central banking scholarship in the period of QE vindicate the broader perspective that I have advanced in this book. My argument has been that we should focus our analyses on central banks' concrete operational relationships and infrastructural entanglements with financial sectors, rather than conceptualizing these organizations' activities in terms of disembodied policies that purportedly follow hard-money interests and/or pro-market beliefs (Braun and Gabor 2020). More particularly, as comes out ever more clearly in the QE period, central bankers conduct a situated version of problem-solving, with the primary intent of securing governability from the position of organizations that are situated at the very heart of financial systems. As one consequence of this, and notwithstanding authorities' new enlightened views and ideals, this leads to policies that reinforce the infrastructural dependency of macroeconomic policy on financial markets. Higher inequality, as well as other problematic developments after 2008, are consequences of this. I will thus use this chapter to demonstrate that there exists a striking continuity between the logics of policy innovation before and after 2008.

The argument presented so far also needs to be extended and modified, however, in light of the QE period. As I have suggested in previous pages, market-based financial systems mattered to central bankers before 2008 primarily because they offered infrastructures that helped authorities to establish particular policy implementation and transmission channels for inflation-targeting policies. That is, policymakers cared about their interactions with markets because they strengthened their hold on inflation and opened up some room to maneuver for activist macroeconomic stabilization. This infrastructural linkage between central banks and finance has remained significant after 2008. But another nexus is becoming increasingly important, determining central banks' actions. As markets grow and become more concentrated and more deeply ingrained in the workings of financialized economies, they more frequently produce crashes. Not only have central bankers been the policymakers most vigorously promoting the view that aggressive responses to these crashes are needed to forestall broader financial and economic calamities (e.g., Geithner 2014). But it is they that have authoritatively enacted these beliefs. With every crisis, then, central banks' balance sheets and their perceived importance as first lines of defense increase. As I shall discuss in this chapter, one of the key features of the period 2010–2020 is that the infrastructural relationships between central banking and financial sectors and the more direct relationships associated with financial instability have become practically and cognitively intertwined.

In this chapter, I also want to elaborate a second aspect that has become apparent in the period of QE. Counterintuitively, while central bank dominance appears to be as inescapable as ever, monetary authorities are exposed to considerable risk of losing their governing capacities and political authority. With ever *more* activism (market support and asset purchases), policy effects increasingly appear particularistic and distributional rather than general and diffuse. Larger and larger interventions help to save and support particular finance-related actors, markets, and strategies, but they do not instigate broad-based growth. We can make sense of this in terms of such diagnoses as "too much finance" (Arcand, Berkes, and Panizza 2015) and secular stagnation (Rachel and Summers 2019). More frequent crises in oversized financial systems produce significant macroeconomic costs, and central bank support helps to keep this destructive cycle going. Moreover, while QE is critical for maintaining debt growth and asset-price appreciation, these credit and wealth effects do not lead to sustainable aggregate demand. They rather reinforce economic distributions and decision-making logics in the economy that can structurally weaken growth (Blyth and Matthijs 2017). The Covid-19 crisis has temporarily rendered invisible these self-defeating dynamics of QE because it has directed attention to exogenous sources of distress. Moreover, because major fiscal action has accompanied central banks' balance-sheet expansions during the pandemic, the problematic side of QE has been less apparent. But the fact that this phase is temporary or exceptional does not resolve the deeper problem of central bank dominance guiding us into a financialization trap.

Looking back at the period 2008 to 2020, I here offer an analysis of how QE has developed in different core economies, how it is entangled with frictions inside financial systems, and how it reinforces secular stagnation in the broader economy. The material that I have relied on in the previous chapters—archival files that inform us about the deliberations inside central banks—is not yet available for the period after 2008. This chapter therefore draws on published sources, newspaper articles from the financial press, interviews, and an emerging (gray) literature on the implementation and transmission of QE. At times, the conclusions I draw are speculative as they rely on interpretations of disparate sources and preliminary findings from existing studies. Moreover, while I discuss QE programs by the Federal Reserve (Fed), ECB, and Bank of England (BoE), I cannot flesh out systematic differences between cases. I also neglect the foreign exchange aspects of QE, which are significant, especially for the Swiss case, which I do not include in my discussion here.

The chapter is structured as follows. I first give a brief overview of the QE programs of the three central banks mentioned above. I then discuss intertwinements between asset purchases and finance-internal distributional processes, before engaging with how QE acts upon financialized economies. I conclude by describing how Covid-19 has helped central bankers to consolidate their influence as capitalism's first line of defense at a time when QE has all but exhausted its macroeconomic powers.

Central Banking after 2008

Central banks have engaged in large-scale asset purchases in the past (Coppola 2019: 14–18). But the Fed can be regarded as the initiator of post-2008 rounds of QE. This innovation evolved out of the emergency interventions during the financial crisis. The Fed's balance sheet expanded rapidly to over $2 trillion after the Lehman crash as the central bank conducted large lending operations (particularly via the "Term Auction Credit" facility) and large foreign exchange swaps with other central banks. Still in late April 2009, these liquidity operations contributed more (around $983 billion) to the Fed balance sheet than outright asset holdings (around $891 billion). Moreover, when the Fed started to increase these holdings in early 2009, it initially concentrated its purchases on mortgage-backed securities, with the intention of simultaneously reviving the real estate market and supporting the ailing financial sector that held large stocks of these devalued assets (Reisenbichler 2020). The Troubled Asset Relief Program, or TARP, the government program to buy up distressed assets, reinforced the Fed's focus on these asset classes and on the group of financial firms that were immediately affected by the crisis. In December 2008, the central bank lowered its federal funds target to 0–0.25 percent and announced in March 2009 that rates would remain zero for "an extended period of time"—forward guidance on future policy that the Fed has used ever since.

While initially planned as an extraordinary program, QE persisted in the United States in the 2010s for three reasons. First, the Fed itself realized that the recovery was exceptionally weak; as Ben Bernanke noted in 2012, "the rate of improvement in the labor market has been painfully slow."[15] Moreover, Congress called an early halt to the government's stimulus and social support programs launched in 2008.[16] Last but certainly not least, "in 2013 hints that asset purchases might begin to slow led to a 'taper tantrum' in bond markets, with the 10-year yield rising by nearly one percentage point over several months" (Bernanke 2020: 946). In another instance during September 2019, the repo and federal funds market rates rose dramatically during a phase in which the Fed attempted to reduce the banks' reserves, which coincided with large public debt issuance, as well as other special factors that increased the banks' as well as nonbanks' funding demands.[17] Again, the Fed was called upon to provide liquidity support.

All this pales, however, in comparison with what happened during the Covid-19 pandemic. In late February 2020, Fed chairman Jay Powell was still claiming that "the fundamentals of the U.S. economy remain strong."[18] But financial markets suddenly panicked, leading the Fed to initiate its largest support operation yet. Within just one quarter, it purchased more government paper than under each of the previous QE1, QE2, and QE3 programs. The primary reason for this $1-trillion-dollar operation was that hedge funds and other investors were suddenly in need of cash liquidity and therefore sold their large government bond holdings. The Fed thus initially started QE4 in March 2020 to primarily help out shadow banks (Vissing-Jorgensen 2020). Various other support programs, from facilities for primary dealers, money-market funds, and large corporations, as well as smaller (Congress-mandated) programs for municipalities and small- to mid-sized companies, were launched within a month. As the pandemic continued, asset purchases increased, expanding the Fed's balance sheet to over $8 trillion.

The European development of QE was less consistent. On the one hand, when the 2008 crisis hit, the ECB responded with a different assessment of its own political role, its legal mandate, and the political-economic situation surrounding it (Tooze 2018). It remained focused on inflation risks even as Great Depression–level unemployment rates and output losses were observed in the South. This attitude was reflected in the ECB's initial refusal to intervene in the secondary bond markets of periphery countries, as well as its consistent advocacy of fiscal consolidation during the European sovereign debt crisis (Braun et al. 2021: 135ff.; Clift 2018). In April and July 2011, the ECB even raised its refinancing rates in light of "upside risks to price stability."[19] But there was a second factor preventing the initial adoption of "proper" QE. For the ECB sought to ease credit conditions via its direct counterparties, the banks. Subsidizing the banks and giving them balance-sheet space for additional lending thus was favored over purchasing securities on capital markets. Accordingly, the European equivalent of QE was a long-term lending facility for banks on very favorable terms, announced in December 2011. The effects of this program can be discerned from the ECB's 2012 end-of-year balance sheet. This indicated a loan size of €1.1 trillion in contrast to only €586.133 million in security holdings. Instead of adopting QE in the face of continuing stagnation, Trichet's ECB thus engaged in "the largest liquidity injection in the history of central banking" (Crosignani, Faria-e-Castro, and Fonseca 2017: 13).

A significant switch in strategy then came under the ECB's new president, Mario Draghi. Following his statement in ultimate defense of the

euro ("whatever it takes"), in 2013 the ECB adopted US-style forward guidance and two asset-purchase programs, which developed into a comprehensive QE program in 2015 (in particular with the Public Sector Purchase Program and the Corporate Sector Purchase Program). In that year,
ECB securities holdings passed the €1-trillion limit and rose to almost €3
trillion in 2018. Draghi initially combined such expansionary monetary
policy with recommendations to fiscal policymakers to restrain spending;
at a press conference in May 2013, he recommended that "in order to
bring debt ratios back on a downward path, euro area countries should
not unravel their efforts to reduce government budget deficits."[20] Only
during the late 2010s did the ECB abandon its austerity stance, encouraging more substantial fiscal action.

During the pandemic, the ECB then accelerated its expansionary policies. These responded simultaneously to three forces. First, market distress
led to spikes in Southern European bond yields yet again, particularly for
Italy and Greece. The ECB responded with its Pandemic Emergency Purchase Programme and was quickly able to close bond-market spreads. The
official justification for these operations was to "counter the serious risks to
the monetary policy transmission mechanism" in the Eurozone.[21] Second,
while the European banking sector had already struggled with undercapi-
talization and defaulted debt on balance sheets before the pandemic, this
new crisis gave the ECB another opportunity to step up its subsidized lending
to the sector under targeted longer-term refinancing operations. These
lending operations constitute a significant part of the ECB's balance-
sheet expansion, indicating a distinctive element in European QE. Lastly,
the ECB's aggressive QE response suggests a significant change in attitudes
among ECB leaders from Trichet to Lagarde, as the central bank emphasized low growth and unemployment as more significant macroeconomic
problems than inflationary risks.

The Bank of England went through equally striking transitions. As discussed in Chapter 5, the UK central bank and its Governor initially remained in denial of the critical role that monetary authorities play in a
deep financial crisis. It took until the Lehman crash before the Bank's Governor Mervyn King appreciated the extent of the financial sector's liquidity problems and the urgent need to step up as a lender of last resort.[22]
From that moment onward, the Bank combined extensive short- and long-
term lending to the banking sector with purchases of government bonds.

Moreover, in contrast to the ECB, the unwinding of emergency loans was overcompensated from 2009 onward with more aggressive asset purchases. This also implied the primacy of monetary versus fiscal policy in fighting the recession. King publicly supported the austerity policies of Chancellor George Osborne, warning of debt accumulation and structural deficits, while expanding the Bank's own operations.[23] In 2013, the Bank then paused its program when the volume of purchased assets stood at £375 billion. QE was reactivated in the wake of Brexit, when the Bank bought another £60 billion in gilts and £10 billion in privately issued bonds.

But the most significant round of QE was in response to Covid-19, when the Bank bought double the volume of assets purchased under all previous QE rounds. Two striking aspects were evident in this latest phase. First, just as in the United States, a sudden spike in liquidity demand within the financial sector initiated the central bank's aggressive response. In 2008, problems in banking had driven central bank action, but this time, the *shadow* banking sector was at the center of attention, and the Bank figured that it could "backstop liquidity in market-based finance" with aggressive asset purchases, that is, as a market-maker of last resort.[24] Second, close alignments between the Bank's sovereign bond purchases and the Treasury's calendar of bond issuances indicated that, without an explicit public commitment, the Bank was helping the government to finance its aggressive fiscal response to Covid-19 (Gabor 2021).

In the following two sections, I will use these brief accounts of Fed, ECB, and BoE policies to elaborate on two features of post-2008 central banking. The first concerns the altered role of financial markets in central banking; in the second section, I discuss how, notwithstanding central bankers' commitments to support broad economic well-being, their limited instruments ultimately support particular finance-related activities, whose structural predominance comes out as one key feature of secularly stagnating economies.

Financial Markets in Structural Disrepair

Central bank–financial market relations have changed significantly from the era of inflation targeting to the post-2008 period. While markets have served mainly as effective and almost invisible infrastructures (Bowker and

Star 1999) for macroeconomically oriented policies during inflation targeting, they are now the central and problematic objects of attention and intervention in central banking. I here distinguish two levels at which this transformation has occurred. On a practical policy level, operations to support dysfunctional markets and struggling financial firms have developed into a persistent feature of post-2008 central banking and have been closely intertwined with policies to support the broader economy. This is evidently true for the 2008–2009 period, when emergency lending and market-making interventions initiated a first phase of QE. In the case of the Fed, this involved large purchase programs for distressed assets, combined with support operations for various money markets (commercial paper, repo, and so on) (Murau 2017). At the Bank and ECB, subsidized lending for ailing banking institutions actually initiated the central banks' balance-sheet expansions in the first phase. But even as the immediate effects of the 2008 crisis subsided, market and balance-sheet support remained key elements. The Fed developed its spontaneous support programs from 2008 into more permanent facilities to backstop the growing shadow-banking sector, for instance through a reverse repo facility. This new backstopping role was massively upgraded during March 2020, when the Fed did not just restart most of its 2008 money-market programs, but effectively offered hedge funds and other nonbanks a standing facility to transform government bond holdings into cash (Gabor 2021).[25] This triggered the largest QE round so far, in which monetary and financial policy motives were inextricably linked. In Europe, the ECB's term funding has played an equivalent role for traditional banks to give them breathing space for balance-sheet repair. As part of this program, banks could, for instance, practice a kind of "collateral trade" (Crosignani, Faria-e-Castro, and Fonseca 2017). They bought southern European bonds with high yields, deposited these bonds as collateral with the ECB, and received term funding that matched the bonds' maturities. Banks could thereby reap a return on holding high-return periphery debt without carrying credit and liquidity risk. Supporting what they regarded as the systemically important elements of finance is thus part and parcel of central banks' expansionary post-2008 policies, with considerable effects on the size, risk-taking behaviors, and distributional patterns in these sectors (Petrou 2021a: 63).[26]

The intertwinement of financial sector–directed and monetary policies is reinforced through the cognitive frameworks that policymakers have adopted to give QE a macroeconomic rationale. As a reminder, let me briefly summarize how policy transmission via financial markets was conceived under inflation targeting. In the inflation-targeting framework, central bankers exercise *conditional influence* over interest rates through changes in their short-term operational targets and expectational communication. That is, policymakers aimed to alter real medium-term interest rates by credibly committing to contain inflation and by conveying science-based assessments of macroeconomic development in their reports. On the horizon was always the idea of a real natural interest rate plus the tolerated level of inflation, which anchored and constrained the actions of central banks as well as markets. Despite its shaky epistemic foundations (Blanchard 2018; Blinder 2004), this inflation-targeting framework was a plausible abstraction of actual policies and gave coherence to policy rationalities, central bank operations, and market signals in the period up until 2008.

When QE was initiated, however, it was first as a practical innovation in money-market and funding operations, for which the authorities had no consistent cognitive framework. For instance, at the Bank of England, this led to prolonged internal controversies over the question of whether the large supply of bank reserves—a direct consequence of asset purchases—had any meaningful economic consequences in itself, through monetary mechanisms (Cassar 2021). But this monetarist view was soon discarded in central bank circles as authorities converged toward a New Keynesian interpretation. As Bernanke remembers, "Fed policymakers and staff understood that, with short-term interest rates near zero, the demand for bank reserves would be highly elastic and the velocity of base money could be expected to fall sharply" (2020: 961; see also Fullwiler 2013: 186).

A more thorough theorization then gradually emerged as New Keynesian economists tried to incorporate large-scale asset purchases into the hegemonic monetary policy conception developed during the period of inflation targeting (Woodford 2003b). One idea to emerge from this theorization was that, while central banks could no longer drive real interest rates lower with changes in their operational targets—which had already hit an effective lower boundary—their announcements, together with asset purchases, would help to signal intentions to keep rates low for longer (Gern et al. 2015). Central bankers, and particularly Ben Bernanke, endorsed this idea, but this raised two problems. First, a growing number of *long-term* interest rates in the 2010s hit their lower limits, exhausting the possibility of stimulative interest-rate policies altogether. Second, in the second half of the 2010s, central bankers discovered an uncomfortable disconnect: While their models of equilibrium interest rates would have suggested that continuing QE led to rising expected inflation, such changes in expectations and actual inflation rates did not happen. There apparently was no stable relation between projected interest rates and changes in inflation and growth.[27] By implication, inflation targeting's cognitive framework was no longer consistent with policy action or observed effects during QE.

What then emerged is a different theorization of QE, built on the intertwinement of monetary with financial policy. This is the portfolio-rebalancing view (see figure 6.2). The idea was that, as central banks buy government bonds or other safe assets from investors, these investors will purchase other securities to re-fill their portfolios with the cash received from central banks. Because investors are not indifferent to the kinds of assets they own in their portfolios, they go into almost equivalent long-term assets, such as corporate bonds (Bernanke 2020: 947). Lower funding costs for these (usually large) corporations, as well as the rising prices for

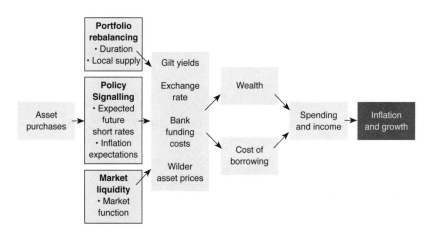

FIGURE 6.2. QE transmission mechanisms, according to the Bank of England.
Source: Andrew Bailey, Jonathan Bridges, Richard Harrison, Josh Jones, and Aakash Mankodi, "The Central Bank Balance Sheet as a Policy Tool: Past, Present and Future," Bank of England Staff Working Paper No. 899. Figure 2. ©2020 Bank of England

broader classes of assets, then allegedly exert stimulative effects via credit and wealth channels (Joyce et al. 2016: 279). Note that, in stark contrast to the inflation-targeting framework, this new cognitive framework relies on the idea that investors do *not* hold perfectly rational expectations (if they did, assets would be functionally equivalent in terms of their risk / return profiles) and that markets are *not* frictionless (which justifies the assumption that reduced availability of one asset—government bonds—influences the prices of others). Indeed, as the father of New Keynesianism, Michael Woodford, made clear, in his own equilibrium theory framework, portfolio-rebalancing mechanisms could not work.[28] Subsequent studies then reinforced empirically that portfolio rebalancing essentially rests on financial frictions—QE can push investors into riskier assets when general risk aversion is high. In economics lingua, this means that QE is "state-contingent," and the situations it works in best are financial crises.[29]

In short, then, central banking between 2008 and 2020 consisted of the systematic intertwinement of monetary with financial policy. With QE, central banks continued to rely on markets for transmitting policies to the broader economy, but these markets themselves turned into problematic objects of governance that require constant support and repair. At the practical as well as cognitive levels, central bankers systematically confounded their sectoral support operations with their macroeconomic objectives, creating a new constellation of monetary policy dominance, which rests less on the welfare promises of financialization than on the perceived inevitability of supporting markets and firms in an economy that has become increasingly vulnerable to developments in finance.

Financialization as an Exhausted Growth Driver

These problems with QE's practices and cognitive frameworks are inseparable from the deeper predicaments that arise for a macroeconomic policy that relies excessively on the structures of financialized capitalism to affect the broader economy. These predicaments shine through in the results delivered by QE after more than ten years of superexpansive policies. To be sure, central bankers have reasons to claim that their policies helped temporarily to lower interest rates, stabilize growth, support employment, and reduce the refinancing burdens for high-debt economies (Bernanke 2020).

But given QE's reliance on financial market–related mechanisms to generate these effects, we have seen extremely weak recoveries, rising inequalities, and entrenched problems of secular stagnation. This is also increasingly seen in studies on QE effectiveness, which indicate exhaustion over the span of ten years.[30]

A first aspect that I have already mentioned concerns the effects of QE in support of financial and other assets, from stocks and bonds to real estate. As the growing literature on inequality has shown, ownership of such assets and access to possibilities for their debt-financed acquisition are distributed highly unequally, even more so than in the case of income (Piketty 2014). Moreover, the very logic of wealth is that an unequal distribution is self-reinforcing over time (Milanovic 2019). Growing inequality then feeds into secular stagnation because propensities to consume are high at the bottom but low at the top. By transmitting policies via wealth effects, QE has thus made a major contribution to cementing and enhancing these long-term and regressive distributional mechanisms. The idea that QE boosts consumption and thereby increases economic activity (Joyce et al. 2016) is hardly convincing on this basis, given that wealth effects today are concentrated overwhelmingly at the top. Karen Petrou (2021a) argues plausibly that central bankers miss this because their models tend to capture averages rather than distributions. Moreover, the increasingly skewed distributions of wealth do not just affect growth and employment today. They rather shape how economies develop into the future, as relatively persistent structural properties. Therefore, even small gains in consumption generated through massive QE interventions can *enlarge* macroeconomic problems over longer periods of time. The economic consequences of such wealth concentration are captured in a study by Atif Mian, Ludwig Straub, and Amir Sufi (2020). These authors show that growing financial wealth at the top goes hand in hand with dissaving among the rest of the population and more government debt. Accumulated wealth at the top does *not* contribute to domestic investment.

A second, related mechanism that links QE with secular stagnation runs though the consolidation and growth of household debt. As a wide-ranging literature has argued, we see this trend among key economies such as the United States as poorer and middle-class households try to compensate for stagnating wages and rising socioeconomic inequalities (van Treeck 2015). Household indebtedness can be a temporary driver of growth but becomes a burden over time, reducing growth directly as well as indirectly (Mian 2019). The problem with household debt is that, for the middle classes (and to a lesser extent, the working classes), it is usually used to finance nondiversified assets, such as real estate. Temporarily, such investments may increase net household wealth as the assets purchased with such debt inflate in value procyclically together with debt. As Alina Bartscher and coauthors (2020) report for the United States, debt expanded most strongly among the middle class prior to 2008, but this class temporarily experienced an even stronger growth in its housing wealth. In fact, most debt was incurred as a *result* of positive net wealth effects because households borrowed more and more on the basis of appreciating house prices. But these temporarily enriched, and increasingly leveraged (Mian, Straub, and Sufi 2020), households ultimately turned from "being an anchor of financial stability to being the epicenter of financial risk in the U.S. economy," as Bartscher and colleagues note (2020: 6). One risk obviously was that households would face higher borrowing costs. But central banks mostly mitigated that risk with lower and lower interest rates from 1983 to 2008. The key vulnerability became a reversal in house-price development in 2006, combined with negative shocks to labor incomes after 2008.[31] After the crisis, QE provided an immediate response to these problems. By lowering interest rates and interventions in particular markets (for example, purchases of mortgage-backed securities), central banks like the Fed eased private debt burdens and reduced refinancing costs for some groups. QE has also helped to stabilize or raise real estate values as the primary assets held by middle-class households. But by making the carrying of debt burdens more palpable and / or more attractive, the Fed's and other central banks' actions have arguably helped to consolidate the structural macroeconomic significance of household debt, at least in economies such as the United States. Under given policies, incurring such debt is a way of profiting from real estate cycles and finance consumption (Petrou 2021a: 84), even if such strategies imply huge macro-risks. One interpretation of QE is thus that it has consolidated "privatized Keynesianism" as an unstable pillar of Western welfare systems (Crouch 2011; Offer 2017; Prasad 2012; Quinn 2019).

A third set of pathologies concerns corporate financing. One of the express intents of QE has been to improve corporate funding conditions, either through portfolio rebalancing or direct credit channels (for example, in funding for lending schemes). The hope is that firms with better funding conditions will invest more, create jobs, and raise overall output. However, the attempt to induce growth via these channels entails the risk of reproducing structural problems and corporate strategies that stand in the way of broad, inclusive growth. At one end of the spectrum, small and medium-sized firms have not profited sufficiently from QE to expand investments, especially in a broader environment of depressed demand; QE may have done just enough to help ailing firms to roll over their debts. At the other end, more successful large corporations have used their low funding costs for activities that either do not bring forth investments or that have a small positive impact on jobs and growth. Ismail Erturk (2016) explains the absence of investments in terms of "financialized corporate behavior." Such behavior involves, for instance, firms using lower debt-financing costs to buy back their own stock, thereby boosting the companies' return on equity and their stock-market valuations. CEOs and other managers with performance-related compensation benefit from these strategies, but the employees and the broader economy do not. Erturk also suggests that, by lowering funding costs and boosting stock values, QE has contributed to an environment in which firms attempt large-scale mergers and acquisitions, consolidating their positions in ever more concentrated markets. Accordingly, we find a trend whereby private investment does not pick up, despite ever easier monetary policy.

But even when firms in thriving sectors such as information technology *do* invest, the marginal benefits of these investments for workers and the economy remain small. That is because we tend to find "superstar firms" in such sectors. These firms have economies of "scale without mass" (that is, with a shrinking employee share), often invest in intangible capital, and adopt aggressive outsourcing strategies (Davis 2016). These factors, together with the firms' oligopoly / monopoly powers, mean that "superstars" can charge high markups, which directly translate into lower relative benefits for workers. Accordingly, superstar firms have done most to foster a reduced labor share of income in highly developed economies, and that helps to explain why this share has dropped so dramatically in the United States since 2000 (Autor et al. 2020). In turn, the rising share of profits going to capital lead to overaccumulation and investments in finance. All in all, then, focusing crisis management on improved corporate financing has arguably meant reproducing rather than challenging the predicament of poor investments, insufficient aggregate demand, growing market concentration, and reduced labor shares of income.

The Broken Promise of Welfare through Financial Sector Growth and Financialization

Financialization helped to support growth leading up to 2008, by sustaining demand at low levels of investment and in times of reduced labor income shares. Likewise, financial globalization helped to reconcile the growth models of export- and debt-oriented economies in the "post-Fordist" era (Baccaro and Pontusson 2016; Schwartz 2019). Inflation targeting was deeply implicated in these developments at the macro-level by facilitating coordination via yield curves and inflation targets—coordination devices that were perfectly adapted to accelerated credit expansion, large global imbalances, the dominance of capital over workers, and elevated levels of domestic inequality. As I argued in Chapter 4, inflation targeting was also aligned with financialization at the meso-level, through central bankers' co-construction of money-market architectures, which were critical for sustaining the money-issuing and liquidity-distribution process that fuels financial growth. What we thus observe prior to 2008 is a constellation of mutual support between the policy dominance of central banks and the expansion and deepening of financialization.

This chapter has discussed developments after a monumental crisis, which brought to light the fundamental contradictions and predicaments that result from these interdependencies. The irony is that postcrisis developments have by and large consolidated the powerful positions of central banks and financial sectors. Central bankers recognized the inability or unwillingness of fiscal authorities to assume more responsibility. This provided a window of opportunity for central bankers to further expand their authority.

Key protagonists of these policy innovations are convinced that QE has worked (Bernanke 2020). Without aggressive first responses by central banks, many financial firms would have failed (Bernanke et al. 2020), and without extremely expansive monetary policies, interest rates would be higher, and we would have more unemployment and less growth. Several studies have questioned these benign assessments, however, particularly for the latter phase of QE. A key argument to emerge from this literature is that post-2008 policies have favored financial market actors and rich groups in society that own excessive financial wealth. My own work is intended to broaden this critique by revealing the deep entanglements of contemporary central banking with oversized financial sectors and mechanisms of financialization. First, as I have argued, financial and monetary policy have become inextricably connected through QE and its various subprograms. Schemes such as subsidized term funding or market-making of last resort have all been incorporated into QE. This has led to a massive expansion of certain segments (such as shadow banking) and has favored the large, established firms at the center of today's financial systems. Moreover, as I have discussed, the dominant theory adduced to justify QE, portfolio rebalancing, justifies such interventions in terms of frictions within finance that require central bank repair. As a result, the rationales for prioritizing finance in public policy have shifted since before 2008. While the earlier promise was that efficient markets and expansive finance would bring welfare for all (Beckert 2020), the new logic after the crisis is that, because the dominance of finance is already entrenched in our economies, refraining from financial market support is too risky. Crashes would unleash major economic shocks, and our fragile debt-dependent welfare systems could further deteriorate if central banks failed to prop up asset markets and sustain debt manageability. In other words, we are in a captive situation, and central banks and financial market logics remain dominant by default.

The problems with this situation become all the more apparent when we look at how central banks aim to reach the broader economy through QE. Relying on the wealth effects generated by asset purchases means entrenching the root causes of secular stagnation; wealth inequality is reinforced, and the consequences of this inequality go far beyond immediate swings in employment and output. Central banks have also increased the risks of household overindebtedness and overleverage because, under current policy conditions, middle-class families continue to invest in nondiversified assets while poorer families, especially in the United States, continue to consume on debt. While it was partly possible to protect these social groups with QE from stronger adverse shocks after 2008, central banks cannot commit themselves forever to maintaining inflated price levels and unsustainable debt. Deleveraging then unleashes deflationary forces on the downturn. Moreover, the idea that economic policy should concentrate on improving the financing conditions for corporate actors has increasingly been called into question by evidence about the actual use of cheap financing in financialized economies. Instead of capital investments, many corporations have turned to financial market–related strategies, such as equity buybacks or mergers and acquisitions. In consequence, higher corporate debt in the United States has *not* been matched by higher investments. Moreover, by improving financing conditions, another problem remains unaddressed. Even when firms *do* invest (increasingly in intellectual property rights, such as patents), workers get a small share of the revenues generated. As a result, we observe no persistent improvement in labor's income share over the period of expansionary central bank policies. In short, then, the structural predicaments of secular stagnation have been more deeply entrenched during a decade of QE.

The broader argument I wish to make here is that, even when central bankers have moved beyond cognitive denial and recognized the various problems confronted in advanced capitalist economies, their actions have remained constrained through their organizations' deep entanglements with finance, driving us ever deeper into unsustainable conditions. It is this structural and infrastructural constraint on central banking in financialized capitalism that scholars should address, rather than trying to repair the current regime through small amendments and institutional tweaks. Let us look at two domains in which progressive proposals do not appear to have helped or perhaps have even backfired. One concerns monetary financing. Modern monetary theory (Tymoigne and Wray 2013) and growing numbers of mainstream economists (e.g., De Gauwe 2020) have revived the discussion around this practice, which involves central banks explicitly and deliberately supporting governments' funding needs. This is not just theory: Short of central banks directly taking on public debt (which is prohibited in many jurisdictions), monetary authorities have already been doing their utmost to ease financing conditions among states. For instance, the Euro system's massive engagement in member states' bond markets, expanded during Covid-19, has been decisive in saving the currency block and generating legitimacy for the central bank (at least in the southern parts). The problem is, however, that the very same operations greeted in Italy have *also* helped shadow banks to recycle their massive bond holdings into cash. Monetary financing, under current conditions, thus means simultaneously facilitating public debt-financing *and* the growth of financial sectors, which rely on this debt as a new form of money—secured by comprehensive backstops from central banks (Gabor 2021). In consequence, what on the surface appears to be a change toward more progressive policies and attitudes structurally consolidates oversized finance. Under these conditions, taxation appears to be a more sustainable solution to finance public spending because it would make it possible to keep financial markets and central banks out of the loop.

A second domain concerns various practices of direct or indirect central bank lending for politically favored sectors. For instance, during the Covid-19 pandemic, central banks lent directly to debtor groups that were deemed vulnerable and in need of liquidity support. Among these were small and medium-sized enterprises (SMEs) and municipalities. Ultimately, "green central banking" may evolve into a more comprehensive version of such favored direct or indirect credit support. But while targeted lending has a long history as a social policy tool (Quinn 2019), it should not be incorporated into central banks' QE. Central banks have no special competencies or legitimacy for such activities (Menand 2020), and liberal economists rightly suggest that such developments problematically confound macroeconomic stabilization operations (for example, for low inflation and maximum employment) with industrial policy. The latter should be conducted in public investment banks with explicit political mandates and frameworks of accountability to carry out such policies.

A key motive for raising doubts about these new, seemingly more progressive elements in recent central banking is that, as the Covid-19 crisis has shown, when push comes to shove, central bank resources are available primarily for the highly concentrated, most leveraged parts of finance. Just remember that American central bankers were able to mobilize $1 trillion in a couple of days during March 2020 to save shadow banks. By implication, even with the best of intentions, central bankers reinforce self-defeating cycles of financial expansion, while their approach to macroeconomic policy leads us ever more deeply into the financialization trap.

Conclusion

THIS BOOK HAS reconstructed the ascendency of central banks since the 1970s. Focusing on a few prominent and formative cases, I have shown how monetary officials have found ways to exploit the particular governing capacities of their organizations by designing instruments that allowed them to tap infrastructural power. While in the German and Swiss contexts, this infrastructural power came from conservative institutional configurations—universal banking and corporatist wage coordination—Anglo-Saxon central bankers taught the world how to capitalize on the globalizing logic of market-based finance.

This in turn had consequences for the development of markets. Central bankers co-constructed a global funding infrastructure (centered on repo markets) that helped to fuel a liquidity illusion—the belief, among financial actors, that balance-sheet positions could always be refinanced in market-based systems. Moreover, inflation targeting led central bankers to focus their efforts on establishing predictability, leading market actors to anticipate very stable developments in inflation and interest rates into the distant future. This then facilitated aggressive term-transformation strategies beyond classic deposit-banking, which proved unsustainable as soon as risk perceptions changed. Moreover, even though central bankers had traditionally been the key regulators and supervisors of money markets and banks' reserve management, in the run-up to the 2008 crisis, authorities failed to react to growing systemic risks in these domains. I have argued that the reason for this inaction was strategic dissociation. Central banks continued to shape money markets and liability management for their monetary policy purposes, but avoided any prudential regulatory interventions that could have damaged the legitimacy and efficacy of their inflation targeting.

In the last chapter, I then showed how authorities innovatively reacted to the fact that they could no longer alter operational targets for interbank money-market rates as inflation targeting's most important tool. The new tool—large-scale asset purchases—developed out of central banks' lender and market-maker of last-resort operations during the crisis and, subsequently, due to persistent economic stagnation and fiscal retrenchment, became the dominant macroeconomic management device. However, quantitative easing (QE) is deeply entangled with defunct features of financialized capitalism. This becomes evident in its double role. On the one hand, as the Covid-19 crisis again brought home, central banks' massive interventions remain in high demand. Expanding shadow banking and unprecedented levels of peacetime debt have rendered it necessary for central banks to operate as ultimate insurers and backstops for financial and economic systems. The threats of major market crashes, debt crises, and deeper secular stagnation make their almost unlimited balance-sheet capacities indispensable. But at the same time, with QE, central banks have exhausted their capacities to generate specific, widely desired macroeconomic outcomes. More than that: Central bank backstops help to make financial markets more unstable over time and reinforce a finance-dependent development that brings forth unignorable structural problems. Central banking thus operates as an endemic feature of a regime whose instabilities and inequalities are increasingly coming to be recognized and felt.

I would like to undertake three remaining tasks in the final pages of this book. First, I will summarize my key contributions to the extant literature on central banking. I will then go beyond central banking to discuss how my analysis can advance state-centric approaches in the study of economic policies (Weir 1989; Weir and Skocpol 1985). Lastly, I will indicate some possible future avenues of research on central banks. My idea here is to theorize central banking in terms of regime preservation in financialized capitalism, which gives monetary officials a new and highly problematic source of legitimacy.

Beyond Interests and Ideas: A New Account of Central Banks' Ascendency and Its Effects

Central banking is not an understudied topic. At the start of this project, and as mentioned in the Preface, a political science colleague had even advised me against working on it on the grounds of epistemic saturation. So in what ways does my analysis add anything new to the vast literature? I want to distinguish two main contributions here. The first consists in providing a complementary explanation for central banks' changing roles in Western capitalist democracies that specifies the processes and timings of their ascendency. The second contribution consists in looking differently at the consequences of monetary policies, particularly for financial markets.

I will start with my particular perspective on how central banks have gained in influence and importance in Western advanced economies. As I discussed in the Introduction and Chapter 1, dominant accounts of this process focus on central banks' key roles in neoliberalism. Different schools of political economy emphasize two aspects of neoliberal institutional and policy change. A first one looks at anti-inflationary interests of capital owners and how the crisis period of the 1970s led to a veritable counterrevolution by these actors. They allegedly mobilized their structural and instrumental powers and thereby led Western states to delegate (if not abdicate) competencies to those institutions that could cater to capitalist demands. The beneficiaries of these neoliberal reforms were central banks. A second group of political economists plausibly argues that "structures do not come with an instruction sheet" (Blyth 2003). For that reason, ideas matter. For instance, politicians could induce significant, "third order" change (Hall 1993) in policies, instruments, and institutions by mobilizing voters around monetarism as an appealing solution to stagflation problems. In an alternative strand of the ideational literature, scholars argue that decision-making on complex topics such as monetary policy is partly dissociated from capitalist pressures or electoral demands. In the relatively self-contained spheres of elite discourse, programs and institutional norms are formulated on the basis of expert ideas.

As I showed in this book, changing constellations of interests among capitalists and voters, as well as ideational reorientations within politics and developments in expert circles, have all played their part in rendering central banks more powerful and leading to a primacy of monetary policies in Western advanced economies. However, the respective forces only loosely influenced the precise processes of policy adoption and institutional change. Interests were often contradictory. For instance, representatives of export sectors simultaneously wanted stable exchange rates as well as low inflation; and banks demanded stable inflation but also stable refinancing rates. More often than not, it was up to policymakers to interpret different demands and resolve dilemmas. More importantly, when policymakers first confronted monetary and macroeconomic instabilities during the 1970s, it was fundamentally uncertain how they could solve these problems and satisfy stability demands (dominant or not). Expert proposals or politicians' electorally appealing ideas usually did not offer viable solutions. And if policymakers went on to adopt policies based on politicians' or experts' ideas, they usually generated unexpected and sometimes highly undesirable effects, as was the case with Margaret Thatcher's early and short-lived attempts to use monetarist monetary policy to reduce inflation (which had extremely detrimental effects on the tradable goods sector). Even in the case of inflation targeting, which has become an extreme case of "scientized" policymaking, New Keynesian models and concepts were of little relevance for its early innovation. Far more important were practical solutions found in the course of policy conduct.

As Ben Braun and Daniela Gabor note, one of the key problems in the political economy literature is that it "has tended to abstract from the operational details of central banking" (2020: 243). I have zeroed in on this neglected aspect and shown that we can better understand the precise processes and timings of central banks' ascendency when looking much closer at the organizations, their policy innovations, and the conditions shaping possibilities for these innovations. Take the case of the Swiss National Bank and the Bundesbank and how these two central banks redefined their policymaking roles after the turn to flexible exchange rates in

1973. As I have shown, neither external pressures by interest groups, nor electoral developments, nor the spread of Friedman's monetarism can explain these transformations. Rather, Swiss and German central bankers were able to gain new roles because they enjoyed sufficient leeway to engage in experiments with monetary targeting, encountered felicitous conditions for this new practice (universal banking and corporatist institutions), and over time recognized the distinctive power of practical monetarism as a version of "incomes policy in disguise." The Bank of England did not enjoy the same room for experimentation during the 1970s, due to its lack of independence and its more circumscribed role as a financial sector institution. Another aspect of the story is that UK central bankers actively decided against more radical innovations because they had, by the mid-1970s, recognized the inoperability of proposed solutions (i.e., monetarism) in the UK context and therefore opted for continued reliance on "private influence" with government. But the Bank's assessments changed over the course of the 1980s. By the early 1990s, neither the Bank's institutional status nor the political context had altered much. But the Bank started to advocate and strategize for independent authority because it had recognized that interest-rate manipulations vis-à-vis a market-based financial system *could* constitute a powerful policy tool. Accordingly, when the opportunity came (after the European Exchange Rate Mechanism disaster), the Bank reformed policy procedures and introduced a new expectational coordination with markets based on its *Inflation Reports*. This innovation in 1992–1993 was the crucial moment leading to central bank dominance. Last but not least, Paul Volcker fundamentally changed the Fed's status, not because he had come to believe in monetarism or because of any significant political change. Nor was Volcker a radical conservative to disregard the macroeconomic costs of his actions. Rather, what made Volcker distinct is that he boldly used the leeway given to the Fed (and the power of its chairman) in order to address what he recognized as the key problem in policy transmission: financial markets' expectations of ever higher inflation. For that purpose, Volcker engaged in a failed episode of monetarist nonborrowed reserves targeting, only to come out of this experiment as a proto-inflation targeter. Again, the central bankers themselves, their policy innovations, and the conditions for these innovations decisively altered their institutional status and the role of monetary policy.

I am now turning to the second contribution that I have made in this book, namely to advance our thinking on the consequences of central banks' ascendency and the effects of their policies, particularly for finance. In brief, extant scholarship has linked monetary policy dominance to the growth of financial markets with two arguments. The first one is that central banks allegedly have a disinflationary, hard-money bias. Disinflationary politics have undermined the interests of workers and supported those of capital. Political economists argue that these regressive policies have raised the structural importance and fueled the growth of finance. Following the disinflation of the 1980s, capitalists felt emboldened by the promise for monetary stability and were keen to grant credit and invest. Disinflationary policies also fueled credit growth in the household sector because workers experiencing losses in labor incomes turned to credit instead. A complementary, widely endorsed argument is that the growing power of central banks is coterminous with the "rise of the liberal creed" (Fourcade-Gourinchas and Babb 2002). As monetary policymakers became more influential after the 1970s, they acted as the champions of free markets. Their influence within the state and their direct policy actions led to deregulations in financial systems, which in turn contributed to an unsustainable growth of credit and the introduction of dangerous financial instruments.

These arguments are not wrong, but incomplete. First, evidence on pre-2008 policies (Cieslak and Vissing-Jorgensen 2018), together with the now-extensive analyses of QE, reveals that central bankers can support financialization with *expansionary,* soft-money policies. Second, the deregulation argument is incomplete because it fails to capture central bankers' distinct policy motives that influence their attitudes and decisions concerning regulatory issues (remember the Bundesbank's and Swiss National Bank's oppositions to innovative money-market instruments). Moreover, the liberalization story misses that central bankers have been actively involved in shaping and regulating financial systems in accordance with their governing interests.

More generally, the weakness of structural power and ideational approaches is that they divide the world into the separate spheres of policies and markets. Following such reasoning, central bankers have been most adamant in their support for finance when they sought to deregulate markets and reduce activist economic policy to establish price stability. But as a growing number of scholars have argued, finance is anything but a free-market realm (Hockett and Omarova 2017; Konings 2011; Pistor 2013); and financialization is anything but the outcome of *laissez-faire* (Quinn 2019).

My own analysis has therefore shifted emphasis to the concrete entanglements and recursive causalities that have integrated central banking and market-based finance. As Chapter 3 on expectation management discussed, central bankers, rather than concentrating on hard money, have emerged during neoliberalism as hyperactive policymakers who constantly adjust interest rates to changing financial and macroeconomic conditions and the expectational dynamics associated with them. In turn, financial markets were able to massively expand in the period before 2008 based on the policy-induced expectation that macroeconomic and financial conditions would remain stable into the distant future. This arguably led to a stability illusion in markets. Another critical area of recursive causalities is that of money markets. Their expansion, driven by private profit motifs, was critical for the failure of embedded liberalism and of postwar regulations—the rise of the Eurodollar is emblematic of this disruptive change. But with the adoption of new policy implementation techniques, central bankers learned to capitalize on banks' growing price sensitivity and the arbitrage relationships that have emerged in marketized financial systems. The consolidation of a proper architecture of money markets involved active support from central bankers (Birk 2017), who helped to formalize key legal, regulatory, and operational arrangements. Where central bankers' support was strongest (in the repo segment), market liquidity grew most strongly (Gabor 2016). There is little recognition of these mechanisms of central bankers assisting financialization in the mainstream literatures because, for conceptualizing and studying the respective processes, we need to complement more standard methods focusing on linear causal effects with those that reveal how public and market actors coproduce institutions and structures that they jointly depend on (Carruthers 2015).

Bureaucrats in Economic Policymaking

The next question I want to address in this Conclusion is how my study can inform research in the social sciences on (transformations in) economic policy more broadly. While central banking is special in many respects, I will try to distill concepts that may help to theorize processes in this broader field and serve to compare particular sites. I will do so by indicating how my work enriches a tradition of research that highlights the importance of state bureaucrats in developing policies and in shaping institutions (Carpenter 2001; Carruthers 1994; Quinn 2019; Weir and Skocpol 1985). I revisit this tradition in light of changes in state–economy relations since the 1970s, with the idea that, while some parts of the public sector have lost capacities because of structural and institutional changes in capitalism, others have gained. Among the winners are central bankers, but presumably also other bureaucrats, who occupy strategic positions at the intersections of politics and markets (Sassen 2006). I therefore single out three concepts—*bureaucratic entrepreneurship, policy instruments,* and *infrastructural power*—that might serve as powerful, flexible tools to conduct research on these actors.

(a) The first concept is *bureaucratic entrepreneurship*. Without denying the importance of changing electoral coalitions, elites' structural and instrumental powers, and / or ideational shifts, authors in the abovementioned tradition have demonstrated that state officials have considerable agency in the policymaking process and in shaping institutional relationships between the state and the economy. To be sure, such agency varies from context to context. For instance, Bruce Carruthers (1994) has argued that, in the 1930s, the UK Treasury was far more autonomous than its US peer, with consequences for economic policy patterns (high consistency in the United Kingdom, volatility in the United States). Moreover, bureaucratic agency is itself institutionalized, organizationally structured, and cultured in different ways. Margaret Weir and Theda Skocpol (1985) show in their now-classic study that, during the 1930s and 1940s, finance ministries in different state structures responded differently to the Great Depression because they were differently receptive to new, Keynesian ideas. More broadly, this line of literature has established that officials in key bureaucratic organizations have several strategic advantages in shaping policies and institutions. They control various resources that give them considerable leverage over policy preparation and implementation; they monopolize certain forms of expertise concerning, for example, contents and procedures; they have privileged access to, and influence over, the elected heads of government; and in some areas (for example, regulation), they have executive decision-making powers of their own. Daniel Carpenter (2001) adds another important aspect to this larger argument. Long tenures do not only make career bureaucrats partially independent from political patronage and other external forces. They also allow them to accumulate experiences over successful and failed policy experimentation. This in turn gives officials invaluable knowledge about policy design. Complementarily, long tenures allow officials to build "reputation networks" with social actors that are essential to successfully implement policies and legitimate bureaucratic organizations. According to Carpenter, officials use these advantages to secure and increase the autonomy of their bureaucratic organizations, thereby shaping not just policies, but the institutional architectures of states.

My own study advances this concept of bureaucratic entrepreneurship in two ways. First, the case of central banking particularly helps to reveal that, in areas with significant cognitive and technical complexity, the translation of political demands, ideas, and proposals into concrete designs, instruments, and programs is a significant aspect of policymaking in its own right. Moreover, whenever policy implementation generates unexpected outcomes (such as failures), actors are needed who can understand these outcomes and learn from them. I mentioned Margaret Thatcher's failed monetarism above. Bank of England officials were the ones who steered Thatcher away from certain versions of monetarism (namely monetary base targeting), which they regarded as incompatible with UK banking structures. More importantly, these officials took their lessons from the repeated failures of UK monetarism and embarked on a search for policy solutions that better reflected the financialization of the economy and structural changes in London's financial sector. In other instances, we saw that, while legal mandates, political demands, and available ideas from macroeconomics changed little in crucial episodes of change, innovation happened at the level of instrumentalization (Lascoumes and Le Galès 2007). The Volcker shock is the most prominent example of this. The broader point here thus is that, rather than being mere technical issues of how to realize "big" political ideas, the concrete operationalization and implementation of policies are significant steps in complex policymaking fields. Officials have significant organizational control and resources with which to shape these steps.

A second, related point is that policy experimentation constitutes a particularly strong version of bureaucratic entrepreneurship. Experimentation occurs when officials have room to try new programs and strategies, and when they have reasons to use this room in proactive ways. In the case of central banking, there is clear evidence for this. Officials have innovated new policy tools, remodeled their own organizations, and engaged in market design. These actions often happened under uncertainty, and more often than not, they generated unexpected results. The monetarist experiments by the German Bundesbank and the Swiss National Bank are a case in point. When authorities engaged in them, they were uncertain whether their targeting would work, how targets could be achieved, and how various stakeholders would react. More importantly, what then became practical monetarism in these countries was an unexpected outcome of these trials. A similar pattern applies to QE, as introduced by the Fed in 2009. Large-scale asset purchases naturally followed on from the Fed's market making of last resort during the crisis of 2008. But, initially, the mechanisms through which asset purchases served monetary policy purposes remained unclear. This raises another important aspect of experimentation: The central bankers discussed in this book have successfully influenced interpretations of their own trials and have claimed ownership over successes (while downplaying failures and costs). For instance, after an initial phase of uncertainty, German and Swiss central bankers drew causal connections between their practical monetarism and the rapid reduction of inflation rates in their countries (but failed to explicate the consequences for employment and growth); and practitioners of QE, after some initial confusion, have introduced the portfolio-rebalancing theory to foreground the benign effects of their massive interventions (while downplaying distorting financial market effects).

(b) Beyond elaborating on the concept of bureaucratic entrepreneurship, a second major contribution of my book is to refine our understanding of *policy instruments,* which received attention in the early state-centric literature (Weir and Skocpol 1985) and more recently in studies on the influence of macroeconomics on economic policy (Hirschman and Berman 2014). My own study refocuses attention on the role of instruments in reconfiguring and reframing specific linkages between public and economic actors (Rose and Miller 1992; Walter and Wansleben 2019). Indeed, going beyond Skocpol and Weir, I radicalize the argument. I posit that policies are conditioned upon specific instrumentalizations, which in turn depend on structural as well as institutional features in different contexts. One example of this is when central bankers started to engage in control inflation during the 1970s. Over the course of different policy experiments, officials realized that their available instruments depended on particular financial sector structures and their own transactional relationships with commercial banks. German and Swiss central bankers learned to capitalize on universal banks' commercial practices to conduct a peculiar version of practical monetarism. Such policies were impossible in contexts with market-based (or marketizing) financial systems, as officials in both the United States and United Kingdom painfully experienced. These latter actors then turned to different policy techniques better adapted to the financial structures in their economies, which consisted in sending price signals to liquid and interconnected markets. The broader point here is thus that much of the bureaucratic entrepreneurship that I have discussed happened in designing, adapting, and improving instruments to align policies with institutional and structural contexts. Instrument choice, in turn, had significant consequences for the substance of policies and their effects. In this book, I have discussed the different financial stability implications of practical monetarism versus inflation targeting. I have also engaged with the now extensive literature on QE as an instrument that fuels wealth inequalities and the financialization of corporate strategies.

(c) A third, related contribution made in this book consists in advancing Michael Mann's concept of *infrastructural power* for understanding instances in which linkages between public and private actors strengthen the former's policymaking capacities. Mann emphasizes two sides of infrastructural power relations. On the one hand, because state actors govern "through," rather than over society, they depend more strongly on the behavior and perceptions of those they govern (Braun 2018a); "[i]nfrastructural power is a two-way street: It also enables civil society parties to control the state" (Mann 1996: 59). At the same time, infrastructural power makes it possible that more and more of "social life is now coordinated through state institutions" (ibid.); it enhances state power through means that would be unavailable in despotic regimes. In this book, I have adapted Mann's concept for the purpose of analyzing how bureaucratic actors raise their policymaking capacities through relations with market actors. My focus was thus on how *some* state actors can use infrastructural powers that are more or less exclusively available to them. Central banks and their relationships with financial markets are a case in point.

As financial markets became more important in the overall economy, they enhanced the infrastructural powers of these particular state bodies. In other words, capitalist transformations redistributed infrastructural powers within the state and changed the latter's shape.

My analysis then looked at how such positive-sum relations between particular economic sectors and state bodies come about—that is, how "infrastructuration" (Edwards 2019) between public policy and private markets concretely happened. The observation motivating this investigation was that expansions of financial markets did *not* invariably and effortlessly enhance the governing powers of central banks. We see considerable variation between cases and over time. For instance, the operational officers at the Bank of England initially confronted serious policy implementation problems when clearing banks turned to active liability-management techniques during the 1970s. Therefore, in the 1970s and into the 1980s, the Bank tried to protect the "old" elements in the City of London (the discount houses, bill market, and so on) against the arrival of overseas competitors and the introduction of new products. Only through innovations in its own policy instruments did the Bank come to appreciate and capitalize on the "market revolution" in the City. The broader point is thus that, in order to use sources of infrastructural power in their environments, policymakers need to configure these relations in particular ways, through the adequate use of instruments. This then allows them to functionalize relations with economic actors as vehicles for the achievement of policy goals. But such configuration succeeds only when economic actors, in turn, connect their own practices and profit interests to the policy-based modes of coordination. Over time, habits, norms, and routines precipitate, which make up what Paul Edwards (2019) calls "infrastructuration." This then gives stable infrastructural power to particular policymakers.

To what extent do these findings about bureaucratic entrepreneurship, policy instruments, and infrastructural power have wider applicability? Admittedly, central banking is an extreme case, in which officials have extensive latitude in fulfilling their (often quite broad) legal mandates, task complexity is very high, officials have exclusive control over a distinct set of instruments, and officials possess ample organizational resources (for example, a large apparatus of expert staff). Moreover, the inflationary problems of the 1970s, crises of fiscal activism, and central banks' exclusive relationships with financial markets have given them unique opportunities to gain influence within the political-economic orders of the late twentieth and early twenty-first centuries. But on smaller scales, I suggest that we can use the concepts of bureaucratic entrepreneurship, policy instruments, and infrastructural power to understand a broader set of contexts associated with economic policy.

Several developments legitimate this assumption. First, states have increasingly become observed, compared, and assessed based on their "outputs"—on the results that public policies should achieve in economic, monetary, environmental, and health-related domains. Such assessments are made by citizens, media, and various "rationalized others" (Meyer et al. 1997). Sociological neo-institutionalism initially observed the remaking of such rationalistic state agency in the context of a US-dominated world culture. But we can expect that pressures to deliver on observed, compared, and evaluated outputs remain relevant even in a more polycentric order. Accordingly, there is a big political prize for those actors in the state who can purportedly deliver desired outputs, and elected governments are under pressure to give problem-solvers more influence or even control over the respective policy domains. Relatedly, "agencification" (Jordana, Levi-Faur, and Fernández i Marín 2011)—the establishment of separate organizational units for specific policy tasks—has broadened the organizational conditions for bureaucratic entrepreneurship and given officials instrument control in more and more domains, from environmental and economic regulation to financial policymaking and public debt management. Agencification can happen for a number of reasons. But one possible avenue consists in bureaucratic actors demonstrating the "superiority" of such organizational forms, based on their capacities to tap infrastructural powers from the market domains over which they govern. Third, since the 1970s, policy areas with considerable technical and epistemic complexity have grown. To name just one example, governments have set themselves targets for decarbonization. However, how to translate such targets into workable industrial, economic, and fiscal policies (e.g., in the energy domain) is far from trivial. How do authorities know which types of intervention (taxes, tax expenditure, public investments) in which sectors actually achieve how much decarbonization? How do they assess the cost-benefit ratios of diverse measures? What are the technical preconditions for implementing these measures (for example, in terms of technical infrastructures)? I expect that, in those countries where decarbonization remains a significant political objective, officials who (experimentally) gain problem-solving capacities and expertise to address these tricky questions will gain considerable influence over policy design and assume influential positions within the state.

More prosaically, there now exists a vast field of research using survey designs and other methods to understand public attitudes and new electoral coalitions behind economic policies (e.g., Barnes and Hicks 2021; Beramendi et al. 2015; Hübscher, Sattler, and Wagner 2021). In many domains, we know, however, that policy patterns do *not* reflect majority views. This leads scholars to return to various versions of elite influence (Culpepper 2011; Culpepper 2015) as the preferred theoretical alternative. What gets lost in these controversies is that economic policies ultimately are governing practices of the state. They entail aspects of organization; they rely on certain instruments and procedures; and they raise complex problems of infrastructuration— only think of the large public-private apparatuses that are needed to raise taxes. The state-centric tradition, and its advancement with ideas from organizational sociology, the sociology of practices, and science and technology studies, offers rich resources to understand these crucial, neglected aspects. If anything, my study of central banking has strengthened the case for such a sociological project.

Logics of Regime Preservation

A last issue I want to address concerns the question of how we can think about central banking going forward. I believe that future research could leverage and advance "policy feedback" concepts (Pierson 1993) and study endogenous crisis mechanisms (Blyth and Matthijs 2017) to understand how neoliberal institutions and policies first reinforced and were supported by financialized economic structures, before entering a downward, vicious cycle. Going beyond the current state of knowledge, we could explore such feedbacks at the meso- and micro-levels.

There exists a curious parallel here. Scholars first explored policy feedbacks and endogenous crisis mechanisms in the study of a defunct Keynesian-Fordist regime. As the literature has shown, in this regime, government commitments to full employment, welfare-state expansions, and strengthened labor unions all supported each other to produce high growth rates, rising wages, and ample opportunities for industrial investment (Baccaro and Pontusson 2016). But, over time, research suggests that several internal mechanisms combined with shifting structural world-economic and technological conditions to unmake this regime. First, labor's increased bargaining power turned into a problem as workers came to regard governments' full employment commitments and expansionary fiscal measures as a license to claim larger shares of firm revenues (Goldthorpe 1978). After exhausting opportunities to raise productivity, firms reacted by hiking prices and thereby induced an inflationary spiral. Simultaneously, governments were unable to address this problem precisely because large constituencies saw full employment, high growth, and generous welfare provisions as political entitlements (Pierson 1993: 602). In these situations, it was easier for governments to accept wage-price spirals than to deflate their constituencies' expectations or to intervene rigorously in corporate and investment decisions (Streeck 2014). Over time, not just capital owners, but also growing sections of the population recognized inflation as a crisis of government, opening up an opportunity for political actors to restabilize state–economy relations on new principles.[1]

Authors have begun to identify equivalent endogenous mechanisms that first strengthened and have subsequently come to undermine financialized capitalism. Particularly in the 1990s, the peak of neoliberalism, it seemed that liberalized financial markets, combined with labor's weakened bargaining power, and inflation-targeting monetary policies produced stable patterns of output and a new promise for welfare through "shareholder capitalism" (Beckert 2020; Davis 2010). The politically volatile factor of labor was taken out of the equation, while (at least in a significant group of advanced economies) credit growth sustained the necessary level of demand (Baccaro and Pontusson 2016). Central banks managed to encourage credit growth and stabilized asset values while ensuring, in conjunction with broader institutional configurations, that no spillovers into inflation occurred. Export economies learned to deal with the prevailing doctrine of "dirty floats" (nominally floating exchange rates) through currency manipulations, currency unions, and global value chains.

But especially since the crisis of 2008, researchers have turned their attention to the various bugs that are built into this regime. First, and most importantly, as many authors have noted, this regime is characterized by growing inequalities in incomes and wealth. At the top, the expansion of finance reflects and helps to reinforce the formation of an extremely wealthy class (with a significant share of finance professionals). This class now finds itself confronted with the problem of capital abundance. Where to invest in economies with no sources of demand that are not themselves products of financial activities? Moreover, capital abundance has led to secularly declining interest rates on safe assets (Rachel and Summers 2019), a process that has intensified an aggressive search for yields. Second, accumulation of household debt among middle-class and lower-income households has provided only fragile sources of prosperity as the respective households usually hold all or most of their wealth in just one asset: their own homes. Reductions in these values then translate into over-indebtedness and deleveraging pressures, which in turn depress overall demand.

This is just a brief and necessarily incomplete list of mechanisms by which financialized capitalism undermines itself—through both economic feedbacks and political reactions to inequalities and crises. The interesting point is that central banks now find themselves in an equivalent situation to that of social democratic governments in the 1970s—that of upholding an unsustainable regime. Participants in financial markets expect support against possible market reversals and expansionary measures to sustain the boom. Debtors also rely on benign financing conditions to roll over vast volumes of existing debt, and issue more. These expectations are already incorporated into asset prices and debt-management strategies. What central banks do under these circumstances is to confirm and uphold these expectations as a strategy of regime preservation. Other courses of action seem too risky in economic and political terms. At the same time, in this situation, monetary authorities lose output legitimacy as their policy space shrinks.

To be sure, I have condensed here complex causal chains in economies and financial systems as feedback mechanisms. Moreover, most of the suggested mechanisms discussed so far are informed by macro-research, particularly in economics. I would therefore see as a major task for sociological research to understand how such feedbacks and "institutional entrainments" (Blyth and Matthijs 2017: 213) work at the meso- and micro-levels. For instance, how do traders in particular money and capital markets incorporate expectations of QE and market-making of last resort into their strategies? And how does this influence the set of feasible policy courses from the perspective of authorities? Also, what are the structural implications of such mutual "lock-ins" from the perspective of economic sociology?

Clearly, because central banks are core actors of regime preservation in a mature financialized capitalism, they give us privileged points of access for understanding broader features of this defunct regime. However, it is important to stress that the story likely to emerge from new research on central banking will differ significantly from the one told in this book. The windows of opportunity that opened up for monetary authorities during the Great Inflation of the 1970s and the expansive phase of financialization— which these authorities used innovatively to transform central banking into a powerful branch of macroeconomic governing—have probably closed.

Appendix

Archives and Interviews

Archives Used for This Research

Britain

Bank of England Archive, London (BoE Archive)
Margaret Thatcher Foundation Archive (https://www.margaretthatcher.org/)
Financial Times Historical Archive (newspaper) (via Gale)

Germany

Bundesbank Historical Archive, Frankfurt
Spiegel (newspaper) (via spiegelonline.de)

Switzerland

Archive of Swiss Bankers Association (SBA Archive)
Neue Zürcher Zeitung Historical Archive (newspaper) (via nzz.ch)
Swiss National Bank Archive, Zurich (SNBA)

Swiss National Archive, Berne (SNA)

Swiss online archive of parliamentary debates (www.amtsdruckschriften.bar
.admin.ch)

United States

Board of Governors of the Federal Reserve System, Federal Open Market Committee, transcripts and other historical materials (https://www.federalreserve
.gov/monetarypolicy/fomc_historical.htm)

FRASER, Federal Reserve Bank of St. Louis (https://fraser.stlouisfed.org). Fraser
also features the Robert Hetzel Oral History Collection (https://fraser
.stlouisfed.org/archival-collection/robert-hetzel-oral-history-collection-4927),
from which I have used various interviews.

International

Bank for International Settlements (BIS) Archive, Basel

Euromoney (magazine) (via EBSCO Host)

Interviewees

Bank of England

Bill Allen   (interviewed by author in October 2018)

Bank of England staff in different positions (1972–2004): Deputy Director for
Monetary Analysis (1994–1998), Deputy Director for Financial Market Operations
(1999–2002), and Deputy Director for Financial Stability and Director for Europe
(2002–2003)

Michael Foot   (interviewed by author in March 2017)

Senior member of the Money Market, Foreign Exchange, European Affairs and
Banking Supervision at Bank of England (1969–1997); Deputy Director of the
Financial Services Authority (1997–2004)

Charles Goodhart   (interviewed by author in May and July 2016)

Monetary policy adviser (1969–1980), chief adviser (1980–1985), and member of the
Monetary Policy Committee (1997–2000) at the Bank of England

Anthony Hotson (interviewed by author in May 2016 and March 2017)

Member of Monetary Policy Group and the Money Market Division, Bank of England (1978–1988)

Andrew Large (interviewed by author in September 2017)

Chairman, Securities and Investments Board (1992–1997); Deputy Chairman of Barclays Bank (1998–2002); Deputy Governor (responsible for Financial Stability); and member of Monetary Policy Committee, Bank of England (2002–2006)

Rachel Lomax (interviewed by author in March 2017)

Official and senior official at HM Treasury (1968–1994) and Deputy Governor of the Bank of England (2003–2008)

Mervyn King (interviewed by author in May 2020)

Non-Executive Director (1990–1991) and chief economist at the Bank of England (1991–1998); subsequently Bank of England's Deputy Governor (1998–2003) and Governor (2003–2013)

Ian Plenderleith (interviewed by author in May 2017)

Junior Assistant to the Governor (1968–1969); member of Foreign Exchange Division, Private Secretary to the Governor (1973–1976); senior member of Money Market Division, Head of Market Operations (1980–1994); Executive Director (Markets) (1994–1997); and Member of the Monetary Policy Committee (1997–2004) at the Bank of England

Paul Tucker (interviewed by author in December 2017)

Joined the Bank of England in 1980 and assumed various roles, including Personal Secretary to the Governor; he subsequently worked in the Bank's different markets divisions (foreign exchange, gilt, and money markets) before becoming Executive Director for Markets (2002–2009) and the Bank's Deputy Governor (2009–2013).

Bundesbank

Gert Häusler (interviewed by author in March 2020)

From 1978 until 1996, various positions at Deutsche Bundesbank, including a secondment to the Bank for International Settlements (1983–1984) and membership in the Central Bank Council

Federal Reserve

Ted Balbach   (Interviewed by Robert Hetzel in May 2002)

Director of research at the Federal Reserve Bank of St. Louis between 1975 and 1992

Ed Boehne   (Interviewed by Robert Hetzel in March 2003)

Started with the Philadelphia Fed as a research economist in 1968 and steadily rose through the ranks, eventually being named president in 1981; Boehne served as president of the Federal Reserve Bank of Philadelphia from 1981 until his retirement in 2000 (longest serving president in the history of the Reserve Bank).

Bill Dudley   (Interviewed by author in June 2020)

Goldman Sachs chief US economist from 1986 to 2007; systems manager at the Federal Reserve Bank of New York (2007–2009); president (2009–2018)

Benjamin Friedman   (interviewed by author in May 2015)

Research assistant at the Federal Reserve Banks of Boston and New York as well as the Federal Reserve Board in the late 1960s; member of the economics faculty at Harvard University since 1972 and full professor since 1980

Allan Meltzer (†2017)   (interviewed by author in May 2015)

PhD degree from UCLA (1958) under supervision of Karl Brunner; faculty member at Carnegie Mellon since 1959 and full professor after 1964; chair of the Shadow Open Market Committee and the authoritative historian of the Federal Reserve (1973–1999)

Swiss National Bank

Werner Abegg   (interviewed by author in March 2015)

Linguistics degree from University of Zurich; journalist with Reuters; became the first SNB press officer in the late 1970s and later Head of Communications

Ernst Baltensperger   (interviewed by author in November 2013)

Assistant, associate, and full professor, Ohio State University (1968–1979); member of Economic and Statistical Section of the SNB (1977–1978)

Peter Bernholz   (interviewed by author in October 2013)

Economics professor at University of Basle (since 1971); regular adviser to the Swiss National Bank

Nikolaus Blattner   (interviewed by author in September 2017)

Secretary General of the Swiss Bankers Association (1987–2000); member of the Directorate of the Swiss National Bank (2001–2007) and its Vice President (2003–2007)

Peter Buomberger   (interviewed by author in April 2014)

Member of the Economic and Statistical Section of the SNB (1975–1984)

Susanne Brandenberger   (interviewed by author in October 2015)

Member of the Swiss Federal Banking Commission (regulatory agency) (1994–1999), responsible for banks' risk management

Serge Gaillard   (interviewed by author in August 2016)

Swiss Trade Union Congress (1997–2007); in this role, Gaillard was also member of the Bank Council of the Swiss National Bank.

Alexander Galli   (interviewed by author in November 2013)

Member of the Economic and Statistical Section of the SNB (1971–1979)

John Lademann   (interviewed by Bernholz in February and March 2005)

Member of Economic and Statistical Section at least since the 1950s; later its Head and Deputy Director (1968–1977)

Carlos Lenz   (interviewed by author in August 2016)

Head of Inflation Forecasting, SNB (since 2013) and professor at University of Berne

Georg Rich   (interviewed by author in December 2013)

Member and later head of Economic and Statistical Section of the SNB (1977–1985); SNB chief economist and Deputy Director (1985–2001)

Jean-Pierre Roth   (interviewed by author in March 2014)

Member of Economic and Statistical Section and other departments in the SNB (1979–1996); SNB Director and President (1996–2009)

Kurt Schiltknecht   (interviewed by Bernholz in September 2004 and by author in November 2013)

Member and later head of Economic and Statistical Section of the SNB (1974–1984); Deputy Director (1982–1984)

Daniel Zuberbühler   (interviewed by author in June 2015)

Joined the secretariat of the Swiss Federal Banking Commission in 1976; from 1996 until 2008, he served as Director.

N.N. (upon request for anonymity)   (interviewed by author in March 2014)

Ex-member of the Directorate of the Swiss National Bank during the 1990s

NOTES

REFERENCES

INDEX

Notes

Preface

1. Unknown author, "The Structure of Financial Markets," November 4, 1983, BoE Archive 2A71.

Introduction

1. Quoted in *Süddeutsche Zeitung,* July 28, 1972, p. 8.

2. A full transcript and video of Ford's speech are available at https://millercenter.org/the-presidency/presidential-speeches/october-8-1974-whip-inflation-now-speech; all quotes here are from the transcript.

3. Bundesbank *Monthly Report,* December 1974, p. 8.

4. Chris Giles, "Central Bankers Have Been Relegated to Second Division of Policymakers," *Financial Times,* October 1, 2020.

5. "The Covid-19 Pandemic Is Forcing a Rethink in Macroeconomics," *Economist,* July 25, 2020.

6. I should note at the outset that, whenever I claim that central banks have gained power, I do not mean to say that central banks have gained more

possibilities to impose their own will on others even if these others find that this will violates their own interests. I rather speak of power in the qualified sense of bureaucratic actors assuming more influential roles in state governing. In my book, power thus means the following: "If you want to achieve objectives that are relevant for society and the political system, you have go via us, involve us in their attainment."

7. This was reported in Planet Money, *The Great Inflation,* July 17, 2021, https://www.npr.org/2021/07/16/1017031811/the-great-inflation-classic.

8. Henning Hesse, Boris Hofmann, and James Weber, "The Macroeconomic Effects of Asset Purchases Revisited," BIS Working Papers No. 680, Monetary and Economic Department, December 2017.

9. Kat Devlin, Shannon Schumacher, and J. J. Moncus, "Many in Western Europe and US Want Economic Changes as Pandemic Continues," Pew Research Center media release, April 22, 2021, https://www.pewresearch.org/global/2021/04/22/many-in-western-europe-and-u-s-want-economic-changes-as-pandemic-continues.

10. My translation is from the following quote: "Z.B. übt jede große Zentralbank . . . kraft monopolistischer Stellung auf dem Kapitalmarkt oft einen 'beherrschenden' Einfluss aus. Sie können den Kreditsuchenden Bedingungen der Kreditgewährung oktroyieren, also deren ökonomische Gebarung im Interesse der Liquidität ihrer eigenen Betriebsmittel weitgehend beeinflussen, weil sich die Kreditsuchenden im eigenen Interesse jenen Bedingungen der ihnen unentbehrlichen Kreditgewährung fügen und diese Fügsamkeit eventuell durch Garantien sicherstellen müssen" (Weber 1976 [1921]: 542).

11. Michael Steen, "Draghi Urges Eurozone Governments to Stay the Course on Austerity," *Financial Times,* May 2, 2013.

1. Neoliberalism and the Rise of Central Banks

1. In her book on public credit policies in the United States, Sarah Quinn gives a good example of these innovations. She writes that "in a fragmented and veto-ridden system, a subset of market-loving, state-hating Americans has long used the array of veto points to slow or redirect state action. In that context, simple pragmatic problem solving can lead officials to discover how a variety of government capacities—guarantees, tax expenditures, incentives, regulations, authority over property rights, and the state's own position as a consumer of goods—move money and exert influence by other means" (2019: 202).

2. See also Foucault (1991 [1978]; 2007 [1978]) and Joyce and Mukerji (2017), as well as Rose and Miller (1992) on this point.

3. "[M]onetary policy has roared . . . into view as the principal—perhaps the only—real tool available to governments . . . In Europe and the United States, in

fact, the ECB and the Fed were pretty much the only games in their respective towns" (Frieden 2013: 3). Adam Tooze in his book *Crashed* cited a financial market actor who said that "everything revolves around monetary policy. It's not the underlying economics that's driving things, it's central bank liquidity" (2018: 473). Wolfgang Streeck similarly observes that "[c]entral banks . . . have become the most important, and indeed effectively the only, players in economic policy, with governments under strict austerity orders and excluded from monetary policy making" (2016: 16).

4. On the electoral success of Ronald Reagan and Margaret Thatcher among working-class voters, see Prasad (2006); on the different attitudes of UK banks vis-à-vis inflation, see Tucker (2018); on the banking sector's pressure to allow for *more* inflation for the sake of *financial* stability, see Copelovitch and Singer (2008).

5. "A former board staffer told me with some fervor: Bankers don't know anything about monetary policy" (Wooley 1984: 81).

6. See Paul Krugman, "How Did Economists Get It So Wrong?," *New York Times Magazine,* September 6, 2009.

7. For instance, the broader regime type (authoritarian vs. democratic) is decisive for what kind of power relations and priorities are institutionally enshrined (Boylan 2001); a state with many veto players is particularly conducive for central bank independence because elected governments confront higher hurdles for reversing such independence (for example, in federal settings) (Frieden 2002); less stable governing coalitions confer more benefits on independence (Bernhard, Broz and Clark 2002); and supposed deep-seated national dispositions and identities (Tognato 2012) can undergird central banks' legitimacy.

8. Max Weber (1976 [1921]) argued for a nuanced analysis of different forms and sources of domination in capitalist state formations; and in this context he also mentioned central banks. And in their much-discredited, but very rich *Economy and Society,* Parsons and Smelser offer a highly interesting theory of credit, in which they theorize its generation through political processes and the "exercise of power" (1956: 56).

9. By situating central banks within these broader configurations, Lebaron (2010) can also make sense of (increasingly small, but telling) differences between central banks. For instance, scientization has been less relevant for Japanese central bankers because the Bank of Japan maintains a version of political authority that remains strongly aligned to the country's large corporate sector.

10. Giving public evidence about one's dominance in struggles over economic policy entails the risk of becoming accountable for an ever-broader array of macroeconomic outcomes—which is why, as reconstructed by Benjamin Friedman (2002), central bankers have rather demonstrated how focusing on narrow objectives and single target variables of price stability can generate beneficial power effects. This means that the most advantageous situation to be striven for is not visible

dominance over the entire set of macroeconomic policy tools. It rather consists of maintaining narrow accountability combined with a hegemonic vision in which one's objectives are given primacy; this may be combined with significant *informal* influence over those areas of policymaking and regulation that affect one's ability to accomplish publicly acknowledged tasks.

11. To be sure, this policy focus is historically contingent. State organizations could in principle reproduce their autonomy without any such concern about policy legitimacy and efficacy, but rely instead on, for example, primordial notions of entitlement. Desmond King and Patrick Les Galès (2017) capture the relevant change with the concept of "policy states." In these state formations, various "agents" of governing—officials, publics, experts, and so on—gain authority by displaying their capacity to generate desirable "outcomes" or "outputs" (Luhmann 2002: 27; Scharpf 2004).

12. Alexander Barkawi and Simon Zadek, "Governing Finance for Sustainable Prosperity," *CEP Discussion Note,* April 2021.

13. Claudio Borio, "Monetary Policy Operating Procedures in Industrial Countries," *BIS Working Papers,* March 1, 1997, p. 287.

14. The role of governments and central banks in inducing or destroying trust in monetary order and in guiding macroeconomic expectations was first exposed with the collapse of the "old" gold standard during the 1930s (Keynes 1973 [1936]) and was reinforced by the abandonment of the Bretton Woods gold-dollar parity system in 1971 (Krippner 2011; Offe 1973).

15. This is why sociologists of central banking use the term "epistemic authority" to describe how central banks gain hegemony over the interpretation of their own policy decisions and (anticipated) effects. But we should not conceptualize expertise as uniform objectified "capital" here. For what it needs to produce are expectations about policy that align with financial infrastructure; in other words, symbolic interventions rely on concrete operational foundations. Moreover, expectational politics is not a process confined to "agents of rationalization," but involves heterogenous stakeholders (bankers, trade unionists, employers, fund managers, and so on), most of whom have specific economic stakes. In that sense, what post-Marxists such as Kirshner describe as the "politics of money" reappears in my conceptual framework as struggles among actors over interpretations of economic policy that are conditioned by the symbolic power available to them.

16. Two types of money markets have assumed a particularly important role. One is the (asset-backed) commercial paper market that expanded massively in the two decades before 2007 (Thiemann and Lepoutre 2017). The other is for repurchase agreements (repos). Repo is a secured form of money-market lending, whereby the borrower pledges "collateral"—an asset that is deemed safe and stable in its value—with a lender to acquire short-term (usually overnight) funds.

17. Shadow banking is fueled by the expansion of "asset-manager capitalism" and by banks' decisions to outsource parts of their balance sheets in order to circumvent restrictions imposed by minimum capital requirements (Thiemann 2014). Due to an inability to create deposit money, shadow banks also play a key role as borrowers, but also as lenders, in money markets.

18. "The Interest Rate Transmission in the United Kingdom and Overseas," *BoE Quarterly Bulletin,* July 1990, p. 198.

19. "The Bank was founded with a capital of £1.2 million, which was immediately lent to the government. The loan was a perpetuity, paying 8 percent interest plus £4,000 annually in management fees. In return the Bank's subscribers received the following rights: (1) The exclusive right to manage all government loans, (2) the exclusive right to lend money to the government, (3) the right to form a joint-stock banking company, (4) the exclusive privilege of limited liability in banking, and (5) the right to issue banknotes backed by government bonds, to the amount of the Bank's capital" (Broz 1998: 244).

20. "[O]nce central banks were given monopoly powers over legal tender, and stood ready and willing to extend emergency liquidity, central bank money emerged naturally as the asset best able to perform the role of settlement medium" (Haldane and Qvigstad 2016: 635).

21. There are a variety of reasons for this, which mattered to varying degrees in different countries. In the Western bloc led by the United States, the Bretton Woods regime of pegged, variable exchange rates, lasting from 1945 to 1973, meant that central bankers were charged primarily with maintaining the exchange rates between domestic currencies and the US dollar; this was a task that, depending on an economy's size and openness, gave little room for maneuver for dynamic, future-oriented macroeconomic management. Moreover, to the extent that such room existed, it was used primarily to accomplish objectives associated with postwar reconstruction, industrial policy, and economic growth; central banks were supposed to keep (sovereign) credit costs low. Finance ministries and other central planning units set these policy objectives so that hardly any purposeful macroeconomic management was devised at central banks. Additionally, a key factor contributing to central banks' low profile and underdeveloped policy role was that, even though some of these organizations had been nationalized, their peculiar institutional positions and organizational forms sat uneasily with the procedures of macroeconomic management and the exercise of formal governing power. For instance, one constitutive feature of central banking was the organizations' interstitial position between public finance and private credit that, in the eyes of central bankers, required a rather secretive and delicate version of public financial management. Moreover, because most problems and conflicts associated with the state-banking nexus were addressed within elite circles, central bankers preferred to operate "in the shadows and behind the scenes" (King 2016: xi). The resultant lack

of explicit conceptions of central bank governing is reflected in Allan Meltzer's comments on the Federal Reserve during the 1960s, when he complained that the US central bank focused only on "short-run week-to-week, day-to-day, or hour-to-hour events in the money and credits market" and that the central bank's "viewpoint is frequently that of a banker rather than that of a regulating authority for the monetary system and the economy" (cited in Wood 2005: 4).

2. Monetarism and the Invention of Monetary Policy

1. For an excellent synoptic assessment of these issues, see Snowdon and Vane (2005).

2. One of them was Karl Brunner, the famous monetarist. In an autobiographical note, he recounted that he "took a job in the Economics Department of the Swiss National Bank. Within a few months, I understood that this department was a blind alley where one grew old peacefully by not ever writing or saying anything substantial, particularly not about monetary problems" (1996: 20).

3. "According to the Coinage Law of 1952, the government was obliged to ask parliament when considering a change in the parity of the Swiss franc" (Straumann 2010: 281–82).

4. "It seems that different representatives of the machines-industry have met with government officials and have not been wholly unsuccessful in giving the impression that an appreciation of the Swiss franc would be a catastrophe for industry" (SNB Directorate, May 25, 1969, SNBA). Federal Finance Minister Celio equally spoke out for a fixed parity in the name of export industry in a parliamentary session on October 7, 1970. Arguably, the Swiss undervaluation regime was even stronger than that of Germany, where the government had resolved to accept an appreciation of the mark in 1961 and in 1969. When Germany devalued in 1969, the Swiss government explicitly stated that it had "no intention" of adjusting the Swiss franc–dollar parity (press release, Bundeskanzlei, October 6, 1969, my translation, SNA).

5. "The banks wanted fixed exchange rates. This made their transborder transactions much easier" (Lademann, interview with Bernholz). "The international currency order created at Bretton Woods has on the whole proven successful. Therefore, we have no reason to abandon fixed exchange rates" (*Bulletin of the Schweizerischen Bankvereins* No. 3 [1966], p. 55, my translation; see also a UBS note from 1973, SNBA J.217). Loepfe (2011: 244, 392) also demonstrates that Swiss banks were in favor of maintaining fixed exchange rates.

6. "All the noise being made by partial interest groups cannot eliminate the fact that we cannot address the huge inflation pressure with regulatory interventions alone, i.e., without exchange rate adjustment" (Dr. Gal, "Note for the Director

General Dr. F. Leutwiler," November 20, 1969, SNBA 2253). "Our current parity with the dollar is not entirely realistic" (SNB Directorate, May 1, 1969, SNBA).

7. "The role that our country plays in international financial markets and that it derives considerable benefits from gives us a special responsibility to maintain stable and orderly international currency relations and a duty to participate in international cooperation" (Nello Celio, answer to an intervention by members of parliament, December 9, 1968; SNA Dossier Währungsfragen, E2807#1974 / 12#576*).

8. The Swiss Coinage Law was changed in 1971 to give the government the authority to adjust the exchange rate. The Federal Council agreed a small (7 percent) revaluation and temporarily left the dollar–Swiss franc exchange rate floating in August 1971.

9. Various Swiss actors realized that Germany, the United States, and others were promising cooperation but acting according to their self-interest. Cf. the parliamentary debates on "protecting the currency" on September 28, 1971, and September 26, 1972.

10. See debate in parliament on December 2, 1971.

11. "One morning, [Leutwiler] received a call from the foreign exchange division, they informed him that a large bank would like to purchase Swiss francs with one billion US dollars. He said that this was impossible. The division should convey to the respective bank that the SNB would close shop and buy no more dollars. Leutwiler then thought that, after two, three days, the storm would be gone, and one could return to normality. But this turned out more difficult than he had anticipated. People didn't realize that they had actually transitioned to a flexible exchange rate regime" (Kurt Schiltknecht, interview with Bernholz). "I got the impression that the SNB Directorate, let alone the government, did not know that the transition to flexible exchange rates implied a tremendous increase in power for the central bank . . . Nobody here in the house understood the implications" (Lademann, interview with Bernholz).

12. "In February 1973 an attempt was made to stop revaluations by interventions in the exchange market. The effect was trifling" (Schiltknecht 1979 [1976]: 337).

13. "We don't have the constitutional foundations for an active fiscal and budgetary policy!" (Furgler, CVP in the parliamentary debate on business cycle policies on June 17, 1971; see also the statements by Federal Minister Ernst Brugger in the same debate).

14. See Message by the Government to Parliament on the revision of the central bank law ("Nationalbankgesetz"), June 24, 1968. "The state must regulate societal and economic processes to a growing extent" (Weber, SP, parliamentary debate on business cycle policies, March 5, 1974).

15. As just one example, for much of the postwar period, the Swiss state actually did not have any developed statistical and scientific apparatus for producing

forecasts for key macroeconomic variables (Prader 1981: 369). The fact that forecasts were unavailable obviously limited economic-policy options. Indeed, the first econometric models of the Swiss economy were developed in Paris, at OECD headquarters, rather than in Berne. Only in 1972 was a national Working Group for Economic Forecasts formed.

16. The Swiss bank lobby wrote in a press release in 1968 that they were strongly opposed to a law (Bankpolitische Korrespondenz der Schweizerischen Bankiervereinigung, 68 / 40). The circumstances of and reasons for parliamentarians' opposition to the Federal Minister's proposal are obscure. In response to the proposal, the Swiss banking lobby commissioned a report by a Swiss constitutional law expert, Professor Nef (Zürich). The Swiss National Bank also commissioned two reports by Professors Huber and Imboden. While Nef thought that the proposed law was unconstitutional, the two other experts thought otherwise. Still, when a commission debated the law in 1969, one parliamentarian from the conservatives demanded that the consultation be halted until the law's constitutionality could be approved. The majority of the commission followed this proposal and the parliament finally rejected the Federal Minister's bill. One theory thus is that the banking lobby "won" the political battle over the law against an alliance of the Swiss National Bank and the Federal Minister. *Neue Zürcher Zeitung* wrote, "The escalation of inflation is a consequence of the fact that our economic policy only has a weak ordo-political foundation, that its lack of effectiveness is disguised as pragmatism, and that talk about the Swiss 'exception' in fact only masks the influence of partial interests" (December 7, 1972).

17. "In summer 1971, we could only receive from the banks the concession that they would accept a prolongation of credit restrictions for another year" (SNB Central Bank Council, December 15, 1972). The SNB was actually reluctant to impose restrictions: "Already on the first key date, it became apparent that the calling in of all excess amounts would have led to serious disturbances in the money market. Therefore, only part of the excess amount was called in" (Schiltknecht 1979 [1976]: 334).

18. See, for example, the transcripts of parliamentary debates on March 5 and September 18, 1974.

19. In a parliamentary initiative—the "Motion Franzoni" (named after the initiator Enrico Franzoni)—in September 1974, some twenty conservative parliamentarians asked the government and central bank to bring monetary growth into line with the growth of real GDP and additionally urged the government to reduce the federal deficit (see Motion Franzoni, parliamentary debate on September 17, 1974). Nello Celio agreed with these proposals, arguing that "excessive liquidity and a circulation of too much money are the main causes of inflation. We must, by all means, try to reduce the money supply" (parliamentary debate on October 5, 1972). Also see SNB Directorate on October 23, 1974 (SNBA).

20. The *Neue Zürcher Zeitung* wrote, for instance, that "the government has accepted with today's decision that an economic policy, which should serve more than just decorative purposes, cannot work without an effective money supply control component" (December 7, 1972). This was two years *before* the SNB actually adopted monetary targeting.

21. "The money supply, that is the volume of bank notes, coins, and the deposits of the non-bank sector on the one hand, and the gross domestic product on the other hand, should expand in equilibrium" (Edmund Stopper, SNB Central Bank Council, December 12, 1972, SNBA). "For the central bank, among the aims of economic policy, the fight against inflation is prioritized" (President Edmund Stopper, SNB Central Bank Council, June 22, 1973, SNBA). "Considering its view about money and inflation, not surprisingly, the SNB opted for a monetarist approach to policymaking" (Rich 2007: 284).

22. Skepticism about monetary policy becomes explicit in internal discussions, where experts argued that "it is more difficult to achieve effective results with monetary policy than in the past. If one too aggressively intervenes too early, banks will try to circumvent credit restrictions even before the crisis is acute" (meeting of the "Professorium" [Professors' Circle], June 19, 1972, SNBA 2.1 2383).

23. Schiltknecht remembers that senior officials rejected monetarist econometric analyses and decision-making based on such knowledge (Schiltknecht, interview with Bernholz). In a session of the Directorate in 1974, one Governor argued that "those who propose to practice central banking just by manipulating the quantity of money overlook the political reality. The implications of such a policy for the money and capital markets would be intolerable" (SNB Directorate, May 9, 1974, SNBA). "A reasonably stable price level cannot be achieved in a small, open economy like Switzerland, which is exposed to the various inflationary pressures from abroad . . . On the other hand, we cannot judge with precision, how large the quantity of money should be in order to achieve price stability. Under these conditions, we must contend with steering rather crudely into the right direction, that means, to pragmatically constrain credit expansion" (SNB Directorate, July 31, 1969, SNBA).

24. "[T]here existed an enormous difference in the quality: This concerned the technical, but also the intellectual level. Actually, the differences between USA and the German-speaking countries were much greater than they are nowadays; Anglo-Saxon economics was much more analytic" (Ernst Baltensperger, interview with author). This position was confirmed by all interviewees and by an analysis of publications in the *Swiss Journal of Economics and Statistics* since 1945.

25. Jürg Niehans, "Geldpolitik unter geänderten Vorzeichen," *Neue Zürcher Zeitung,* April 14, 1974.

26. Brunner is a founding member of two academic journals (the *Journal of Money, Credit and Banking* and the *Journal of Monetary Economics*), two important

conference series (Rochester-Carnegie Conference Series on Public Policy; Konstanz Seminars on Monetary Theory and Monetary Policy), and the Shadow Open Market Committee.

27. In a classic defense of "traditional" central banking, SNB Director Leutwiler claimed at the very same conference where Brunner promoted his scientific monetarism that, when it came to the question of how to control the money supply, "theory gets lost in the lofty heights . . . Always, in the economic sphere, there will exist a gap between theoretical ideas and political reality" (Leutwiler 1971: 278, my translation). Swiss Finance Minister Nello Celio believed that in no other field was academic advice as misleading as in monetary and economic questions (parliamentary debate on June 26, 1973). Another good example of the feeble role of economics is provided by the absence of serious interventions by economists in the debate about fixed versus flexible exchange rates. For instance, within the SNB's own advisory body, containing several professors from Swiss universities, economists expressed diverging opinions regarding exchange-rate policies. Even strong advocates of flexible exchange rates, associated with the Mont Pèlerin Société, failed to challenge the central bank on that matter. Moreover, while being more cautious than Minister Celio in their critique of economics, the two SNB presidents, Edwin Stopper and Fritz Leutwiler, also expressed skepticism about the formalization of economic expertise (see SNBA 2.1 2383). Karl Brunner aimed to change this situation but he personally was too busy with his cross-Atlantic crusade for monetarism and free-market policies to do the necessary empirical work to develop specific monetarist-policy prescriptions for Switzerland (Schiltknecht, interview with Bernholz). Halbeisen confirms that "[w]hen the Swiss National Bank discontinued its dollar purchases for exchange rate support purposes on January 23, 1973, no theoretically-backed monetary policy procedure existed that could be applied in a flexible exchange rate environment" (2005: 103). Indeed, the whole central bank organization at the time seemed unfit for implementing something like a monetary strategy. The 400 or so employees were trained and employed in order to administer the SNB's reserve holdings, implement transactions with banks, control the issuance of currency, and, above all, produce proper documentation of all these operations; but they were not trained in addressing conceptual problems of monetary policy. Alexander Galli, who joined the central bank's Economics and Statistics Department (VOSTA) in 1973, gives a nice description of the corresponding organizational culture: "At the beginning of the 1970s, the SNB was just one state institution among many. I still remember my first days there: This was a dusty organization with many old ladies, who would sit at their rumbling calculators and produce files. They were all very industrious. And at 12 o'clock, everybody went for lunch. Silence. And at half past one, everybody returned and work continued until five. After that, it turned dark" (Alexander Galli, interview with author).

28. Some attempts in that direction had been made during the late 1960s and early 1970s (by Professor René Erbe in 1969 and the Basel Centre for Economic and Financial Research in 1970); but they had remained unsystematic. As a result, in the early 1970s, the SNB still published monetary statistics whose meaning was unclear and whose calculative basis was dubious. Galli was the first to address this shortcoming (see particularly Alexander Galli, "Die Definition der Geldmenge," June 16, 1972, SNBA 2.1/2406).

29. In their first Proposals for Money Supply Policy in 1975 from October 21, 1974, Schiltknecht and Galli wrote, "In order to better capture the importance of the monetary base for the central bank's money supply policy, we assume that the National Bank can determine the monetary base" (SNBA 2.13.11).

30. SNB press release on January 8, 1975 (SNBA).

31. In a speech in April 1975, Leutwiler argued that flexible exchange rates brought more problems than previously assumed and that monetary policy, even under these conditions, was not independent of foreign influences. He explicitly expressed his support for a return to fixed parities ("Die Notenbank zwischen Inflation und Konjunkturrückgang," *Neue Zürcher Zeitung,* April 24, 1975). Six weeks after the first announcements of monetary targets, the economist Kurt Schiltknecht contacted Leutwiler to complain that the SNB's actions did not correspond to its strategy. In particular, Schiltknecht criticized that the Directorate continued to intervene in the foreign exchange markets in an attempt to avoid further Swiss franc appreciation and thereby expanded the monetary base beyond the target (Schiltknecht, interview with Bernholz).

32. SNB Directorate, November 25, 1976 (SNBA).

33. See, for instance, articles in the *Neue Zürcher Zeitung* from November 27, 1976; February 2, 1978; September 16/17, 1978; May 12/13, 1979; August 21, 1979; and December 15/16, 1979.

34. For instance, in a public defense of the proposed central banking law, the Finance Department stated, "Because money influences the economy, monetary policy focuses on controlling the money supply. Its optimal volume depends on economic growth . . . It is beyond doubt that control of the money supply provides a necessary condition for a stable level of prices over the long term and is inevitable for the smooth functioning of money and capital markets" (message from the Federal Department of Finance in support of a change of the federal central banking law, February 27, 1978, pp. 773–775, SNA).

35. Protocol of the SNB Bank Council meeting, June 12, 1981 (SNBA).

36. This happened in 1978. In that year, the central bank expanded M1 by 16 percent instead of the announced 5 percent. Indeed, political pressure continued to increase throughout 1978. Industry interest groups successfully lobbied parliament to hold a session on exchange-rate policy (Loepfe 2011: 406–7). Because the federal government at the time still held formal authority over the exchange rate,

the central bankers feared that the government would decide to re-regulate the foreign exchange markets, for instance by establishing an official rate for nonfinancial Swiss franc trading. In that case, the SNB would have lost its newly won political powers. As a response to this scenario, those members of the SNB who believed least in the effectiveness of such policies (VOSTA economists Kurt Schiltknecht and Georg Rich) came up with a proposal to control the Swiss franc / German mark exchange rate (Bernholz 2007: 192). Accordingly, the SNB published a press release just before the corresponding parliament session on October 1, 1978, declaring unlimited intervention in order to keep the value of 100 German marks clearly above 80 Swiss francs.

37. As one director remarked at a meeting in 1984, by focusing on monetary policy the central bank had successfully "increased its room to maneuver towards the federal government as well as towards the banks" (SNB Directorate, July 12, 1984, SNBA).

38. When the Swiss were asked about their central bank in a public survey in 1981, "almost all respondents said that they would readily consider anything that the SNB does as right." Reported during a board meeting of the Swiss Bankers Association on June 29, 1981, SBA Archive.

39. In a note from August 1978, he claimed that the central bank was the only bureaucracy that conducts a "credible," "comprehensible," and "economically relevant" policy (Thomann, "Notiz für Le. Zur Geldmengenpolitik der Nationalbank," August 8, 1978, SNBA 2.1 / 2489).

40. Unknown author, "Another note," June 24, 1977, BoE Archive 7A127 / 1.

41. Labour Party, Financial Institutions Group, January 28, 1975, BoE Archive, BoE Archive 7A127 / 1; Gordon Pepper, "Paper for the Money Study Group," monetary policy symposium, November 28, 1973, BoE Archive 2A128 / 11.

42. Joe Grice, "Report of a Visit to the Bundesbank and to the German Federal Ministry of Finance," May 12–14, 1987, BoE Archive 2A182 / 10.

43. The respective legal act entailed no explicit statement about the policy aims to be pursued by central banking, but simply handed control over to the government; the latter gained the authority to appoint members to the Court and Governors, now for tenures of five years.

44. Rachel Lomax, interview with author.

45. The 1946 Bank of England nationalization gave it the power "'if so authorised by the Treasury' to 'issue directions to any banker', but this power of compulsion was never used, despite the fact that for most of the post-war years banks were under instructions to restrain lending and to direct their loans in directions favoured by the government . . . [T]hese . . . were always issued as 'requests' by the Bank . . . yet the language [also] signified the Bank's determination to carry out an increasingly wide range of public duties without resort to the statute book, and to

the range of political forces which a statute book involved" (Moran 1984: 20). Only as an ultima ratio did the Bank threaten statutory action and intrusion from government (Allen 2014: 196; Turner 2014: 185).

46. Unknown author, "The Position of the Bank," August 16, 1977, BoE Archive 7A127/1.

47. "The much bigger part of the economics division was the forecasting group, which had the macro-model that replicated what the Treasury had—and that was part of, if you like, the kind of 'Keynesian' forecasting system, that was the standard policy formulation that had been established in what, the 1960s? I'm not sure when it started. But you have the budget each year, and there would be an exercise in demand management to decide whether there would be a fiscal stimulus or a fiscal contraction, what taxes should be raised and so forth. The Treasury was obviously in the lead, but the Bank had its own model, and there was an interaction between the Bank and the Treasury on that in the run-up to the budget (that was a sort of endless cycle) . . . It was a long period when the Bank viewed economists with suspicion . . . Back then the governor was almost invariably a past chairman of one of the merchant banks. Lee Pemberton when he came was unusual because he came from a clearing bank. The Bank was run by people who were not economists, and if they had specialist training it was as a market-practitioner type. Mervyn King was certainly the first Governor I think who we had as a real self-styled economist" (Anthony Hotson, interview with author).

48. "Cobbold objected against prescribed holdings of short term debt by the banks, saying 'his Court would never stand for this' . . . Cobbold's opposition was important because, as the Treasury discovered, it would not compel the Bank of England to give directions to commercial banks" (Allen 2014: 15).

49. John Fforde, "The United Kingdom—Setting Monetary Objectives," in Paul Meek (ed.), *Central Bank Views on Monetary Targeting*, 51–59 (New York: Federal Reserve Bank of New York, 1983).

50. The draft "The Money Supply and Expenditure," by A. D. Crockett, May 29, 1968 and October 15, 1968; and a note by Dicks-Mireaux in the September 12, 1968, express strong skepticism toward the "American literature" (both from BoE Archive 2A128/1). For journalistic accounts of monetarism in Britain during that period, see, for example, "The Money Supply: The Great Debate," *Financial Times*, October 25, 1968.

51. In their paper on the "Importance of Money," published in the *BoE Quarterly Bulletin* in June 1970 (pp. 159–98), Goodhart and Crockett argued that the interest-elasticity of money demand provided no strong evidence for the view, articulated for instance in the Radcliffe Report of 1959, of a continuum between money and financial assets, but also no strong evidence for the monetarist assumption of a negligible substitutability between monetary and financial assets. This

implied, for the Bank economists, that the traditional British doctrine of an impotent monetary policy had to be abandoned (Needham 2014b: 26), but that, at the same time, any understanding of monetary policy presupposed the careful study of the peculiarities of the British monetary system. Moreover, the Bank economists, while initially identifying relatively strong correlations between money supply and money income, stressed that correlation had to be distinguished from causation, and that money supply could not be treated as exogenous.

52. John Fforde, "The United Kingdom—Setting Monetary Objectives," in Paul Meek (ed.), *Central Bank Views on Monetary Targeting*, 51–59 (New York: Federal Reserve Bank of New York, 1983).

53. Christopher Kit MacMahon, "Another Note on Externalising the Bank," June 24, 1977, BoE Archive 7A127 / 1; Michael Foot, Charles Goodhart, and Anthony Hotson, "Monetary Base Control," *BoE Quarterly Bulletin*, July 1979, 149–59.

54. "The Conservative Economic Reconstruction Group was then persuaded by a coterie of monetarists that the primary cause was . . . the money supply growth of 1972–3" (Needham 2014b: 3). In their 1976 manifesto, *The Right Approach to the Economy,* Conservatives suggested that "it would now be right to announce clear targets for monetary expansion as one of the objectives of economic management." Thatcher, the new leader of the Conservative party, drew extensively on monetarist vocabulary to establish a morally charged distinction between the "half-baked" fight against inflation allegedly pursued by Labour versus a more resolute, consequential version of anti-inflationism promised by the Conservatives themselves (on this, see Ian Gilmour, "Monetarism and History," *London Review of Books,* January 21, 1982). See also Margaret Thatcher, speech at Conservative Local Government Conference, London, March 3, 1979, Margaret Thatcher Foundation Archive.

55. For example, Gordon Pepper, "A Monetary Base for the UK," *W. Greenwell and Co Monetary Bulletin* No. 61; Brian Griffiths, "How the Bank Has Mismanaged Monetary Policy," *The Banker* 126 (610) (1977): 1411–1419.

56. A. L. Coleby, "The Bank of England's Operational Procedures for Meeting Monetary Objectives," in Paul Meek (ed.), *Central Bank Views on Monetary Targeting,* 62 (New York: Federal Reserve Bank of New York, 1983).

57. Charles Goodhart, "Bank of England Research on the Demand of Money Function," September 2, 1974, BoE Archive 2A128 / 12; "attempts to fit demand for money equations to the post-1971 period yield generally unsatisfactory results. The implausible parameter estimates on the lagged dependent variable confirm the trend towards such instability suggested by Hacche's earlier work" (unknown author, "Paper on Special Deposits," January 31, 1977, BoE Archive 6A50).

58. "The problems of restraining public expenditures to planned limits could still prove difficult. In these circumstances we judge it all the more necessary to

include in the package an explicit monetary target for this year, with a commitment to a further and lower target for next year. Influential opinion abroad, including the IMF and the predominant contributors to the GAB, regards the adoption of a normative monetary target as a matter of great importance" (unknown author, "Money Supply Target," September 19, 1976, BoE Archive 6A50/18).

59. Unknown author, "Externalising the Bank—Second Note," May 23, 1977, BoE Archive 7A127/1.

60. Ibid.

61. Ibid. Unknown author, "Externalising the Bank—Internal Memorandum of a Discussion on the Executive Level, First Circulated to the Deputy Governor and Different Directors," May 18, 1977, BoE Archive 7A127/1.

62. As Paul Tucker states, "[M]uch of the Bank's influence over monetary policy came from the markets side, including leveraging advice of actual or expected adverse reactions in the gilt market or the foreign exchange markets, plus its operational roles" (cited in Acosta et al. 2020: 11).

63. Helmut Schlesinger and Friedrich W. Bockelmann, "Statement on German Position," in Proceedings of the BIS meeting, *The Developments of the Money Supply and Its Relation to Economic Activity and Prices,* November 4–6, 1971, BIS Archive.)

64. *Bundesbank Monthly Report,* February 1990, 8. And in a subsequent report, the Bundesbank stated that "[m]onetary policy, in particular, is called upon to make a credible contribution towards reducing inflationary expectations, and thus the risk premiums in market interest rates, by pursuing a consistent stability policy. Any 'premature' relaxation of monetary policy could jeopardize the imminent return to greater price stability. Monetary policy would be overtaxed, however, were it alone required to combat inflation. Ancillary support, above all by wage and fiscal policy makers, remains indispensable if tensions in further economic developments are to be avoided" (*Bundesbank Monthly Report,* June 1992, 10).

65. To take one example, the Bundesbank urged trade unions in its monthly bulletin of September 1977 to lower their demands: "restraint in the 'distributional struggle' is . . . urgently required to prevent the rekindling of inflationary expectations, which might deter savers and disrupt the capital market" (*Bundesbank Monthly Report,* September 1977, 3).

66. In the critical post-reunification period, Bundesbank officials warned about excessive deficits and claimed that "expecting monetary policy alone to safeguard stability would be tantamount to overrating its capabilities. The fiscal policy of the Federal and *Land* governments and local authorities therefore faces the difficult task of setting a course in the direction of fiscal consolidation as soon as possible" (*Bundesbank Monthly Report,* February 1991, 8).

67. Special report on Germany, *Euromoney,* September 1, 1992.

68. For Germany, Bibow (2003) has analyzed the huge costs of the Bundesbank's monetarist dogmatism. In Switzerland, currency appreciation plus restrictive

monetary policies meant that the SNB in effect imposed domestic deflation on the economy, especially under President Markus Lusser, whose reign lasted until 1996. In Japan, the central bank abandoned monetarism in the second half of the 1980s. But monetary targeting had given the central bank the role of independent guardian of price stability that it unduly exploited in the early 1990s, in a nonaccommodative response to consumption tax increases and in its attempt to counteract asset-price inflation.

3. Hegemonizing Financial Market Expectations

1. Similarly, Frederic Mishkin, at a FOMC meeting on December 11, 2007, stated that "keeping inflation expectations contained" among these key interlocutors "is the most critical thing that we do" (see also Blinder 2001: 25).

2. Rachel Lomax, interview with author.

3. "Firstly, prior to the late 1970s the traditional corporate lending business of banks proved highly profitable. This, when combined with restrictions on their lending, meant that banks had no incentive to diversify their lending away from their corporate and unsecured personal lending business [. . .] Secondly, . . . banks have in the past been subject of lending constraints of one form or another . . . Hence banks were constrained from lending significant amounts in the mortgage market for most of the 1970s" (Drake 1989: 44–46).

4. "You can see a lot of that stuff and what Terry Burns and Allen Budd were writing when they were in the London Business School, and they went on writing the stuff when they came in. In many ways, they were the intellectual architects in this approach" (Lomax, interview with author).

5. Peter Lilley, *Ten Policy Questions about the Medium-Term Financial Strategy* (cited in Payne 2010: 144).

6. J. Odling, "Notes of a Meeting by the Chancellor of the Exchequer with Internal Staff and External Advisers, Held 5th October 1979," October 12, 1979, BoE Archive 7A1333 / 1. Advisers were Alan Budd, Patrick Minford, Tim Congdon, Terry Burns, John Flemming, Brian Griffiths, and Gordon Pepper. In 1989, Peter Middleton, a key Treasury official, still defended the medium-term strategy on "credibility" grounds: "Medium term horizons are important in three respects. They give policy a sense of purpose which can be presented with simplicity, coherence and clarity. Second, it implies the intention to eschew measures which might bring short-term benefits but long-term costs. Third, the medium-term dimension to policy itself adds greatly to *market credibility* and the chances of success" (Middleton 1989: 49, my emphasis).

7. Letter, Geoffrey Howe to Margaret Thatcher, February 20, 1980, Margaret Thatcher Foundation Archive.

8. The Conservative Ian Gilmour pointed this out and came to regard the Thatcher government's ideological deafness toward labor's orientations and rationales as one of its key failures. See Ian Gilmour, "Monetarism and History," *London Review of Books,* January 21, 1982.

9. Offer argues that, in the Thatcher era, "housing wealth held out the promise of financial security for a growing part of the population, as an alternative and complement to social insurance, and another pillar of personal security" (2017: 1063).

10. John Townsend, "The Orientation of Monetary Policy and the Monetary Policy Decision-Making Process in the United Kingdom," 1991, BoE Archive 10A114/25.

11. Nigel Lawson here gives an (incomplete) list of "his" deregulations: "The unannounced ending, virtually as soon as the new Government took office in May 1979, of the restrictive guidelines on building society lending; the abolition of hire-purchase restrictions in July 1982; the collapse of the building societies' cartel in October 1983; some aspects of the Building Societies Act, 1986; the withdrawal of mortgage lending 'guidance' in December 1986; the effective abolition of the control of borrowing order in March 1989 . . . Until 1981 the building societies, and to a lesser extent the local authorities, had almost a monopoly over housing finance. Building societies took in funds on retail terms and lent them to home buyers at rates of interest fixed by the Building Societies Association. The cartel broke up as a result of a burgeoning of the competitive instinct among the bigger building societies themselves, followed by the massive invasion of the mortgage lending business by the banks, who were growing increasingly disenchanted with the joys of lending to Latin American and other governments overseas. Competition for mortgage business was further increased in the second half of the 1980s by the entry of specialist mortgage lenders, many of them American, who raised finance in the wholesale capital markets" (1992: 626–27). "Whereas banks had previously had a 5 per cent market share, by the end of 1982 they were providing 40 per cent of all new loans . . . The 1983 Finance Act would help the building societies compete more effectively for consumers as they were to be granted more access to wholesale markets" (Payne 2010: 156).

12. "Broad money targeting was formally suspended in 1985 and abandoned in the March 1987 Budget" (Cobham 2002: 14).

13. There is supportive evidence for that view: "Total consumer credit from the monetary sector rose annually at rates of 17 per cent and more between 1983 and 1988, loans for house purchase increased even more rapidly, and the growth of bank lending in sterling to industrial and commercial companies accelerated from a 1983–5 average of 10.2 per cent to 17.3 per cent in 1986, 21.6 per cent in 1987 and over 32 per cent in each of 1988 and 1989. The phenomenon of equity withdrawal in the housing market—householders, as a group, borrowing for house purchase more

than they needed and diverting the excess into consumers' expenditure—also became more prominent" (Cobham 2002: 56).

14. If there was one powerful constituency that profited from this indecisiveness, it was homeowners with mortgages (Greider 1987). But other financial market actors, corporate leaders, political representatives, and even general popular sentiment increasingly perceived inflation as the country's number one problem.

15. FOMC, transcript, June 2, 1979, p. 10, cited in Lindsey et al. (2013: 493).

16. Greider cites Stuart Eizenstat, the US president's domestic policy adviser, who "explained Jimmy Carter's fateful choice: 'Volcker was selected because he was the candidate of Wall Street. This was their price, in effect. What was known about him? That he was able and bright and it was also known that he was conservative'" (1987: 47).

17. Ted Balbach, interview with Robert Hetzel. "Consistent with his early background in financial markets at the New York Fed and with his oversight of the Bretton Woods system at the Treasury, Volcker focused on expectations. Moreover, he acted on the belief that credible monetary policy could shape those expectations" (Hetzel 2008: 150).

18. Greenbook for the FOMC meeting on August 18, 1981.

19. "Two-thirds of funds rate changes were due to judgmental actions of the Fed and only one-third resulted from automatic adjustment" (Goodfriend 1993: 4).

20. Greenspan's concern for bond-market rates is reflected in the following exchange at an FOMC meeting: "Black: 'I agree [about the establishment of a noninflationary environment] that that's exactly the position of everybody in this room, but I'm not sure that the public is completely convinced.' Greenspan: 'That may be. They will be convinced only after a period of time; and we will know they are convinced when we see the 30-year Treasury at 5-1/2 percent'" (cited in Hetzel 2008: 201).

21. "The Interest Rate Transmission in the United Kingdom and Overseas," *BoE Quarterly Bulletin*, July 1990, p. 198.

22. "Official Transactions in the Gilt Market," *BoE Quarterly Bulletin*, June 1966, p. 142.

23. "The Gilt-Edged Market," *BoE Quarterly Bulletin*, June 1979, p. 138.

24. M. J. Hamburger, "Expectations, Long-Term Interest Rates, and Monetary Policy in the United Kingdom," *BoE Quarterly Bulletin*, March 1971, p. 364. See also Allen (2019: 94).

25. "In the eight years to 1970, the PSBR [Public Sector Borrowing Requirement] averaged a little over £3/4 billion (2 per cent of GDP at current market prices). Since then, it has averaged £6 billion (6 per cent of GDP), with a peak of over 10 1/2 billion (lo 1/4 percent of GDP) in 1975" ("The Gilt-Edged Market," *BoE Quarterly Bulletin*, June 1979, p. 139).

26. Ibid., p. 138.

27. Ian Plenderleith, interview with author.

28. "Gilt Futures Likely to Be Popular," *Financial Times,* October 25, 1982.

29. Plenderleith, interview with author. See also Creon Butler and Roger Clews, "Money Market Operations in the United Kingdom," *BIS Conference Papers (Implementation and Tactics of Monetary Policy),* 1997, pp. 45–70.

30. In designing this system and rethinking the Bank's role, the officials explicitly took the Fed-Treasury securities market as their blueprint; as one official stated, "An American system lends itself more easily to a market in which Government securities are auctioned as funds are needed and in which the operations of the central bank are aimed primarily at the conduct of monetary policy" (J. G. Hill, "The Future Structure of the Gilt-Edged Market," March 20, 1984, BoE Archive 2A7-1 and 2).

31. A bulletin piece from 1985 finds no systematic arbitrage opportunities between the spot and futures markets: "In the absence of transactions costs or other market imperfections in the futures and spot markets, the implied forward rate and the futures rate should be identical, both being based on all information currently available to traders. If they are not equal, arbitrageurs can make riskless gains . . . Over the last three years, there has been a tendency for the pricing of futures contracts to become more efficient" ("Arbitrage between the Spot and Futures Markets for Eurodollars," *BoE Quarterly Bulletin,* December 1985, p. 561).

32. "Inflation Report," *BoE Quarterly Bulletin,* February 1993, p. 27. In Cobham's summative words, "there seems little reason to doubt that the Bank of England made efforts (mostly not observable) to protect and strengthen its autonomy and to further the case for central bank independence. In particular, it worked to improve its monetary expertise (notably its inflation forecasting capacity) and made use of the mechanisms of accountability such as the *Inflation Report* and the Governor's contributions to the minutes of the monthly Monetary Meetings . . . to establish its technical reputation" (2002: 103).

33. Butler and Clews, "Money Market Operations in the United Kingdom," p. 48.

34. Ibid.

35. Ed Boehne, interview with Hetzel (2008). See also Axilrod (2009: 138) and Krippner (2011: 130).

36. Peter Schmid and Henner Asche, "Monetary Policy Instruments and Procedures in Germany: Evolution, Deployment and Effects," *BIS Conference Papers (Implementation and Tactics of Monetary Policy),* 1997, p. 91.

37. Schmid and Asche, "Monetary Policy Instruments and Procedures in Germany," p. 94.

38. Erich Spörndli and Dewet Moser, "Monetary Policy Operating Procedures in Switzerland," *BIS Conference Papers (Implementation and Tactics of Monetary Policy),* 1997, pp. 142–43.

39. To be precise, the ECB initially tried to develop a hybrid of inflation targeting and monetarism, mainly to create continuity between the German "success" of monetary stability and the new institution as yet without a reputation (McNamara 1998). However, due to erratic M3 growth that was inconsistent with price developments, the ECB soon abandoned monetarism and fully committed to inflation targeting in 2003.

40. Hans Lindberg, Kerstin Mitlid, and Peter Sellin, "Monetary Tactics with an Inflation Target: The Swedish Case," *BIS Conference Papers (Implementation and Tactics of Monetary Policy)*, 1997, pp. 231–49.

4. Money Markets as Infrastructures of Global Finance and Central Banks

1. "The operational target of monetary policy is a variable with the following characteristics: (i) it can sufficiently be controlled by the central bank; (ii) it is economically relevant, in the sense that it effectively influences the ultimate target of monetary policy (e.g. price stability); (iii) it defines the stance of monetary policy, in the sense that it is set by the policy decision-making body of the central bank (e.g. the Federal Open Market Committee for the Federal Reserve or the Governing Council for the European Central Bank); (iv) it gives the necessary and sufficient guidance to the monetary policy implementation officers in the central bank on what to do" (Bindseil 2014: 10).

2. Repos (repurchase agreements) involve the temporary exchange of securities, as collateral, against cash, and an agreement to reverse this transaction, with the return of the same or equivalent securities at a later, predetermined date. Depending on the perceived risk of the underlying collateral, the cash borrower pays a "margin rate" or "haircut" on the repo. Due to this haircut, repos usually are "over-collateralized" loans (Sissoko 2019), meaning that the cash lender holds more value in collateral than they have lent out in cash. Moreover, in bilateral repos, the lender can "rehypothecate" (relend) the borrowed securities for the duration of the loan (some limits apply in the United States). The price differential between the initial purchase and the later repurchase, agreed on at the start of the contract, constitutes the interest on the loan.

3. "First created in 1971 under the Investment Act of 1940, money market mutual funds emerged as a serious challenger to bank deposits in the context of high and rising inflation . . . In 1976, Merrill Lynch introduced a money market mutual fund account against which customers could write checks, further increasing the institutional similarities between these funds and deposit accounts of banks" (Thiemann 2018: 83).

4. The three laws being cited are Kennedy's Interest Equalization Tax, which came into force in 1964; the foreign Credit Restraint Program (1965); and the Foreign Investment Program (1968).

5. "The Federal Reserve advocated subjecting the money market funds to reserve requirements (administered by the Federal Reserve, of course) to put them on the same competitive basis as the banks. However, any hopes for this proposal were dashed when it turned out that the money market funds could mobilize political support as effectively as the banks and the savings and loans combined" (Wooley 1984: 85).

6. According to Konings (2011), another force at work against significant regulatory reforms came from within the government. By the 1970s, the US Treasury had realized that Eurodollar markets were useful in generating demand for US dollars, mitigating fears about a potential loss of its global reserve status and America's "exorbitant privilege" (Eichengreen 2010).

7. The Fed only officially adopted interest-rate signaling in the 1990s and early 2000s, through the decision to announce a fed funds target (1994), through the definition of federal funds rate targets as key policy objectives in the Domestic Policy Directive (1998), and ultimately through an attempt to "de-stigmatize" discount window lending (2003), the latter serving as a way to give rigidity to targets by setting a "ceiling" for market rates. For a reconstruction of this development, and of an equally delayed and reluctant adoption of the "short-term interest rate doctrine" in academia, see Bindseil (2004b).

8. In US bankruptcy proceedings, firms are given "automatic stay," meaning that assets remain in the ownership of the failing company during a "breathing space." These generous rules have a clear economic and political rationale, but they contradicted the logic of repo markets, in which lenders want security through control over collateral.

9. Hearing before the Subcommittee on Monopolies and Commercial Law of the Committee on the Judiciary, House of Representatives, Ninety-Eighth Congress, Second session, H.R. 2852 and H.R. 3418 "Bankruptcy Law and Repurchase Agreements," May 2, 1984, Serial No. 128, US Government Printing Office, Washington, DC, 1985.

10. "When the Discount Houses came in to borrow, and they had physically to come in to do this . . . there would be a message to go with it. And the message would say something like, 'we are not happy about . . .' and then immediately they would go back and say, 'The Bank of England is insisting that . . .' Because we could issue Treasury Bills effectively at any time, we could always manipulate that and make the discount market short of cash within 24 hours if we wanted to" (Michael Foot, interview with author). See also Bank of England, "The Management of Money Day by Day," *BoE Quarterly Bulletin,* March 1963, pp. 15–21.

11. A. L. Coleby, "Sterling Money Market Banks," September 26, 1979, BoE Archive 10A211-1 + 2. The LDMA was highly supportive of informality, as expressed by its representatives: "The Members of the LDMA have an important role to play in the conduct of the Bill Market. They are concerned to maintain the quality of the Bill on London while wishing to encourage its use. The more codified market practices become, the less skills and expertise participants in a market are required to exercise . . . The operation of such a system does not require the Bank of England to state publicly (i) that some names are more eligible than others; (ii) that some bills are more eligible than others" (LDMA, "The Conduct of Open Market Operations," December 23, 1980, BoE Archive 10A211-1 and 10A211-2).

12. Unknown author, "Note on 'Eligibility,'" December 23, 1980, BoE Archive 10A211-1 and 10A211-2.

13. Unknown author, "The Money Market," 1980, BoE Archive 2A182/1.

14. Paul Tucker and Ian Plenderleith, interviews with author. See also "Proposal for a Revised Directing Structure," April 19, 1979, BoE Archive 7A127-1. "One relic from the past has been a degree of ambiguity about the relationship between the Executive Directors of the Bank and the areas of the Bank whose policy work they coordinate; on some subjects they have not been in the line of command between Heads of Department and the Governors" (confidential letter by C. to the Governor, Deputy, MacMahon and Blunden, November 2, 1979, BoE Archive 6A262/1).

15. Letter, Gerald & National to Chief Cashier Coleby, July 10, 1986, BoE Archive 10A211-1 and 10A211-2.

16. David White, "United Kingdom," *Euromoney,* September 1992.

17. To be precise, banking firms registered under Section 123 or 127 of the 1967 Companies Act only had to hold a 10 percent rather than a 12.5 percent reserve ratio.

18. "Sterling Certificates of Deposit," *BoE Quarterly Bulletin,* December 1972.

19. Charles A. E. Goodhart, "Implementation of Federal Reserve Open Market Operations (Comment)," in Paul Meek (ed.), *Central Bank Views on Monetary Targeting,* p. 52 (New York: Federal Reserve Bank of New York, 1983).

20. Paul Tucker, "Managing the Central Bank's Balance Sheet: Where Monetary Policy Meets Financial Stability," *BoE Quarterly Bulletin,* July 2004, pp. 359–82.

21. A. L. Coleby, "Money Market Management," February 18, 1981, and Coleby to Lankester, "Review of 1981 Monetary Control Arrangements," November 12, 1984, BoE Archive 2A182/2 + 8. "The modifications to monetary control arrangements introduced last August [1981, LW] were designed, inter alia, to provide for more flexible management of short-term interest rates allowing for greater degree of market influence and a lower political profile than with MLR [the Bank of England's discount lending rate, LW], in the hope that this might reduce any 'bias

to delay' in more rigorously administered arrangements . . . The arrangements have not functioned as originally envisaged for two important reasons . . . Persistent money market shortages and the resulting rigidity of our dealing rates has meant much less 'noise' than expected. [Second,] political interest in the precise levels of base rates seems certain to persist" (unknown author, "Undisclosed band," April 22, 1982, BoE Archive 2A182/4).

22. A. R. Latter, "Easing Liquidity by Abandoning the 12 1/2 Per Cent Minimum Reserve Ratio," July 11, 1980, BoE Archive 2A182/1. "It is tempting—having given the clearing banks due warning of the nature and extent of the expected problem, which I am sure they would not sufficiently heed—to leave them to stew in their own juice. But I think that course must be rejected" (A. L. Coleby, "Money Markets in the Next Weeks," February 16, 1981, BoE Archive 2A182/2). "We have no alternative but to accommodate the demand for reserve assets which the banks generate" (A. L. Coleby, "Money Market and Reserve Asset Assistance—Banking August," July 31, 1980, BoE Archive 2A182/2).

23. Paul Tucker, interview with author.

24. "Corsetry Removed Layer by Layer," *Financial Times,* October 7, 1985.

25. "We shall shortly have to accept the enlargement of the list, or stand up to defend a practice that has become explicitly discriminatory" (Coleby, "Sterling Money Market Banks"). "Our present compromise allowing a proportion of 'impure' transactions . . . is logically untenable . . . I think we must now make a choice between reverting to total 'purity' or abandoning the current notions of what is pure . . . For my part . . . I recommend that we should reject the whole approach, because I think it would unduly restrict the availability of bills for our operations" (A. L. Coleby, "Eligible Bills," BoE Archive 10A211-1 and -2). "Adherence to the traditional form of the real bill doctrine—the self-liquidating transaction in goods—would drastically restrict the supply of eligible bills at a time when, for monetary control purposes, it would be desirable to increase the supply quickly . . . Banks would . . . hold more liquid assets than before and hence as a second-round portfolio adjustment would be less likely, other things being equal, to maintain the level of their liquid deposits with the discount market" (unknown author, "Primary Liquidity in the Context of Monetary Control," January 28, 1981, BoE Archive 10A211-1 + 2, 4). "Once we move from that narrow interpretation of 'self-liquidating' [where the bills relates to some goods, LW] we do, however, have some difficulty in finding precise definitions" (A. L. Coleby to Keswick, February 28, 1985, BoE Archive 2A182/8).

26. Paul Tucker, interview with author.

27. From the early 1980s onward, the central bankers had demanded that banks predict their daily shortages in central bank (that is, final settlement) money so that the central bank could calculate with some precision how much daily liquidity support was needed. The central bank, in turn, published its own daily forecast of

system shortages in its own liability via Reuters, thereby signaling its intended operations for the day to a broad group of market participants.

28. Unknown author, "The Structure of Financial Markets," November 4, 1983, BoE Archive 2A71.

29. Ian Plenderleith, interview with author.

30. Ibid.

31. Ibid.

32. Georg Rich, "Finanzplatz Schweiz und Euromarkt," talk given to the Higher Economic and Administrative School, Lucerne, April 23, 1979, SNBA.

33. Georg Rich, "Die Staatliche Kontrolle der Euromärkte," published in a supplementary publication of the *Neue Zürcher Zeitung* on the Euromarket, November 23, 1982, SNBA.

34. Letter from Credit Suisse, SNB Directorate, August 19, 1976, and August 18, 1977, SNBA.

35. Special report on Germany, *Euromoney,* September 1, 1992.

36. Peter Schmid and Henner Asche, "Monetary Policy Instruments and Procedures in Germany: Evolution, Deployment and Effects," *BIS Conference Papers (Implementation and Tactics of Monetary Policy),* 1997, p. 81.

37. Joe Grice, "Report of a Visit to the Bundesbank and to the German Federal Ministry of Finance," May 12–14, 1987, BoE Archive 2A182 / 10. "There appears to have been little discussion in Germany about the cost imposed on banking intermediation by the existence of minimum reserve requirements and its effects in driving business elsewhere, probably for a number of reasons. Prime amongst these no doubt is the dominance of the universal banking system and the lack of development of other markets" (John Townsend, "The Implementation of Monetary Policy in Germany," November 21, 1985, BoE Archive 2A182 / 22).

38. Special report on Germany, *Euromoney,* April 1992.

39. "Since . . . 1986, banks have been permitted to issue *certificates of deposit* (CDs). However, the market has never developed because of two structural impediments, as well as the relative unattractiveness of this source of financing for German banks compared to conventional retail deposits. The first impediment was the so-called stock exchange turnover tax (Börsenumsatzsteuer) . . . the second impediment [is] the Bundesbank's minimum reserve requirements . . . *Commercial paper* was brought to life by the lifting of the so-called stock exchange turnover tax (Börsenumsatzsteuer), which was imposed on all securities trades involving a German counterparty until January 1991 . . . Banks and finance companies are prevented from issuing, however, by the imposition of minimum reserve requirements on their debt in maturities under two years" (Special report on Germany, *Euromoney,* September 1992, p. 20). Money-market funds were introduced in 1994, but cautiously; initially, no secondary trading in such funds existed (Schröder, Münchmeyer Hengst and Co., "Letter from Germany," *Euromoney,* December 1994).

40. "With its substantial lowering of the reserve ratios as of March 1, 1993 and March 1, 1994, respectively, the Bundesbank has paid due heed to considerations of competition among European financial centres and to the strong tendency towards shifting deposits from Germany to the Euromarkets" (Häusler 1994: 257).

41. Georg Rich, interview with author, December 2013.

42. Thomas Jordan, "Risikominimierung und Liquiditätssicherung mittels Einsatz von Repo-Geschäften," talk given at the conference "Liquidität—eine Herausforderung für die Banken," Swiss National Bank, Zürich, January 11, 2005.

43. Committee for the Global Financial System, "Implications of Repo Markets for Central Banks," Bank for International Settlements, Basel, 1999, p. 3; Committee for the Global Financial System, "Market Liquidity: Research Findings and Selected Policy Implications," Bank for International Settlements, Basel, 1999, p. 11.

44. Committee for the Global Financial System, "Implications of Repo Markets for Central Banks," p. 3.

45. Counterparty Risk Management Policy Group, "Improving Counterparty Risk Management Practices," New York, p. 4. Manuals written by derivatives lawyers advised market participants to seek positions in derivatives and repos backed by "super-priority" laws as a smart solution for hedging risk (Roe 2011: 555).

46. Directive 2002 / 47 / EC of the European Parliament and the Council of 6 June 2002 on financial collateral arrangements, *Official Journal of the European Communities,* June 27, 2002, p. 43.

47. Stephanie Cooke, "Too Many Crooks Spoil the Froth," *Euromoney,* July 1994.

48. The figures given here are based on biannual surveys conducted by International Securities (later renamed: Capital) Markets Association (ISMA / ICMA); they bear the risk of double-counting because reported figures from banks are simply added up.

49. Tucker, "Managing the Central Bank's Balance Sheet," p. 363.

5. The Organization of Ignorance

1. Ben S. Bernanke, "The Great Moderation," speech at the meeting of the Eastern Economic Association, February 20, 2004, Board of Governors of the Federal Reserve System, Washington, DC.

2. Isabel Cairó and Jae Sims, "Income Inequality, Financial Crises, and Monetary Policy," Finance and Economics Discussion Series 2018-048, 2018, Board of Governors of the Federal Reserve System, Washington, DC.

3. Masciandaro and Quintyn propose that "[w]hile regulation concerns the drafting and implementation of rules and regulations governing the activities of the financial system, supervision is about ensuring that financial institutions obey the

regulatory framework, and imposing sanctions on those institutions that do not abide by the rules and regulations. Such sanctions can go as far as 'closing' insolvent institutions, with attendant consequences on individuals' property rights" (2013: 263).

4. Two subcommittees, the so-called Cooke Committee and the Sandberg group, worked out relatively detailed plans to introduce international norms prescribing banks to keep secure liquidity for emergency periods during the 1980s. But these proposals were not taken up by senior negotiators.

5. The Swiss Bankers' Association successfully represented the sector by serving as a powerful voice for banking interests and by eliciting support among its diverse members for its lobbying and decision-making (Guex and Mazbouri 2013).

6. These meetings, usually dinners, were a regular part of the SNB directors' schedules (SNBA).

7. Annual report of SBA 1933–1934, SBA Archive; letter of SNB to the SBA Council, July 28, 1961, SNBA.

8. Council meeting of the SBA, April 3, 1968, SBA Archive.

9. One regulator recognized this state of affairs: "Control is only exerted by private circles and the Federal Banking Commission created by the law is not part of public administration, and in reality has no right to monitor either the internal affairs of the banks or the reports of the auditors" (Paul Rossy, cited in Mazbouri and Schaufelbuehl 2015: 681).

10. As reported in the *Neue Zürcher Zeitung* ("Uhren- und Textilindustrie in der Absatzkrise," May 24, 1975), the central bankers saw an imbalance between "financial" and trade-related foreign exchange activities. They suggested different policies to rein in speculation, such as registration of all traders on a central exchange, a stamp duty tax on foreign exchange transactions, or a general prohibition on foreigners investing money in Switzerland (Loepfe 2011).

11. "Last week Sindona's Geneva-based Banque de Financement (Finabank) was shut down by Swiss authorities after it was announced that it had lost $60 million speculating on behalf of another Sindona operation, Edilcentro International, on the foreign exchange market. Financial sources have begun to predict a chain reaction of bank troubles caused by Finabank's losses" (Inter Press Service press release, January 14, 1975, SNBA).

12. Most damaging was a case that became public in 1977. The head of a Credit Suisse branch in Chiasso and several employees, as well as business partners, had, over the years, channeled wealth from rich Italians into a dubious fund in Liechtenstein, providing investors with a guarantee on their expected returns. When these investors redeemed their money, Credit Suisse had to realize losses of CHF 1.4 billion (Mabillard and de Weck 1977). For a time, "Chiasso" came to symbolize the intimate connection between offshore banking and white-collar crime, very lax to nonexistent oversight, and a widening gulf between financial and broader national interests.

13. During a speech at Bankers' Day, an annual gathering organized by the SBA, Leutwiler stated that the "cooperation between the central bank and the banks has not met expectations in these hard times because the fundamental concept of policymaking was wrong. The regulation of money supply and its influence on credit expansion is a task that the central bank exercises as one of its constitutional duties. This task cannot be accomplished by the central bank and banks as equal partners. The oft-cited argument of missing gentlemen fails to capture the actual problem; it is not the main task of bankers or indeed central bankers to be gentlemen" (Fritz Leutwiler, "Zusammenarbeit zwischen Noteninstitut und Banken in schwierigen Zeiten," September 26, 1975, SNBA). One year earlier, the bankers conceded that cooperative policymaking belongs to the past (Council of the SBA, May 15, 1974). See also *Neue Zürcher Zeitung*, "Die Notenbank im Spannungsfeld der Politik," February 27, 1975. In an SNB expert commission, economics professor Otto Wuergler claimed that the behavior of banks, from an ethical point of view, was no longer acceptable (Meeting of the "Professorium," May 21, 1969, SNBA 2.1 2383). Alfred Sarasin recognized this change: He perceived as a great danger that the cooperative spirit between the central bank and the banks might be destroyed and "politics" might enter the central bank (meeting of SBA Council, September 20, 1968). And in the SBA Council session from July 3, 1972, Max Oetterli reiterated this line of reasoning. He posited that "we are at a crossroads with monetary policy. Turning away from cooperative solution, the central bank has now used legal means" (SBA Archive). Especially the SNB's planned credit restrictions raised concerns about "authoritative rule" (SNB Bank Council, September 13, 1968, SNBA).

14. The president of the SNB conceded that "the Federal Banking Commission has clearly failed in its treatment of the cases of Finabank and Edilcentro. Under these circumstances, it would appear advantageous to have more control over regulatory matters. We have to instruct Federal Minister Chevallaz accordingly." As another central bank director added, "[I]n public, the central bank will probably be made responsible for the failures of the FBC" (SNB Directorate, February 6, 1975, SNBA).

15. This issue was discussed during a Directorate meeting on November 14, 1974, with different Directors expressing divergent opinions. The Directors also considered other options, such as the establishment of a federal agency responsible for revisions.

16. Session of the SNB Directorate, April 7, 1983, SNBA.

17. Session of the SNB Directorate, July 12, 1984, SNBA.

18. Markus Lusser, "Notenbank und Bankenaufsicht: Trennung oder Vermischung der Aufgaben?," speech at the General Assembly of the Spanish-Swiss Chamber of Commerce, Zurich, July 5, 1994, SNBA.

19. Nikolaus Blattner, interview with author.

20. Rich, letter to Directorate, December 6, 1985, SNBA. In a complementary protocol note, it says that, "personally, Mr Rich originally thought that the liquidity provisions are irrelevant for monetary policy. But in the course of his work, he has changed his opinion. Liquidity rules are not necessary, but they complement the disciplining effect of interest rate changes" (SNB Directorate, April 24, 1986, SNBA).

21. "It belongs to one of our tasks to monitor liquidity. We do this without conviction because to our knowledge (1) no bank has ever failed only because of liquidity problems, (2) the legal provisions are not adequate in all respects, and (3) the existing possibilities to circumvent the rules raise serious questions about compliance" (Secretariat to Members of the Swiss Banking Commission, April 26, 1982, SNBA 1.3 / 1237).

22. Internal Report Working Group, "Liquidity Rules," SNBA.

23. Ibid.

24. UBS acquired O'Connor Partners, a securities trading firm, in 1992 and Kidder Peabody and PaineWebber in 2000. It also created the internal hedge fund, Dillon Read Capital Management. Credit Suisse had already acquired shares in First Boston in 1978 and became the majority shareholder in 1988. It acquired Donaldson, Lufkin & Jenrette in 2000.

25. After about a decade of negotiations, the experts working on a revision of banking law finally abandoned the entire project. Also, the finance minister, after creating a few new posts at the Federal Banking Commission secretariat in the late 1970s, stopped this expansion in the early 1980s.

26. Blattner, interview with author.

27. "The planned revision would lead to an abandonment of today's liquidity rules (Art. 15–18 BankV). Every bank will have to adopt its own liquidity policy, which will be adequate to its activities and organizational structure. The details of banks' policies would be left to themselves and their auditors, who would have to monitor the adequacy of the adopted provisions" (annual report of Swiss Banking Commission, 1997).

28. Annual report of Swiss Banking Commission, 2007.

29. Paul Tucker, "Regimes for Handling Bank Failures: Redrawing the Banking Social Contract," speech at the British Bankers' Association Annual International Banking Conference, June 30, 2009, Bank of England, London.

30. Edward George, "The Pursuit of Financial Stability," *BoE Quarterly Bulletin,* February 1994, pp. 60–66.

31. Private schools and Oxford and Cambridge universities ("Oxbridge") were formative for this elite. Chairmen of clearing banks and merchant banks had usually attended these educational institutions (Grueter 2016; Lisle-Williams 1984).

32. As Eddie George comments, "[T]he Banking Act of 1946 . . . gave us a power to 'make recommendations' to bankers, or to issue directions, but none of

this was considered a supervisory power. Rather, the Act was seen as justifying the qualitative lending guidance that was part of monetary policy in the 1950s and 1960s" (George, "The Pursuit of Financial Stability," p. 62).

33. Unknown author, "The Treasury, the Bank and the Constitution," August 25, 1977, BoE Archive 7A127 / 1.

34. The special regulations were as follows: "First . . . houses' holdings of 'undefined' assets (in effect, assets other than public sector debt), are limited to a maximum of 20 times their capital resources. Secondly, as a prudential control, their total balance sheet must not exceed 30 times capital resources" (unknown author, "The Money Market," 1980, BoE Archive 2A182 / 1).

35. Reserves included Treasury bills, "call money" (wholesale accounts) with the discount houses, and central bank money. See Allen (2015) for a detailed discussion of the Bank of England's asset choices.

36. "Other UK banks," among them the fringe institutions, had grown from constituting 8.6 percent of the British banking system in 1962 to 13 percent in 1970.

37. As Grueter describes it, "60 per cent or more of each fringe banks' investments were in the property sector, with it eventually becoming common practice to lend up to and over 100 per cent of asset values for such investments" (2016: 4).

38. Unknown author, "Fringe Banks (Speaking Notes)," January 15, 1974, BoE Archive 6A395 / 2.

39. John Fforde, "The Supervisory Function," December 20, 1973, BoE Archive 7A222 / 1.

40. For instance, the Bank's Governor Gordon Richardson claimed that "[t]he arguments for making such distinctions [between insiders and outsiders, LW], whether overt or not, rest mainly on the history of self-regulation among fully recognised U.K. banks and the degree of flexibility and individuality which the self-regulation has permitted them . . . It would be a great shame if this [self-regulatory] process were halted or impaired by the advent of legislation . . . The arguments for a two-tier control are, first, that the Bank has acquired all its experience of control in an environment of trust. It is consequently not equipped to deal with the more suspicious, legalistic attitude which would probably be required in dealing with institutions in which the ethic of self-regulation and trustworthiness was less well established. Moreover, the legalistic attitude which the Bank might come to adopt with this element might, in time, spill over into its treatment of the elite group with unfortunate consequences to its working relationships with the more important group" (Gordon Richardson, "The Supervisory Function," BoE Archive 7A222 / 1). This emphasis on self-regulation neglects, however, that with the separation of regulation from money-market management, the informal power that the Bank wielded over banking practices had been impaired. See also George Blunden, "The Supervision of the UK Banking System," *BoE Quarterly Bulletin,* June 1975.

41. Jasper Hollom to Gordon Richardson, "Cashier's Department. The Chief Cashier's Note of 6 February," February 21, 1974, BoE Archive 0A46/2.

42. Unnamed author, "The Bank of England: Proposal for a Revised Directing Structure," April 19, 1979, BoE Archive 7A152/1.

43. "The Capital and Liquidity Adequacy of Banks," *BoE Quarterly Bulletin,* September 1975.

44. Unknown author, "The Measurement of Liquidity," March 1980, BoE Archive 10A21 1/1.

45. Unknown author, "The Arrangements to Follow the Reserve Asset Ratio," December 31, 1980, BoE Archive 10A21 1/1. The clearing banks used the same reasoning: "The question of primary liquidity should be discussed separately and divorced from consideration of individual banks' functional need for liquidity" (Committee London Clearing Bank, "The Measurement of Liquidity," December 1980, BoE Archive 10A21 1/1). A *Financial Times* journalist reiterated this point of view and described liquidity requirements as "an uneasy medley of monetary and prudential controls that obliged all banks, whatever their mix of business, to hold a certain proportion of assets in prescribed near-liquid form on each monthly balance sheet day" ("More Flexibility in the London Money Markets," *Financial Times,* September 27, 1982).

46. Unknown author, "Sterling Liquidity," September 19, 1984, BoE Archive 2A71-5.

47. "Bankers See Snags in Plan for Liquidity Requirements," *Financial Times,* December 7, 1988; unknown author, "Report on a Conversation with National Westminster on Primary Liquidity at the Bank," August 13, 1986, BoE Archive 10A21 1/2. British Bankers' Association representatives argued in a meeting with Bank staff in 1986 that "it would be more appropriate—and in line with current supervisory practice—to agree the stock levels that should be held by banks in the course of the normal supervisory dialogue, not through a comprehensive regulation" (unknown author, "Primary Liquidity: Meeting with the BBA," November 21, 1986, BoE Archive 10A21 1/2).

48. Andrew Large, interview with author.

49. John Townend, "Supervision of the Wholesale Money Markets," *BoE Quarterly Bulletin,* January 1988, p. 69.

50. Brian Quinn, "The Bank of England's Role in Prudential Supervision," *BoE Quarterly Bulletin,* May 1993, pp. 260–64.

51. Financial Services Authority, "The Failure of the Royal Bank of Scotland," board report, Financial Services Authority, London, 2011.

52. The only liquidity regulation in place in Britain at the outbreak of the crisis was the Sterling Stock Regime, which included only major UK retail banks. It was also deficient because, as the FSA later noted, it "did not protect against longer liquidity stresses due to it only capturing wholesale flows out to a five-day period;

did not capture non-sterling flows; excluded off balance sheet contingent liabilities; and assumed only 5 per cent of retail deposits would be withdrawn over the five day period"—an amount exceeded in the Northern Rock case (see Financial Services Authority, "The Failure of the Royal Bank of Scotland"). Willem Buiter concluded in a parliamentary hearing in 2007 that "the FSA is an institution that thinks more about capital adequacy and solvency issues than about liquidity issues" (House of Commons Treasury Committee, *The Run on the Rock,* Fifth Report of Session 2007–2008, p. 26).

53. George, "The Pursuit of Financial Stability," p. 66. George's colleague Brian Quinn had given one important reason why: "[M]onetary policy cannot be carried out effectively unless the infrastructure and institutions through which operations are conducted are stable and sound. The infrastructure includes the payment system and, in particular, the wholesale payments mechanism." In that context, George and Quinn had also stressed that, as a lender of last resort, a central bank needed to know its ailing borrowers. Because such expertise was gained through supervision, the respective task belonged within central banks. See Quinn, "The Bank of England's Role," p. 262.

54. Rachel Lomax, interview with author.

55. Chris Giles, "The Court of King Mervyn," *Financial Times,* May 2, 2012.

56. "The Bank did not now have a culture of regulation . . . In view of these considerations, the Bank had concluded that where statutory regulation was required it should fall to the existing regulator, namely the FSA" (minutes of nonexecutive Directors Committee meeting, June 13, 2007, BoE Archive; see also Willem Buiter, "The Unfortunate Uselessness of Most 'State of the Art' Academic Monetary Economics," *Financial Times,* March 3, 2009).

57. Bill Allen, interview with author. Bindseil explains the associated dogma in the following words: "In principle, monetary macroeconomists in central banks do not need to understand monetary policy implementation and, symmetrically, implementation experts do not need to understand much about monetary policy strategy and the transmission mechanism" (2014: 12).

58. Andrew Large, "Financial Stability—Managing Liquidity Risk in a Global System," speech given at the Fourteenth City of London Central Banking and Regulatory Conference, London, November 28, 2005, Bank of England, London.

59. Bank of England Governor Mervyn King still argued in August that year that "the banking system as a whole is strong enough to withstand the impact of taking onto the balance sheet the assets of conduits and other vehicles" (cited in Hutter and Lloyd-Bostock 2017: 69). King also rejected early requests from Northern Rock for emergency lending, delaying a rescue until a veritable run was already under way (House of Commons Treasury Committee, *The Run on the Rock*).

60. These problems became evident in 2007–2008, because the Bank of England's emergency liquidity measures required coordination between money-market

managers and those managing relations with banks. As Plenderleith documents, the separation of these two functions raised obstacles for lender and market-maker of last-resort operations (emergency liquidity assistance, ELA); see Ian Plenderleith, *Review of the Bank of England's Provision of Emergency Liquidity Assistance in 2008–09,* Report to the Court of the Bank of England, October 2012, p. 64.

61. Bundesbank, "The Bundesbank's Involvement in Banking Supervision," *Deutsche Bundesbank Monthly Report,* September 2000, p. 34.

6. Plumbing Financialization in Vain

1. Denmark, the Euro Area, Japan, Sweden, Switzerland, the United Kingdom, and the United States have been said to follow quantitative easing, while some central banks have largely not (Australia, Canada, New Zealand, and Norway).

2. Jerome Powell, "New Economic Challenges and the Fed's Monetary Policy Review," speech at the economic policy symposium sponsored by the Federal Reserve Bank of Kansas City, August 27, 2020, Federal Reserve Board, Washington, DC.

3. Vitor Constâncio, "Past and Future of the ECB Monetary Policy," speech at the Conference on "Central Banks in Historical Perspective," Valletta, May 4, 2018, European Central Bank, Frankfurt.

4. See https://www.populardemocracy.org/campaign/building-national -campaign-strong-economy-fed.

5. See https://blockupy.org/en/.

6. Martin Arnold and Mehreen Khan, "Lagarde Calls on European Governments to Launch Fiscal Stimulus," *Financial Times,* September 4, 2019.

7. See https://www.epi.org/publication/why-is-recovery-taking-so-long-and -who-is-to-blame/.

8. Federal Reserve Distributional Financial Accounts, https://www.federalreserve .gov/releases/z1/dataviz/dfa/distribute/chart/.

9. Office of National Statistics, "Household Income Inequality, UK: Financial Year Ending 2020," https://www.ons.gov.uk/peoplepopulationandcommunity /personalandhouseholdfinances/incomeandwealth/bulletins/householdincomeineq ualityfinancial/financialyearending2020; Arun Advani, George Bangham, and Jack Leslie, "The UK's Wealth Distribution and Characteristics of High Wealth," Resolution Foundation Briefing, December 2020, https://www.resolutionfoundation .org/app/uploads/2020/12/The-UKs-wealth-distribution.pdf.

10. Geraldine Dany-Knedlik and Alexander Kriwoluzky, "Einkommensunglei-chheit in Deutschland sinkt in Krisenzeiten temporär," German Institute for

Economic Research (DIW), Wochenbericht 46, 2021, https://www.diw.de/de/diw
_01.c.829920.de/publikationen/wochenberichte/2021_46_1/einkommensungleichheit
_in_deutschland_sinkt_in_krisenzeiten_temporaer.html#:~:text=Erste%20
Auswertungen%20von%20Teilbefragungen%20des,w%C3%A4hrend%20der%20
Corona%2DPandemie%20leicht.

11. For instance, the *Economist* noted in July 2020 that, in the United States,
"of the stock of debt that companies have added since 2012, that lent by banks has
increased by just 2 percentage points of GDP. The stock that the non-bank sector
holds has risen by 6 percentage points"; a similar trend has occurred in private real
estate lending, where "[i]n 2007, almost 80 per cent of mortgages were created by
banks," while a "decade later, more than half were originated by non-banks."
Shadow-banking actors such as hedge funds have taken over significant parts of
securities trading. See "Banks Lose Out to Capital Markets When It Comes to
Credit Provision," *Economist*, July 25, 2020. For the Euro area, ECB senior official
Vítor Constâncio states that "the importance of banks in funding non-financial
firms has declined everywhere, including in the euro-area. There has been a
dramatic change, as non-bank financing sources have become much more important since the onset of the financial crisis. Total assets of investment funds in
percentage of total bank assets increased from 16 per cent in 2007 to 44 per cent
last year" (Constâncio, "Past and Future of the ECB Monetary Policy").

12. Financial Stability Board, "Global Monitoring Report on Non-bank
Financial Intermediation," December 16, 2020.

13. Ben Bernanke, "Monetary Policy and Inequality," blog post, *Brookings
Institute,* June 1, 2015; Mario Draghi, "Stability, Equity and Monetary Policy,"
2nd DIW Europe Lecture, Berlin, October 25, 2016, European Central Bank,
Frankfurt. See Monnin (2019) for an excellent review of the impact of QE on
income distribution.

14. "A Monetary Policy for the 1 Per Cent," *Economist,* July 5, 2012.

15. Ben Bernanke, "Monetary Policy since the Onset of the Crisis," speech at
the economic policy symposium sponsored by the Federal Reserve Bank of Kansas
City, August 31, 2012, Federal Reserve Board, Washington, DC.

16. Jason Furman, "The New View of Fiscal Policy and Its Application," speech
at the conference "The Global Implications of Europe's Redesign New York," New
York, October 5, 2016, https://obamawhitehouse.archives.gov/sites/default/files/page
/files/20161005_furman_suerf_fiscal_policy_cea.pdf.

17. For a reconstruction of the September 2019 events, see the Fed's own
analysis, https://www.federalreserve.gov/econres/notes/feds-notes/what-happened-in
-money-markets-in-september-2019-20200227.htm.

18. Statement from Federal Reserve chairman Jerome H. Powell, February 28,
2020, https://www.federalreserve.gov/newsevents/pressreleases/other20200228a
.htm.

19. Press conference transcripts, April and July 2011, ECB, Frankfurt.

20. Michael Steen, "Draghi Urges Eurozone Governments to Stay the Course on Austerity," *Financial Times,* May 2, 2013.

21. See https://www.ecb.europa.eu/mopo/implement/pepp/html/index.en.html.

22. See Chapter 5. The landmark document is Bank of England, *The Development of the Bank of England's Market Operations,* Consultative Paper October 2008, Bank of England, London.

23. Larry Elliott, "Bank Governor Mervyn King Backs Spending Cuts in Coalition's First Budget," *Guardian,* May 12, 2010.

24. Andrew Bailey, Jonathan Bridges, Richard Harrison, Josh Jones, and Aakash Mankodi, "The Central Bank Balance Sheet as a Policy Tool: Past, Present and Future," Bank of England Staff Working Paper No. 899, p. 24.

25. In a detailed study, the legal scholar Lev Menand (2020) argues that the Fed actually exposes itself through these support operations beyond its legal mandate—a mandate that was written in the spirit of functional separation between the money-creating bank sector and nonbank firms.

26. For instance, Di Maggio and Kacperczyk show that the reduction in US interest rates has "triggered significant responses of [money-market funds] and the broader asset management industry in terms of their product offerings, pricing policy, and organizational structure" (2017: 60). While funds associated with larger banks have often been closed, independent money-market funds have decided to invest in more risky assets to address the predicament of lowered returns. The problem with this development is that shares in money-market funds are treated in the United States as money-like assets. But with riskier investments, money-market funds increasingly expose themselves to runs.

27. Chris Giles, "Central Bankers Face a Crisis of Confidence as Models Fail," *Financial Times,* October 11, 2017.

28. Michael Woodford, "Methods of Policy Accommodation at the Interest-Rate Lower Bound," paper presented at the Federal Reserve Bank of Kansas City Symposium on "The Changing Policy Landscape," Jackson Hole, Wyoming, August 31, 2012.

29. Gertjan Vlieghe, "Revisiting the 3D Perspective on Low Long Term Interest Rates," public lecture at the London School of Economics and Political Science, July 26, 2021.

30. Henning Hesse, Boris Hofmann, and James Weber, "The Macroeconomic Effects of Asset Purchases Revisited," BIS Working Papers No. 680, Monetary and Economic Department, December 2017.

31. Martin Wolf summarizes the long-term macroeconomic implications in succinct terms: "If the central bank wants to raise inflation in an economy with structurally weak demand, it will do so by encouraging the growth of credit and debt. It might then fail to raise inflation, but create a debt crisis. That is defla-

tionary, not inflationary." Martin Wolf, "Monetary Policy Has Run Its Course," *Financial Times,* March 12, 2019.

Conclusion

1. Similar mechanisms fueled the crisis of the fiscal state as welfare promises made at earlier times came to weigh on budgets under reduced growth rates and aging populations (Pierson 2001). Beyond these domestic feedbacks, there also existed destructive ones at the transnational level. Demand from American consumers had made the rise of European export economies (particularly Germany) possible. But that very same demand turned into a problem for the international currency order (Bretton Woods), upon which international trade was based. The United States could not, at the same time, promise a stable exchange rate with gold and other currencies, while financing US consumption and the external surpluses of other economies; and export-oriented economies could not absorb surplus dollars endlessly without, at some point, risking revaluations or inflation. Therefore, in the 1970s, the Fordist regime was ripe for a major crisis that enabled the "re-formation of capitalism" and its nexus with the state (Streeck 2009).

References

Abbott, Andrew D. 1988. *The System of Professions: An Essay on the Division of Expert Labor.* Chicago: University of Chicago Press.

———. 1992. "What Do Cases Do? Some Notes on Activity in Sociological Analysis." Pp. 53–82 in *What Is a Case? Exploring the Foundations of Social Inquiry,* edited by Charles C. Ragin and Howard S. Becker. Cambridge: Cambridge University Press.

Abolafia, Mitchell Y. 1996. *Making Markets: Opportunism and Restraint on Wall Street.* Cambridge, MA: Harvard University Press.

———. 2012. "Central Banking and the Triumph of Technical Rationality." Pp. 94–112 in *Handbook of the Sociology of Finance,* edited by Karin Knorr Cetina and Alex Preda. Oxford: Oxford University Press.

———. 2020. *Stewards of the Market: How the Federal Reserve Made Sense of the Financial Crisis.* Cambridge, MA: Harvard University Press.

Acosta, Juan, Beatrice Cherrier, François Claveau, Clément Fontan, Aurélien Goutsmedt, and Francesco Sergi. 2020. *A History of Economic Research at the Bank of England (1960–2019).* Universidad de Los Andes.

Adolph, Christopher. 2013. *Bankers, Bureaucrats, and Central Bank Politics: The Myth of Neutrality.* Cambridge: Cambridge University Press.

Adrian, Tobias, and Nellie Liang. 2016. "Monetary Policy, Financial Conditions, and Financial Stability." *FRBNY Staff Reports,* No. 690, New York.

Adrian, Tobias, and Hyun Song Shin. 2008. "Financial Intermediaries, Financial Stability, and Monetary Policy." *FRBNY Staff Report,* No. 346, New York.

Ahamed, Liaquat. 2009. *Lords of Finance: The Bankers Who Broke the World.* New York: Penguin.

Albertini, Flurin von, ed. 1994. *Schweizer Geldpolitik im Dilemma.* Zurich: Verlag Ruegger.

Allen, Christopher S. 1989. "The Underdevelopment of Keynesianism in the Federal Republic of Germany." Pp. 231–62 in *The Political Power of Economic Ideas: Keynesianism across Nations,* edited by Peter Hall. Princeton, NJ: Princeton University Press.

Allen, Franklin, Michael K. F. Chui, and Angela Maddaloni. 2004. "Financial Systems in Europe, the USA, and Asia." *Oxford Review of Economic Policy* 20(4):490–508.

Allen, William A. 2013. *International Liquidity and the Financial Crisis.* Cambridge: Cambridge University Press.

———. 2014. *Monetary Policy and Financial Repression in Britain, 1951–59.* Basingstoke, UK: Palgrave Macmillan.

———. 2015. "Asset Choice in British Central Banking History, the Myth of the Safe Asset, and Bank Regulation." *Journal of Banking and Financial Economics* 2(4):18–31.

———. 2019. *The Bank of England and the Government Debt: Operations in the Gilt-Edged Market, 1928–1972.* Cambridge: Cambridge University Press.

Arcand, Jean Louis, Enrico Berkes, and Ugo Panizza. 2015. "Too Much Finance?" *Journal of Economic Growth* 20(2):105–48.

Argy, Victor, Anthony Brennan, and Glenn Stevens. 1990. "Monetary Targeting: The International Experience." *Economic Record* 66(1):37–62.

Auclert, Adrien. 2019. "Monetary Policy and the Redistribution Channel." *American Economic Review* 109(6):2333–67.

Autor, David, David Dorn, Lawrence F. Katz, Christina Patterson, and John Van Reenen. 2020. "The Fall of the Labor Share and the Rise of Superstar Firms." *Quarterly Journal of Economics* 135(2):645–709.

Axilrod, Steven H. 2009. *Inside the Fed: Monetary Policy and Its Management.* Cambridge, MA: MIT Press.

Baccaro, Lucio, and Chris Howell. 2017. *Trajectories of Neoliberal Transformation: European Industrial Relations since the 1970s.* Cambridge: Cambridge University Press.

Baccaro, Lucio, and Jonas Pontusson. 2016. "Rethinking Comparative Political Economy: The Growth Model Perspective." *Politics & Society* 44(2):175–207.

Bagehot, Walter. 1873. *Lombard Street: A Description of the Money Market.* London: H. S. King & Co.

Baldwin, Robert. 2013. "Trade and Industrialization after Globalization's Second Unbundling: How Building and Joining a Supply Chain Are Different and Why It Matters." Pp. 165–212 in *Globalization in an Age of Crisis: Multilateral Economic Cooperation in the Twenty-First Century,* edited by Robert C. Feenstra and Alan M. Taylor. Cambridge, MA: NBER Books.

Baltensperger, Ernst. 1984. "Geldmengenpolitik und Inflationskontrolle." *Mitteilungen der Kommission für Konjunkturfragen,* Bern: Schweizerische Kommission für Konjunkturfragen.

Ban, Cornel. 2016. *Ruling Ideas: How Global Neoliberalism Goes Local.* New York: Oxford University Press.

Barnes, Lucy, and Timothy Hicks. 2021. "All Keynesians Now? Public Support for Countercyclical Government Borrowing." *Political Science Research and Methods* 9(1):180–88.

Barro, Robert J., and David B. Gordon. 1983. "Rules, Discretion and Reputation in a Model of Monetary Policy." *Journal of Monetary Economics* 12:101–21.

Bartscher, Alina K., Moritz Kuhn, Moritz Schularick, and Ulrike I. Steins. 2020. "Modigliani Meets Minsky: Inequality, Debt, and Financial Fragility in America, 1950–2016." *FRBNY Staff Report,* No. 924. New York: Federal Reserve Bank of New York.

Beck, Mareike. 2021. "Extroverted Financialization: How US Finance Shapes European Banking." *Review of International Political Economy:*1–23.

Beckert, Jens. 2016. *Imagined Futures: Fictional Expectations and Capitalist Dynamics.* Cambridge, MA: Harvard University Press.

———. 2020. "The Exhausted Futures of Neoliberalism: From Promissory Legitimacy to Social Anomy." *Journal of Cultural Economy* 13(3):318–30.

Beckert, Jens, and Richard Bronk. 2018. "An Introduction to Uncertain Futures." Pp. 1–36 in *Uncertain Futures: Imaginaries, Narratives, and Calculation in the Economy,* edited by Jens Beckert and Richard Bronk. Oxford: Oxford University Press.

Bell, Daniel. 1967. "The Year 2000: The Trajectory of an Idea." *Daedalus* 96(3):639–51.

Beramendi, Pablo, Silja Häusermann, Herbert Kitschelt, and Hanspeter Kriesi. 2015. "Introduction: The Politics of Advanced Capitalism." Pp. 1–64 in *The Politics of Advanced Capitalism,* edited by Hanspeter Kriesi, Herbert Kitschelt, Pablo Beramendi, and Silja Häusermann. Cambridge: Cambridge University Press.

Bernanke, Ben. 2020. "The New Tools of Monetary Policy." *American Economic Review* 110(4):943–83.

Bernanke, Ben, Timothy F. Geithner, Henry M. Paulson, and J. Nellie Liang. 2020. *First Responders: Inside the U.S. Strategy for Fighting the 2007–2009 Global Financial Crisis.* New Haven, CT: Yale University Press.

Bernanke, Ben, and Frederic S. Mishkin. 1997. "Inflation Targeting: A New Framework for Monetary Policy?" NBER Working Paper No. 5893. Cambridge, MA: National Bureau of Economic Research.

Bernhard, William, J. Lawrence Broz, and William R. Clark. 2002. "The Political Economy of Monetary Institutions." *International Organization* 56(4):693–723.

Bernholz, Peter. 1974. *Währungskrisen und Währungsordnung.* Hamburg: Hoffmann und Campe.

———. 2007. "Die Nationalbank 1945–1982: Von der Devisenbann-Wirtschaft zur Geldmengensteuerung bei flexiblen Wechselkursen." Pp. 119–213 in *Die Schweizerische Nationalbank 1907–2007,* edited by Schweizerische National-bank. Zürich: NZZ Libro.

Best, Jacqueline. 2019. "The Inflation Game: Targets, Practices and the Social Production of Monetary Credibility." *New Political Economy* 24(5):623–40.

Bibow, Jörg. 2003. "On the 'Burden' of German Unification." *BNL Quarterly Review* 225:137–69.

Bindseil, Ulrich. 2004a. *Monetary Policy Implementation.* Oxford: Oxford University Press.

———. 2004b. *The Operational Target of Monetary Policy and the Rise and Fall of the Reserve Position Doctrine.* Frankfurt: European Central Bank.

———. 2014. *Monetary Policy Operations and the Financial System.* Oxford: Oxford University Press.

Birk, Marius. 2017. "Liquidity without Tears: The Paradox of Regulating Liquidity through Designing Liquidity." Master's thesis, Johann Wolfgang Goethe-Universität, Frankfurt a.M.

Blanchard, Olivier. 2018. "Should We Reject the Natural Rate Hypothesis?" *Journal of Economic Perspectives* 32(1):97–120.

Blinder, Alan S. 2001. *How Do Central Banks Talk?* London: CEPR.

———. 2004. *The Quiet Revolution: Central Banking Goes Modern.* New Haven, CT: Yale University Press.

Blyth, Mark. 2002. *Great Transformations: Economic Ideas and Institutional Change in the Twentieth Century.* Cambridge: Cambridge University Press.

———. 2003. "Structures Do Not Come with an Instruction Sheet: Interests, Ideas, and Progress in Political Science." *Perspectives on Politics* 1(4):695–706.

Blyth, Mark, and Matthias Matthijs. 2017. "Black Swans, Lame Ducks, and the Mystery of IPE's Missing Macroeconomy." *Review of International Political Economy* 24(2):203–31.

Bockman, Johanna, and Gil Eyal. 2002. "Eastern Europe as a Laboratory for Economic Knowledge: The Transnational Roots of Neoliberalism." *American Journal of Sociology* 108(2):310–52.

Bodea, Cristina, and Raymond Hicks. 2015. "International Finance and Central Bank Independence: Institutional Diffusion and the Flow and Cost of Capital." *Journal of Politics* 77(1):268–84.

Boix, Carles. 2015. "Prosperity and the Evolving Structure of Advanced Econo-mies." Pp. 67–88 in *The Politics of Advanced Capitalism,* edited by Pablo

Beramendi, Silja Häusermann, Herbert Kitschelt, and Hanspeter Kriesi. Cambridge: Cambridge University Press.

Bonner, Clemens, and Paul Hilbers. 2015. "Global Liquidity Regulation—Why Did It Take So Long?" DNB Working Papers. Amsterdam: De Nederlandsche Bank.

Booth, Alan. 2001. "Britain in the 1950s: A 'Keynesian' Managed Economy?" *History of Political Economy* 33(2):283–313.

Bordo, Michael D., and Harold James. 2007. "Die Nationalbank 1907–1946: Glückliche Kindheit oder schwierige Jugend?" Pp. 29–118 in *Die Schweizerische Nationalbank 1907–2007,* edited by Schweizerische Nationalbank. Zürich: NZZ Libro.

Borio, Claudio. 2011. "Central Banking Post-Crisis: What Compass for Uncharted Waters?" BIS Working Papers. Basel: Bank for International Settlements.

Borio, Claudio, and Haibin Zhu. 2012. "Capital Regulation, Risk-Taking and Monetary Policy: A Missing Link in the Transmission Mechanism?" *Journal of Financial Stability* 8(4):236–51.

Bourdieu, Pierre. 1996 [1989]. *The State Nobility: Elite Schools in the Field of Power.* Cambridge: Polity Press.

———. 2014. *On the State.* Cambridge: Polity Press.

Bowker, Geoffrey C., and Susan Leigh Star. 1999. *Sorting Things Out: Classification and Its Consequences.* Cambridge, MA: MIT Press.

Boyer, Robert. 1990. *The Regulation School: A Critical Introduction.* New York: Columbia University Press.

Boylan, Delia M. 2001. *Defusing Democracy: Central Bank Autonomy and the Transition from Authoritarian Rule.* Ann Arbor: University of Michigan Press.

Braudel, Fernand. 1992 [1979]. *The Wheels of Commerce.* Berkeley: University of California Press.

Braun, Benjamin. 2015. "Governing the Future: The European Central Bank's Expectation Management during the Great Moderation." *Economy and Society* 44(3):367–91.

———. 2018a. "Central Banking and the Infrastructural Power of Finance: The Case of ECB Support for Repo and Securitization Markets." *Socio-economic Review* 18(2):395–418.

———. 2018b. "Central Banks Planning: Unconventional Monetary Policy and the Price of Bending the Yield Curve." Pp. 194–216 in *Uncertain Futures,* edited by Jens Beckert and Richard Bronk. Oxford: Oxford University Press.

Braun, Benjamin, Donato Di Carlo, Sebastian Diessner, and Maximilian Düsterhöftd. 2021. *Polanyi in Frankfurt: Supranational Money and the National Disembedding of Labor.* Cologne: Max Planck Institute for the Study of Societies.

Braun, Benjamin, and Daniela Gabor. 2020. "Central Banking, Shadow Banking, and Infrastructural Power." Pp. 241–52 in *The Routledge International Handbook of*

Financialization, edited by Philipp Mader, Daniel Mertens, and Natascha van der Zwan. London: Routledge.

Braun, Benjamin, Arie Krampf, and Steffen Murau. 2021. "Financial Globalization as Positive Integration: Monetary Technocrats and the Eurodollar Market in the 1970s." *Review of International Political Economy.* 28(4):794–819.

Brenner, Robert. 2006. *The Economics of Global Turbulence.* New York: Verso.

Broz, J. Lawrence. 1998. "The Origins of Central Banking: Solutions to the Free-Rider Problem." *International Organization* 52(2):231–68.

Brunner, Karl. 1968. "The Role of Money and Monetary Policy." *Federal Reserve Bank of St. Louis Review,* Federal Reserve Bank of St. Louis, St. Louis.

———. 1971. "A Survey of Selected Issues in Monetary Theory." *Schweizerische Zeitschrift für Volkswirtschaft und Statistik* 107(1):1–146.

———. 1996. "My Quest for Economic Knowledge." Pp. 18–30 in *Economic Analysis and Political Ideology: The Selected Essays of Karl Brunner, Volume One,* edited by Thomas Z. Lys. Cheltenham, UK: Edward Elgar.

Brunnermeier, Markus, Andrew Crocket, Charles A. E. Goodhart, Avinash D. Persaud, and Hyun Song Shin. 2009. "The Fundamental Principles of Financial Regulation." *Geneva Reports on the World Economy.* Geneva: ICMB International Center for Monetary and Banking Studies.

Brunnermeier, Markus K., and Lasse Heje Pedersen. 2009. "Market Liquidity and Funding Liquidity." *Review of Financial Studies* 22(6):2201–38.

Buggeln, Marc, Martin Daunton, and Alexander Nützenadel. 2017. "The Political Economy of Public Finance since the 1970s: Questioning the Leviathan." Pp. 1–31 in *The Political Economy of Public Finances,* edited by Marc Buggeln, Martin Daunton, and Alexander Nützenadel. Cambridge: Cambridge University Press.

Bühlmann, Felix, Thomas David, and André Mach. 2012. "The Swiss Business Elite (1980–2000): How the Changing Composition of the Elite Explains the Decline of the Swiss Company Network." *Economy and Society* 41(2):199–226.

Burgess, W. Randolph 1927. *The Reserve Banks and the Money Market.* New York: Harper & Brothers.

Burn, Gary. 1999. "The State, the City and the Euromarkets." *Review of International Political Economy* 6(2):225–61.

———. 2006. *The Re-emergence of Global Finance.* Houndsmills, UK: Palgrave Macmillan.

Burns, Arthur. 1979. *The Anguish of Central Banking.* Belgrade: Per Jacobsson Foundation.

Calomiris, Charles, and Luc Laeven. 2016. "Political Foundations of the Lender of Last Resort: A Global Historical Narrative." *Journal of Financial Intermediation* 28:48–65.

Calomiris, Charles W. 1998. "Universal Banking 'American-Style.'" *Journal of Institutional and Theoretical Economics* 154(1):44–57.

Campbell, John L. 2020. "The Evolution of Fiscal and Monetary Policy." Pp. 787–811 in *The New Handbook of Political Sociology,* edited by Cedric de Leon, Isaac William Martin, Joya Misra, and Thomas Janoski. Cambridge: Cambridge University Press.

Capie, Forrest H. 2010. *The Bank of England, 1950s to 1979.* Cambridge: Cambridge University Press.

Carpenter, Daniel. 2001. *The Forging of Bureaucratic Autonomy: Reputations, Networks, and Policy Innovation in Executive Agencies, 1862–1928.* Princeton, NJ: Princeton University Press.

Carruthers, Bruce G. 1994. "When Is the State Autonomous? Culture, Organization Theory, and the Political Sociology of the State." *Sociological Theory* 12(1):19–44.

———. 2013. "Diverging Derivatives: Law, Governance and Modern Financial Markets." *Journal of Comparative Economics* 41(2):386–400.

———. 2015. "Financialization and the Institutional Foundations of the New Capitalism." *Socio-economic Review* 13(2):379–98.

Carruthers, Bruce G., Sarah Babb, and Terence C. Halliday. 2001. "Institutionalizing Markets, or the Market for Institutions? Central Banks, Bankruptcy Law, and the Globalization of Financial Markets." Pp. 94–126 in *The Rise of Neoliberalism and Institutional Analysis,* edited by John L. Campbell and Ove K. Pedersen. Princeton, NJ: Princeton University Press.

Cassar, Dylan. 2021. "Down to (a) Science? Epistemic Struggles, Socio-technical Configurations, and the Enacting of Quantitative Easing at the Bank of England." Unpublished manuscript, University of Edinburgh, Edinburgh.

Cieslak, Anna, and Annette Vissing-Jorgensen. 2018. "The Economics of the Fed Put." NBER Working Paper No. 26894. Cambridge, MA: National Bureau of Economic Research.

Cleveland, Harold van B., and Thomas F. Huertas. 1985. *Citibank, 1812–1970.* Cambridge, MA: Harvard University Press.

Clift, Ben. 2018. *The IMF and the Politics of Austerity in the Wake of the Global Financial Crisis.* Oxford: Oxford University Press.

———. 2020. "The Hollowing out of Monetarism: The Rise of Rules-Based Monetary Policy-Making in the UK and USA and Problems with the Paradigm Change Framework." *Comparative European Politics* 18(3):281–308.

Cobham, David P. 2002. *The Making of Monetary Policy in the UK, 1975–2000.* Chichester, UK: J. Wiley.

Collins, Michael, and Mae Baker. 1999. "Bank of England Autonomy: A Retrospective." Pp. 13–33 in *The Emergence of Modern Central Banking from 1918 to the Present,* edited by Carl-Ludwig Holtfrerich, Jaime Reis, and Gianni Toniolo. Aldershot, UK: Ashgate.

Conti-Brown, Peter. 2016. *The Power and Independence of the Federal Reserve.* Princeton, NJ: Princeton University Press.

Copelovitch, Mark S., and David Andrew Singer. 2008. "Financial Regulation, Monetary Policy, and Inflation in the Industrialized World." *Journal of Politics* 70(3):663–80.

Coppola, Frances. 2019. *The Case for People's Quantitative Easing.* Cambridge: Polity Press.

Crosignani, Matteo, Miguel Faria-e-Castro, and Luis Fonseca. 2017. "The (Unintended?) Consequences of the Largest Liquidity Injection Ever." Finance and Economics Discussion Series No. 2017-011. Washington, DC: Divisions of Research & Statistics and Monetary Affairs Federal Reserve Board.

Crouch, Colin. 2011. *The Strange Non-death of Neoliberalism.* Cambridge: Polity Press.

Culpepper, Pepper D. 2011. *Quiet Politics and Business Power. Corporate Control in Europe and Japan.* Cambridge: Cambridge University Press.

———. 2015. "Structural Power and Political Science in the Post-crisis Era." *Business and Politics* 17(3):391–409.

Cusack, Thomas R. 1999. "Partisan Politics and Fiscal Policy." *Comparative Political Studies* 32(4):464–86.

D'Arista, Jane W. 1994. *The Evolution of US Finance, Volume II: Restructuring Markets and Institutions.* New York: M. E. Sharpe.

Davies, Aled. 2012. "The Evolution of British Monetarism: 1968–1979." Discussion Papers in Economic and Social History. Oxford: University of Oxford.

Davies, Howard, and David Green. 2010. *Banking on the Future: The Fall and Rise of Central Banking.* Princeton, NJ: Princeton University Press.

Davis, Gerald F. 2010. "Is Shareholder Capitalism a Defunct Model for Financing Development?" *Review of Market Integration* 2(2–3):317–31.

———. 2016. *The Vanishing American Corporation: Navigating the Hazards of a New Economy.* Oakland, CA: Berrett-Koehler.

De Gauwe, Paul. 2020. "The Need for Monetary Financing of Corona Budget Deficits." *Intereconomics* 55(3):133–34.

de Roover, Raymond. 1946. "Le contrat de change depuis la fin du treizième siècle jusqu'au début du dix-septième." *Revue Belge de Philologie et d'Histoire* 25(1–2):111–28.

Deeg, Richard. 1999. *Finance Capitalism Unveiled: Banks and the German Political Economy.* Ann Arbor: University of Michigan Press.

Dewey, John. 1915. "The Logic of Judgements of Practise." *Journal of Philosophy, Psychology and Scientific Methods* 12(19):505–23.

Di Maggio, Marco, and Marcin Kacperczyk. 2017. "The Unintended Consequences of the Zero Lower Bound Policy." *Journal of Financial Economics* 123(1):59–80.

Drake, Leigh. 1989. *The Building Society Industry in Transition.* Houndmills, UK: Macmillan.

Edwards, Paul N. 2019. "Infrastructuration: On Habits, Norms and Routines as Elements of Infrastructure." *Research in the Sociology of Organizations* 62:355–66.

Eichengreen, Barry J. 2008. *Globalizing Capital: A History of the International Monetary System.* Princeton, NJ: Princeton University Press.

———. 2010. *The Rise and Fall of the Dollar and the Future of the International Monetary System.* Oxford: Oxford University Press.

El-Erian, Mohamed A. 2016. *The Only Game in Town: Central Banks, Instability, and Avoiding the Next Collapse.* New York: Random House.

Emminger, Otmar. 1988. "The Evolution of the Exchange Rate from 'Sacrosanct' Parity to Flexible Monetary Policy Instrument." Pp. 1–16 in *German Yearbook on Business History 1987,* edited by Hans Pohl and Bernd Rudolph. Berlin: Springer.

Englund, Peter. 1999. "The Swedish Banking Crisis: Roots and Consequences." *Oxford Review of Economic Policy* 15(3):80–97.

Ertman, Thomas. 1997. *Birth of the Leviathan: Building States and Regimes in Medieval and Early Modern Europe.* Cambridge: Cambridge University Press.

Erturk, Ismail. 2016. *Post-crisis Central Bank Unconventional Policies and Financialised Transmission Channels.* Manchester Business School, University of Manchester.

Evans, Peter B. 1995. *Embedded Autonomy: States and Industrial Transformation.* Princeton, NJ: Princeton University Press.

Filc, Wolfgang. 1994. "Die Bundesbank zwischen Geldmengenorientierung und Zinsverantwortung." *Wirtschaftsdienst* 74(6):282–86.

Fisher, Stanley. 1994. "Modern Central Banking." Pp. 262–329 in *The Future of Central Banking: The Tercentenary Symposium of the Bank of England,* edited by Forrest Capie, Stanley Fischer, Charles Goodhart, and Norbert Schnadt. Cambridge: Cambridge University Press.

Fletcher, Gordon Alan. 1976. *The Discount Houses in London: Principles, Operations and Change.* London: Macmillan.

Fligstein, Neil. 2001. *The Architecture of Markets: An Economic Sociology of Twenty-First-Century Capitalist Societies.* Princeton, NJ: Princeton University Press.

Fligstein, Neil, Jonah Stuart Brundage, and Michael Schultz. 2017. "Seeing Like the Fed: Culture, Cognition, and Framing in the Failure to Anticipate the Financial Crisis of 2008." *American Sociological Review* 82(5):879–909.

Fontan, Clément, François Claveau, and Peter Dietsch. 2016. "Central Banking and Inequalities: Taking off the Blinders." *Politics, Philosophy and Economics* 15(4):319–57.

Foucault, Michel. 1991 [1978]. "Governmentality." Pp. 87–104 in *The Foucault Effect: Studies in Governmentality,* edited by Graham Burchell, Colin Gordon, and Peter Miller. Chicago: University of Chicago Press.

———. 2007 [1978]. *Security, Territory, Population: Lectures at the Collège de France, 1977–78.* Basingstoke, UK: Palgrave Macmillan.

Fourcade, Marion. 2006. "The Construction of a Global Profession: The Transnationalization of Economics." *American Journal of Sociology* 112(1):145–94.

Fourcade, Marion. 2009. *Economists and Societies: Discipline and Profession in the United States, Great Britain, and France, 1890s to 1990s.* Princeton, NJ: Princeton University Press.

Fourcade, Marion, and Rakesh Khurana. 2013. "From Social Control to Financial Economics: The Linked Ecologies of Economics and Business in Twentieth Century America." *Theory and Society* 42:121–59.

Fourcade-Gourinchas, Marion, and Sarah Babb. 2002. "The Rebirth of the Liberal Creed: Paths to Neoliberalism in Four Countries." *American Journal of Sociology* 108(3):533–79.

Franzese, Jr., Robert J. 2000. "Credibly Conservative Monetary Policy and Labour-Goods Market Organisation: A Review with Implications for ECB-Led Monetary Policy in Europe." Pp. 97–124 in *The History of the Bundesbank: Lessons for the European Central Bank,* edited by Jakob de Haan. London: Routledge.

Frieden, Jeffry. 2002. "Real Sources of European Currency Policy: Sectorial Interests and European Monetary Integration." *International Organization* 56(4):831–60.

———. 2013. "The Coming Battles over Monetary Policy." Manuscript, Harvard University, Cambridge, MA.

Friedman, Benjamin M. 2002. "The Use and Meaning of Words in Central Banking: Inflation Targeting, Credibility, and Transparency." NBER Working Paper No. 8972. Cambridge, MA: National Bureau of Economic Research.

Friedman, Milton. 1956. "The Quantity Theory of Money—a Restatement." Pp. 3–21 in *Studies in the Quantity Theory of Money,* edited by Milton Friedman. Chicago: University of Chicago Press.

———. 1968. "The Role of Monetary Policy." *American Economic Review* 58(1):1–17.

———. 1970. "A Theoretical Framework for Monetary Analysis." *Journal of Political Economy* 78(2):193–238.

———. 1990 [1961]. "Lag in Effect of Monetary Policy." Pp. 40–65 in *Milton Friedman: Critical Assessments,* edited by John C. Wood and Ronald N. Woods. London: Routledge.

Friedman, Milton, and Anna Jacobson Schwartz. 1963. *A Monetary History of the United States: 1867–1960.* Princeton, NJ: Princeton University Press.

Fullwiler, Scott T. 2013. "An Endogenous Money Perspective on the Post-crisis Monetary Policy Debate." *Review of Keynesian Economics* 1(2):171–94.

———. 2017. "Modern Central-Bank Operations: The General Principles." Pp. 50–87 in *Advances in Endogenous Money Analysis,* edited by Louis-Philippe Rochon and Sergio Rossi. Cheltenham, UK: Edward Elgar.

Funk, Russell J., and Daniel Hirschman. 2014. "Derivatives and Deregulation." *Administrative Science Quarterly* 59(4):669–704.

Gabor, Daniela. 2016. "The (Impossible) Repo Trinity: The Political Economy of Repo Markets." *Review of International Political Economy* 23(6):967–1000.

———. 2021. *Revolution without Revolutionaries: Interrogating the Return of Monetary Financing* Working Paper. Bristol: University of the West of England.

Garbade, Kenneth D. 2006. "The Evolution of Repo Contracting Conventions in the 1980s." *FRBNY Economic Policy Review.*

Gebauer, Wolfgang. 1983. "The Euromarkets and Monetary Control: The Deutschemark Case." EUI Working Paper No. 66. Florence: European University Institute.

Geithner, Timothy F. 2014. *Stress Test: Reflections on Financial Crises.* New York: Crown.

George, Alexander L., and Andrew Bennett. 2004. *Case Studies and Theory Development in the Social Sciences.* Cambridge, MA: MIT Press.

Gern, Klaus-Jürgen, Nils Jannsen, Stefan Kooths, and Maik Wolters. 2015. "Quantitative Easing in the Euro Area: Transmission Channels and Risks." *Intereconomics* 50(4):206–12.

Giddey, Thibaud. 2010. *La genèse et les premières années d'activités de la Commission fédérale des banques (1931–1943).* Mémoire de Maitrise universitaire des lettres en histoire contemporaine, Université de Lausanne, Lausanne.

———. 2012. "Gendarme ou médecin des banques? Les premières années d'activité de la Commission fédérale des banques (1935–1943)." *Traverse: Zeitschrift für Geschichte/Revue d'histoire* 19:145–63.

———. 2013. "The Regulation of Foreign Banks in Switzerland (1959–1972)." Pp. 449–85 in *EABH Annual Conference,* edited by Melanie Aspey, Peter Hertner, Krzysztof Kaczmar, Jakub Skiba, Dieter Stiefel, and Nuno Valério. Warsaw, Poland: European Association for Banking and Financial History.

———. 2016. "La surveillance bancaire en Suisse: Mise en place et évolution d'un régime de régulation financière (1914–1975)." In *Faculté des lettres.* Lausanne: Université de Lausanne.

Ginalski, Stéphanie, Thomas David, and André Mach. 2014. "From National Cohesion to Transnationalization: The Changing Role of Banks in the Swiss Company Network, 1910–2010." Pp. 107–24 in *The Power of Corporate Networks: A Comparative and Historical Perspective,* edited by Thomas David and Gerada Westerhuis. New York: Routledge.

Goldthorpe, John Harry. 1978. "The Current Inflation: Towards a Sociological Account." Pp. 186–216 in *The Political Economy of Inflation,* edited by Fred Hirsch and John Harry Goldthorpe. London: Martin Robertson.

Golub, Stephen, Ayse Kaya, and Michael Reay. 2015. "What Were They Thinking? The Federal Reserve in the Run-Up to the 2008 Financial Crisis." *Review of International Political Economy* 22(4):657–92.

Goodfriend, Marvin. 1993. "Interest Rate Policy and the Inflation Scare Problem: 1979–1992." *Federal Reserve Bank of Richmond, Economic Quarterly* 79(1): 1–23.

———. 2007. "How the World Achieved Consensus on Monetary Policy." *Journal of Economic Perspectives* 21(4):47–68.

Goodfriend, Marvin, and Monica Hargraves. 1983. "A Historical Assessment of the Rationales and Functions of Reserve Requirements." *Federal Reserve Bank of Richmond Economic Review,* March/April, Federal Reserve Bank of Richmond, Richmond, IL.

Goodhart, Charles A. E. 1986. "Financial Innovation and Monetary Control." *Oxford Review of Economic Policy* 2(4):79–102.

———. 1988. *The Evolution of Central Banks.* Cambridge, MA: MIT Press.

———. 1989. "The Conduct of Monetary Policy." *Economic Journal* 99(June): 203–346.

———. 2000. *The Organisational Structure of Banking Supervision.* Basel: Bank for International Settlements.

———. 2002. "The Organizational Structure of Banking Supervision." *Economic Notes* 31(1):1–32.

———. 2004. "The Bank of England over the Last 35 Years." *Bankhistorisches Archiv* Beiheft 43: Welche Aufgaben muss eine Zentralbank wahrnehmen? Historische Erfahrungen und europäische Perspektiven:29–54.

———. 2011a. *The Basel Committee on Banking Supervision: A History of the Early Years, 1974–1997.* Cambridge: Cambridge University Press.

———. 2011b. "The Changing Role of Central Banks." *Financial History Review* 18(2):135–54.

Goodhart, Charles A. E., and Duncan J. Needham. 2018. "Historical Reasons for the Focus on Broad Monetary Aggregates in Post–World War II Britain and the 'Seven Years War' with the IMF." *Financial History Review* 24(3):331–56.

Goodhart, Charles A. E., and Dirk Schoenmaker. 1992. "Institutional Separation between Supervisory and Regulatory Agencies." *Giornale degli Economisti e Annali di Economia* 51(9):353–439.

Goodman, John B. 1992. *Monetary Sovereignty: The Politics of Central Banking in Western Europe.* Ithaca, NY: Cornell University Press.

Gorton, Gary, and Lixin Huang. 2002. "Banking Panics and the Origin of Central Banking." NBER Working Paper No. 9137. Cambridge, MA: National Bureau of Economic Research.

Gorton, Gary, and Andrew Metrick. 2012. "Securitized Banking and the Run on Repo." *Journal of Financial Economics* 104(3):425–51.

Grant, Wyn. 2002. *Economic Policy in Britain.* Houndmills, UK: Palgrave.

Gray, Julia. 2013. *The Company States Keep: International Economic Organizations and Investor Perceptions.* Cambridge: Cambridge University Press.

Gray, William Glenn. 2007. "Floating the System: Germany, the United States, and the Breakdown of Bretton Woods, 1969–1973." *Diplomatic History* 31(2): 295–323.

Green, Jeremy. 2015. "Anglo-American Development, the Euromarkets, and the Deeper Origins of Neoliberal Deregulation." *Review of International Studies* 42(3): 425–49.

Greider, William. 1987. *Secrets of the Temple: How the Federal Reserve Runs the Country.* New York: Simon and Schuster.

Grueter, Andreas. 2016. *Outsiders In: The Secondary Banking Crisis of the 1970s as a Renegotiation of Legitimacy and Control in the British Banking System.* Master's thesis, London School of Economics and Political Science, London.

Guex, Sébastien. 2012. "L'etat fédéral et les crises economiques du début du XXe diècle à nos jours: La Suisse, un bastion anti-Keneséien." *Annuaire Suisse d'Histoire Économique et Sociale* 27(27):151–69.

Guex, Sébastien, and Malik Mazbouri. 2013. "Une grande association patronale dans la sphère publique: L'exemple de l'Association suisse des banquiers (de 1912 à nos jours)." Pp. 205–35 in *Les organisations patronales et la sphère publique,* edited by Danièle Fraboulet, Clotilde Druelle-Korn, and Pierre Vernus. Rennes: Presses Universitaires de Rennes.

Guex, Sébastien, and Yves Sancey. 2010. "Les dirigeants de la Banque Nationale Suisse au XXe siècle." Pp. 143–79 in *Gouverner une banque centrale: Du XVIIe siècle à nos jours,* edited by Olivier Feiertag and Michel Margairaz. Paris: Albin Michel.

Halbeisen, Patrick. 2005. "Cool Lover? Switzerland and the Road to European Monetary Union." Pp. 99–117 in *European Central Banks and Monetary Cooperation after 1945,* edited by Piet Clement and Juan Carlos Martinez Olivia. Frankfurt: Adelmann.

Halbeisen, Patrick, and Tobias Straumann. 2012. "Die Wirtschaftspolitik im internationalen Kontext." Pp. 977–1075 in *Wirtschaftsgeschichte der Schweiz im 20. Jahrhundert,* edited by Margrit Müller, Béatrice Veyrassat, and Patrick Halbeisen. Basel: Schwabe Basel.

Haldane, Andrew G. 2018. "How Monetary Policy Affects Your Gross Domestic Product." *Australian Economic Review* 51(3):309–35.

Haldane, Andrew G., and Jan F. Qvigstad. 2016. "The Evolution of Central Banks: A Practitioner's Perspective." Pp. 627–71 in *Central Banks at a Crossroads: What Can We Learn from History?,* edited by Michael D. Bordo, Marc Flandreau, and Jan F. Qvigstad. Cambridge: Cambridge University Press.

Hall, Peter A. 1986. *Governing the Economy: The Politics of State Intervention in Britain and France.* Cambridge: Polity Press.

———. 1993. "Policy Paradigms, Social Learning, and the State: The Case of Economic Policymaking in Britain." *Comparative Politics* 25(3):275–96.

Hall, Peter A., and Robert J. Franzese. 1998. "Mixed Signals: Central Bank Independence, Coordinated Wage Bargaining, and European Monetary Union." *International Organization* 52(3):505–35.

Hall, Peter A., and David Soskice. 2001. "An Introduction to Varieties of Capitalism." Pp. 1–68 in *Varieties of Capitalism: The Institutional Foundations of Comparative Advantage,* edited by Peter A. Hall and David Soskice. Oxford: Oxford University Press.

Hancké, Bob. 2013. *Unions, Central Banks, and EMU: Labour Market Institutions and Monetary Integration in Europe.* Oxford: Oxford University Press.

Hardie, Iain, David Howarth, Sylvia Maxfield, and Amy Verdun. 2013. "Banks and the False Dichotomy in the Comparative Political Economy of Finance." *World Politics* 65(4):691–728.

Hardie, Iain, and Sylvia Maxfield. 2013. "Market-Based Banking as the Worst of All Worlds: Illustrations from the United States and United Kingdom." Pp. 56–76 in *Market-Based Banking and the International Financial Crisis,* edited by Iain Hardie and David Howarth. Oxford: Oxford University Press.

Haubrich, Joseph G., and James B. Thomson. 2008. "Umbrella Supervision and the Role of the Central Bank." *Journal of Banking Regulation* 10(1):17–27.

Häusler, Gert. 1994. "The Competitive Position of Germany as a Financial Centre as Seen by a Central Banker." Pp. 253–63 in *The Competitiveness of Financial Institutions and Centres in Europe,* edited by Donald E. Fair and Raymond Robert. Dordrecht: Kluwer Academic.

Hay, Colin. 2001. "The 'Crisis' of Keynesianism and the Rise of Neoliberalism in Britain: An Ideational Institutionalist Approach." Pp. 193–218 in *The Rise of Neoliberalism and Institutional Analysis,* edited by John L. Campbell and Ove Kaj Pedersen. Princeton, NJ: Princeton University Press.

Haydu, Jeffrey. 1998. "Making Use of the Past: Time Periods as Cases to Compare and as Sequences of Problem Solving." *American Journal of Sociology* 104(2): 339–71.

Hayo, Bernd, and Carsten Hefeker. 2010. "The Complex Relationship between Central Bank Independence and Inflation." Pp. 179–217 in *Challenges in Central Banking. The Current Institutional Environment and Forces Affecting Monetary Policy,* edited by Pierre L. Siklos, Martin T. Bohl, and Mark E. Wohar. Cambridge: Cambridge University Press.

Helleiner, Eric. 1994. *States and the Reemergence of Global Finance: From Bretton Woods to the 1990s.* Ithaca, NY: Cornell University Press.

Hetzel, Robert L. 2008. *The Monetary Policy of the Federal Reserve: A History.* Cambridge: Cambridge University Press.

Hibbs, Douglas A. 1977. "Political Parties and Macroeconomic Policy." *American Political Science Review* 71(4):1467–87.

Hirschman, Daniel, and Elizabeth Popp Berman. 2014. "Do Economists Make Policies? On the Political Effects of Economics." *Socio-economic Review* 12(4):779–811.

Hirshman, Albert O. 1970. *Exit, Voice, and Loyalty: Responses to Decline in Firms, Organizations, and States.* Cambridge, MA: Harvard University Press.

Hockett, Robert C., and Saule T. Omarova. 2017. "The Finance Franchise." *Cornell Law Review* 102:1143–218.

Holmes, Douglas R. 2013. *Economy of Words: Communicative Imperatives in Central Banks.* Chicago: University of Chicago Press.

Höpner, Martin. 2019. "The German Undervaluation Regime under Bretton Woods: How Germany Became the Nightmare of the World Economy." MPIfG Discussion Paper No. 19/1. Cologne: Max-Planck-Institut für Gesellschaftsforschung.

Hotson, Anthony. 2010. *British Monetary Targets, 1976 to 1987: A View from the Fourth Floor of the Bank of England.* London: London School of Economics.

———. 2017. *Respectable Banking: The Search for Stability in London's Money and Credit Markets since 1695.* Cambridge: Cambridge University Press.

Hübscher, Evelyne, Thomas Sattler, and Markus Wagner. 2021. "Voter Responses to Fiscal Austerity." *British Journal of Political Science* 51(4):1751–60.

Hug, Peter. 2002. "Steuerflucht und die Legende vom antinazistischen Ursprung des Bankgeheimnisses. Funktion und Risiko der moralischen Überhöhung des Finanzplatzes Schweiz." Pp. 269–322 in *Gedächtnis, Geld und Gesetz. Zum Umgang mit der Vergangenheit des Zweiten Weltkriegs,* edited by Jakob Tanner and Sigrid Weigel. Zürich: vdf Hochschulverlag.

Hung, Ho-fung, and Daniel Thompson. 2016. "Money Supply, Class Power, and Inflation: Monetarism Reassessed." *American Sociological Review* 81(3):447–66.

Hutter, Bridget M., and Sally M. Lloyd-Bostock. 2017. *Regulatory Crisis: Negotiating the Consequences of Risk, Disasters and Crises.* Cambridge: Cambridge University Press.

Ingham, Geoffrey Keith. 2004. *The Nature of Money.* Cambridge: Polity Press.

Issing, Otmar. 1997. "Monetary Targeting in Germany: The Stability of Monetary Policy and of the Monetary System." *Journal of Monetary Economics* 39(1): 67–79.

Iversen, Torben. 1998. "Wage Bargaining, Hard Money and Economic Performance: Theory and Evidence for Organized Market Economies." *British Journal of Political Science* 28(1):31–61.

Jahan, Sarwat. 2017. "Inflation Targeting: Holding the Line." Pp. 72–73 in *Back to Basics: Economics Concepts Explained,* edited by International Monetary Fund. Washington, DC: International Monetary Fund.

James, Harold. 2012. *Making the European Monetary Union.* Cambridge, MA: Harvard University Press.

————. 2020. *Making a Modern Central Bank: The Bank of England 1979–2003.* Cambridge: Cambridge University Press.

Janssen, Hauke. 2006. *Milton Friedman und die 'monetaristische Revolution in Deutschland.'* Marburg: Metropolis.

Jobst, Clemens, and Stefano Ugolini. 2016. "The Coevolution of Money Markets and Monetary Policy, 1815–2008." Pp. 145–94 in *Central Banks at a Crossroads,* edited by Michael D. Bordo, Marc Flandreau, Oyvind Eitrheim, and Jan F. Qvigstad. Cambridge: Cambridge University Press.

Johnson, Harry G. 1990 [1971]. "The Keynesian Revolution and the Monetarist Counter-Revolution." Pp. 72–88 in *Milton Friedman: Critical Assessments,* edited by John C. Wood and Ronald N. Woods. London: Routledge.

Johnson, Peter A. 1998. *The Government of Money. Monetarism in Germany and the United States.* Ithaca, NY: Cornell University Press.

Johnson, Simon, and James Kwak. 2010. *13 Bankers: The Wall Street Takeover and the Next Financial Meltdown.* New York: Vintage, 2011.

Jones, Daniel Stedman. 2012. *Masters of the Universe: Hayek, Friedman, and the Birth of Neoliberal Politics.* Princeton, NJ: Princeton University Press.

Jordà, Òscar, Björn Richter, Moritz Schularick, and Alan M. Taylor. 2017. "Bank Capital Redux: Solvency, Liquidity, and Crisis." Federal Reserve Bank of San Francisco Working Paper.

Jordà, Òscar, Moritz Schularick, and Alan M. Taylor. 2014. "The Great Mortgaging: Housing Finance, Crises, and Business Cycles." NBER Working Paper No. 20501. Cambridge, MA: National Bureau of Economic Research.

Jordana, Jacint, and David Levi-Faur. 2004. "The Politics of Regulation in the Age of Governance." Pp. 1–28 in *The Politics of Regulation: Institutions and Regulatory Reforms for the Age of Governance,* edited by Jacint Jordana and David Levi-Faur. Cheltenham, UK: Edward Elgar.

Jordana, Jacint, David Levi-Faur, and Xavier Fernández i Marín. 2011. "The Global Diffusion of Regulatory Agencies: Channels of Transfer and Stages of Diffusion." *Comparative Political Studies* 44(10):1343–69.

Joyce, Michael, David Miles, Andrew Scott, and Dimitri Vayanos. 2016. "Quantitative Easing and Unconventional Monetary Policy—an Introduction." *Economic Journal* 122:271–88.

Joyce, Patrick. 2013. *The State of Freedom: A Social History of the British State since 1800.* Cambridge: Cambridge University Press.

Joyce, Patrick, and Chandra Mukerji. 2017. "The State of Things: State History and Theory Reconfigured." *Theory and Society* 46(1):1–19.

Kallinikos, Jannis, Hans Hasselbladh, and Attila Marton. 2013. "Governing Social Practice: Technology and Institutional Change." *Theory and Society* 42(4): 395–421.

Kane, Edward J. 1981. "Accelerating Inflation, Technological Innovation, and the Decreasing Effectiveness of Banking Regulation." *Journal of Finance* 36(2):355–67.

Kapstein, Ethan Barnaby. 1992. "Between Power and Purpose: Central Banks and the Politics of Regulatory Convergence." *International Organization* 46(1): 265–87.

Karamouzis, Nicholas, and Raymond Lombra. 1989. "Federal Reserve Policymaking: An Overview and Analysis of the Policy Process." *Journal of Monetary Economics* 30(1):7–62.

Katzenstein, Peter J. 1985. *Small States in World Markets: Industrial Policy in Europe.* Ithaca, NY: Cornell University Press.

Keynes, John Maynard. 1973 [1936]. *The General Theory of Employment Interest and Money.* London: Macmillan.

King, Desmond, and Patrick Le Galès. 2017. "The Three Constituencies of the State: Why the State Has Lost Unifying Energy." *British Journal of Sociology* 68(S1):S11–S33.

King, Mervyn A. 1994. "Monetary Policy in the UK." *Fiscal Studies* 15:109–28.

———. 1997. "Changes in UK Monetary Policy: Rules and Discretion in Practice." *Journal of Monetary Economics* 39(1):81–97.

———. 2016. *The End of Alchemy: Money, Banking, and the Future of the Global Economy.* New York: W. W. Norton.

King, Michael. 2005. "Epistemic Communities and the Diffusion of Ideas: Central Bank Reform in the United Kingdom." *West European Politics* 28(1):94–123.

Kirshner, Jonathan. 2003. "Money Is Politics." *Review of International Political Economy* 10(4):645–60.

Knafo, Samuel. 2013. *The Making of Modern Finance: Liberal Governance and the Gold Standard.* London: Routledge.

Kneeshaw, J. T., and P. Van den Bergh. 1989. "Changes in Central Bank Money Market Operating Procedures in the 1980s." BIS Economic Papers. Basel: Bank for International Settlements.

Knorr Cetina, Karin. 2007. "Economic Sociology and the Sociology of Finance. Four Distinctions, Two Developments, One Field?" *Economic Sociology* 8(3):4–10.

Konings, Martijn. 2011. *The Development of American Finance.* New York: Cambridge University Press.

Kriesi, Hanspeter. 1980. *Entscheidungsstrukturen und Entscheidungsprozesse in der Schweizer Politik.* Frankfurt: Campus.

Krippner, Greta R. 2005. "The Financialization of the American Economy." *Socioeconomic Review* 3(2):173–208.

———. 2011. *Capitalizing on Crisis: The Political Origins of the Rise of Finance.* Cambridge, MA: Harvard University Press.

Kwak, James. 2014. "Cultural Capture and the Financial Crisis." Pp. 71–98 in *Preventing Regulatory Capture: Special Interest Influence and How to Limit It*, edited by Daniel Carpenter and David A. Moss. Cambridge: Cambridge University Press.

Kydland, Finn E., and Edward C. Prescott. 1977. "Rules Rather Than Discretion: The Inconsistency of Optimal Plans." *Journal of Political Economy* 85(3): 473–92.

Laidler, David. 2003. "Monetary Policy without Money: Hamlet without the Ghost." *Research Report, No. 2003-7,* University of Western Ontario, Department of Economics, London (Ontario).

———. 2007. *Successes and Failures of Monetary Policy since the 1950s.* Ontario: RBC Financial Group Economic Policy Research Institute.

Langley, Paul. 2015. *Liquidity Lost: The Governance of the Global Financial Crisis.* Oxford: Oxford University Press.

Lascoumes, Pierre, and Patrick Le Galès. 2007. "Introduction: Understanding Public Policy through Its Instruments—From the Nature of Instruments to the Sociology of Public Policy Instrumentation." *Governance* 20(1):1–21.

Laubach, Thomas, and Adam S. Posen. 1997. "Disciplined Discretion: The German and Swiss Monetary Targeting Framework in Operation." Research Paper. New York: Federal Reserve Bank of New York.

Lawson, Nigel. 1992. *The View from No. 11: Memoirs of a Tory Radical.* London: Bentam Press.

Lebaron, Frédéric. 2010. "European Central Bankers in the Global Space of Central Bankers: A Geometric Data Analysis Approach." *French Politics* 8(3):294–320.

Leeper, Eric M. 2010. "Monetary Science, Fiscal Alchemy." NBER Working Paper No. 16510. Cambridge, MA: National Bureau of Economic Research.

Leutwiler, Fritz. 1971. "Theorie und Wirklichkeit der Notenbankpolitik." *Schweizerisches Journal for Volkswirtschaft und Statistik* 107(1):275–89.

Lindblom, Charles Edward. 1977. *Politics and Markets: The World's Political and Economic Systems.* New York: Basic Books.

Lindow, Wesley. 1972. *Inside the Money Market.* New York: Random House.

Lindsey, David E., Athanasios Orphanides, and Robert H. Rasche. 2013. "The Reform of October 1979: How It Happened and Why." *Federal Reserve Bank of St. Louis Review* (November / December):487–542.

Lisle-Williams, Michael. 1984. "Beyond the Market: The Survival of Family Capitalism in the English Merchant Banks." *British Journal of Sociology* 35(2):241.

Loepfe, Willi. 2011. *Der Aufstieg des schweizerischen Finanzplatzes in der Nachkriegszeit.* Weinfelden (CH): Wolfan.

Lucas, Jr., Robert E. 1981. *Studies in Business-Cycle Theory.* Cambridge, MA: MIT Press.

Luhmann, Niklas. 2002. *Die Politik der Gesellschaft.* Frankfurt: Suhrkamp.

Lynch, Julia. 2020. *Regimes of Inequality: The Political Economy of Health and Wealth.* Cambridge: Cambridge University Press.

Mabillard, Max, and Roger de Weck. 1977. *Scandale au Crédit Suisse.* Geneva: La Tribune de Genève.

Maerowitz, Seth P. 1981. "The Market for Federal Funds." *Federal Reserve Bank of Richmond Economic Review* 67(4):3–7.

Maier, Charles. 2004. "Two Sorts of Crisis? The 'Long' 1970s in the West and the East." Pp. 49–62 in *Koordinaten deutscher Geschichte in der Epoche des Ost-West-Konflikts,* edited by Hans Günter Hockerts. München: R. Oldenbourg.

Majone, Giandomenico. 1994. "The Rise of the Regulatory State in Europe." *West European Politics* 17(3):77–101.

Mallaby, Sebastian. 2017. *The Man Who Knew: The Life and Times of Alan Greenspan.* London: Bloomsbury.

Maman, Daniel, and Zeev Rosenhek. 2009. "The Contested Institutionalization of Policy Paradigm Shifts: The Adoption of Inflation Targeting in Israel." *Socio-economic Review* 7(2):217–43.

Mann, Michael. 1984. "The Autonomous Power of the State: Its Origins, Mechanisms and Results." *European Journal of Sociology/Archives Européennes de Sociologie/Europäisches Archiv für Soziologie* 25(2):185–213.

———. 1996. *The Sources of Social Power, Volume 2: The Rise of Classes and Nation States 1760–1914.* Cambridge: Cambridge University Press.

———. 2011. *The Sources of Social Power, Volume 4: Globalizations, 1945–2011.* Cambridge: Cambridge University Press.

Manow, Philip. 2020. *Social Protection, Capitalist Production: The Bismarckian Welfare State in the German Political Economy, 1880–2015.* Oxford: Oxford University Press.

Marcussen, Martin. 2009. "Scientization of Central Banking: The Politics of A-politicization." Pp. 373–90 in *Central Banks in the Age of the Euro,* edited by Kenneth Dyson and Marcus Marcussen. Oxford; New York: Oxford University Press.

Marsh, David. 1992. *The Most Powerful Bank: Inside Germany's Bundesbank.* London: Times Books.

Masciandaro, Donato, and Marc Quintyn. 2013. "The Evolution of Financial Supervision: The Continuing Search for the Holy Grail." Pp. 263–318 in *50 Years of Money and Finance: Lessons and Challenges,* edited by Morten Balling and Ernest Gnan. Vienna: SUERF.

Maxfield, Sylvia. 1991. "Bankers' Alliances and Economic Policy Patterns: Evidence from Mexico and Brazil." *Comparative Political Studies* 23(4):419–58.

Mayes, David G., and W. A. Razzak. 2001. "Transparency and Accountability: Empirical Models and Policy-Making at the Reserve Bank of New Zealand."

Pp. 93–110 in *Empirical Models and Policy-Making: Interaction and Institutions,* edited by Frank A. G. den Butter and Mary S. Morgan. London: Routledge.

Mazbouri, Malik, Sébastien Guex, and Rodrigo Lopez. 2012. "Finanzplatz Schweiz." Pp. 468–518 in *Wirtschaftsgeschichte der Schweiz im 20. Jahrhundert,* edited by Margrit Müller, Béatrice Veyrassat, and Patrick Halbeisen. Basel: Schwabe Basel.

Mazbouri, Malik, and Janick Marina Schaufelbuehl. 2015. "A Legislator under Surveillance: The Creation and Implementation of Swiss Banking Legislation 1910–1934." *European History Quarterly* 45(4):662–88.

McCallum, Bennett T. 1997. "Inflation Targeting in Canada, New Zealand, Sweden, the United Kingdom, and in General." NBER Working Paper No. 5579. Cambridge, MA: National Bureau of Economic Research.

McLeay, Michael, Amar Radia, and Thomas Ryland. 2014. "Money Creation in the Modern Economy." *BoE Quarterly Bulletin* Q1 (March):14–27.

McMichael, Philip. 1990. "Incorporating Comparison within a World-Historical Perspective: An Alternative Comparative Method." *American Sociological Review* 55(3):385–97.

McNamara, Kathleen R. 1998. *The Currency of Ideas: Monetary Politics in the European Union.* Ithaca, NY: Cornell University Press.

Mee, Simon. 2019. *Central Bank Independence and the Legacy of the German Past.* Cambridge: Cambridge University Press.

Mehrling, Perry. 2011. *The New Lombard Street: How the Fed Became the Dealer of Last Resort.* Princeton, NJ: Princeton University Press.

Meltzer, Allan H. 2003. *A History of the Federal Reserve, Volume I, 1913–1951.* Chicago: University of Chicago Press.

Menand, Lev. 2020. "Unappropriated Dollars: The Fed's Ad Hoc Lending Facilities and the Rules That Govern Them." ECGI Law Working Papers No. 518 / 2020. Brussels: European Corporate Governance Institute.

———. 2021. "Why Supervise Banks? The Foundations of the American Monetary Settlement." *Vanderbilt Law Review* 74:951–1021.

Meulendyk, Ann-Marie. 1998. *US Monetary Policy and Financial Markets.* New York: Federal Reserve Bank of New York.

Meyer, John W., John Boli, George M. Thomas, and Francisco O. Ramirez. 1997. "World Society and the Nation-State." *American Journal of Sociology* 103(1): 144–81.

Mian, Atif R. 2019. "How to Think about Finance?" Research brief, Economists for Inclusive Prosperity.

Mian, Atif R., Ludwig Straub, and Amir Sufi. 2020. "The Saving Glut of the Rich." NBER Working Paper No. 26941. Cambridge, MA: National Bureau of Economic Research.

Michie, Ranald C. 2004. "The City of London and the British Government: The Changing Relationship." Pp. 31–58 in *The British Government and the City of*

London in the Twentieth Century, edited by Ranald C. Michie and Philip Williamson. Cambridge: Cambridge University Press.

Middleton, Peter. 1989. "Economic Policy Formulation in the Treasury in the Post-War Period: NIESR Jubilee Lecture." *National Institute Economic Review* 127:46–51.

Milanovic, Branco. 2019. *Capitalism, Alone.* Cambridge, MA: Harvard University Press.

Minford, Patrick. 1991. *The Supply Side Revolution in Britain.* Cheltenham, UK: Edward Elgar.

Minsky, Hyman P. 1957. "Central Banking and Money Market Changes." *Quarterly Journal of Economics* 71(2):171–87.

———. 1975. *John Maynard Keynes.* London: Macmillan.

———. 1986. *Stabilizing an Unstable Economy.* New Haven, CT: Yale University Press.

———. 1988. "Review of: Secrets of the Temple: How the Federal Reserve Runs the Country." *Challenge* 31(3):58–62.

Mishkin, Frederic S. 2007. *Monetary Policy Strategy.* Cambridge, MA: MIT Press.

Mizruchi, Mark S. 2013. *The Fracturing of the American Corporate Elite.* Cambridge, MA: Harvard University Press.

Monnet, Eric. 2015. "La politique de la Banque de France au sortir des trente glorieuses: Un tournant néolibéral et monétariste?" *Revue d'Histoire Moderne et Contemporaine* 62(1):147–74.

Monnin, Pierre. 2019. "The Risks and Side Effects of UMP: An Assessment of IMF Views and Analysis." IEO Background Paper. Washington, DC: Independent Evaluation Office of the International Monetary Fund.

Moran, Michael. 1984. *The Politics of Banking: The Strange Case of Competition and Credit Control.* London: Macmillan.

———. 1991. *The Politics of the Financial Services Revolution: The USA, UK and Japan.* London: Macmillan.

———. 2003. *The British Regulatory State: High Modernism and Hyper-innovation.* Oxford: Oxford University Press.

Morgan, Kimberly J., and Andrea L. Campbell. 2011. *The Delegated Welfare State: Medicare, Markets, and the Governance of Social Policy.* Oxford: Oxford University Press.

Morgan, Mary S. 2006. "Measuring Instruments in Economics and the Velocity of Money." Working papers on the Nature of Evidence: How Well Do "Facts" Travel? No. 13/06. London: London School of Economics and Political Science.

Morrison, James A. 2016. "Shocking Intellectual Austerity: The Role of Ideas in the Demise of the Gold Standard in Britain." *International Organization: IO* 70(1):175–204.

Mosley, Layna. 2003. *Global Capital and National Governments.* Cambridge: Cambridge University Press.

Mudge, Stephanie L., and Antoine Vauchez. 2016. "Fielding Supranationalism: The European Central Bank as a Field Effect." *Sociological Review Monograph* 64(2):146–69.

Mudge, Stephanie Lee. 2008. "What Is Neo-liberalism?" *Socio-economic Review* 6(4):703–31.

Murau, Steffen. 2017. "Shadow Money and the Public Money Supply: The Impact of the 2007–2009 Financial Crisis on the Monetary System." *Review of International Political Economy* 24(5):802–38.

Needham, Duncan. 2014a. "The 1981 Budget: 'a Dunkirk, not an Alamein.'" Pp. 148–80 in *Expansionary Fiscal Contraction: The Thatcher Government's 1981 Budget in Perspective,* edited by Duncan Needham and Anthony Hotson. Cambridge: Cambridge University Press.

———. 2014b. *UK Monetary Policy from Devaluation to Thatcher, 1967–1982.* Basingstoke, UK: Palgrave Macmillan.

Needham, Duncan, and Anthony Hotson. 2018. *The Changing Risk Culture of UK Banks.* Cambridge: University of Cambridge.

Nelson, Stephen C., and Peter J. Katzenstein. 2014. "Uncertainty, Risk, and the Financial Crisis of 2008." *International Organization* 68(2):361–92.

Nyborg, Kjell G., and Per Östberg. 2014. "Money and Liquidity in Financial Markets." *Journal of Financial Economics* 112(1):30–52.

Oatley, Thomas, and Robert Nabors. 1998. "Redistributive Cooperation: Market Failure, Wealth Transfers, and the Basel Accord." *International Organization* 52(1):35–54.

O'Connor, James. 1973. *The Fiscal Crisis of the State.* New York: St. Martin's Press.

Oesch, Daniel. 2011. "Swiss Trade Unions and Industrial Relations after 1990." Pp. 82–102 in *Switzerland in Europe: Continuity and Change in the Swiss Political Economy,* edited by Christine Trampusch and André Mach. London: Routledge.

Offe, Klaus. 1973. *Strukturprobleme des kapitalistischen Staates.* Frankfurt: Suhrkamp.

Offer, Avner. 2014. "Narrow Banking, Real Estate, and Financial Stability in the UK c. 1870–2010." Pp. 158–73 in *British Financial Crises since 1825,* edited by Nicholas Dimsdale and Anthony Hotson. Oxford: Oxford University Press.

———. 2017. "The Market Turn: From Social Democracy to Market Liberalism." *Economic History Review* 70(4):1051–71.

Oliver, Michael J. 2014. "The Long Road to 1981: British Money Supply Targets from DCE to the MTFS." Pp. 210–28 in *Expansionary Fiscal Contraction: The Thatcher Government's 1981 Budget in Perspective,* edited by Duncan Needham and Anthony Hotson. Cambridge: Cambridge University Press.

Orléan, André. 2008. "Monetary Beliefs and the Power of Central Banks." Pp. 7–21 in *Central Banks as Economic Institutions,* edited by Jean-Philippe Touffut. Cheltenham, UK: Edward Elgar.

Orphanides, Athanasios, and John Williams. 2011. "Monetary Policy Mistakes and
the Evolution of Inflation Expectations." NBER Working Paper No. 17080.
Cambridge, MA: National Bureau of Economic Research.

Özgöde, Onur. 2021. "The Emergence of Systemic Risk: The Federal Reserve,
Bailouts, and Monetary Government at the Limits." *Socio-economic Review*
(forthcoming).

Parsons, Talcott, and Neil J. Smelser. 1956. *Economy and Society: A Study in the
Integration of Economic and Social Theory.* London: Routledge and Kegan Paul.

Payne, Christopher. 2010. *The Consumer, Credit and Debt: Governing the British
Economy.* PhD thesis, London School of Economics and Political Science,
London.

Peden, George C. 2000. *The Treasury and British Public Policy, 1906–1959.* Oxford:
Oxford University Press.

Pepper, Gordon T., and Michael J. Oliver. 2001. *Monetarism under Thatcher: Lessons
for the Future.* Northampton, MA: Edward Elgar.

Persson, Torsten, and Guido Tabellini. 1993. "Designing Institutions for Monetary
Stability." *Carnegie-Rochester Conference Series on Public Policy* 39:53–84.

Petrou, Karen. 2021a. *Engine of Inequality: The Fed and the Future of Wealth in
America.* Hoboken, NJ: John Wiley and Sons.

Petrou, Karen. 2021b. *A Central Bank Mandate for Our Time: The Fed's De Facto
Fiscal Role and Its Anti-Equality Impact.* Paper presented at the conference
"Populism and the Future of the Fed," Cato Institute, Washington, DC,
November 18, 2021.

Pierson, Paul. 1993. "When Effect Becomes Cause: Policy Feedback and Political
Change." *World Politics* 45(4):595–628.

———. 2001. "From Expansion to Austerity." Pp. 54–80 in *Seeking the Center,*
edited by Martin A. Levin, Marc K. Landy, and Martin Shapiro. Washington,
DC: Georgetown University Press.

———. 2004. *Politics in Time: History, Institutions, and Social Analysis.* Princeton,
NJ: Princeton University Press.

———. 2014. "Power and Path Dependence." Pp. 123–46 in *Advances in Comparative-
Historical Analysis,* edited by James Mahoney and Kathleen Thelen. Cambridge:
Cambridge University Press.

Piketty, Thomas. 2014. *Capital in the Twenty-First Century.* Cambridge, MA:
Belknap Press of Harvard University Press.

Pincus, Steven C. A., and James A. Robinson. 2011. "What Really Happened during
the Glorious Revolution?" NBER Working Paper No. 17206. Cambridge, MA:
National Bureau of Economic Research.

Pistor, Katharina. 2013. "A Legal Theory of Finance." *Journal of Comparative
Economics* 41(2):315–30.

Pixley, Jocelyn. 2018. *Central Banks, Democratic States and Financial Power.* Cambridge:
Cambridge University Press.

Polak, Jacques J. 1997. *The IMF Monetary Model at Forty.* Washington, DC: International Monetary Fund.

Polillo, Simone, and Mauro F. Guillén. 2005. "Globalization Pressures and the State: The Worldwide Spread of Central Bank Independence." *American Journal of Sociology* 110(6):1764–802.

Pozsar, Zlotan, Tobias Adrian, Adam Ashcraft, and Hayley Boesky. 2010. *Shadow Banking.* New York: Federal Reserve Bank of New York.

Prader, Gaudenz. 1981. *50 Jahre Schweizerische Stabilisierungspolitik: Lernprozesse in Theorie und Politik am Beispiel der Finanz- und Beschäftigungspolitik des Bundes.* Zürich: Schulthess.

Prasad, Monica. 2006. *The Politics of Free Markets: The Rise of Neoliberal Economic Policies in Britain, France, Germany, and the United States.* Chicago: University of Chicago Press.

———. 2012. *The Land of Too Much: American Abundance and the Paradox of Poverty.* Cambridge, MA: Harvard University Press.

Preda, Alex. 2009. *Framing Finance: The Boundaries of Markets and Modern Capitalism.* Chicago: University of Chicago Press.

Quinn, Sarah L. 2017. "The Miracles of Bookkeeping: How Budget Politics Link Fiscal Policies and Financial Markets." *American Journal of Sociology* 123(1): 48–85.

———. 2019. *American Bonds: How Credit Markets Shaped a Nation.* Princeton, NJ: Princeton University Press.

Rachel, Lukasz, and Lawrence H. Summers. 2019. "On Secular Stagnation in the Industrialized World." *Brookings Papers on Economic Activity* (Spring):1–54.

Rademacher, Inga. 2020. "One State, One Interest? How a Historic Shock to the Balance of Power of the Bundesbank and the Ministry of Finance Laid the Path for German Fiscal Austerity." Unpublished manuscript, Kings College, London.

Reid, Margaret I. 1982. *The Secondary Banking Crisis, 1973–75: Its Causes and Course.* London: Macmillan.

Reinicke, Wolfgang H. 1995. *Banking, Politics and Global Finance: American Commercial Banks and Regulatory Change, 1980–1990.* Aldershot, UK: Edward Elgar.

Reisenbichler, Alexander. 2020. "The Politics of Quantitative Easing and Housing Stimulus by the Federal Reserve and European Central Bank, 2008–2018." *West European Politics* 43(2):464–84.

Rich, Georg. 1987. "Swiss and United States Monetary Policy: Has Monetarism Failed?" *Federal Reserve Bank of Richmond Economic Review* 73:3–17.

———. 2007. "Swiss Monetary Targeting 1974–1996: The Role of Internal Policy Analysis." *Schweizerische Zeitschrift für Volkswirtschaft und Statistik* 143(3): 283–329.

Ricks, Morgan. 2016. *The Money Problem: Rethinking Financial Regulation.* Chicago: University of Chicago Press.

Riles, Annelise. 2011. *Collateral Knowledge: Legal Reasoning in the Global Financial Markets.* Chicago: University of Chicago Press.

———. 2018. *Financial Citizenship: Experts, Publics, and the Politics of Central Banking.* Ithaca, NY: Cornell University Press.

Roberts, Alasdair. 2011. *The Logic of Discipline: Global Capitalism and the Architecture of Government.* Oxford: Oxford University Press.

Roe, Mark J. 2011. "The Derivatives Market's Payment Priorities as Financial Crisis Accelerator." *Stanford Law Review* 63:539–89.

Rogoff, Kenneth. 1985. "The Optimal Degree of Commitment to an Intermediate Monetary Target." *Quarterly Journal of Economics* 100:1169–90.

Rosanvallon, Pierre. 2013. *The Society of Equals.* Cambridge, MA: Harvard University Press.

Rose, Nicolas, and Peter Miller. 1992. "Political Power beyond the State: Problematics of Government." *British Journal of Sociology* 43(2):173–205.

Ross, Duncan M. 2004. "Domestic Monetary Policy 1945–1971." Pp. 298–321 in *The British Government and the City of London in the Twentieth Century,* edited by Ranald C. Michie and Philip Williamson. Cambridge: Cambridge University Press.

Rueschemeyer, Dietrich. 2003. "Can One or a Few Cases Yield Theoretical Gains?" Pp. 305–36 in *Comparative Historical Analysis in the Social Sciences,* edited by James Mahoney and Dietrich Rueschemeyer. Cambridge: Cambridge University Press.

Ruggie, John Gerard. 1982. "International Regimes, Transactions, and Change: Embedded Liberalism in the Postwar Economic Order." *International Organization* 36(2):379–415.

Saad Filho, Alfredo. 2007. "Monetary Policy in the Neo-liberal Transition: A Political Economy Critique of Keynesianism, Monetarism and Inflation Targeting." Pp. 89–120 in *Political Economy and Global Capitalism: The 21st Century, Present and Future,* edited by Bob Jessop, Richard Westra, and Robert Albritton. London: Anthem Press.

Saez, Emmanuel, and Gabriel Zucman. 2019. *The Triumph of Injustice: How the Rich Dodge Taxes and How to Make Them Pay.* New York: W. W. Norton.

Sassen, Saskia. 2006. *Territory, Authority, Rights: From Medieval to Global Assemblages.* Princeton, NJ: Princeton University Press.

Sayers, Richard S. 1976. *The Bank of England 1891–1944, Volume 1.* Cambridge: Cambridge University Press.

Scharpf, Fritz W. 1976. *Does Organization Matter? Task Structure and Interaction in the Ministerial Bureaucracy.* Berlin: Wissenschaftszentrum Berlin.

———. 1987. *Sozialdemokratische Krisenpolitik in Europa.* Frankfurt: Campus.

———. 2004. "Legitimationskonzepte jenseits des Nationalstaats." MPIfG
    Working Paper. Cologne: Max Planck Institut für Gesellschaftsforschung.

Schenk, Catherine R. 2010. *The Decline of Sterling: Managing the Retreat of an
    International Currency, 1945–1992.* Cambridge: Cambridge University Press.

———. 2014. "Summer in the City: Banking Failures of 1974 and the Development
    of International Banking Supervision." *English Historical Review* 129(540):
    1129–56.

Scheve, Kenneth. 2004. "Public Inflation Aversion and the Political Economy of
    Macroeconomic Policymaking." *International Organization* 58(1):1–34.

Schiltknecht, Kurt. 1979 [1976]. "Monetary Policy under Flexible Exchange Rates:
    The Swiss Case." Pp. 321–49 in *Inflation, Unemployment, and Monetary
    Control. Collected Papers from the 1973–1976 Konstanz Seminars,* edited by Karl
    Brunner and Manfred J. Neumann. Berlin: Duncker and Humblot.

Schularick, Moritz, and Alan M. Taylor. 2012. "Credit Booms Gone Bust: Mon-
    etary Policy, Leverage Cycles, and Financial Crises, 1870–2008." *American
    Economic Review* 102(2):1029–61.

Schwartz, Herman Mark. 2019. "American Hegemony: Intellectual Property
    Rights, Dollar Centrality, and Infrastructural Power." *Review of International
    Political Economy* 26(3):490–519.

Schweizerische Nationalbank. 1982. *75 Jahre Schweizerische Nationalbank. Die Zeit
    von 1957 bis 1982.* Zürich: Schweizerische Nationalbank.

Seabrooke, Leonard, and Eleni Tsingou. 2009. *Revolving Doors and Linked Ecologies
    in the World Economy: Policy Locations and the Practice of International
    Financial Reform.* Coventry, UK: University of Warwick.

Seabrooke, Leonard, and Duncan Wigan. 2014. "Global Wealth Chains in the
    International Political Economy." *Review of International Political Economy*
    21(1):257–63.

Shabani, Mimoza, Judith Jan Tyson, Jan Toporowski, and Terry McKinley. 2014.
    The Financial System in the U.K. London: School of Oriental and African
    Studies.

Sherwin, Murray 2000. "Strategic Choices in Inflation Targeting: The New
    Zealand Experience." Pp. 15–27 in *Inflation Targeting in Practice: Strategic and
    Operational Issues and Application to Emerging Market Economies,* edited by
    Mario Bléjer, Alain Ize, Alfredo Leone, and Sérgio Werlang. Washington, DC:
    International Monetary Fund.

Siklos, Pierre L. 2002. *The Changing Face of Central Banking: Evolutionary Trends
    since World War II.* Cambridge: Cambridge University Press.

Simmel, Georg. 1989 [1900]. *Philosophie des Geldes.* Frankfurt: Suhrkamp.

Singleton, John. 2011. *Central Banking in the Twentieth Century.* Cambridge:
    Cambridge University Press.

Sissoko, Carolyn. 2010. "The Legal Foundations of Financial Collapse." *Journal of
    Financial Economic Policy* 2(1):5–34.

———. 2016. "How to Stabilize the Banking System: Lessons from the Pre-1914 London Money Market." *Financial History Review* 23(1):1–20.

———. 2019. "Repurchase Agreements and the (De)construction of Financial Markets." *Economy and Society*:1–27.

Skocpol, Theda. 1985. "Bringing the State Back In: Strategies of Analysis in Current Research." Pp. 3–37 in *Bringing the State Back In,* edited by Peter B. Evans, Dietrich Rueschemeyer, and Theda Skocpol. Cambridge: Cambridge University Press.

Snowdon, Brian, and Howard R. Vane. 2005. *Modern Macroeconomics: Its Origins, Development and Current State.* Cheltenham, UK: Edward Elgar.

Stasavage, David. 2003. "Communication, Coordination and Common Knowledge in Monetary Policy." Pp. 183–203 in *Institutional Conflicts and Complementarities,* edited by Franzese Robert, Peter Mooslechner, and Martin Schürz. Boston: Springer.

Steinmo, Sven. 1993. *Taxation and Democracy: Swedish, British, and American Approaches to Financing the Modern State.* New Haven, CT: Yale University Press.

Stephens, Philip. 1996. *Politics and the Pound: The Conservatives' Struggle with Sterling.* London: Macmillan.

Stock, James H., and Mark W. Watson. 2003. "Has the Business Cycle Changed and Why?" Pp. 159–230 in *NBER Macroeconomics Annual 2002,* edited by Mark Gertler and Kenneth Rogoff. Cambridge, MA: MIT Press.

Strange, Susan. 1998. *Mad Money.* Manchester: Manchester University Press.

Straumann, Tobias. 2010. *Fixed Ideas of Money: Small States and Exchange Rate Regimes in Twentieth Century Europe.* New York: Cambridge University Press.

Streeck, Wolfgang. 2009. *Re-forming Capitalism: Institutional Change in the German Political Economy.* Oxford: Oxford University Press.

———. 2014. *Buying Time: The Delayed Crisis of Democratic Capitalism.* London: Verso.

———. 2016. *How Will Capitalism End?* London: Verso.

Streeck, Wolfgang, and Kathleen Ann Thelen. 2005. *Beyond Continuity: Institutional Change in Advanced Political Economies.* Oxford: Oxford University Press.

Suzuki, Yoshio. 1985. "Japan's Monetary Policy over the Past 10 Years." *Bank of Japan Monetary and Economic Studies* 3(2):1–9.

Swank, Duane. 2016. "Taxing Choices: International Competition, Domestic Institutions and the Transformation of Corporate Tax Policy." *Journal of European Public Policy* 23(4):571–603.

Tanner, Jakob. 2015. *Die Geschichte der Schweiz im 20. Jahrhundert.* Muenchen: C. H. Beck.

Taylor, Alan M. 2015. "Credit, Financial Stability, and the Macroeconomy." *Annual Review of Economics* 7(1):309–39.

Thelen, Kathleen. 1999. "Historical Institutionalism in Comparative Politics." *Annual Review of Political Science* 2:369–404.

Thiemann, Matthias. 2014. "In the Shadow of Basel: How Competitive Politics Bred the Crisis." *Review of International Political Economy* 21(6):1203–39.

———. 2018. *The Growth of Shadow Banking: A Comparative Institutional Analysis.* Cambridge: Cambridge University Press.

Thiemann, Matthias, and Jan Lepoutre. 2017. "Stitched on the Edge: Rule Evasion, Embedded Regulators, and the Evolution of Markets." *American Journal of Sociology* 122(6):1775–821.

Thiemann, Matthias, Carolina Raquel Melches, and Edin Ibrocevic. 2021. "Measuring and Mitigating Systemic Risks: How the Forging of New Alliances between Central Bank and Academic Economists Legitimize the Transnational Macroprudential Agenda." *Review of International Political Economy* 28(6):1433–58.

Tilcsik, Andras. 2010. "From Ritual to Reality: Demography, Ideology, and Decoupling in a Post-communist Government Agency." *Academy of Management Journal* 53(6):1474–98.

Tilly, Charles. 1990. *Coercion, Capital, and European States, AD 990–1990.* Cambridge, MA: B. Blackwell.

Tilly, Charles, and Robert Goodin. 2006. "It Depends." Pp. 3–32 in *The Oxford Handbook of Contextual Political Analysis,* edited by Robert Goodin and Charles Tilly. Oxford: Oxford University Press.

Tognato, Carlo. 2012. *Central Bank Independence: Cultural Codes and Symbolic Performance.* New York: Palgrave Macmillan.

Toma, Mark. 1988. "The Role of the Federal Reserve in Reserve Requirement Regulation." *Cato Journal* 7(3):701–25.

Toniolo, Gianni. 2005. *Central Bank Cooperation at the Bank for International Settlements, 1930–1973.* Cambridge: Cambridge University Press.

Tooze, J. Adam. 2018. *Crashed: How a Decade of Financial Crises Changed the World.* New York: Penguin Random House.

Tucker, Paul. 2014. "The Lender of Last Resort and Modern Central Banking: Principles and Reconstruction." BIS Papers. Basel: Bank for International Settlements.

———. 2018. *Unelected Power: The Quest for Legitimacy in Central Banking and the Regulatory State.* Princeton, NJ: Princeton University Press.

Turner, John D. 2014. *Banking in Crisis: The Rise and Fall of British Banking Stability, 1800 to the Present.* Cambridge: Cambridge University Press.

Tymoigne, Éric, and L. Randall Wray. 2013. *Modern Money Theory 101: A Reply to Critics.* Levy Economics Institute of Bard College.

van der Zwan, Natascha. 2014. "Making Sense of Financialization." *Socio-economic Review* 12(1):99–129.

Van Gunten, Tod. 2015. "Cycles of Polarization and Settlement: Diffusion and Transformation in the Macroeconomic Policy Field." *Theory and Society* 44(4):321–54.

van Treeck, Till. 2015. "Inequality, the Crisis, and Stagnation." *European Journal of Economics and Economic Policies* 12(2):158–69.

Vaughan, Diane. 1996. *The Challenger Launch Decision: Risky Technology, Culture, and Deviance at NASA.* Chicago: University of Chicago Press.

Vissing-Jorgensen, Annette. 2020. "Bond Markets in Spring 2020 and the Response of the Federal Reserve." Unpublished manuscript, University of California, Berkeley and NBER, Berkeley, CA.

Walter, Timo, and Leon Wansleben. 2019. "How Central Bankers Learned to Love Financialization: The Fed, the Bank, and the Enlisting of Unfettered Markets in the Conduct of Monetary Policy." Socio-economic Review 18(3):625–53.

Walters, Gary. 1982. "Repurchase Agreements and the Bankruptcy Code: The Need for Legislative Action." *Fordham Law Review* 52(5):828–49.

Wansleben, Leon. 2018. "How Expectations Became Governable: Institutional Change and the Performative Power of Central Banks." *Theory and Society* 47(6):773–803.

———. 2020. "Formal Institution Building in Financialized Capitalism: The Case of Repo Markets." *Theory and Society* 49(2):187–213.

Wasserfallen, Fabio. 2019. "Global Diffusion, Policy Flexibility, and Inflation Targeting." *International Interactions* 45(4):617–37.

Weber, Max. 1976 [1921]. *Wirtschaft und Gesellschaft.* Tübingen: J. C. B. Mohr (Paul Siebeck).

Weir, Margaret. 1989. "Ideas and Politics: The Acceptance of Keynesianism in Britain and the United States." Pp. 53–86 in *The Political Power of Economic Ideas: Keynesianism across Nations,* edited by Peter Hall. Princeton, NJ: Princeton University Press.

Weir, Margaret, and Theda Skocpol. 1985. "State Structures and the Possibilities for 'Keynesian' Responses to the Great Depression in Sweden, Britain, and the United States." Pp. 107–64 in *Bringing the State Back In,* edited by Dietrich Rueschemeyer, Peter B. Evans, and Theda Skocpol. Cambridge: Cambridge University Press.

Wexler, Ralph J. 1981. "Federal Control over the Money Market." *Arizona State Law Journal* 159:159–210.

Wildavsky, Aaron B., and Naomi Caiden. 1992. *The New Politics of the Budgetary Process.* New York: HarperCollins.

Willis, Henry Parker. 1914. "The Federal Reserve Act." *American Economic Review* 4(1):1–24.

Wood, John H. 2005. *A History of Central Banking in Great Britain and the United States.* Cambridge: Cambridge University Press.

Woodford, Michael. 2003a. "Inflation Targeting and Optimal Monetary Policy."
     Paper prepared for the Annual Economic Policy Conference, Federal Reserve
     Bank of St. Louis, Princeton University, Princeton, NJ.
———. 2003b. *Interest and Prices.* Princeton, NJ: Princeton University Press.
———. 2009. "Convergence in Macroeconomics: Elements of the New Synthesis."
     American Economic Journal: Macroeconomics 1(1):267–79.
Wooley, John T. 1984. *Monetary Politics: The Federal Reserve and the Politics of
     Monetary Policy.* Cambridge: Cambridge University Press.
Zimmermann, Hubert. 2012. "No Country for the Market: The Regulation of
     Finance in Germany after the Crisis." *German Politics* 21(4):484–501.
Zysman, John. 1983. *Governments, Markets and Growth: Financial Systems and the
     Politics of Industrial Change.* Oxford: Robertson.

Index

The letter *f* or *t* following a page number denotes a figure or table.